RESEARCH
METHODS
IN
PSYCHOLOGY

RESEARCH METHODS IN PSYCHOLOGY

Philip J. Dunham

Dalhousie University

HARPER & ROW, PUBLISHERS, New York
Cambridge, Philadelphia, San Francisco, Washington,
London, Mexico City, São Paulo, Singapore, Sydney

1817

Sponsoring Editor: Leslie Carr
Project Editor: Carla Samodulski
Text Design Adaptation: Barbara Bert/North 7 Atelier
Cover Design: Roseanne Lufrano
Text Art: Volt Information Sciences, Inc.
Production Manager: Willie Lane
Compositor: Ruttle, Shaw & Wetherill, Inc.
Printer and Binder: R. R. Donnelley & Sons Company
Cover Printer: NEBC

RESEARCH METHODS IN PSYCHOLOGY

Library of Congress Cataloging in Publication Data

Dunham, Philip J.
    Research methods in psychology.

    Includes index.
    1. Psychology—Research—Methodology.   2.   Psychology,
Experimental.   I.   Title.
BF76.5.D86   1988   150'.72   87-23636
ISBN 0-06-041807-9

88 89 90 91 9 8 7 6 5 4 3 2 1

For Hoy and Kate

CONTENTS

9   QUASI-ANALYTIC EXPERIMENTS: EX POST FACTO DESIGNS   195

10   QUASI-ANALYTIC EXPERIMENTS: BIVARIATE CORRELATION DESIGNS   223

11   QUASI-ANALYTIC EXPERIMENTS: MULTIVARIATE CORRELATION DESIGNS   248

12   CITIZEN SCIENCE: AN EPILOGUE   263

TO THE INSTRUCTOR

Experience tells me that most people will not bother to read a lengthy preface, yet I think that it is very important for you to know exactly how this book has been organized to accomplish its goals, and why these goals may be worthwhile. To solve this problem, I have departed somewhat from tradition. Instead of putting this material in the preface, I have explained the purpose and organization of the book in the first chapter. This chapter is important because it sets the stage for those that follow. The subsequent chapters should then be read in the order in which they are presented. Each chapter builds to some extent on the information in the preceding one.

This book was developed for use in a one-semester course on research methods in psychology that I have been teaching for the past 20 years. I have used different versions of the manuscript for several years and direct feedback from my students has contributed substantially to its organization and content.

I start with the assumption that the reader has absolutely no background in psychological research methodology and has never had a course in descriptive or inferential statistics. In the first half of the book, my goal is to present the basic logic and architecture of research designs ranging from simple experiments with two treatment groups to experiments using more complex factorial methods. These designs are presented with examples to illustrate the logic of the scientific method in its purest form (i.e., random assignment of subjects to treatments, simultaneous manipulation and control of relevant variables, and so on). I call these designs *analytic experiments*. In the second half of the book, the student is introduced to research questions that force the scientist to deviate from the logic of the analytic experiment and adopt what are now generally called *quasi-analytic* procedures. Throughout the book, the emphasis is on the strengths and weaknesses of particular methodological approaches as the means of searching for probabilistic causes. I want the student to think critically about the different strategies we use as scientists and the legitimacy of the inferences we draw from those strategies.

Course testing has revealed several features of the book that have proved popular with students and particularly effective in helping them acquire the skills described above. Foremost among these are the journal articles reprinted at the ends of certain chapters. For example, in the first part of Chapter 6 the student is introduced to simple factorial designs and the concepts associated with them (i.e., main effects, additivity, interactions, and so on). These concepts are illustrated with a hypothetical example intended to make them as clear as possible. Once students have read the chapter, they are then asked to read the journal article selected to illustrate these same concepts. The chapter exercises then test the students' abilities to apply the knowledge acquired in the chapter to the journal article. I want them to identify the independent and dependent variables in an actual factorial design, to be able to interpret an interaction that is presented in a table or graph, to search for confounded variables, and so on.

The advantages that I have observed of this hands-on approach have been a pleasant surprise. Rather than fear the prospect of going to a primary source, students leave the course feeling that they *can* go to the journals for information. The use of actual journal articles as required reading also helps them write their own laboratory reports by providing models they can follow. Some of the articles awaken personal and research interests that students pursue in subsequent courses. Finally, and most importantly, the students gain some sense of power and control over scientific information; and, although it can sometimes be misdirected, they develop a healthy skepticism about scientific information that is, in my opinion, at the heart of the complex, self-corrective process we call science.

I suspect that most will agree that the goals described above are important in any methodology text. Other features of the book, however, may or may not be of value, depending on your particular point of view. For example, my approach to the matter of inferential statistics is to assume that the students need to understand the logic and architecture of various experimental designs before they are introduced to the many different inferential statistical models that we use in the context of these different designs. I have therefore limited my discussion of inferential statistics to a brief explanation of the process of statistical inference and why scientists use these statistical procedures on their data. In our program, students are introduced to inferential statistics after the introductory methods course, not before it. If you don't share this approach, you may want to use an introductory statistics book to supplement this text.

Although many students will not pursue a research career, I have also attempted to present a frank discussion of the ethics of both human and animal research. After six years on the research ethics committee of Dalhousie University, I know that these issues are important and sensitive. In my opinion, an informed general public is an absolute necessity if rational decisions are to be made about research ethics. I hope I have given the students a glimpse of the very real questions we struggle with in this domain.

Finally, please note that I have included a *conceptual* introduction to the logic of some basic multivariate methods discussed in Chapter 11. I realize that it is unusual to find discussions of methods like multiple correlation/regression in an introductory methodology text, and some instructors may choose not to assign this chapter. I believe, however, that the tremendous recent growth of interest in these methods in the contemporary psychological literature justifies exposing the beginning student to them at a logical, conceptual level.

PERSONAL ACKNOWLEDGEMENTS

Anyone who has written a textbook knows the frustration of not being able to thank the large number of people who contribute to it in so many subtle and important ways. I hope my gratitude has been obvious to all of them. The following should receive special thanks. First, several thousand students have passed through my methodology courses in the past 20 years. Every year I learn something new from them. Second, thanks to my wife Fran, who perused an early draft of the manuscript and proceeded to become, without doubt, my most severe and valued critic. Her contribution is easily described. If it is readable, thank her; if it is not, blame me. Also, special thanks to Ron Hoffman and Lilyan White. We have worked together as a team in undergraduate courses for over a decade, and their critical appraisal of this material has contributed substantially to its development. Lilyan died recently in the prime of her young life, and it helps me to know that some part of this gentle soul survives in the pages that follow and in the students she taught over the years.

Thanks also to Gail Eskes, Sharon Longard, Teresa Alexander, Alan Hurshman, Nancy Gibbons, Carolyn Jean Graham, and Christine Dore, all of whom know the special ways in which they helped in the production of the manuscript. I would also like to express my appreciation to the following manuscript reviewers for their helpful suggestions: David F. Berger, State University of New York, Cortland; Gary E. Brown, University of Tennessee at Martin; Steven Buck, University of Washington; Douglas K. Candland, Bucknell University; J. F. Campbell, Carleton University; Frank Durso, The University of Oklahoma; Charles G. Halcomb, Texas Tech University; James Pate, Georgia State University; Michael H. Siegel, State University College, Oneonta; James L. Spencer, West Virginia State College.

Finally, it has once again been a pleasure to write for the talented people at Harper & Row. The quality of their psychology list is well-known and I am pleased to be associated with it and with editors like Leslie Carr, Carla Samodulski, Susan Mackey, and George Middendorf, who are never more than a phone call away with good advice and a sense of humor.

Philip J. Dunham

TO THE STUDENT

As we walk down the hallway toward the observation room, Mrs. K cradles her 3-month-old infant in a particularly close, protective manner. Following a few steps behind, Mr. K glances nervously into each room as we pass. Their baby is asleep, oblivious to the unspoken concerns of his parents and the strange surroundings.

This scene is repeated many times each day in our research laboratory. The young families who participate in our studies of infant social development are always nervous when they first arrive. Once they have relaxed and started to enjoy themselves, however, their parental concerns inevitably surface. Can Kelly see the colors on the chart? Do other babies this age sleep through the night? Will Ashley miss me when I go back to work next week? Should I pick him up every time he cries? Do you think day care for babies this age is a good idea? And so on.

As they are leaving, Mr. and Mrs. K make one last comment. They want to move into a larger apartment in the south end of Halifax next month. Both are concerned that the move might be stressful and risky for the baby. "Why?" I ask. Mrs. K replies, "Because I read in a magazine that babies who have a lot of stress in their lives are more likely to develop cancer as children." Obviously, the scientific claims reported in the magazine were having a definite impact on this young couple. If the move was in fact risky, they had decided to stay in their present apartment.

This is a very common story. The problem is always the same, only the specific content changes. A journalist accurately reports the results of some scientific research which, if valid, could have considerable impact on our lives. Unfortunately, most people, including the journalist, do not have a very good understanding of the methods used to obtain these results. Consequently, they are unable to judge the legitimacy of the inferences drawn from the research.

Mrs. K's comment reminded me once again of this dilemma and my primary reason for writing this book. I believe every person needs a basic understanding of the research methods that are used by scientists. Only then is it possible to critically evaluate scientific information. The purpose of this book is to help you develop a basic understanding of scientific research methodology, particularly as it is used in psychological research. While some of you might eventually use these skills as research psychologists, my goal, first and foremost, is to help all of you become critical, intelligent consumers of the research that psychologists report.

I will explain the content and organization of the book in more detail in Chapter 1. At this point, however, I want to draw your attention to one specific feature of this book that I think you will find interesting and useful. At the end of certain critical chapters I have reprinted articles selected from various scientific journals. One of your tasks will be to read them and then answer the questions that I have provided. They will test the extent of your understanding of the methodology involved, and the degree to which you are becoming a critical, intelligent consumer of scientific information. If I have done my job, in each chapter you should be able to (1) read and understand these journal articles, (2) recognize the particular research strategies employed by the scientists, (3) identify the strengths and weaknesses of these strategies, and, most importantly, (4) reach your own conclusions about the validity of the claims made by the scientists.

At this point, it might also interest you to know that the journal article reprinted at the end of Chapter 10 is concerned with the effects of early stress on the development of cancer during childhood. It is the original source of the information Mrs. K read in her magazine. By the time you reach Chapter 10, my sincere hope is that you will be able to read this research with a critical eye, recognize its strengths and weaknesses, and draw your own conclusions about the validity of the claims made. Because Mrs. K did not have these skills, she had to settle for my opinion on the matter.

Philip J. Dunham

CHAPTER 1

PURPOSE AND ORGANIZATION OF THIS BOOK

This first chapter will suggest why you might want to read this textbook and describe how it has been organized.

WHY STUDY BEHAVIORAL RESEARCH METHODOLOGY?

The general purpose of courses on research methodology is to familiarize students with the scientific method as a way of studying behavioral phenomena. But the teacher often finds the advanced courses easier to teach than the introductory or basic course. The reason is simple: Most of the students in advanced courses plan to pursue careers as professional psychologists. They hope to go on to graduate study, where they will make heavy use of the concepts and principles they have learned. Hence, such students already realize that research methodology is directly relevant to their needs.

In the introductory course, however, the students are typically in their first or second year; their career plans are less definite, and many may not be committed to psychology as a major area of study. Indeed, only some 2 or 3 percent of them will ever become directly involved in behavioral research. Hence, these beginning students may not see the subject matter as clearly relevant to their needs. If only a small percentage of them pursue a professional research career, who are the others and what do they intend to do with their lives?

If they are typical North American university students, a substantial per-

1

centage of those who will read this book do not yet have specific career plans; most, after they graduate, will probably take jobs in the business world. Others have more definite plans. In fact, increasing numbers of students in psychology courses apparently hope to pursue careers in one of the health professions—for example, behavioral medicine, speech therapy, audiology, occupational therapy, nursing, physiotherapy, and so on. Most of these disciplines look favorably on students with some background in psychology, assuming that the subject matter is strongly relevant. This argument also holds for such social science disciplines as criminology, community planning, social work, recreation, and education.

It should be obvious, then, that a basic problem in teaching an introductory course on behavioral research methodology (or writing a textbook for it) is finding a way to present the subject matter that will fit the needs of each of these students.

Consider first the easy case: that small percentage who intend to pursue careers as professional psychologists. The relevance and value of the material to be presented in the following chapters should be obvious to them. The concepts and principles to be introduced will be among the most basic tools that they will require. The study of behavioral phenomena will be their job, and they will be required to use—or at least understand the use of—research methods in order to do their job well. In other words, one may assume that such students do not need to be motivated to read the following chapters and learn what they have to offer. Behavioral research methodology is already part of their business.

Consider next those who might be headed for a career in one of the health professions or social sciences other than psychology. In addition to finding courses in psychology relevant to their careers, many health professionals may well have a specific interest in behavioral research methods for at least two reasons: (1) the typical health professional now recognizes that he or she will be working in an environment that requires the ability to read and properly interpret a wide variety of scientific information and (2) individuals in many of these callings are expected to carry out work-related research programs. Judging from the journal articles published in these areas, a great deal of this research involves the study of health-related behavior. Indeed, when they are offered some directly relevant examples, most students planning careers in the health professions can easily see the value of a solid background in behavioral research methodology. A passionate editorial (Downs, 1982) in the journal *Nursing Research* is directly to the point. It expresses concern that nurses are simply not reading a growing body of research literature in the health professions and are therefore not incorporating these research findings into their nursing practices. With reference to this problem, the editor states:

> My guess is that a lot of people are unaware of how dated their information is; they continue to believe that experience derived from practice will suffice. Some soul-searching is in order. If the answer you arrive at is that research reports are too difficult to read, I hope you will sharpen your skills. You are definitely out of date.

The same point can be made to students planning to work in any of the social sciences. The first step in solving the problem mentioned in this editorial is to develop a basic grasp of research methodology. This certainly makes it much easier to read and understand published research reports; it is an absolute necessity if you hope to generate research of your own. In this book, I have tried to introduce concepts and use examples that permit students in the various health professions and social sciences to see the relevance of behavioral research methodology.

Perhaps the most difficult challenge in teaching the introductory methodology course is the student who plans to earn a living in the business world. These students are perhaps the least likely to require training in the direct application of behavioral research methods, although there are some contexts in which such skills would come in handy. Again, however, it can be argued that a basic knowledge of research methodology can be of value, if not in generating actual research then in consuming scientific information. Specifically, we are all faced with important decisions in our lives which, in many instances, require us to think critically about information produced by scientific research. Some people can think about such information in an intelligent and critical manner; others are *illiterate* in this respect. A basic course in research methodology can serve as the first step toward becoming a literate, critical consumer of such information. Indeed, for many students who do not pursue a career in science, this basic course may be the *only* step they take toward developing such skills. In order to emphasize this point, we shall look at a few examples.

Consider first a businessman who spends a lot of time flying around the country in commercial airliners. Over the past year, for reasons he cannot understand, he has developed such a great fear of flying that he is unable to board a plane without having a severe anxiety attack. He sweats profusely, feels dizzy, and eventually becomes physically ill each time he must fly. On consulting his doctor, he was told that his fear of flying was not particularly unusual and given a prescription for a tranquilizer. The pills seemed to solve the problem, and he now uses this medication each time he flies.

Recently, this same gentleman read a magazine article suggesting that tranquilizers can be addictive. Having called his doctor to express concern, he was assured that his medication would not be addictive in the prescribed dosage. Whom should he believe, the family physician or the doctor who wrote the magazine column?

Consider next a high school student who, in spite of being very bright, was failing in school. Living in constant fear that a teacher would call on her to speak, she dealt with the problem by skipping classes. Arrangements were eventually made for the girl to see a psychologist, who claimed that he could help her by using a procedure called biofeedback training.

To make a long story short, the sessions with the psychologist were expensive and—after six weeks of treatment—the girl did not seem to be making progress. Her parents discussed the situation with some friends, who suggested that the psychologist was using the wrong treatment procedure. What should they do now?

Finally, consider the claims made by a child psychologist on a radio program. The psychologist suggested that too much television is bad for children. She personally believed that some of the more violent cartoons could have adverse effects upon the development of very young children. To buttress her argument, she pointed to recent research demonstrating that a "TV diet" was good for children. The scientific studies to which she referred had apparently shown that the children in the experiment benefited greatly when their exposure to TV was limited to an hour a day. Children placed on such a TV diet were observed to behave in a more mature manner, to perform better in school, and to have fewer behavioral problems.

Obviously a great many parents must have heard this radio program. Since most people are genuinely concerned about the development of their children, many would probably have accepted these claims and adopted the prescribed TV diet. If you were a parent who heard this program, would you do so?

These three stories have much in common. They all involve real people faced with very real problems. To deal with these, they depend on advice from professionals, and the advice they receive has serious consequences for them. Is the drug addictive or not? Is the therapy effective or not? Is the TV diet necessary or not? The businessman in the first example, the young girl in the second example, and the parents in the third example must feel some degree of helplessness. They must make important decisions on the basis of conflicting or inadequate information. Not exactly the ideal position in which to find yourself, is it?

These cases exemplify just a few of the many ways in which we are forced to deal with scientific information in our everyday lives; they also show how difficult it can be to interpret that information. It is likely that most people do not manage such problems very effectively.

Whatever the actual outcome of these three examples, it is possible to do more than just take the advice of "authorities" on such matters, particularly when that advice is conflicting. As suggested earlier, you can become a more active and informed consumer of the scientific information that touches your life and you can make more informed judgments about it. There are just two simple prerequisites for becoming a good "consumer-critic": First, you must develop a healthily *skeptical* attitude, recognizing that scientists are, in fact, fallible in their efforts to understand nature. Good scientists are always skeptical and suspicious of their knowledge; why shouldn't you be too? Second, you must develop an understanding of the methods scientists use to get their information. Doing this may not solve all the problems you will meet in dealing with scientific information, but it can make the difference between feeling lost and victimized and feeling in reasonable control of your life. To the extent that this book can further these aims, it will have accomplished its basic purpose and been of some value to you.

ORGANIZATION OF THIS BOOK

If you had the chance to observe the activities of a research scientist over several months, you would find that almost all of his or her behavior during that period could be placed into one of three categories. Specifically, the scientist:

1. Will be in the process of observing and describing some phenomenon in nature
2. Will be in the process of thinking about that phenomenon in a manner intended to generate some questions about it
3. Will be in the process of actively manipulating nature in some manner designed to provide answers to the questions being asked

If you are a person who uses the scientific method to learn more about the world—whether you are a chemist, physicist, psychologist, social worker, or gas station operator—your working day will include the three basic categories of behavior described above. And these three categories also provide a good basis for organizing our discussion of behavioral research methodology in the present context. *Indeed, everything you will encounter in the following chapters can be viewed as an attempt to describe the various special rules and problems that a behavioral scientist encounters when engaging in these three basic activities.* The next few paragraphs will describe this organizational scheme in enough detail to give you a general idea of the material that will be covered.

Observation and Description

A graduate student who works part-time as a volunteer at a rape crisis center says that, once rape victims have recovered from their initial shock and injury, it is not uncommon for them to suffer from severe bouts of depression. This student has taken the first step in the three categories of behavior described earlier. She has observed a phenomenon, it has attracted her interest, and she wants to know more about it. All scientific research begins with such observations; it is therefore appropriate to focus our initial attention on this phase of the research process. Chapters 2 and 3 will be specifically concerned with the observation and description phase of scientific activity. We will consider the rules and regulations that must be followed if informal observations such as the one reported above are to be admissible for further analysis. We will also focus on some of the more prominent hazards that can interfere with this phase of the process.

Asking Questions

Next, in Chapter 4, we will consider the phase of scientific activity that can be described very simply as "thinking about the phenomenon and asking questions." This is the phase that calls for the most creativity. Test yourself. When you first read about postrape depression, did any questions about this phenomenon pop into your mind? Why does it occur—or, in other words, what factors would promote or discourage the development of these depressive episodes?

One might wonder, for instance, whether postrape depression would be less likely in cases where the rapist was quickly prosecuted and punished. Admittedly, this is not an especially ingenious idea. Do you have any additional thoughts about the matter? If so, hold onto them for now, because they may be useful later when we discuss the tactics that can be used to answer such questions. Perhaps you do not realize it now, but any question you might pose about the postrape depression phenomenon will present some very difficult problems when it comes to finding a way of answering it. Some phenomena are like that, and you will eventually be able to recognize the types of questions that pose special problems and those that do not.

Answering Questions

Beginning with Chapter 5, the remainder of the book will be devoted to explaining the tactics scientists use to answer the questions they ask. Some strategies are better than others; that is, they are less likely to produce misleading answers. You will learn, however, that *none* are foolproof, and that it pays to view the results obtained with different methods with different degrees of skepticism. Chapters 5 and 6 will be specifically concerned with a method called the *analytic experiment*. In Chapter 5 we will consider the simplest case of an analytic experiment and learn about its logic and architecture; in Chapter 6, we will explore more complex variations of the simple case. We open the discussion of research tactics with the analytic experiment because it is generally considered to be the least risky of the various methods scientists use to answer questions about nature.

Chapters 7 through 12 will elaborate upon two general themes. First there are a great many questions that force you to deviate in some important ways from your most powerful tool, the analytic experiment. In these chapters we will consider the logic and architecture of some of the most common deviations. Some authors refer to these as "quasi-experimental" procedures (e.g., Campbell & Stanley, 1966). Second, as we consider each of these deviations from the analytic experiment, we will also emphasize the hazards that you are most likely to encounter when you indulge in any particular deviation. By learning the "weaknesses" of each particular type of deviation, you will inevitably sharpen your own skills as a researcher and/or critic of scientific information.

Appendixes

You will have noted in the table of contents that a number of appendixes follow the last chapter. Depending upon background and previous course work, some students may find that they do not need to read every appendix. For this reason and to preserve the flow of the text, these special topics have been included as separate sections to be read at your discretion.

Very briefly, Appendix A is intended to improve your skills at using a library to find information relevant to any phenomenon that might attract your interest. Appendix B attempts to deal with many students' misgivings about the ethics of using humans or laboratory animals as experimental subjects. All scientific disciplines have developed codes of ethics designed to guide the scientist on these matters. Obviously, there are no right or wrong answers to ethical questions; they become a matter of informed judgment. The material in Appendix B is designed to introduce you to the problem of research ethics and make you think about it from various points of view. You will eventually have to reach your own conclusions, and it is important to consider all sides of the issue.

In some methodology courses, students are required to conduct research projects and to write research reports in the style required by journals that publish psychological research. The most widely accepted style for such reports is described in detail in the *Publication Manual of the American Psychological Association.* Appendix C is designed to help you write research reports in "APA style." The organization and basic elements of a research report are described and a copy of a student's report is reprinted to illustrate various details of a proper format. Should you require additional information, most university libraries have copies of the *Publication Manual of the American Psychological Association.*

You will learn later that most scientific research eventually involves some calculational procedures called *inferential statistics.* These statistical procedures can, in some cases, be very elaborate, and instructors differ in the degree to which they choose to emphasize them. Our bias, reflected in the organization of this book, is quite clear: it is that inferential statistics should be taught as a separate course *following* the introductory course in research methods. That is, once the basic logic and architecture of various research methods have been understood, statistical theory becomes more meaningful. Hence, this textbook introduces a bare minimum of inferential statistics. Appendix D is not intended to provide training in the use of statistical procedures. It is designed to illustrate why and how inferential statistics are a part of scientific research. It is best read after you have completed Chapter 5.

CHAPTER EXERCISES

At the end of most chapters, you will find at least one major exercise. These exercises are intended to test your understanding of the major concepts and principles that have just been discussed. Generally, they require you to *apply* what you have learned in some manner that will illustrate and elaborate upon the important concepts. Indeed, one such exercise is presented below. It shouldn't take much time, and it is designed to confirm the point made earlier in this chapter: that it pays to be skeptical about scientific information. Appendix E provides answers to selected questions from the exercises at the end of each chapter.

1.1. *The Case of the TV Diet.* You will recall the story, earlier in this chapter, about the child psychologist who claimed that research had shown a TV diet to be good for children. You might be interested to know that there is more to this story. As I was listening to that radio program, I had some doubts about the claims being made and decided to explore the matter. I called the radio station and asked for the name and address of the psychologist who had been interviewed. I then wrote the psychologist a letter to request any information that might be available on the topic of a TV diet, expressing particular interest in the research cited as evidence for its positive effects.

I later received a letter thanking me for my interest and enclosing a copy of the research on which the claims had been based. Surprisingly, this research had been reported a number of years ago by a journalist in *Redbook* magazine. This was obviously not a scientific journal, and the research had not been done by trained behavioral scientists. Hence, it would appear that my skepticism was justified. For your interest, the article from *Redbook* magazine follows. There are many reasons to question the conclusions drawn from the research reported in it. Read the article and test your own critical skills by listing as many criticisms as you can of the methods used to demonstrate that a TV diet is good for children.

HOW TV CHANGES CHILDREN

CLAIRE SAFRAN

Do your children need to go on a "television diet"? What would they lose? What would they—and you—gain? A Redbook experiment indicates that TV may be affecting your children more than you know.

Susie, who once hung back, playing in corners by herself, now joins in with the other three and four year olds of her nursery class. Young Mark has stopped playing at "blowing things up." It is two weeks since his last fist fight, and he doesn't tease and poke at the family pets as often as before. Mary, who was getting Ds and Fs on her third grade spelling tests, came home the other day with a B plus.

These are some of the changes in some of the children who took part in a recent Redbook experiment. Young children, according to most surveys and polls, watch television an average of two or three hours per day. What effect, Redbook's editors wondered, does this amount of TV watching have on them? Some of what the children see is good, even educational. Much of what they see has been called "bubble gum for the mind." Can this spoil a child's appetite for better kinds of nourishment? Can it make her sick?

Looking for answers, we asked a group of parents in New Milford, Connecticut to put their children on a "television diet," cutting them back to no more than an hour a day for a four-week test period. The differences in the children's behavior and in the quality of family life in just that short time are something that we think other parents should know about.

Like most diets, ours wasn't easy. Asked to change a habit, some of the children began by being cranky, fidgety, downright nervous, almost as if they were having "withdrawal pangs," as adults do when they cut back on food or cigarettes.

There were parental pangs too. In one family, the wife attends graduate school in the early evenings and the husband prepares dinner and looks after their three year old. He'd been using the television as an electronic cookie, something to offer when the child was fussy or bored or underfoot. Now, he invited the youngster to join in cooking. "It is not an unmitigated joy," he reports, "to have a three year old help you fix lasagna."

Note to Reader

At this point the article continues for several paragraphs offering descriptions of the adverse effects that TV is suspected to have on children's behavior. These include stories of boys who, wearing towels as capes, imitated Batman by jumping out of windows; babies who can't sleep unless the TV set is turned on; and youngsters who break their legs trying to imitate Evel Knievel's motorcycle stunts on their bicycles. The article then continues with reference to a study done in a nursery school in New York City.

Last year, Eleanor Brussels, principal of the Horace Mann School for the Nursery Years, a highly regarded private school in New York City, decided to do something about this. She sent a letter to parents explaining her concern about television and urging them to monitor the programs their children watched and to limit them to an hour a day. Most of the parents cooperated, and within three weeks there were some remarkable changes. The children seemed calmer and more relaxed at school. Instead of acting out Superman or the Flintstones, they began to play out their own minidramas and games that grow out of a child's own imagination. They were less easily distracted and could work creatively either alone or as a group—something only a few had been able to do before.

We talked with Ms. Brussels and her staff of teachers about their experience in limiting television. Would the same thing happen with other children? What would the children do during the hours that once were filled by TV? What would a mother do if she couldn't rely on her handy-dandy combination pacifier and baby sitter?

We decided to repeat the experiment, this time following up on it so that we could know what happened at home as well as in the classroom. In the quiet suburb of New Milford, Connecticut, we worked with the Family Resource Center, which includes nursery, kindergarten, and day care facilities, and with the First Congregational Church CO-OP Nursery. About 15 mothers agreed to join the television study, monitoring the shows their children watched and keeping diaries of what happened as they limited their viewing. Some of the teachers also contributed their observations, and when the test period was over, parents, teachers, and editors met for an exchange of impressions and feelings.

Here then are the results, concentrating on just a few of the families, whose experiences seem typical of the others, and changing their names for the sake of privacy.

If there were a prize for the most changed child, it would go to Susie Richards, a bright, usually well behaved four year old. Before the Redbook study she was a passive child, a bit too quiet, very much a loner. During her mornings at nursery school she fluttered on the edge of things. Despite her teacher's urgings, she refused to join the other children or to work by herself with clay, paints—anything that took real involvement.

During the first week, Susie had "fits of temper" over not being allowed to watch "Batman." At nursery school she was moodier than usual, sitting and staring at the ground. During the second week though, she began to ask her mother to invite a playmate home for the afternoons, something she'd rarely wanted before. Her teacher noticed that she played more with the other children and seemed happier and more talkative. By the end of four weeks, Susie seemed a different girl. She was no longer just an onlooker. Now she was a participant, playing creatively by herself or joining willingly in a dodge-ball game or a group project. To both her mother and her teacher, she seemed a happier child.

Did Susie change just because she was watching less television? There always have been shy or withdrawn children, of course, and many of them become less retiring in the natural course of time. Could that be what had happened to Susie?

During our study Susie kept asking when the "test" would be over. After four weeks her mother allowed her to resume her normal television watching habits. A couple of weeks after that, Susie's mother and teacher talked again. Susie was doing so well, the teacher said, but now she is off by herself, alone again. When the fantasies and adventures of television were taken away from her, Susie had felt a real need to reach out, to be involved, to find her own adventures. When they were returned, she withdrew again. There seems to be a definite cause and effect relationship between Susie's behavior and her television watching, and her mother has put her back on a "television diet."

Note to Reader

The article, at this point, describes several more examples of how the children's behavior improved according to the observations of the parents and the nursery school teacher. For example, Mark was calmer, listened to directions better, and quit teasing the family pet. Mary got her homework done on time and got better grades. Based on these descriptions, the article concludes:

The parents who took part in Redbook's experiment were loving and concerned mothers and fathers to begin with. For the most part their children were happy and healthy. With less television in their lives, the family members are a bit more involved with one another now; they seem a shade happier.

A couple of months after the test period ended, we checked back with some of the families. Now that they're no longer counting the video minutes to record them in diaries, some parents have added a bit to their children's viewing time. But they are still monitoring the shows, carefully filtering out the violence. Almost all are confident they will never slip back into the old patterns, the automatic click of the "on" button, the mindless watching.

These families have broken the habit. They have looked closely at their children, at the television that they were watching—and back again. For any parent, that can be an eyeful.

Concluding Comments

If you do not have many criticisms at this point, read on. I guarantee that you will find some help in the chapters that follow. But even at this point you will probably agree that it pays to be skeptical about some of the claims made in the name of science. Perhaps every claim made in this article about a TV diet is true—or maybe none of them are true. The point is that the tactics used to answer these questions would not be acceptable to a well-trained behavioral scientist— nor will they be acceptable to you once you have read the following chapters.

CHAPTER 2

OBSERVATION AND DESCRIPTION

SOME TYPICAL OBSERVATIONS

Located in the basement of an office building in the heart of Halifax, Nova Scotia, is a small business called Backstreet Imports. However, it does not sell imported goods, as the name would imply. Instead, its activity takes place in a dimly lit room filled with young people between 10 and 20 years of age and numerous electronic video games. Backstreet Imports is one of the many video-game arcades now found in every city in North America. Those who are very skilled at particular games in this arcade are held in high esteem by their peers. For example, "LOP" had the high score on a game called Zaxon for six weeks last winter. He was later displaced by "JET," a 15-year-old who holds the current record on both Zaxon and Battlezone.

For the uninitiated, the strange three-letter names used by the patrons of Backstreet Imports are usual in most video arcades. At the end of a game, each machine asks the player to input three identifying letters. If the score for that game is among the top scores for the day, the machine is programmed to display the three letters (e.g., LOP) along with the appropriate ranking on the video screen. This system lets all the players know the top ten on a daily basis; it also allows LOP and JET to display their achievements (or perhaps avoid displaying them by entering a false set of letters).

Consider next a student's weekend at a nearby ski resort where she and 14 of her friends had managed to stay overnight in a single motel room. Needless to say, the quarters were cramped; to make matters worse, the students were kept awake for most of the night by someone who was grinding and gnashing his teeth. Apparently the noise sounded like fingernails scraped rhythmically across a chalkboard. Our student found this somewhat bizarre until someone explained

13

that the phenomenon was not uncommon. It is called bruxism and apparently occurs in 20 percent of the general population (Glaros & Rao, 1977).

Finally, let's turn to a topic a student wanted to pursue as a research project. He was intrigued by some observations reported by the well-known ethologist Eckhard Hess. Hess (1975) had prepared two identical photographs of a female face and retouched one of them so as to enlarge the pupils of the eyes. When males were asked to rate these photographs, Hess found, curiously, that they tended to rate the female with the larger pupils as more friendly, sympathetic, and attractive than the one with the smaller pupils. On the basis of these and other similar results, Hess suggested that pupil size may serve as an important nonverbal signal between males and females during social interactions. As indicated above, the student found this phenomenon interesting and is now proceeding with his own plans for independent research on the topic.

The preceding paragraphs describe three phenomena that can be designated as follows: (1) video-game addiction, (2) bruxism, and (3) nonverbal communication. With the help of these examples, we can now discuss some general characteristics of the observation-and-description phase of scientific activity.

SOME CHARACTERISTICS OF SCIENTIFIC OBSERVATIONS

Spontaneous Discovery vs. Premeditated Observation

Scientific observation is often portrayed as an intense emotional process that always leads to exciting discoveries. When a major discovery is *serendipitous* (i.e., occurs through a lucky accident), it seems all the more thrilling. Sir Alexander Fleming's discovery of the drug penicillin in the 1920s is commonly cited as an example of this. While growing bacteria, Fleming noticed that a green mold had developed on his cultures and that this mold killed the bacteria. As you probably know, this green mold eventually led to the development of penicillin.

Although such an account makes interesting reading, it tells of the exception rather than the rule, presenting a distorted view of the way in which most scientists go about their daily business. The falsity of such portrayals becomes clear when students in advanced methodology courses are asked to find some phenomenon upon which to base their research projects. Typically, such students will return in a state of panic and report that, after several days, they have still not observed anything important. It may well be that those who fail in this initial task do so because they have been reading too many stories about great discoveries in the history of science. They are desperately searching for their own version of an "exotic green mold," and they cannot manage to find one. They fail to realize that such discoveries do not occur every day.

The cure for the "exotic-green-mold syndrome" is to consider a few observations like those that introduced the present chapter. These examples are more typical. A social psychologist might focus her attention on the video-arcade behavior of LOP and JET and ask some interesting questions about their behavior. Or a geriatric nurse, noticing that her patients preferred certain types of food over others, might ask questions about their diet and food preferences. Or a

researcher in behavioral medicine, observing widespread depression among sur-
vivors of major heart attacks, might wonder how such depression can be prevented.

The point of all these examples is that the overwhelming bulk of scientific
research does not begin with accidents, such as the dramatic discovery of a green
mold that eats bacteria! It starts when some individual makes a premeditated
decision to focus on an interesting event. Often, the event is a very commonly
observed phenomenon or one that has already been the focus of numerous
experiments and journal articles. Once students realize this, they tend to develop
the opposite problem. They see *too many* events about which they would like to
ask questions.

Passive vs. Active Observation

Another feature of the examples described at the outset of this chapter is that
the observer was, for the most part, a passive agent. In reality, however, the
observation process seldom remains passive for long. As your interest in a
phenomenon develops, you will inevitably ask some questions and be tempted
to arrange a situation that will provide some answers. At that point you have
moved past the preliminary stage of passive observation and into the more active
process of designing an experiment. In fact, it is almost impossible not to slip
into this active mode. A simple example will illustrate the point.

Suppose you became interested in the video-arcade behavior of LOP and
JET. Every afternoon, you would go to the arcade and observe these two; you
would keep records of the games they played, their scores, the amount of time
they spent on each game, and any interactions they might have with others in
the arcade. At this point, you would still be a passive observer, describing their
behavior as it occurred under natural conditions. However, if you were a curious
person, you would not be able to tolerate this passivity for long. Eventually, you
would probably want to change one of the games in the arcade. Suppose, for
example, that you modified the Zaxon game so that it no longer displayed the
top scores for the day. Having made the change, you would return each day to
see what happened. Would you still be a passive observer? Obviously not.
Implicit in your actions would be the question: Is the public ranking of scores
necessary to maintain interest in this game? In changing the machine, you would
be creating the conditions that could provide the answer to this question. Although the tactics you used would not (as you will discover) be the best available,
this example illustrates the basic point. There is a very short distance between
passive observation and the later activities required to obtain answers. In other
words, the three phases of scientific activity described in Chapter 1 are not as
neatly separated as our discussion might have implied.

GROUND RULES FOR OBSERVATION AND DESCRIPTION

In this section, we will consider two basic rules the scientist must follow during
observation and description. The first recognizes that our everyday language is

not precise enough to prevent confusion. This rule states that *the phenomena we observe must be defined in terms of the operations used to measure those phenomena*. Such definitions are called *operational definitions* (Bridgman, 1927); their main purpose is to prevent confusion by making scientific observations publicly reproducible and reliable. The second rule states that *the procedures used to make our observations should not introduce distortions*. In future discussion, we shall refer to these two rules as the *operational-definition rule* and the *distortion rule*. The rest of this chapter will explain and explore some of the more important implications of these rules.

The Operational-Definition Rule

If ten dentists told you the percentage of their patients that suffered from bruxism, you would probably get ten very different answers—not because their patients were so different but because each dentist might have a unique idea of what the term "bruxism" means. One might simply ask patients if they grind their teeth during sleep; another might actually measure the amount of wear on the grinding surfaces; and so on. You can see how these different definitions would produce different estimates of the disorder. Each estimate is correct, but only "in the eye of the observer."

For scientific purposes, the appropriate approach to the problem of counting bruxists would be to say:

> O.K., I will count bruxists, but first we will have to agree on an operational definition. When I use the term, I am referring to any patient who exhibits at least 0.2 mm of wear on the grinding surfaces of at least two molars over a period of six months of observation. If you agree, we can proceed to count bruxists; if not, what changes would you like to make in the definition?

This more rigorous approach removes, for the most part, any confusion by defining bruxism in terms of the *publicly reproducible operations necessary to measure the phenomenon*. Such is the beauty of a good operational definition. It permits anyone who looks at a patient's teeth to decide whether that person is a bruxist or not. Ten different dentists can look at the same patient and reach the same conclusions, or one dentist can look at the same patient on ten different occasions and make the same judgment each time. In this sense, operational definitions make our observations and descriptions of phenomena publicly *reproducible* and *reliable*.

Several characteristics of the operational-definition rule deserve additional discussion. The first is that a knowledge of this rule can turn you into a real bore! You will find that people hate to have their conversations restricted in this way. For example, in a discussion of pornography on a recent TV news program, it was argued that pornographic magazines tend to alter men's attitudes toward women in various negative ways. If the moderator had asked your opinion, would you have agreed with this point of view? It may seem that any reasonable person could easily offer an opinion on this, but it is not enough to be reasonable if there is no mutual agreement on the meaning of the term "pornography." The "pictures" in the moderator's mind could be very different from the "pictures" in yours. Consequently, your best reply would be to ask for an operational definition before you attempted to discuss the question. In everyday conversation, such a reply may be taken as an effort to avoid the issue. But it is plain that no issue can be seriously discussed if it is not first defined!

Perhaps most people find the operational-definition rule objectionable because terms seem to lose some of their conventional meaning when they are operationally defined. Scientists are also concerned about this loss of meaning. They call it a loss of *construct validity*.

This dilemma can be illustrated by continuing with our pornography example. For argument's sake, let us say that *a pornographic magazine is any magazine containing at least one picture of a male or female with complete frontal nudity*. Do you agree that this is a good operational definition? You may feel sure that it is not, but in fact it is. You may dislike the definition because it is too narrow and restricted. In your mind, the term "pornography" conjures up a much wider range of images than simple frontal nudity. Recall, however, that the basic purpose of the operational definition is to prevent confusion. If, using this definition, you were to look through a given group of ten magazines, you would surely be able to tell which of them were pornographic. In other words, this definition of pornography is now publicly reproducible and can be reliably used by anyone else.

The point is that operational definitions eliminate confusion in scientific observation and description; they do not guarantee that the definition will capture all the conventional meaning that a term carries for everyone using it. Hence, your objections to our prudish definition are not directed at its *reliability*; they are directed at its failure to capture the various meanings of "pornography" beyond mere frontal nudity (that is, the *construct validity* of the term). Indeed, it often seems that the better a definition is at eliminating confusion, the worse it is at capturing the everyday meaning of a term. This is a basic dilemma. In using an operational definition, we usually gain reliability and eliminate confusion, but we also lose construct validity. Operational definitions that maximize reliability and minimize the loss of construct validity should be cherished.

In practice, scientists usually escape from this dilemma by working with many different operational definitions of the same concept. If you object to our definition of pornography, you are welcome to propose your own and to make your own measurements and observations based on your definition. Given enough time and a variety of definitions, we should eventually reach a reasonable understanding of the properties of pornographic material. The vital point is that each definition must be publicly reproducible and reliable.

Another important characteristic of operational definitions becomes obvious once you understand that there are many possible operational definitions for a single term. Specifically, it should not surprise you to find that different operational definitions of the same term will often produce conflicting observations. For example, it is possible for one scientist to claim that pornography has no effect on male attitudes while another claims that pornography does have an effect. You should now understand that these statements are not necessarily contradictory: the two scientists may simply have used very different operational definitions in the course of trying to answer the same question. Of course, to the outsider who is not familiar with the operational-definition rule, these scientists appear to be crazy. One appears to be saying one thing and the other the opposite. In fact, conflicting observations based on different operational definitions should not be viewed as a problem. Instead, it can be argued that it is good for scientists to work with a variety of operational definitions. The results obtained with many different definitions will eventually reveal the complexities of concepts such as pornography.

An article in *MacLean's Magazine* (Law, 1980) illustrates the preceding point very effectively. In this article, entitled "Yes, Virginia, Drinking Is Good for Your Health," the author reports that alcohol prevents the development of various types of heart disease. Of course, this information would seem to contradict much other evidence about the effects of alcohol. In other words, after reading this article, we find ourselves with conflicting advice. How can drinking be good for our health and bad for our health at the same time? Somebody has to be wrong, crazy, or both!

If you have understood the preceding discussion of the operational-definition rule, you now have at least one possible explanation for this conflicting advice. It is possible that both conclusions are correct. If "alcohol" is operationally defined in terms of very small quantities, the conclusions concerning the prevention of heart disease might be correct for that particular operational definition. If, however, "alcohol" is operationally defined in terms of larger quantities, the more traditional conclusions concerning the negative effects of alcohol on health might be correct, again for that particular operational definition. In other words, the scientists are neither wrong nor crazy. It is conceivable that drinking is both good and bad for your health *depending upon the particular operational definition of alcohol* that was employed. Furthermore, the use of more than one operational definition of alcohol consumption has given us more complete information on the properties of alcohol than we had with only one operational definition (i.e., heavy alcohol consumption).

If you are persistent enough to search the library for the scientific report on which the *MacLean's* article was based, you will discover that this hunch about the different operational definitions is correct. Very small quantities of alcohol were used by the scientists (Hennekens, Willet, Rosner, Cole, & Mayrent, 1979) who observed the positive effects of alcohol on heart disease. (If you are interested in considering this particular medical question in more detail, you might wish to consult a discussion of the issue by Castelli, 1979.)

The Distortion Rule

As described earlier, the second basic rule to be followed during the observation-and-description phase of scientific enquiry is the distortion rule. If we ignore, for practical reasons, philosophical questions about the reality of the world, the purpose of this rule is obvious. We want to be sure our observations are accurate.

You might think that distorted observations are rare in science. Not so. One of the classic examples occurred when early astronomers reported that various planets had color fringes around them. This led them to assume that the planets were emitting different wavelengths of light—that is, until someone discovered that the color fringes were chromatic aberrations produced by the imperfect lenses used in early telescopes. Although this example comes from astronomy, the avoidance of distorted observations is also one of the most difficult problems faced by the behavioral scientist. Indeed, the following discussion will probably convince you that it is almost impossible for the behavioral scientist to meet the requirements of the distortion rule.

Three basic types of distortion can occur when you are observing behavior: (1) those introduced by instruments used to observe and measure behavior, (2) those introduced by observer bias, and (3) those introduced by sampling procedures. We will consider each and illustrate how difficult it is to find appropriate solutions.

Distortion Produced by Instruments   Behavioral scientists use movie cameras, video cameras, high-speed photographic analysis, and numerous other technological devices to record and analyze behavioral events. Given the technology that we have today, it is unusual to find distortion of the sort encountered by the astronomers described above. A more likely and serious problem is the impact of the observer and all the technical equipment on the person or animal under observation. Put quite simply, the very act of observing an individual is sufficient to cause distortions in the behavior of that individual. Imagine, if you will, walking into a video arcade like Backstreet Imports with a movie camera on your shoulder and filming LOP and JET. Do you think you would obtain an undistorted, natural record of their activities? The point is as obvious as it is problematic. How do you observe these individuals without influencing their usual patterns of behavior? There might be a number of devious ways to go about the task, but these are usually prohibited by ethical rules intended to protect people's privacy (see Appendix B for a discussion of these issues).

The same basic problem will arise if you try to obtain an undistorted measurement of a phenomenon like bruxism. Any device you use to measure the jaw's grinding movements will very likely interfere with the activity or perhaps accentuate it. I have challenged students to find a solution to this particular problem, and the scenarios generated would qualify as scripts for a James Bond movie. The solution most frequently proposed involves implanting tiny pressure sensors and transmitters in each of the teeth and monitoring the grinding activity at a distance with a telemetry device. Little concern seems to be wasted on the poor subject, who is left with a mouth full of useless hardware once the observations have been completed.

These problems and solutions sound humorous in the abstract, but they are not too far from reality. If you wish to observe behavior in a video arcade or monitor the jaw movements of a bruxist without distortion, it does require considerable ingenuity. If you are interested in a more extensive analysis of this source of distortion and artifact, Rosenthal and Rosnow (1969) have devoted an entire volume to the many variations on the theme. The basic problem has not changed in the time since they wrote their influential book. The presence of an observer and observation equipment is a major source of distortion. You should always take this problem into account in analyzing the results of your own observations or the observations of other scientists.

Distortion Produced by Observer Bias   Another serious and difficult source of distortion is the bias introduced by any preconceived ideas and assumptions you may have about the phenomenon you are observing. An excellent example of this comes once again from the field of astronomy. T. S. Kuhn, in his classic book *The Structure of Scientific Revolutions,* notes that prior to the Copernican revolution, western astronomers operated on the basic assumption that the universe was a static, unchanging system. Under this assumption, one would not expect to observe, for example, new planets emerging in the system. Accordingly, no new planets were reported. After the Copernican revolution, a different set of assumptions was accepted: namely, that the universe was a developing system in which regular changes and new planets might be observed. Curiously, in the first half-century following the Copernican revolution, western astronomers discovered many new and interesting events. It was during this period, for example, that Sir William Herschel discovered the plant Uranus. Apparently what one believes can determine what one will observe! You might propose that technological improvements after the Copernican revolution accounted for the new discoveries. No so. The Chinese astronomers, with far less sophisticated instruments, had reported the planet Uranus long before the western astronomers. Of course, the Chinese view of the universe did not assume that it was static and unchanging.

Do you think similar bias and distortion can occur when you observe behavioral phenomena? I have no doubt that it does; if anything, such bias is more prominent in the context of behavioral observations. A recent example, although not yet completely resolved, probably makes the argument as well as any single example could.

Anyone interested in anthropology has heard of Margaret Mead and her first book called *Coming of Age in Samoa,* which has become a classic. It is an account of her observations of the Samoan culture and, in particular, of the attitudes and behavior of Samoan adolescents. After extensive study, Mead concluded that the Samoan culture was a very casual society with little evidence of the guilt, conflict, and adolescent turmoil that is so typical of North American culture. She observed that Samoans permitted free love among their adolescents, and she thought that this practice in particular might account for the lack of sexual violence and adolescent stress.

Approximately sixty years have passed since Mead made these observations, and her research on this culture has now been challenged for the first time by Derek Freeman, an anthropologist who has also done extensive research on the Samoan culture. His book on the topic is titled *Margaret Mead and Samoa: The Making and Unmaking of an Anthropological Myth.* As the title implies, Freeman argues that Margaret Mead's observations of this culture were very much distorted. Based on his own observations of the Samoans in the 1940s and a considerable amount of other evidence, Freeman describes a Samoan culture very different from the one reported by Mead. According to Freeman: (1) adolescent Samoans are puritanical in their sexual mores and place a high value on virginity; (2) there is a high frequency of violent crime, including rape, in the culture; and (3) there is considerable evidence for adolescent stress and turmoil.

How can this happen? Two anthropologists observe the same culture and report events of an entirely different nature. Given our previous discussion of operational definitions, you might think that some of the confusion might originate from lack of precise operational definitions. Given the degree of difference, that seems an unlikely explanation. Where the one saw happiness and free love, the other saw rape and violence. This suggests that something other than operational definitions was amiss.

Freeman (1983) argues persuasively that Mead's view of the Samoans was, in fact, distorted by her preconceived beliefs about their culture, and that these distortions were inevitable given that she was not fluent in the Samoan language and consequently had only very indirect exposure to the Samoan culture. Is Freeman correct in these accusations? Did Margaret Mead have strong preconceived ideas about the nature of the culture she was observing? Did these ideas distort her perceptions? Unfortunately, Mead died before Freeman's claims were published. Hence it is not possible to obtain her answer to the question.

Freeman points out that a major question of interest at the time Margaret Mead was making her observations was whether adolescent turmoil is a product of cultural practices per se or a consequence of heredity. If adolescent problems are a product of cultural practices (e.g., sexual repression), one should be able to find cultures that do not produce the typical "troubled teenager." If, alternatively, this stress is hereditary, then troubled teenagers should be observable in all cultures regardless of their characteristics. Freeman suggests that Margaret Mead was convinced, prior to her visit to Samoa, that adolescent turmoil was a product of cultural practices, not heredity. He suggests that she therefore saw what she wanted to see and was blind to things that failed to fit her preconceptions.

No matter how the dust settles on this controversy, the example serves to make several important points about observation and description in science. First, it shows that our preconceived ideas as observers can distort our observations. You should recognize that all observers are subject to this bias, including world-class anthropologists like Margaret Mead and Derek Freeman. Second, you should note that this type of bias and distortion has nothing to do with the *integrity* of the observer. For example, to my knowledge, absolutely no one questions the honesty of either of these anthropologists—nor should it be questioned. Both believed their observations and described them as accurately as they could. Finally, the moral of the story is that no one completely escapes this problem. It is ubiquitous. Every observer has beliefs and attitudes that can distort observations. If, for example, you are involved in a project to monitor the recovery of rape victims from their trauma, to document the development of a retarded child who has been placed in a special classroom, or to describe the recovery of a stroke victim from partial paralysis, you will inevitably begin the process with deep-seated attitudes and beliefs about each of these phenomena. These attitudes can seriously distort your observations and descriptions. You do not have to take a banana boat to Samoa to find examples of this problem; it is always present when you look at the world and try to describe what you see.

As the preceding examples indicate, there would seem to be no simple solution to this source of distortion. An admirable attitude was expressed several decades ago by Hyman (1954). He suggests that "All scientific inquiry is subject to error, and it is far better to be aware of this, to study the sources in an attempt to reduce it, and to estimate the magnitude of such errors in our findings than to be ignorant of the errors concealed in the data."

This is probably the only general solution to these violations of the distortion rule. Besides, we must realize that, since there are many different scientists who eventually observe the same phenomenon, it is unlikely that all of them will share the same set of preconceived ideas about its properties. In short, one individual's distorted view should eventually be tested by the observations of many others. This is just one of the fortunate self-corrective features of scientific inquiry. The controversy between Margaret Mead and Derek Freeman is not a *scandal,* as some popular accounts of the story would imply (see *Time,* Feb. 14, 1983). Instead, as a consumer of scientific information, you should be glad that this self-corrective feature of scientific observation is healthy and at work challenging the inevitable distortions that tend to occur from time to time.

Distortions Produced by Sampling Procedures   Scientists almost always encounter two practical problems when they decide to observe and describe some phenomenon. Unfortunately, the solutions to these practical problems are often a source of distortion and bias. If, for example, you are interested in bruxism, it would obviously be desirable to observe this phenomenon on a *continuous* basis in order to describe its temporal characteristics (occurrence in terms of time). When does it occur? When it does occur, how long does it persist? Continuous observation of an individual would seem to be necessary to obtain data on these questions, but this poses a major practical problem. It is often difficult to arrange for observation 24 hours a day over a period of many days.

The typical solution has been to use one of many *time-sampling* observational procedures. With these, the observer assumes that samples of behavior can be observed during predetermined periods of time; then, the characteristics of the continuous time record can be *inferred* from these samples. As you might imagine, there is considerable room for error in this process.

A second and conceptually related problem is to determine how often a phenomenon like bruxism is observed in a given population. For example, how many students enrolled in your university grind their teeth during sleep? Once again, the practical problem is obvious. It would be difficult to observe every student in the university and to determine whether he or she were a bruxist; that would be an enormous job. Once again, the solution is to obtain a smaller sample of students from this population. If the smaller sample is representative of the larger population, you should be able, from the proportion that you find in your sample, to estimate the proportion of grinders in the entire university. The key word, of course, is *representative*. If the sample is not representative, your estimates will be biased and, as you might imagine, the danger of bias is substantial.

You can see that these two practical problems and their solutions are conceptually similar. In the one case, looking at a particular behavior, we try to find the characteristics of its continuous time record by sampling smaller segments of time and estimating from those. In the other case, considering a particular event, we try to find the frequency of its occurrence in a large population by observing its frequency in a smaller sample and basing our estimate on that. We shall refer to these two basic categories of sampling as *time sampling* and *event sampling* respectively, and we shall complete our discussion of the *distortion rule* by considering each of these cases in more detail. Please note that the use of the terms "time sampling" and "event sampling" is by no means universal in discussions of sampling procedures. Indeed, you may find them used in very different ways by different authors (e.g., Altmann, 1974; Lehner, 1979).

Time Sampling   Of the various forms that mental illness can take, one of the most disturbing and perplexing is the self-injurious behavior sometimes exhibited by autistic children. As a student, I once toured a local mental hospital as a part of a course in abnormal psychology. The purpose of the tour was to explain some of the different treatment programs available in the hospital. As we passed through the children's ward, I noticed that a young girl in one of the cribs was wearing a football helmet. On inquiring about this child, I was told that the helmet was for her own protection. Apparently, she frequently smashed her head against the iron railings on the side of the crib. Without the helmet to protect her, she would literally beat herself unconscious. I asked how frequently these bouts of head bashing occurred and how long they typically lasted. The nurse said that she had seen bouts last as long as 20 or 30 minutes, but she was unable to say how frequently they occurred. She did not have the time to monitor each patient in the ward on a continuous basis.

This long-past but well-remembered experience comes to mind for obvious reasons. It is exactly the sort of situation in which a behavioral scientist often resorts to a time-sampling procedure. If, for example, you wanted to know how frequently this child bashed her head against the crib and how long these bouts typically lasted, you would have two choices. You could arrange to monitor the behavior continuously 24 hours a day, day after day, or to observe the behavior by sampling segments of time according to some prearranged plan.

If, for practical reasons, you are forced to use the time-sampling procedure, how would you schedule your observation periods? From the outset, you should understand that there is no standard formula to guarantee that your sampling procedure will provide an undistorted estimate. Although standard procedures are often proposed in the literature on this topic, they must be used with a heavy dose of common sense. Every situation will require some special considerations. In the present discussion, we shall consider just one example of a popular time-sampling procedure and illustrate some of the problems that you may encounter in using variations on it. If you can generalize what we have to say about these few examples to other situations, you will be able to invent your own time-sampling procedures and be sensitive to the dangers associated with this process.

One of the most frequently encountered time-sampling procedures is called *one-zero time sampling*. With this procedure, the observer establishes some arbitrary unit of time (e.g., 30 minutes, 30 seconds) during which the patient is observed. A number of such intervals are scheduled. If, during a particular observation interval, head-bashing behavior is observed, a "1" is recorded for that interval. If no head bashing occurs during that interval, a "0" is recorded. Given a reliable operational definition of what is meant by "head bashing," this procedure is very easy to use. You should realize, however, that your decisions about the length of each observation interval and the scheduling of these intervals are very important. Every situation calls for a lot of common sense and consideration before these decisions are made. Figure 2.1 illustrates some of the decisions you might make and the problems you will encounter when you make them.

Assume that the first record at the top of Figure 2.1 is an actual continuous time record of head-bashing behavior observed over a period of 24 consecutive hours. As you can see, the continuous observation record indicates that observation commenced at 1200 hours and terminated exactly 24 hours later. During that period, 12 bouts of head bashing occurred. The longest bout commenced at 2400 hours and lasted 3 hours (dark areas of record); the shortest bout started at 1400 hours and lasted about 15 minutes.

Now assume that we tried to estimate the characteristics of this continuous record by time sampling, using *one-zero convenience sampling* as shown in Figure 2.1. This is perhaps the most common variation on one-zero sampling procedures. As the name implies, the observations are made whenever it is most practical or *convenient*. In the example presented in Figure 2.1, the patient was observed for a 30-minute period on six occasions that were convenient (i.e., during a coffee break, after lunch, etc.). This convenience schedule permitted observations of head bashing at 1500 hours and again at 1630 hours. Other observation periods were scored as zero, indicating that no head bashing occurred.

Common sense should tell you that, in spite of its popularity, convenience sampling is not a very good choice. If, for example, the observer's convenience schedule corresponds with the patient's sleep schedule, the observer's time-sample data would underestimate the amount of head bashing. Similarly, coincidences in the other direction would overestimate the frequency of head bashing. The data illustrated for convenience sampling in Figure 2.1 are arranged to demonstrate how a particular schedule can seriously underestimate the frequency and duration of head-banging behavior.

Consider, next, the variation on one-zero sampling called *one-zero fixed-time sampling,* also illustrated in Figure 2.1. As the label implies, observations are made at predetermined, fixed intervals of time. In this particular example, 30-minute observation periods have been scheduled every 4.5 hours throughout the day and night, whether they are convenient or not.

Again, common sense should tell you that this may not always be the best approach. If, for example, the head-bashing behavior (or any behavioral phenom-

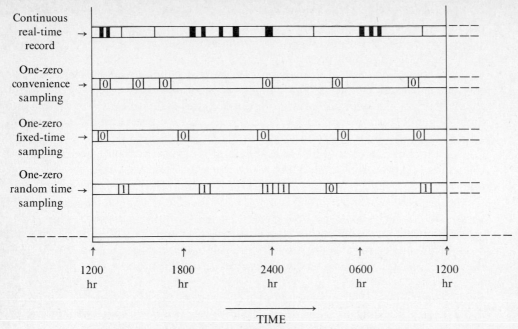

Figure 2.1 Estimating characteristics of a real-time continuous record using three different one-zero time-sampling procedures over a 24-hour period.

enon) happens to occur with some regularity or pattern (that is, if it has a definite rhythm), the fixed interval that you schedule might be in phase with that pattern or out of phase with it. In either case, your time sample would be distorted. In one case, you would grossly overestimate the frequency and duration of the behavior; in the other case, you would underestimate. In the example illustrated in Figure 2.1, the observer's fixed time schedule was out of phase with bouts of head bashing and would lead to the conclusion that the child does not bash its head very frequently.

Finally, consider the illustration of *one-zero random sampling* in Figure 2.1. In this variation on the procedure, the observer first decides on the length of the time-sample interval (e.g., 30 minutes). Next, the 24-hour period is divided into the 48 possible 30-minute periods during which observations can be made. If the observer decides to observe during six of the 48 possible observation intervals, those six are selected *at random*. For example, the 48 periods could be recorded on 48 separate cards, the deck shuffled; then the six cards drawn would represent the periods during which observations would be made.

If you repeated this random-selection process each day over a period of one month, each potential observation period would have an equal probability of being selected as an observation interval. This is what is meant by the term "random" in this context. Common sense should tell you that this random procedure will eliminate some of the problems that were encountered with convenience and fixed-time sampling procedures. The random selection of observation intervals will, by definition, prevent the observer from being in or out of phase with the phenomenon under observation; hence the chances for distortion are reduced. The six sampling intervals illustrated in Figure 2.1 were obtained using a random selection procedure.

Although the random-sampling procedure is generally to be preferred for the reasons described above, you will appreciate that it can be very inconvenient for the person who will be required to observe the patient at any time of day or night depending upon the "luck of the draw." This is probably the reason that random time sampling is not used as often as it should be.

To summarize briefly, Figure 2.1 illustrates several variations on a standard time-sampling procedure called *one-zero sampling*. Each variation has its particular problems and advantages. If there is a moral to the story, it is that you should use common sense in designing these procedures. Each situation will call for special tactics; in the present context, it would not be possible or desirable to describe all the special circumstances you might encounter. If you find yourself having difficulty designing a particular time-sampling procedure, Altmann's (1974) discussion of this topic is still one of the best available.

Event Sampling   When we encounter a behavioral phenomenon that seems interesting and unusual to us, a very common reaction is to ask how frequently the phenomenon occurs in the population. For example, I recently read an article in a medical journal suggesting that breast-fed babies show a lower incidence of childhood allergies than babies that have been fed a commercially available formula (Kajosaari & Saarinen, 1983). This particular study was conducted in Finland, and as I read it, I wondered whether or not breast-feeding is a common practice in North America. How would I proceed to answer this question?

One approach to the problem is to observe every infant born in North America during the next year and count the number of cases in which the infant is breast-fed. This would obviously be a monumental task. A more reasonable and commonly used approach would be to select a smaller *sample* of cases from the entire *population* (i.e., North America). The idea is to estimate how many infants in the entire population were breast-fed by observing the proportion of breast-fed infants in the smaller sample. Any procedure for estimating the frequency of a behavioral event in a population is called *event sampling*. As you will discover, the problems encountered in designing an event-sampling procedure parallel those of *time-sampling* procedures.

All event-sampling procedures share certain characteristics. First, a *population*—that is, any clearly defined group of individuals in whom the observer is interested—must be delineated. It might consist of all individuals living in New York City who are less than 5 feet tall or all females with red hair who live in cities with populations of less than 10,000. In our breast-feeding example, the population is defined as all infants born in North America during the past 12 months. Second, a *sample* is selected from the defined population. The goal is to obtain a *representative sample* of individuals. If it is representative, we should be able to estimate accurately the characteristics of the larger population from the smaller sample. If half the mothers in the population breast-feed their babies, a representative sample would also show approximately the same proportion of breast-feeders (e.g., one half the sample). How does one manage to select a *representative* sample? The answer depends to a large extent on the specific conditions for which a sampling procedure is being designed and, once again, I can outline only a few of the problems you might encounter.

Figure 2.2 illustrates some of the basic variations on *event-sampling* procedures. In order to keep the numbers small, we will start with the assumption that only 100 infants were born in North America during the past 12 months and that you have this complete list at your disposal. In the diagram at the top of Figure 2.2, each infant in this population has been given a number. Assume also that the infants circled in this population are those who are actually being breast-fed. Note that there are, in fact, 20 such cases in this population. Your task is to select a sample of 10 cases from this population which can be assumed to be representative (i.e., that has approximately the same proportion of breast-fed babies as does the population). How do you proceed?

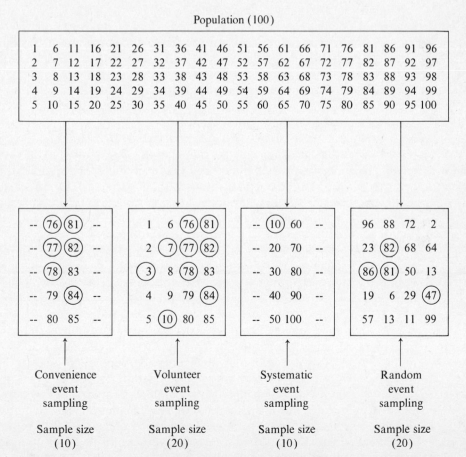

Figure 2.2 Estimating the number of breast-fed babies in a population of 100 cases using four different event-sampling procedures.

The first sample illustrated in Figure 2.2 was obtained by using a *convenience event-sampling* procedure. As the name implies, the observer decided to select the 10 subjects numbered consecutively from 76 to 85. A typical reason for a convenience sample might be that these 10 cases were born in a local maternity hospital. The observer had convenient access to the records and information and no particular reason to suspect that women giving birth at this hospital would be unusual or nonrepresentative of the North American population as a whole. Unfortunately, convenience event sampling is perhaps the most frequently encountered procedure; "unfortunately" because the price of convenience is a high risk of distortion. Almost by definition, a sample that is "convenient" is going to have some unique characteristics. Note in Figure 2.2 that the convenience sample yielded 6 cases of breast-feeding in the 10 cases sampled, suggesting that 60 percent of the population breast-feed their infants. This is obviously an overestimate of the population characteristic (20 percent); it is the type of distortion that might occur if the convenient hospital happened to have a pediatrician on staff who was very enthusiastic about breast-feeding.

Consider next the example titled *volunteer event sampling,* which is also illustrated in Figure 2.2. This procedure is basically a variation on the convenience-sampling procedure described above. As the name implies, volunteer event sampling refers to any procedure in which members of the population volunteer to be a part of the sample. Suppose, for example, that you mailed requests for information to 50 mothers in this population of 100 and that only 20 replied (this rate of return would not be unusual). Assume, as the data in Figure 2.2 indicate, that 9 of these 20 mothers breast-feed their infants.

Common sense should tell you that these 20 volunteers are probably a biased or distorted sample of the population. The fact that they volunteered makes them special by definition. You might predict, for example, that mothers who breast-feed are more likely to reply to a request for information. It is inconvenient to breast-feed an infant in contemporary North American society. Women often work outside the home or maintain a busy schedule of activities within it. Hence there is good reason to think that a woman who decides to breast-feed will feel very strongly about the matter and be more prepared to express these opinions. Whether you are right or wrong in this prediction is beside the point. The fact remains that the dangers of bias are high when you depend in any way on the whims of volunteers to provide you with a sample.

Examine next, the *systematic event-sampling* procedure illustrated in Figure 2.2. As the name implies, the observer starts with a complete numbered list and systematically selects every "nth" person from it. As indicated in Figure 2.2, the selection of every tenth individual from the population gives us a sample of 10 cases. The danger of bias with this procedure is perhaps not as high as it would be in convenience sampling or volunteer sampling *unless* there happened to be some pattern in the enumeration of the population. Suppose, for example, that our population of mothers were numbered consecutively in a manner that just happened to place older women in every tenth position of the numbering system. If older mothers are less likely to breast-feed their infants, this numbering system would bias our systematic sample toward the selection of older mothers, as has been illustrated in Figure 2.2. The basic point is that systematic samples can lead to distortion or bias if there is some underlying pattern in the way the population has been listed or numbered.

It might be noted at this point that people often mistakenly believe that they can overcome the above sampling errors if a large enough sample is taken. The preceding examples should illustrate that the old maxim "the larger your sample the more accurate it will be" is simply not true in all cases. If, for instance, you use a volunteer sampling procedure, it is clear that you run the risk of obtaining a biased sample. If you multiply the size of the sample by 10, all you will do is obtain a larger sample with the same bias! It can, however, be demonstrated that if your sample is representative (i.e., does not have any source of bias or distortion), then it is true that the larger the sample, the more accurate it will be.

Turn your attention now to the *random event sampling* procedure illustrated in Figure 2.2. As was the case with the random time-sampling procedure discussed earlier, a random event sampling procedure should theoretically eliminate the sources of bias and distortion mentioned in the descriptions of event-sampling procedures above.

In order to select a random sample of 20 cases from the population of mothers in Figure 2.2, you must devise a procedure that will permit each mother in the population to have an *equal* chance of being selected. Chance, and chance alone, should be the factor that determines whether or not a particular mother is selected. That is what is meant by the term "random" in the context of event sampling. One way you might accomplish this task is to place the name of each mother on a card and shuffle the deck thoroughly. If you draw 20 cards from the deck of 100, it should be obvious that chance alone will determine which mothers will be selected; you will then have a random sample. It should also be obvious that you have eliminated some of the bias and distortion found in some of the other event-sampling procedures already described. With a random sample, there is no reason to think that we have overestimated or underestimated the number of mothers in the population. As indicated in Figure 2.2, our random sample of 20 mothers produced 4 cases of breast-feeding, which is the same proportion as found in the population.

Several additional points should be made about the random event sampling procedure. First, chance is chance, and the outcome of any random selection procedure will vary each time you select a sample from the population. The next time you sample 20 mothers, you might find 5 cases of breast-feeding, or 3 cases, or 6 cases, and so on. There is even a small probability that chance could deal you a sample of 20 breast-feeding mothers in a random sample of 20. Mathematicians show us, however, that large variations from the actual population proportion are less likely than small variations. Hence, the variations occurring by chance alone are viewed by most scientists as the least offensive of many possible sources of distortion. To help matters, if your sample is truly random, you may assume that the larger the sample, the greater the probability that your sample offers a close estimate of the population characteristics.

A second point is that it is often impossible, for a wide variety of practical reasons, to obtain a truly random sample from your population. To illustrate this point, you must step outside of the nice convenient population provided in Figure 2.2. In reality, the number of mothers having babies every day in North America is extremely large. Can you imagine obtaining a truly random sample from this population? In order to follow the rules of random event sampling, every mother in the population would have to have an equal chance of being selected for the sample; otherwise you would be introducing some source of bias or distortion. The logistical problems of obtaining such a truly random sample are probably insurmountable. Even if you could obtain a complete list of the population, there would probably be some bias in the method you used to contact the people on the list and consequently some bias in the sample. As you can see, there are very few situations in which a scientist can be guaranteed a random sample in the strictest sense of the word.

Finally, you can see that the person making a decision about selecting a sample from a population always faces the same basic dilemma. A truly random sample is the best approach, but the logistical problems that must be overcome to meet the criterion of randomness are often insurmountable. Alternatively, procedures such as convenience and volunteer sampling carry substantial dangers of distortion and bias, but they do not impose insurmountable logistical problems. The net result is that scientists do not often make the effort to be strictly random. They settle on something less than random and take the risk of bias and distortion. As Feinstein (1971) has indicated, even very large and well-funded sampling surveys such as the U.S. Surgeon General's report on smoking and health have used very questionable convenience- and volunteer-sampling procedures. In one extreme case, estimates of smoking-related diseases were based on a sample that consisted of British medical doctors who volunteered to reply to questionnaires. Given the preceding discussion, you should now be aware of the bias that is built into such a sample.

At this point, you might wonder why you should worry about these different sampling procedures and their good and bad characteristics. Once again, the answer depends to some extent on your particular situation. If you are a critical consumer of scientific information, this discussion of sampling problems should add one more weapon to your arsenal. Near the beginning of the chapter, I described bruxism as a behavioral phenomenon that occurs in 20 percent of the population. Chances are that you simply accepted that statement as fact; perhaps you even memorized it in case it should appear as a question on an examination. It is hoped you now understand that it would be very difficult to obtain an estimate of the frequency with which bruxism occurs. You should be thinking "Is this 20 percent figure based on a convenience-sampling estimate? If so, what are the likely sources of distortion and bias? Is the sample likely to be an overestimate or an underestimate of the population frequency?" Once again, half your battle as a consumer is maintaining a skeptical attitude and knowing when and how to ask questions about scientific information.

On the other hand, if you intend to do behavioral research, you will inevitably be required to devise both time- and event-sampling procedures. I am reminded of a counseling psychologist who designed a program to help students suffering from severe "examination anxiety." In order to estimate the number of students in the university who might be interested in this program, she asked me to distribute a questionnaire to my second-year methodology class as a sample upon which to base her estimates. She should have known better! If you find yourself in a similar situation, I hope that you too would know better. Feinstein's (1977) discussion of sampling procedures is a good resource if you wish to extend your knowledge of this topic.

This completes our discussion of sampling as a source of bias and distortion during the observation-and-description phase of science. You should, however, be forewarned that these same basic concepts will emerge again later, when we consider the tactics for doing additional research on our observations.

CHAPTER EXERCISES

2.1. This exercise has three parts, to be completed in the order listed below.

Part 1. Operational Definitions. Ten terms are listed below. You might use any of them quite freely in casual conversations with your friends. Select any *three* of the terms and develop an operational definition for each that meets the criteria discussed in this chapter. You will note that "bruxism" is one of the terms on the list. Do not use this as one of your terms; it is included merely to help jog your memory of our earlier discussion of the operational-definition rule.

bruxism
premenstrual tension
aggression
gambling
heroin addiction
dreaming
depression
hyperactive
walking
play

Part 2. Literature Search. Although it was not mentioned in the preceding discussion, your first task when you encounter a phenomenon that interests you will be to go to the library and find out whether or not it has been of interest to anyone else and, if so, to determine what other people have had to say about it. This task is usually called a *literature search*. Theoretically, any scientist should be completely familiar with every book or article relevant to the phenomenon under examination. Hence, scientists are continually searching and monitoring the scientific literature for information relevant to their interests.

The matter of a literature search was not brought up in the preceding pages for a good reason. Even a very general description of how one goes about the task is somewhat tedious and boring to read. Hence, this material has been put in an appendix, where you can tackle it one day when you are feeling particularly tolerant of life's misfortunes. Should that be the case today, the second part of this exercise should find you seated in the library with Appendix A in front of you. Once you have read Appendix A, you should select one of the three concepts that you have operationally defined in the preceding part of the exercise. Armed with your new-found library skills, you should then try to locate at least one relatively recent (last three years) scientific journal article relevant to that concept.

Part 3. Operational Definition Revisited. Once you have found at least one journal article relevant to the concept that you have operationally defined, read the journal article and see if you can determine how the authors defined this same concept. Is their definition the same as yours, or different? Which of the definitions is better in your opinion, and why?

2.2. Cigarette smoking is an interesting phenomenon. Everyone believes it to be bad for your health, yet an incredible number of people continue to smoke and cannot break this habit. As a behavioral phenomenon, smoking lends itself to both *time-sampling* and *event-sampling* observational procedures.

To test your skills at devising an effective time-sampling procedure, find a friend or a roommate who smokes cigarettes. Ask the friend to keep a diary for one day in which he (or she) records the time at which each cigarette is smoked. In the meantime, you should arrange a time-sampling procedure that you can use to observe the friend during that same 24-hour period. Your task is to design the procedure so that you can obtain an accurate estimate of two characteristics of your friend's smoking behavior: (1) the number of cigarettes the friend smokes during the 24-hour period and (2) the average interval between cigarettes.

Note that the sampling procedure you design can be a one-zero procedure or any other variation you think will work. As indicated in the preceding discussion, there is nothing special about any particular procedure; common sense is often your best guide when approaching these tasks.

If it is possible to arrange the described conditions above, you will be in the fortunate position of checking the accuracy of your estimates by asking to see your friend's diary at the end of the 24-hour period—"fortunate" because we do not usually have the option of seeing the record that we are trying to estimate with our samples.

Finally, to test your knowledge of event-sampling problems, assume that you have been offered a job as a government consultant. Your task is to conduct a survey of the local high school population which will estimate the number of high school students that smoke at least one package of cigarettes per day. You will be limited, for financial reasons, to a 200-student sample on which to base your estimates. How will you proceed?

2.3. If you *have not* read Ken Kesey's book *One Flew over the Cuckoo's Nest* or seen the movie of the same name, you should. If you *have* read the book or seen the movie, you know that the story is concerned with the relationships that develop between patients and staff in a mental hospital. One message developed in the story is that the professional staff in a mental hospital do not interact much with patients; and when they do interact, the patients are treated in various subtle ways that tend to depersonalize them. Much of the story in Kesey's book is concerned with the efforts of one "patient," in this environment that constantly depersonalizes him and refuses to deal with him as a unique individual, to assert himself and maintain a sense of individuality.

Suppose, for a moment, that you decided to observe one of your local mental hospital environments to see whether there is any truth in Kesey's story. Specifically, does the professional staff treat patients in ways that tend to depersonalize them?

Such a task would put all the information you have learned in this chapter to a severe test. First, you would have to devise an observation procedure that would not produce distortions in the normal or usual behavior patterns of patients and staff. For example, once they knew they were being observed, they would probably behave differently. You would also have to examine your own preconceived ideas about mental patients and the professional staff to avoid seeing only those behavior patterns you *believed* you would see. Perhaps your most difficult task would be to define the term *depersonalization* operationally, since it is the phenomenon you are hoping to observe. Which of the behaviors exhibited by the professional staff should be counted as depersonalizing influences and which should not be counted? Similarly, which of the behaviors exhibited by the patients should be counted as evidence of depersonalization and which should not be counted? A simple operational definition might not be adequate. You might want to employ several different operations to measure the depersonalization concept.

In addition to all the preceding problems, you would have to decide whether you were going to observe every mental hospital or just some sample. Obviously the latter choice is your only practical alternative. Similarly, you must decide if you are going to observe the behavior patterns on a continuous basis or whether you will take a time sample. If the latter, how will you proceed so as to avoid distortion and bias?

In short, the task of going into a mental hospital and observing staff-patient interactions would bring everything that has been discussed in the present chapter into play. It would provide a true test of your understanding of concepts such as the *operational-definition rule* and the *distortion rule*.

Since it is unlikely that you will be able to do the observational task, you can do the next best thing. Specifically, you may read the following article. It describes the observations made by some people who decided to undertake the task described above. You will probably find their observations interesting; but, more importantly, you should read the article in order to answer the following questions:

1. Explain how this study demonstrates that our preconceived ideas distort our observations of the world.
2. Explain how the observers in this study avoided the problem of distortions caused by the presence of the observers.
3. Explain how the author of the study operationally defined depersonalization.
4. Explain any time-sampling distortions that might have occurred in the observations of depersonalization.
5. Explain any event-sampling distortions that might have occurred in the selection of the sample of mental hospitals.

ON BEING SANE IN INSANE PLACES

D. L. ROSENHAN

If sanity and insanity exist, how shall we know them?

The question is neither capricious nor itself insane. However much we may be personally convinced that we can tell the normal from the abnormal, the evidence is simply not compelling. It is commonplace, for example, to read about murder trials wherein eminent psychiatrists for the defense are contradicted by equally eminent psychiatrists for the prosecution on the matter of the defendant's sanity. More generally, there are a great deal of conflicting data on the reliability, utility, and meaning of such terms as "sanity," "insanity," "mental illness," and "schizophrenia." Finally, as early as 1934, Benedict suggested that normality and abnormality are not universal. What is viewed as normal in one culture may be seen as quite aberrant in another. Thus, notions of normality and abnormality may not be quite as accurate as people believe they are.

To raise questions regarding normality and abnormality is in no way to question the fact that some behaviors are deviant or odd. Murder is deviant. So, too, are hallucinations. Nor does raising such questions deny the existence of the personal anguish that is often associated with "mental illness." Anxiety and depression exist. Psychological suffering exists. But normality and abnormality, sanity and insanity, and the diagnoses that flow from them may be less substantive than many believe them to be.

At its heart, the question of whether the sane can be distinguished from the insane (and whether degrees of insanity can be distinguished from each other) is a simple matter: do the salient characteristics that lead to diagnoses reside in the patients themselves or in the environments and contexts in which the observers find them? From Bleuler, through Kretchmer, through the formulators of the recently revised *Diagnostic and Statistical Manual* of the American Psychiatric Association, the belief has been strong that patients present symptoms, that those symptoms can be categorized, and, implicitly, that the sane are distinguishable from the insane. More recently, however, this belief has been questioned. Based in part on theoretical and anthropological considerations, but also on philosophical, legal, and therapeutic ones, the view has grown that psychological categorization of mental illness is useless at best and downright harmful, misleading, and pejorative at worst. Psychiatric diagnoses, in this view, are in the minds of the observers and are not valid summaries of characteristics displayed by the observed.

Gains can be made in deciding which of these is more nearly accurate by getting normal people (that is, people who do not have, and have never suffered, symptoms of serious psychiatric disorders) admitted to psychiatric hospitals and then determining whether they were discovered to be sane and, if so, how. If the sanity of such pseudopatients were always detected, there would be prima facie evidence that a sane individual can be distinguished from the insane context in which he is found. Normality (and presumably abnormality) is distinct enough that it can be recognized wherever it occurs, for it is carried within the person. If, on the other hand, the sanity of the pseudopatients were never discovered, serious difficulties would arise for those who support traditional modes of psychiatric diagnosis. Given that the hospital staff was not incompetent, that the pseudopatient had been behaving as sanely as he had been outside of the hospital, and that it had never been previously suggested that he belonged in a psychiatric hospital, such an unlikely outcome would support the view that psychiatric diagnosis betrays little about the patient but much about the environment in which an observer finds him.

This article describes such an experiment. Eight sane people gained secret admission to 12 different hospitals. Their diagnostic experiences constitute the data of the first part of this article; the remainder is devoted to a description of their experiences in psychiatric institutions. Too few psychiatrists and psychologists, even those who have worked in such hospitals, know what the experience is like. They rarely talk about it with former patients, perhaps because they distrust information coming from the previously insane. Those who have worked in psychiatric hospitals are likely to have adapted so thoroughly to the settings that they are insensitive to the impact of that experience. And while there have been occasional reports of researchers who submitted themselves to psychiatric hospitalization, these researchers have commonly remained in the hospitals for short periods of time, often with the knowledge of the hospital staff. It is difficult to know the extent to which they were treated like patients or like research colleagues. Nevertheless, their reports about the inside of the psychiatric hospital have been valuable. This article extends those efforts.

PSEUDOPATIENTS AND THEIR SETTINGS

The eight pseudopatients were a varied group. One was a psychology graduate student in his 20s. The remaining seven were older and "established." Among them were three psychologists, a pediatrician, a psychiatrist, a painter, and a housewife. Three pseudopatients were women, five were men. All of them employed pseudonyms, lest their alleged diagnoses embarrass them later. Those who were in mental health professions alleged another occupation in order to avoid the special attentions that might be accorded by staff, as a matter of courtesy or caution, to ailing colleagues. With the exception of myself (I was the first pseudopatient and my presence was known to the hospital administrator and chief psychologist and, so far as I can tell, to them alone), the presence of pseudopatients and the nature of the research program was not known to the hospital staffs.

The settings were similarly varied. In order to generalize the findings, admission into a variety of hospitals was sought. The 12 hospitals in the sample were located in five different states on the East and West coasts. Some were old and shabby, some were quite new. Some were research-oriented, others not. Some had good staff-patient ratios, others were quite understaffed. Only one was a strictly private hospital. All of the others were supported by state or federal funds or, in one instance, by university funds.

After calling the hospital for an appointment, the pseudopatient arrived at the admissions office complaining that he had been hearing voices. Asked what the voices said, he replied that they were often unclear, but as far as he could tell they said "empty," "hollow," and "thud." The voices were unfamiliar and were of the same sex as the pseudopatient. The choice of these symptoms was occasioned by their apparent similarity to existential symptoms. Such symptoms are alleged to arise from painful concerns about the perceived meaninglessness of one's life. It is as if the hallucinating person were saying, "My life is empty and hollow." The choice of these symptoms was also determined by the *absence* of a single report of existential psychoses in the literature.

Beyond alleging the symptoms and falsifying name, vocation, and employment, no further alterations of person, history, or circumstances were made. The significant events of the pseudopatient's life history were presented as they had actually occurred. Relationships with parents and siblings, with spouse and children, with people at work and in school, consistent with the aforementioned exceptions, were described as they were or had been. Frustrations and upsets were described along with joys and satisfactions. These facts are important to remember. If anything, they strongly biased the subsequent results in favor of detecting sanity, since none of their histories or current behaviors were seriously pathological in any way.

Immediately upon admission to the psychiatric ward, the pseudopatient ceased simulating *any* symptoms of abnormality. In some cases, there was a brief period of mild nervousness and anxiety, since none of the pseudopatients really believed that they would be admitted so easily. Indeed, their shared fear was that they would be immediately exposed as frauds and greatly embarrassed. Moreover, many of them had never visited a psychiatric ward; even those who had, nevertheless had some genuine fears about what might happen to them. Their nervousness, then, was quite appropriate to the novelty of the hospital setting, and it abated rapidly.

Apart from that short-lived nervousness, the pseudopatient behaved on the ward as he "normally" behaved. The pseudopatient spoke to patients and staff as he might ordinarily. Because there is uncommonly little to do on a psychiatric ward, he attempted to engage others in conversation. When asked by staff how he was feeling, he indicated that he was fine, that he no longer experienced symptoms. He responded to instructions from attendants, to calls for medication (which was not swallowed), and to dining-hall instructions. Beyond such activities as were available to him on the admissions ward, he spent his time writing down his observations about the ward, its patients, and the staff. Initially these notes were written "secretly," but as it soon became clear that no one much cared, they were subsequently written on standard tablets of paper in such public places as the dayroom. No secret was made of these activities.

The pseudopatient, very much as a true psychiatric patient, entered a hospital with no foreknowledge of when he would be discharged. Each was told that he would have to get out by his own devices, essentially by convincing the staff that he was sane. The psychological stresses associated with hospitalization were considerable, and all but one of the pseudopatients desired to be discharged almost immediately after being admitted. They were, therefore, motivated not only to behave sanely, but to be paragons of cooperation. That their behavior was in no way disruptive is confirmed by nursing reports, which have been obtained on most of the patients. These reports uniformly indicate that the patients were "friendly," "cooperative," and "exhibited no abnormal indications."

THE NORMAL ARE NOT DETECTABLY SANE

Despite their public "show" of sanity, the pseudopatients were never detected. Admitted, except in one case, with a diagnosis of schizophrenia each was discharged with a diagnosis of schizophrenia "in remission." The label "in remission" should in no way be dismissed as a formality, for at no time during any hospitalization had any question been raised about any pseudopatient's simulation. Nor are there any indications in the hospital records that the pseudopatient's status was suspect. Rather, the evidence is strong that, once labeled schizophrenic, the pseudopatient was stuck with that label. If the pseudopatient was to be discharged, he must naturally be "in remission"; but he was not sane, nor, in the institution's view, had he ever been sane.

The uniform failure to recognize sanity cannot be attributed to the quality of the hospitals, for, although there were considerable variations among them, several are considered excellent. Nor can it be alleged that there was simply not enough time to observe the pseudopatients. Length of hospitalization ranged from 7 to 52 days, with an average of 19 days. The pseudopatients were not, in fact, carefully observed, but this failure clearly speaks more to traditions within psychiatric hospitals than to lack of opportunity.

Finally, it cannot be said that the failure to recognize the pseudopatients' sanity was due to the fact that they were not behaving sanely. While there was clearly some tension present in all of them, their daily visitors could detect no serious behavioral consequences—nor, indeed, could other patients. It was quite common for the patients to "detect" the pseudopatients' sanity. During the first three hospitalizations, when accurate counts were kept, 35 of a total of 118 patients on the admissions ward voiced their suspicions, some vigorously. "You're not crazy. You're a journalist, or a professor [referring to the continual note-taking]. You're checking up on the hospital." While most of the patients were reassured by the pseudopatient's insistence that he had been sick before he came in but was fine now, some continued to believe that the pseudopatient was sane throughout his hospitalization. The fact that the patients often recognized normality when staff did not raise important questions.

Failure to detect sanity during the course of hospitalization may be due to the fact that physicians operate with a strong bias toward what statisticians call the type 2 error. This is to say that physicians are more inclined to call a healthy person sick (a false positive, type 2) than a sick person healthy (a false negative, type 1). The reasons for this are not hard to find: it is clearly more dangerous to misdiagnose illness than health. Better to err on the side of caution, to suspect illness even among the healthy.

But what holds for medicine does not hold equally well for psychiatry. Medical illnesses, while unfortunate, are not commonly pejorative. Psychiatric diagnoses, on the contrary, carry with them personal, legal, and social stigmas. It was therefore important to see whether the tendency toward diagnosing the sane insane could be reversed. The following experiment was arranged at a research and teaching hospital whose staff had heard these findings but doubted that such an error could occur in their hospital. The staff was informed that at some time during the following 3 months, one or more pseudopatients would attempt to be admitted into the psychiatric hospital. Each staff member was asked to rate each patient who presented himself at admissions or on the ward according to the likelihood that the patient was a pseudopatient. A 10-point scale was used, with a 1 and 2 reflecting high confidence that the patient was a pseudopatient.

Judgments were obtained on 193 patients who were admitted for psychiatric treatment. All staff who had had sustained contact with or primary responsibility for the patient—attendants, nurses, psychiatrists, physicians, and psychologists—were asked to make judgments. Forty-one patients were alleged, with high confidence, to be pseudopatients by at least one member of the staff. Twenty-three were considered suspect by at least one psychiatrist. Nineteen were suspected by one psychiatrist *and* one other staff member. Actually, no genuine pseudopatient (at least from my group) presented himself during this period.

The experiment is instructive. It indicates that the tendency to designate sane people as insane can be reversed when the stakes (in this case, prestige and diagnostic acumen) are high. But what can be said of the 19 people who were suspected of being "sane" by one psychiatrist and another staff member? Were these people truly "sane," or was it rather the case that in the course of avoiding the type 2 error the staff tended to make more errors of the first sort—calling the crazy "sane"? There is no way of knowing. But one thing is certain: any diagnostic process that lends itself so readily to massive errors of this sort cannot be a very reliable one.

THE STICKINESS OF PSYCHODIAGNOSTIC LABELS

Beyond the tendency to call the healthy sick—a tendency that accounts better for diagnostic behavior on admission than it does for such behavior after a lengthy period of exposure—the data speak to the massive role of labeling in psychiatric assessment. Having once been labeled schizophrenic, there is nothing the pseudopatient can do to overcome the tag. The tag profoundly colors others' perceptions of him and his behavior.

From one viewpoint, these data are hardly surprising, for it has long been known that elements are given meaning by the context in which they occur. Gestalt psychology made this point vigorously, and Asch demonstrated that there are "central" personality traits (such as "warm" versus "cold") which are so powerful that they markedly color the meaning of other information in forming an impression of a given personality. "Insane," "schizophrenic," "manic-depressive," and "crazy" are probably among the most powerful of such central traits. Once a person is designated abnormal, all of his other behaviors and characteristics are colored by that label. Indeed, that label is so powerful that many of the pseudopatients' normal behaviors were overlooked entirely or profoundly misinterpreted. Some examples may clarify this issue.

Earlier I indicated that there were no changes in the pseudopatients' personal history and current status beyond those of names, employment, and, where necessary, vocation. Otherwise, a veridical description of personal history and circumstances were offered. Those circumstances were not psychotic. How were they made consonant with the diagnosis of psychosis? Or were those diagnoses modified in such a way as to bring them into accord with the circumstances of the pseudopatient's life, as described by him?

As far as I can determine, diagnoses were in no way affected by the relative health or the circumstances of a pseudopatient's life. Rather the reverse occurred: the perception of his circumstances was shaped entirely by the diagnosis. A clear example of such translation is found in the case of a pseudopatient who had had a close relationship with his mother but was rather remote from his father during his early childhood. During adolescence and beyond, however, his father became a close friend, while his relationship with his mother cooled. His present relationship with his wife was characteristically close and warm. Apart from occasional angry exchanges, friction was minimal. The children had rarely been spanked. Surely there is nothing especially pathological about such a history. Indeed, many readers may see a similar pattern in their own experiences with no markedly deleterious consequences. Observe, however, how such a history was translated in the psychopathological context, this from the case summary prepared after the patient was discharged.

> This white 39-year-old-male . . . manifests a long history of considerable ambivalence in close relationships, which begins in early childhood. A warm relationship with his mother cools during his adolescence. A distant relationship to his father is described as becoming very intense. Affective stability is absent. His attempts to control emotionality with his wife and children are punctuated by angry outbursts and, in the case of the children, spankings. And while he says that he has several good friends, one senses considerable ambivalence embedded in those relationships also. . . .

The facts of the case were unintentionally distorted by the staff to achieve consistency with a popular theory of the dynamics of a schizophrenic reaction. Nothing of an ambivalent nature had been described in relations with parents, spouse, or friends. To the extent that ambivalence could be inferred, it was probably not greater than is found in all human relationships. It is true that pseudopatient's relationships with his parents changed over time, but in the ordinary context that would hardly be remarkable—indeed, it might very well be expected. Clearly, the meaning ascribed to his verbalizations (that is, ambivalence, affective instability) was determined by the diagnosis: schizophrenia. An entirely different meaning would have been ascribed if it were known that the man was "normal."

All pseudopatients took extensive notes publicly. Under ordinary circumstances, such behavior would have raised questions in the minds of observers, as, in fact, it did among patients. Indeed, it seemed so certain that the notes would elicit suspicion that elaborate precautions were taken to remove them from the ward each day. But the precautions proved needless. The closest any staff member came to questioning these notes occurred when one pseudopatient asked his physician what kind of medication he was receiving and began to write down the response. "You needn't write it," he was told gently. "If you have trouble remembering, just ask me again."

If no questions were asked of the pseudopatients, how was their writing interpreted? Nursing records for three patients indicate that the writing was seen as an aspect of their pathological behavior. "Patient engages in writing behavior" was the daily nursing comment on one of the pseudopatients who was never questioned about his writing. Given that the patient is in the hospital, he must be psychologically disturbed. And given that he is disturbed, continuous writing must be a behavioral manifestation of that disturbance, perhaps a subset of the compulsive behaviors that are sometimes correlated with schizophrenia.

One tacit characteristic of psychiatric diagnosis is that it locates the source of aberration within the individual and only rarely with the complex of stimuli that surrounds him. Consequently, behaviors that are stimulated by the environment are commonly misattributed to the patient's disorder. For example, one kindly nurse found a pseudopatient pacing the long hospital corridors. "Nervous, Mr. X?" she asked. "No, bored," he said.

The notes kept by pseudopatients are full of patient behaviors that were misinterpreted by well-intentioned staff. Often enough, a patient would go "berserk" because he had, wittingly or unwittingly, been mistreated by, say, an attendant. A nurse coming upon the scene would rarely inquire even cursorily into the environmental stimuli of the patient's behavior. Rather, she assumed that his upset derived from his pathology, not from his present interactions with other staff members. Occasionally, the staff might assume that the patient's family (especially when they had recently visited) or other patients had stimulated the outburst. But never were the staff found to assume that one of themselves or the structure of the hospital had anything to do with a patient's behavior. One psychiatrist pointed to a group of patients who were sitting outside the cafeteria entrance half an hour before lunchtime. To a group of young residents he indicated that such behavior was characteristic of the oral-acquisitive nature of the syndrome. It seemed not to occur to him that there were very few things to anticipate in a psychiatric hospital besides eating.

A psychiatric label has a life and an influence of its own. Once the impression has been formed that the patient is schizophrenic, the expectation is that he will continue to be schizophrenic. When a sufficient amount of time has passed, during which the patient has done nothing bizarre, he is considered to be in remission and available for discharge. But the label endures beyond discharge, with the unconfirmed expectation that he will behave as a schizophrenic again. Such labels, conferred by mental health professionals, are as influential on the patient as they are on his relatives and friends, and it should not surprise anyone that the diagnosis acts on all of them as a self-fulfilling prophecy. Eventually, the patient himself accepts the diagnosis, with all of its surplus meaning and expectations, and behaves accordingly.

The inferences to be made from these matters are quite simple. Much as Zigler and Phillips have demonstrated that there is enormous overlap in the symptoms presented by patients who have been variously diagnosed, so there is enormous overlap in the behaviors of the sane and the insane. The sane are not "sane" all of the time. We lose our tempers "for no good reason." We are occasionally depressed or anxious, again for no good reason. And we may find it difficult to get along with one or another person—again for no good reason that we can specify. Similarly, the insane are not always insane. Indeed, it was the impression of the pseudopatients while living with them that they were sane for long periods of time—that the bizarre behaviors upon which their diagnoses were allegedly predicated constituted only a small fraction of their total behavior. If it makes no sense to label ourselves permanently depressed on the basis of an occasional depression, then it takes better evidence than is presently available to label all patients insane or schizophrenic on the basis of bizarre behaviors or cognitions. It seems more useful, as Mischel has pointed out, to limit our discussions to *behaviors*, the stimuli that provoke them, and their correlates.

It is not known why powerful impressions of personality traits, such as "crazy" or "insane," arise. Conceivably, when the origins and stimuli that give rise to a behavior are remote or unknown, or when the behavior strikes us as immutable, trait labels regarding the *behaver* arise. When, on the other hand, the origins and stimuli are known and available, discourse is limited to the behavior itself. Thus, I may hallucinate because I am sleeping, or I may hallucinate because I have ingested a peculiar drug. These are termed sleep-induced hallucinations, or dreams, and drug-induced hallucinations, respectively. But when the stimuli to my hallucinations are unknown, that is called craziness, or schizophrenia—as if that inference were somehow as illuminating as the others.

THE EXPERIENCE OF PSYCHIATRIC HOSPITALIZATION

The term "mental illness" is of recent origin. It was coined by people who were humane in their inclinations and who wanted very much to raise the station of (and the public's sympathies toward) the psychologically disturbed from that of witches and "crazies" to one that was akin to the physically ill. And they were at least partially successful, for the treatment of the mentally ill *has* improved considerably over the years. But while treatment has improved, it is doubtful that people really regard the mentally ill in the same way that they view the physically ill. A broken leg is something one recovers from, but mental illness allegedly endures forever. A broken leg does not threaten the observer, but a crazy schizophrenic? There is by now a host of evidence that attitudes toward the mentally ill are characterized by fear, hostility, aloofness, suspicion, and dread. The mentally ill are society's lepers.

That such attitudes infect the general population is perhaps not surprising, only upsetting. But that they affect the professionals—attendants, nurses, physicians, psychologists, and social workers—who treat and deal with the mentally ill is more disconcerting, both because such attitudes are self-evidently pernicious and because they are unwitting. Most mental health professionals would insist that they are sympathetic toward the mentally ill, that they are neither avoidant nor hostile. But it is more likely that an exquisite ambivalence characterizes their relations with psychiatric patients, such that their avowed impulses are only part of their entire attitude. Negative attitudes are there too and can easily be detected. Such attitudes should not surprise us. They are the natural offspring of the labels patients wear and the places in which they are found.

Consider the structure of the typical psychiatric hospital. Staff and patients are strictly segregated. Staff have their own living space, including their dining facilities, bathrooms, and assembly places. The glassed quarters that contain the professional staff, which the pseudopatients came to call "the cage," sit out on every dayroom. The staff emerge primarily for caretaking purposes—to give medication, to conduct a therapy or group meeting, to instruct or reprimand a patient. Otherwise, staff keep to themselves, almost as if the disorder that afflicts their charges is somehow catching.

So much is patient-staff segregation the rule that, for four public hospitals in which an attempt was made to measure the degree to which staff and patients mingle, it was necessary to use "time out of the staff cage" as the operational measure. While it was not the case that all time spent out of the cage was spent mingling with patients (attendants, for example, would occasionally emerge to watch television in the dayroom), it was the only way in which one could gather reliable data on time for measuring.

The average amount of time spent by attendants outside of the cage was 11.3 percent (range, 3 to 52 percent). This figure does not represent only time spent mingling with patients, but also includes time spent on such chores as folding laundry, supervising patients while they shave, directing ward clean-up, and sending patients to off-ward activities. It was the relatively rare attendant who spent time talking with patients or playing games with them. It proved impossible to obtain a "percent mingling time" for nurses, since the amount of time they spent out of the cage was too brief. Rather, we counted instances of emergence from the cage. On the average, daytime nurses emerged from the cage 11.5 times per shift, including instances when they left the ward entirely (range, 4 to 39 times). Late afternoon and night nurses were even less available, emerging on the average 9.4 times per shift (range, 4 to 39 times).

Data on early morning nurses, who arrived usually after midnight and departed at 8 a.m., are not available because patients were asleep during most of this period.

Physicians, especially psychiatrists, were even less available. They were rarely seen on the wards. Quite commonly, they would be seen only when they arrived and departed, with the remaining time being spent in their offices or in the cage. On the average, physicians emerged on the ward 6.7 times per day (range, 1 to 17 times). It proved difficult to make an accurate estimate in this regard, since physicians often maintained hours that allowed them to come and go at different times.

The hierarchical organization of the psychiatric hospital has been commented on before, but the latent meaning of that kind of organization is worth noting again. Those with the most power have least to do with patients, and those with the least power are most involved with them. Recall, however, that the acquisition of role-appropriate behaviors occurs mainly through the observation of others, with the most powerful having the most influence. Consequently, it is understandable that attendants not only spend more time with patients than do any other members of the staff—that is required by their station in the hierarchy—but also, insofar as they learn from their superiors' behavior, spend as little time with patients as they can. Attendants are seen mainly in the cage, which is where the models, the action, and the power are.

I turn now to a different set of studies, these dealing with staff response to patient-initiated contact. It has long been known that the amount of time a person spends with you can be an index of your significance to him. If he initiates and maintains eye contact, there is reason to believe that he is considering your requests and needs. If he pauses to chat or actually stops and talks, there is added reason to infer that he is individuating you. In four hospitals, the pseudopatient approached the staff member with a request which took the following form: "Pardon me, Mr. [or Dr. or Mrs.] X, could you tell me when I will be eligible for grounds privileges?" (or ". . . when I will be presented at the staff meeting?" or ". . . when I am likely to be discharged?"). While the content of the question varied according to the appropriateness of the target and the pseudopatient's (apparent) current needs, the form was always a courteous and relevant request for information. Care was taken never to approach a particular member of the staff more than once a day, lest the staff member become suspicious or irritated. In examining these data, remember that the behavior of the pseudopatients was neither bizarre nor disruptive. One could indeed engage in good conversation with them.

The data for these experiments are shown in Table 1, separately for physicians (column 1) and for nurses and attendants (column 2). Minor differences between these four institutions were overwhelmed by the degree to which staff avoided continuing contacts that patients had initiated. By far, their most common response consisted of either a brief response to the question, offered while they were "on the move" and with head averted, or no response at all.

The encounter frequently took the following bizarre form: (pseudopatient)

Table 1 Self-initiated Contact by Pseudopatients with Psychiatrists and Nurses and Attendants, Compared to Contact with Other Groups

| | Psychiatric Hospitals | | University Campus (nonmedical) | University Medical Center | | |
| | | | | Physicians | | |
Contact	(1) Psychiatrists	(2) Nurses and attendants	(3) Faculty	(4) "Looking for a psychiatrist"	(5) "Looking for an internist"	(6) No additional comment
Responses						
Moves on, head averted (%)	71	88	0	0	0	0
Makes eye contact (%)	23	10	0	11	0	0
Pauses and chats (%)	2	2	0	11	0	10
Stops and talks (%)	4	0.5	100	78	100	90
Mean number of questions answered (out of 6)	*	*	6	3.8	4.8	4.5
Respondents (no.)	13	47	14	18	15	10
Attempts (no.)	185	1283	14	18	15	10

"Pardon me, Dr. X. Could you tell me when I am eligible for grounds privileges?" (physician) "Good morning, Dave. How are you today?" (Moves off without waiting for a response.)

It is instructive to compare these data with data recently obtained at Stanford University. It has been alleged that large and eminent universities are characterized by faculty who are so busy that they have no time for students. For this comparison, a young lady approached individual faculty members who seemed to be walking purposefully to some meeting or teaching engagement and asked them the following six questions.

1. "Pardon me, could you direct me to Encina Hall?" (At the medical school: ". . . to the Clinical Research Centre?")
2. "Do you know where the Fish Annex is?" (There is no Fish Annex at Stanford.)
3. "Do you teach here?"
4. "How does one apply for admission to the college?" (At the medical school: ". . . to the medical school?")
5. "Is it difficult to get in?"
6. "Is there financial aid?"

Without exception, as can be seen in Table 1 (column 3), all of the questions were answered. No matter how rushed they were, all respondents not only maintained eye contact, but stopped to talk. Indeed, many of the respondents went out of their way to direct or take the questioner to the office she was seeking, to try to locate "Fish Annex," or to discuss with her the possibilities of being admitted to the university.

Similar data, also shown in Table 1 (columns 4, 5, and 6), were obtained in the hospital. Here too, the young lady came prepared with six questions. After the first question, however, she remarked to 18 of her respondents (column 4), "I'm looking for a psychiatrist," and to 15 others (column 5), "I'm looking for an internist." Ten other respondents received no inserted comment (column 6). The general degree of cooperative responses is considerably higher for these university groups than it was for pseudopatients in psychiatric hospitals. Even so, differences are apparent within the medical school setting. Once having indicated that she was looking for a psychiatrist, the degree of cooperation elicited was less than when she sought an internist.

Note to Reader

The remainder of Rosenhan's article describes additional examples of the ways in which patients are made to feel powerless and depersonalized in the hospital setting. These examples serve primarily to underline and emphasize points that have already been made; so this additional material has not been included. The student who would like to pursue this topic in more detail will find the reference citation on the opening page of this reading.

Although the primary reason for including this article was to

illustrate the various problems of observation and description discussed in Chapter 2, it is also interesting to think about this research
in the context of the ethical principles discussed in Appendix B. Rosenhan's research illustrates a common dilemma encountered by
psychologists interested in human behavior. In order to avoid influencing the behavior of those being observed, it is often necessary to use
some form of deception. However, when you resort to deception you
bring yourself very close to violating some of the ethical principles
discussed in Appendix B. Although debriefing the subjects after the
observations are made is one positive step, there would seem to be
no completely satisfactory solution.

MEASURING BEHAVIOR

Is *Hustler* magazine more or less pornographic than *Playboy*? Are you more or less introverted that most of your friends? These questions assume that we can compare magazines or people along some measurable dimension to see if one has more or less of a given quality than another.

Chapter 3 will consider this process of comparing and quantifying people and events. First, we shall describe and discuss several levels of measurement (also called *scales of measurement*), the most common among which are (1) nominal, (2) ordinal, (3) interval, and (4) ratio. The importance of each will be outlined.

The second part of the chapter will focus on some of the special procedures psychologists use to measure various psychological phenomena. These include methods to measure attitudes, personality traits, learning, memory, and perceptual processes.

Finally, we shall look at some of the basic calculations that are commonly used to summarize or describe the results obtained with these measurement techniques. These calculations are called *descriptive statistics,* and it is important to understand how they are used and misused by scientists.

LEVELS OF MEASUREMENT

Nominal Scale

If you were interested in measuring smoking behavior, your first impulse might be to assign people to one of two categories: those who smoke and those who do not. If you give smokers the label 003 and nonsmokers the label 008, you are using a level of measurement called a *nominal scale*. Blondes vs. redheads, white wine vs. red, and males vs. females are all nominal measurements. You could use letters, numbers, or a combination of both to label the categories; it doesn't really matter.

The restriction of measurements to a nominal scale is not very informative and can be frustrating. Once you have categorized an entire population into smokers and nonsmokers, you cannot say much more about your observations. For example, the nominal scale of measurement does not let you compare one smoker to another or to describe an "average smoker." The same problems arise when you use other nominal categories such as blood type, sex, race, or nationality. When you simply divide things into categories, you usually fail to capture much of the richness and variability observed in nature.

Ordinal Scale

Although there are some contexts in which you will find yourself restricted to a nominal scale of measurement, it is usually possible and desirable to measure behavior along a dimension that at least lets you rank your observations in order. If, for example, you ask a dentist to examine the teeth of 20 bruxists and rank-order the amount of damage, you have moved beyond the nominal scale to an *ordinal* scale, on which different individuals can be *ranked within the category*. Obviously, rank-ordering gives you more information. In addition to knowing that person A is a bruxist (nominal), you can now also state that A has a more severe grinding habit than B, that B has a worse habit than C, and so on.

Of course, an ordinal scale of measurement does not tell you anything about the absolute amount of grinding that person B exhibits or the distances between people who have been rank-ordered along this scale; nor does the ordinal scale let you make any statements about B's condition being twice as severe as A's, or A's being half as severe as C's, and so on. The ordinal scale will, however, permit some limited discussion of the relationship between one individual and others. If F is ranked sixth in a group of 20, we can, for example, talk about the *percentage* of people who fall below or above F; such statements are clearly not possible with a nominal scale. Hence, the ordinal scale helps to capture some of the observable variations within a category.

Interval Scale

The interval scale of measurement has all the properties of the nominal and ordinal scales plus one very important additional feature: it can tell you exactly how far apart the different observations on the scale are. To illustrate, assume you are in a fishing boat on a lake with three stumps showing above the surface of the water (A, B, and C, as in Figure 3.1). As you view the stumps sticking up, you notice that stump C protrudes the most, followed closely by stump B and then by stump A. You have no way of knowing, however, how deep the water is at each of the stump locations. If you use a ruler to quantify your observations of these three stumps, it will tell you that stump A extends 10 cm above the surface of the water. If you proceeded to measure the other two stumps

Figure 3.1 An interval scale of measurement. Three stumps emerge from the surface of the lake. You do not know the lake depth at each stump location, hence you have no absolute zero on your measurement scale. All measurements are relative to the arbitrary zero point at water level.

in the same way, you would produce a pure example of an interval scale. Since our ruler has equal intervals along its length, we can make several statements about the *relative* differences among the three stumps. If the difference between A and B is 3 cm and the difference between B and C is 3 cm, we can say that the differences between the measured parts of the stumps are equal. Given this interval scale, we can also add, subtract, multiply, and divide our measurements of the stumps by a constant; as we do so, the *relative* differences among the three stumps will be maintained. You might say that their "identities" will survive these numerical manipulations.

Observe, however, that we have not yet said anything about the *absolute* height of the three stumps. To do so would require that we measure them from the bottom of the lake, and we have no idea how deep the lake is at the three stump locations. This is like saying that our measurement scale has no *absolute zero point*. This is why the 10 cm measurement of stump A is arbitrary and why we can discuss only *relative* differences among the stumps. Such are the properties of an interval measurement scale. It has equal intervals along the dimension being measured, but it does not have an absolute zero point.

Interval scales are not restricted to the measurement of stumps in a lake. If you think about it, you will realize that the scores on your examinations do not have absolute zero points. A student who receives a grade of zero on a history examination has been given an arbitrary zero point. Even though he received a grade of zero on the examination, he probably knows something about history. The zero refers only to the questions asked on this particular examination. The student's knowledge is analogous to the entire stump; the examination simply measures the part protruding above the surface of the water. An absolute zero would require us to know exactly how deep the water (knowledge of history) was on the day of the examination. (Unfortunately, these observations do not make a score of zero any more palatable to the student.)

In short, the interval scale gives us considerably more information than the ordinal scale, but the lack of an absolute zero still limits our conclusions in a number of ways. For example, we cannot, on the basis of interval measurements, say that stump C is twice as tall as stump B. To make such a statement would require that we measure the stumps on a scale that had an absolute zero point.

Ratio Scale

The ratio scale of measurement has all the basic properties of the other scales discussed thus far plus an absolute zero point. Continuing with our stump example, this means that we know where the bottom of the lake is. If we empty the lake and use a ruler to measure the stumps, we will generate a ratio scale of measurement. The ruler will measure the height of each stump from the ground (zero) to the top in equal units along the way. We can now make all the comparisons and numerical manipulations we did with the interval measurement and, in addition, we can make statements about A being half as tall as B and so on. Such are the characteristics of the ratio scale. Most physical measures of time and space meet the requirements of the ratio scale. If, for example, you wish to measure how long a particular behavior has lasted, how far a person has moved, or how many cigarettes a person has smoked, you are quantifying your observations on a ratio scale of measurement.

To summarize, we have considered the properties of four different levels of measurement, each level building on the characteristics of the preceding one. That is, each succeeding level permits us to represent more information about the world. As a consumer of scientific information, you get the least for your money from the nominal and ordinal scales. When you encounter a claim based upon a nominal scale of measurement, it often pays to think about that claim in terms of more sensitive scales. I have often read, for example, that an alcoholic is unable to consume alcohol in small amounts (i.e., be a social drinker). Although I do not know much about the research on which this claim is based, I am suspicious of the *nominal scale* of measurement implicit in that statement. It divides the world into two categories of people: alcoholics and nonalcoholics. It also divides drinking behavior into two categories: social drinking and alcoholic drinking. I suspect that alcoholism is much more varied and complex than the label (nominal measurement) "alcoholic" implies. With more sensitive scales of measurement, the statement that alcoholics cannot drink in moderation would probably be seen as a gross oversimplification. In general, nature always becomes more interesting and informative when we employ more sensitive scales.

MEASURING MENTAL PROCESSES

It is relatively easy to quantify overt behaviors like jogging, smoking, and fingernail biting and to obtain ratio measurements of such events. However, psychologists are also interested in measuring *mental processes*. Measuring how much you smoke each day is one thing; measuring your attitudes toward people who smoke is quite another. Now that you understand the different scales of measurement, we can turn our attention to some of the special techniques required to measure mental processes like your attitudes toward smoking. In each case, we will consider the special method of measurement, how the method relates to the scales of measurement described earlier, and some of the special problems you may encounter in using these methods.

Measuring Attitudes

Recently, a student who was applying for a part-time job in a residence for retarded adults asked me to write a letter to support her application. The residence provided living accommodations for 12 retarded individuals who were able to work in the community but required assistance in the day-to-day management of household affairs. The student was required to provide some of this assistance, moral support, and friendship.

A person would need very positive attitudes about mental retardation in order to do this type of work, and, from my previous knowledge of this student, I thought she would be good at the job. My judgment was based more on intuition than on precise measurement procedures. If it had been necessary to obtain a more precise idea of her attitudes toward mentally retarded adults, there are several approaches that I could have used. In this part of the chapter, we shall consider some of the more commonly used methods for measuring attitudes. Some are more rigorous than others and—given the extensive use of attitude measurement procedures in behavioral research—these special measurement methods will be examined in some detail.

Interviews   At the least rigorous end of the attitude-measurement continuum are interviews. Essentially, an interview is an interaction between two people in which one persons asks questions and the other provides answers. Interviews tend to be somewhat informal—it is difficult to define them operationally with precision; they can, however, be structured to varying degrees. A highly structured interview is based on a standard set of questions that are asked in a standard sequence. The answers are often tape-recorded for future analysis. Other interviews are less structured and consist simply of some mutual discussion from which the observer draws conclusions about the attitudes of the person being interviewed. The interview has the advantage of permitting a wide-ranging assessment of opinions and attitudes; it does not force the individual into prearranged answers. In other words, because it is "open-ended," it can reveal information that might not be obtained from the more structured procedures to be described below.

The primary disadvantage of even the most structured interview should be obvious if you think back to the operational-definition rule discussed in Chapter 2. A procedure used to measure an attitude is essentially an operational definition of the attitude. If the interview is a good operational definition, it should permit anyone to *repeat the measurement procedure (i.e., the interview) in exactly the same manner.* As you can imagine, an interview would be very difficult to repeat exactly. The interactions and activities are too complex and subtle to be defined precisely.

Of course, precision and reliability are not always most important. Recall, for example, the student hired as an assistant in the residence. Very likely, an extensive interview conducted by several trained social workers would be the most appropriate (and perhaps most effective) method of assessing such a job candidate. It would be difficult to repeat such an interview *reliably* with a number of job candidates, but strict reliability and precision are probably not so important in this context. In the hands of an experienced person, a loosely structured interview can be an excellent basis for making judgments about the suitability of a candidate for a job.

Finally, with reference to scales of measurement, interview procedures are not particularly impressive. Measurements produced by most interviews are at best a nominal scale. You might argue that you could reliably assign people to a particular category (e.g., feminist or sexist) after an interview, but it is more difficult to justify any claims for rank-ordering these same people (i.e., ordinal measurement).

Questionnaires   A questionnaire is a series of written questions designed to measure a person's attitudes or opinions on a particular topic. Many of the problems found with the interviews also apply to questionnaires. These do, however, tend to eliminate the complex and subtle interactions of the interview. In this sense, the questionnaire can be considered a more structured procedure and a more reliable operational definition than the interview.

Questionnaires also differ in the degree to which they are structured. In some cases, a question is written and one is asked to write an answer in the space provided. Scoring the answers to open-ended questions of this type is a problem. Several different observers may read the same answer and give it very different scores. In such cases, the reliability is uncertain; you would not want to place too much confidence in the results. One way around this difficulty is to use a multiple-choice questionnaire in which both the questions and answers are structured. This eliminates any problem with scoring reliability, but it also has its cost. You may not, on any particular question, offer the person a choice appropriate to his or her attitudes. In such cases, the person is forced to give you a distorted answer chosen from those made available.

In short, questionnaires are more structured than interviews and come closer to meeting the requirements of the operational-definition rule. In the scoring of multiple-choice questionnaires, it is reasonable to suggest that an ordinal level of measurement is achieved, since you can rank-order individuals on the basis of the number of yes and no answers. Claims for an interval scale would be seriously questioned, in that no effort is made on the questionnaire to equate the distances between the positive or negative attitudes expressed along the dimension being measured.

Attitude Scales   In general, interviews and questionnaires are convenient procedures for obtaining rough estimates of attitudes on particular topics. If, however, you are confronted with the serious task of measuring attitudes in a way that meets the standards of the operational-definition rule, you will want to use one of several special methods that have been developed to construct an *attitude scale*. Here, we shall consider only one representative example that illustrates the basic principles involved. This method is called the *Likert scale,* after Rensis Likert, the social psychologist traditionally associated with its use. Past experience in methodology courses suggests that students often find themselves in situations where a knowledge of attitude-measurement procedures could prove valuable. For this reason, we shall examine this method in greater detail.

The Likert scale is one of a general class called *summative rating scales;* it consists of a list of 10 to 20 statements expressing opinions about a particular topic (e.g., person, place, object, etc.). Some statements express positive opinions and some express negative ones. A person being tested would be asked to respond to each statement in the list by checking one of the following categories:

(SA) I strongly agree with this statement.

(A) I agree with this statement.

(?) I am uncertain about my feelings about this statement.

(D) I disagree with this statement.

(SD) I strongly disagree with this statement.

Here is an example of a statement that might occur on a Likert scale designed to quantify your attitudes toward the topic of abortion:

Item 1. Abortion should be available to any woman who has a good reason for wanting to terminate her pregnancy.
SA A ? D SD

This statement would be considered positive in that a person who agreed with it would be assumed to have a positive attitude toward abortion and anyone who disagreed would have a negative attitude.

Consider next a second statement on the same topic:

Item 2. Women who have abortions should be prosecuted as criminals.
SA A ? D SD

This statement would be considered negative in that a person who agreed with it would have a negative attitude toward abortion and anyone who disagreed would have a positive attitude toward abortion.

The scoring method for quantifying responses to these statements also requires some explanation. Basically, people with very positive attitudes toward the topic should consistently receive high scores and people with negative attitudes should receive low scores. In the present case, if you answered SA in response to item 1, you would receive a score of 5; if you answered A in response to item 1, you would receive a score of 4; and so on up the scale (there are five possible levels on the scale). You should note again that item 1 is a positively worded statement.

With respect to item 2, a negatively worded statement, the scoring procedure is reversed. Specifically, if you answered SA to item 2, you would receive a score of 1; if you answered A to item 2, you would receive a score of 2; and so on down the scale.

With this scoring system and an equal number of positive and negative statements on the Likert scale, the score on all the statements can be summed. The higher the score, the more positive the person's attitudes toward the topic. Very low scores indicate strong negative attitudes.

These two items illustrate the basic characteristics of a Likert scale and how answers to each statement are quantified. I might also mention that some Likert scales use a seven-point scale of agreement and disagreement and some do not include the "uncertain" category among the options. The scoring principles, however, remain the same. We can now go on to consider how you would construct a complete Likert scale.

The basic procedure can be conveniently divided into three stages. To illustrate each, we shall use the example of measuring the attitudes of college students toward adult mental retardates. The three stages would be as follows: (1) preparing a *trial list* of statements, some of which will eventually be included in the final scale and others which will be discarded; (2) pretesting the trial list of statements on a group of people; and (3) using the pretest information to select the best statements for inclusion in the final scale and discard the bad statements.

Your first problem will be to generate a large number of positively and negatively worded statements about the topic under consideration. A great deal has been written about the process of inventing statements for use in attitude-measurement scales, and opinions are somewhat mixed as to what makes a good statement. Table 3.1 offers a list of criteria representing an informal consensus on the matter. With the help of the suggestions in the table, take a moment to see if you can produce a few statements (some positive and some negative) that

Table 3.1   A LIST OF SUGGESTED CRITERIA FOR EDITING STATEMENTS TO BE USED IN THE DEVELOPMENT OF AN ATTITUDE SCALE

1. Avoid extreme statements with which everyone will either strongly agree or strongly disagree. Such statements are the least sensitive to differences among individuals.
2. Statements should seek opinions, not state facts about the topic.
3. Try to think of statements that cover different ranges of the attitude scale (i.e., some mildly positive, some mildly negative, etc.).
4. Avoid the use of universal words such as *never* and *always*.
5. Avoid neutral statements.
6. Focus the question directly on the topic; do not bring in other topics or concepts.
7. Write all statements in the present tense.

express a range of attitudes toward adult retardates. It is not always easy to meet the criteria outlined, particularly if you are required to generate 75 to 100 statements on a topic. To help you, ten potential statements, with signs showing their positive or negative direction, are listed in Table 3.2.

Once you have a *trial list* of statements (such as those suggested in Table 3.2), your next task consists of *pretesting* this trial list. The people you choose for the pretest should be a sample with characteristics similar to those of the group you eventually hope to measure. If your attitude scale is going to be used with a population of college students, you should pretest it on a sample of college students (following the principles of sampling described in Chapter 2). Similarly, you should keep the conditions of the pretest as close as possible to the conditions under which the final scale will be administered. If, for example, the final test will be given with a time limit, the same time limit should be in effect during the pretest.

Let us assume that you will conduct a pretest of the ten statements in Table 3.2 so as to pinpoint the three best positive statements and the three best negative ones for later use in your final Likert scale. This brings you to the third and most crucial stage. How do you use the results obtained with your pretest to determine which statements are good and which are bad?

Table 3.3 is constructed to illustrate the results of the pretest for three subjects, John, Mary, and Jane. They responded to the ten statements in your trial list, and their responses are recorded in the columns to the right of the statements. Ordinarily, you would have perhaps a hundred such subjects, which would make Table 3.3 much more impressive; but for our present purposes, only three are more convenient.

Before going on to discuss how to select good and bad statements from the trial list, we must go over the information in Table 3.3. Take, for example, the response that John made to each of the statements on the pretest. Looking first at item 1, "Adult retardates should be kept in mental hospitals," you note that a person making this statement reflects a negative attitude (the minus sign in the table would be omitted in actual copies of the scale items). John placed his "X" in the column SA, which means that he strongly agrees with this statement. Using

Table 3.2 SOME TRIAL STATEMENTS FOR POTENTIAL USE IN AN ATTITUDE SCALE CONCERNED WITH ATTITUDES TOWARD ADULT RETARDATES

- 1. Adult retardates should be kept in mental hospitals.
- 2. Adult retardates are potentially dangerous.
- 3. Adult retardates should not have children.
- 4. Adult retardates cannot do some types of work.
- 5. Adult retardates should be kept in prisons.
+ 6. Adult retardates should be integrated into the community.
+ 7. Adult retardates are very pleasant people.
+ 8. Adult retardates should receive government financial support.
+ 9. Adult retardates can be very creative individuals.
+10. Adult retardates can take care of their own finances.

Table 3.3   PRETEST RESULTS FOR TEN STATEMENTS FROM THREE HYPOTHETICAL SUBJECTS IN THE PRETEST SAMPLE

	Responses					Score		
	SA	A	?	D	SD	(X) John	(O) Mary	(√) Jane
1. Adult retardates should be kept in mental hospitals. (−)	X	√			O	1	5	2
2. Adult retardates should be integrated into the community. (+)	O			√	X	1	5	2
3. Adult retardates are potentially dangerous. (−)	√	X			O	2	5	2
4. Adult retardates are very pleasant people (+)	O			√	X	1	5	2
5. Adult retardates should not have children. (−)	X	√		O		1	4	2
6. Adult retardates should receive government financial support. (+)		O		X	√	2	4	1
7. Adult retardates cannot do some types of work. (−)	X	√			O	1	5	2
8. Adult retardates can be very creative individuals. (+)		O		√	X	1	4	2
9. Adult retardates should be kept in prison. (−)	√	X			O	2	5	1
10. Adult retardates can take care of their own finances. (+)	O			X	√	2	5	1
TOTAL						14	47	17

the scoring system discussed earlier, you would give John one point for this strong negative attitude. Look next at item 2: "Adult retardates should be integrated into the community." This statement reflects a positive attitude, and John placed an "X" in the SD column, indicating that he strongly disagrees. As you can see, John is on his way to telling you he has very negative attitudes toward adult retardates, and his total score of 14 confirms this suspicion! (See the bottom of Table 3.3.)

See if you can track the responses made by Mary to each of the ten

statements in Table 3.3 and understand why her total score is very high (47).
Mary marks her responses with an "0"; finally, Jane, who is more similar to
John in her attitudes and uses a "√" to record her responses.

Since you have obtained pretest data from approximately 100 individuals
like John, Mary, and Jane (the more people the better), you are now in a position
to select the very best statements from your trial list of ten and discard the bad
ones. Of course, the "$100 question" is "What do you mean by good and bad
statements?" We can now answer this in one of two ways. One would involve a
long digression to explain some statistical calculations that must be used on these
pretest data to measure certain characteristics of each statement. Instead, we
shall take the easier course and merely explain, in commonsense terms, what
these statistical calculations would accomplish. Later, in Chapter 10, you will be
introduced to these basic calculational procedures—and, if you want a more
advanced discussion, you can consult excellent descriptions of the techniques by
either Nunnally (1970) or Edwards (1957).

Using common sense, how can you determine if statement 1 in Table 3.3 is
a good or bad statement to use in your final list? The answer to this is as follows:
*If a statement on the pretest is good, all of the people who have similar total
scores on the pretest should have similar responses to that particular statement.
If a statement is bad, there will be very little relationship between how people
responded to the statement and their total scores on the pretest.* Another way
of saying the same thing is that people with similar attitudes will consistently
respond in the same way to a good statement or, conversely, people with similar
attitudes will fail to respond in the same way to a bad statement. The correlational
statistics mentioned earlier *quantify* the extent to which statements are good or
bad in the terms described above. Once you have calculated the appropriate
statistic for each statement in your pretest list, you are in a position to select the
very best statements for inclusion in the final form of your attitude scale and to
discard those that are bad.

If you have followed the procedures and reasoning in the preceding paragraph, you can see that behavioral scientists are willing to go to a lot of trouble
to measure the mental processes we call attitudes. Indeed, you might wonder if
all of this effort is really necessary. The answer is yes—it is absolutely necessary,
and the reasons were outlined in detail in Chapter 2, when we discussed the
operational-definition rule.

To illustrate the point in the present context, you will recall that we went
to great lengths in Chapter 2 to explain why it is necessary to define the term
"pornography" operationally. The same arguments hold true with respect to the
use of terms that refer to attitudes and opinions. In everyday language, we think
that we know what it means to have feminist attitudes. However, on close
examination, each of us probably has a slightly different idea. If a behavioral
scientist hopes to examine feminism as an attitude, it will be necessary to eliminate any potential confusion about the meaning of the term. This requires an
operational definition, and you now realize that one of the most effective ways
in which you can define an attitude operationally is to construct a Likert scale.
Once you have constructed the scale, you will be able to state that a feminist is

any man or woman who scores above a particular level on the Likert scale. You can see the advantage of the definition. Everyone who uses the term "feminism" now knows exactly what it means, and anyone can repeat your measurements of feminism simply by administering your Likert scale. In short, just as "pornography" was defined in Chapter 2 as any picture revealing frontal nudity, an effective operational definition of attitudes is provided by the Likert scale.

Several additional points should be noted briefly before we conclude our discussion of attitude measurement. First, the Likert scale is not the only attitude-scaling procedure you can use. For a discussion of other methods and their advantages and disadvantages you should consult Nunnally (1970). Second, it is not always necessary to construct your own attitude-measurement scale. Many such scales are already available. Lists and descriptions of them are provided in Shaw and Wright (1967) and Robinson and Shaver (1973). If you have completed Exercise 2.1 at the end of Chapter 2, you will be familiar with the *Psychological Abstracts* and perhaps already know that this source has separate sections called "Attitude Measurement" and "Attitude Measures," which abstract studies using attitude scales.

Finally, one last word of caution about attitude scales. When these scales are used to measure mental processes, you assume that the respondent's statements are honest and sincere. Unfortunately, this is very often a questionable assumption. Attitude scales are just another approach to the processes of observation and description; as such, they are subject to the same problems of distortion that we discussed in Chapter 2. Some individuals want to appear socially acceptable and pleasant to the observer. Hence, they will respond to the statements on the attitude scale in a manner that portrays them as such, regardless of their honest attitudes and opinions. The opposite can also occur when individuals feel threatened by the observer and react with antagonism to the statements on the scale. In both cases, the attitudes measured will not be valid. You should be aware of these potential distortions.

My own conservative view is that you should never assume validity unless you combine the use of the attitude scale with at least one other operational definition of the attitude you are trying to measure. To illustrate the point, consider the following story (the source of which has long since been forgotten).

A man was driving through a snowstorm to meet his wife. His son was asleep in the front seat of the car. A large truck skidded out of control on a curve and crashed into the car. When the ambulance arrived the father was dead, and his son was unconscious but still alive. Upon arrival at the hospital, the boy was rushed into emergency surgery. The neurosurgeon looked at the patient and said: "I can't operate on this boy, he is my son!"

How can this story be true?

The typical answer to this question is that the boy had been adopted by the man driving the car and the neurosurgeon was the boy's biological father. Often other complicated explanations are offered. But, of most interest, very few people arrive at the simplest and most obvious explanation: the neurosurgeon is the boy's mother!

Now it is entirely possible that an individual who scored very high on a Likert scale designed to measure feminist attitudes would lie in order to appear socially acceptable. This story, or techniques similar to it, provide a second, corroborating operational definition of the attitude. The additional measure permits the observer to determine the extent to which the responses on the two measures are similar. A very thorough approach to the problem might also attempt to measure directly the behavior of the individual during male-female interactions. The essential point is that a number of different operational definitions of the attitudes in question will provide you with converging evidence for the validity of your attitude scale.

Measuring Personality Traits

How do other people describe you? Are you an introverted, shy individual? Are you a slightly anxious person? Would your closest friends describe you as a depressive, perhaps even suicidal person? If someone is described as an introvert, you have some idea what this means and can imagine how that person might behave at a party or in a job interview. Cronbach (1970) defines a personality trait as *a tendency to react in a defined way to a defined class of stimuli*. In this section, we will consider how people measure personality traits.

Although most of us know what is meant by the terms "introverted," "shy," "anxious," and "depressive," any attempt to employ them in the context of scientific observation and description requires us once again to invoke our old friend the *operational-definition rule*. If you want to label someone a depressive, you are required to eliminate any possible confusion by defining this mental condition operationally in terms of the procedures used to measure it. Fortunately, behavioral scientists have been interested in personality traits like depression for well over a century, and there is a standard procedure available for measuring almost every conceivable personality trait. Indeed, in the case of depression you can choose from any of several standard personality tests.

It is not possible, in the present context, to describe all the personality tests available to the psychologist. Instead, we shall briefly consider the way you might proceed if you wanted to select a particular test. Specifically, we shall consider some of the practical problems involved in selecting a good personality test and some of the fundamental criteria that such a test should meet. For a more complete description of various available personality tests, you should consult the excellent discussions by Cronbach (1970) and Anastasi (1976). In addition, two standard guides to commercially available personality tests are Buros (1974), *Tests in Print,* and/or Buros (1978), *Eighth Mental Measurements Yearbook*.

As indicated earlier, there are a number of important questions to consider when you select a particular personality test from among the many available. Some tests are designed to measure a particular trait (e.g., the Beck Depression Inventory, as the name implies, is specifically designed to measure depression). Other personality tests are more comprehensive and will provide information about several different personality traits (e.g., the Minnesota Multiphasic Personality Inventory, also called the MMPI, measures many different traits and is widely used as an instrument for diagnosing mental illnesses ranging from mild neuroses to serious psychotic tendencies). Obviously, you would select the testing instrument best suited to your particular purpose. If you are primarily concerned with an individual's current level of depression, the Beck Depression Inventory is more convenient and easy to use than the MMPI. Hence you would probably choose the Beck.

Another important practical consideration is your training and familiarity with a testing procedure. Some personality tests are objective paper-and-pencil tests that are easy to administer and score. Such tests are often called *personality inventories,* in the sense that a subject simply reads a list of statements and indicates which statements apply to him or her. Once again, the Beck Depression Inventory provides a good example. There are 21 items on this test, each containing four statements. The subject is simply required to circle the statement on each item that describes him or her the best. A sample statement from the Beck reads: "I have to push myself very hard to do anything." It does not take a great deal of skill or practice to administer and score the Beck Depression Inventory. On the other hand, some personality tests are very difficult to administer and score reliably unless you have had considerable background, training, and experience. The Thematic Apperception Test (TAT) is one such example. This test requires the subject to look at a series of 20 pictures and tell a story about each. For example, one picture in the series depicts a young boy examining a violin. The TAT requires the subject to describe what is happening in this picture, what led up to the events in the picture, and what the outcome of the story will be. Such tests are generally called *projective tests,* since the subject is asked to *project* his or her feelings into the unstructured events of the picture. As indicated above, it takes considerable training and experience to score these stories reliably and to arrive at some number that quantifies various personality traits. Hence, it would be unwise—and unethical—for someone who has not had the proper training to use projective testing instruments like the TAT.

Yet another factor to keep in mind in selecting a personality test is the type of person being treated. Some tests are intended for use with adults, others with children. Many tests are limited to a particular language and culture. It may seem obvious, but you should make sure a test is used only in those situations for which it was designed. A bilingual Francophone may not do well on a test that was constructed and validated for Anglophones.

In addition to the factors noted above, there are two additional things you should know about any personality test before you decide to use it as a measuring instrument. Specifically, you will want to know if the test is *reliable* and if it is *valid.* You will perhaps recall that these are the two basic questions that we have asked about all operational definitions. Personality tests are no different in this respect. Indeed, the *reliability* and *validity* of the test are perhaps the two most important criteria on which it should be judged.

Reliability   The ability of the test to produce consistent measurements is called *reliability.* There are several ways that people interested in personality measurement assess the reliability of a test. *Split-half* reliability studies divide questions from the test into two groups and compare the performance of individuals on each half of the test to see if the same measurements are obtained. *Test-retest* reliability studies compare the performance of each individual over a number of successive test sessions to determine if consistent scores are obtained. The more discrepant the scores obtained on each occasion, the less reliable the test.

The point to appreciate is that we want our measuring instruments (whether they are operational definitions of pornography, attitude scales, or personality tests) to give us consistent, reliable, repeatable results when we quantify our observations. Otherwise these instruments are of no use. No one wants to use a "rubber ruler" to measure distance, nor does the behavioral scientist want to use a personality test that measures you as an introvert on one occasion and an extrovert on another.

Test Validity   A more difficult characteristic to pin down is test validity. A personality test is valid if it measures the trait that it is designed to measure. This is easy to say but hard to determine. For example, the Beck Depression Inventory claims to measure the extent to which a person is depressed. The score on this test can vary from 0 to 60, with scores above 24 indicating severe depression. If, every time a person completed the Beck, it produced a score of approximately 30, we would be able to conclude that the test was a reliable measuring instrument. Can we assume, however, that it is valid? Is it really measuring depression, or is it measuring some different personality characteristic such as hostility? If this question sounds similar to the one we discussed in the previous chapter with reference to the term "pornography," it should. It is once again the question of construct validity in a different context, and as you will discover, the answer has not changed.

In order to determine the validity of a test, people interested in personality measurement usually conduct validation studies. A validation study compares the scores obtained on the personality test with some other criterion that is also accepted as a definition of the personality trait under consideration. In the case of the Beck Depression Inventory, Beck and his associates, in 1961, administered their test to a group of psychiatric patients and recorded the scores. At the same time, psychiatrists interviewed these patients and made their own independent judgments as to how depressed each patient was. These psychiatric judgments were the independent criterion against which the Beck scores were validated. A high degree of agreement between the Beck scores and the psychiatric judgments would argue for the validity of the Beck Depression Inventory; a low degree of agreement would argue that the Beck test was not really measuring what it claimed to be. In this case, the results indicated a high level of agreement, and since that time a large number of other validation studies have produced similar results (cf. Beck, 1970). The impressive reliability and validity measures that have been reported for the Beck Depression Inventory are at least partly responsible for the popularity of this test among behavioral scientists interested in quantifying depression. That it is very easy to use and score also adds to its desirability.

You should now have both the terminology and background to understand what we mean when we say that validation studies of personality tests consist essentially of *comparing the extent to which two different operational definitions of a mental process (e.g., depression) sort people into comparable categories.*

If one operational definition of depression (such as the Beck Depression Inventory) measures you as severely depressed and a second operational definition (such as a psychiatric interview) also measures you as severely depressed, the personality test is assumed to have some validity. As this process is repeated many times over and many different operational definitions seem to agree with the test results, confidence in the validity of the testing instrument grows.

Regarding the scores from such personality tests, there is some disagreement about which scale of measurement is generated. Since the test scores range between 0 and 60, your first impression might be that you have a *ratio* scale of measurement and consequently that you can assume Fred is twice as depressed as Joe and so on. It is, however, generally agreed that scores on most personality tests are not ratio measurements. The argument against the ratio assumption is that mental traits probably do not have a meaningful zero point. A score of zero on the Beck Depression Inventory suggests that you are not a depressive, but it does not mean that you absolutely lack the trait. Hence, the absolute zero point required by the ratio scale is not available.

It can also be argued that the scores obtained with a personality test do not meet the requirements of an interval scale. This scale requires, for example, that the difference in amount of depression between scores of 5 and 10 be the same as the difference in amount of depression between scores of 55 and 60 (i.e., equal intervals). In spite of these arguments, people often treat the results obtained from "mental" tests as if they are interval measurements.

Given the preceding description of the various characteristics of personality measurement, what are the implications of this discussion? Once again, it depends on your situation. If you find yourself on the receiving end of one or more of these tests, you should know that they vary considerably in their reliability and validity. A conservative view is that the results obtained with any testing instrument should be taken with a grain of salt. If you discover that there has been very little research on the reliability and validity of the test, a somewhat larger dose of salt is in order. It is very likely that your "mental processes" have been measured at some point in your life (like those intelligence tests they administered in school). Perhaps now you will be more interested in the characteristics of these measurement procedures. Were they reliable? Were they valid? Did people make claims about the measurements that were not justified by the measurement scale? Did, for example, someone suggest that your scores were at least twice as high as some other student's scores? Was this claim justified by the measurement scale? The same considerations also pertain to the behavioral scientist who decides to use these testing instruments in the context of behavioral research. Measurements in science must be reliable and valid. If they are not, the probability of distortion, bias, and error is high. Hence, mental measurements should be adopted and used with caution.

Paradigm Measurements

A friend recently made an interesting personal observation. Apparently his father had undergone serious heart surgery twice within a very short period, the second operation having been required to repair an error made the first time! The father has now returned to work and is feeling reasonably well considering what he had experienced. The friend, however, claims that his father's memory is not as good as it had been prior to the surgery. The father forgets business appointments and occasionally doesn't recall the names of close personal acquaintances. He suggested that some aspect of the surgical procedure might have produced brain damage that, in turn, caused memory problems. I suggested, alternatively, that his father might simply be distracted by physical symptoms (e.g., minor palpitations, pains, etc.). Given these distractions, which would not be unusual for someone recovering from a serious illness, one might expect lapses in memory. In other words, distractions and lack of attention, rather than brain damage, could explain the memory deficits. The friend did not seem particularly impressed by my explanation and suggested that research should be done to determine if surgical procedures can affect postoperative mental processes. You will probably agree that the question is an interesting one.

Over the years, certain mental processes like human learning and memory have been recognized as phenomena of central importance in our attempts to understand behavior. Consequently, a number of standard procedures for measuring these processes have been developed. Taken together, the term *paradigm measurements* describes this collection of procedures. Space does not permit a description of all the various paradigm measurements. Entire volumes, for example, are devoted to methods of measuring human learning and memory. Instead, we shall briefly describe a few of the more prominent methods to give you some idea of what paradigm measurements are and the wealth of methodology that exists in this area. Perhaps the best overviews are textbooks in general experimental psychology that concentrate on methods of studying mental processes such as learning, memory, perception, cognition, and motivation (e.g., Sidowski, 1966; Kling & Riggs, 1971; Dunham, 1977; Mook, 1982).

Human Learning and Memory Paradigms   The friend described earlier was interested in measuring human memory before and after surgical treatment. There is no shortage of methods available to him. Almost all the procedures consist basically of asking a subject to learn a list of verbal materials (e.g., words, letters, phrases) that must be recalled at a later time. The interval between the original learning and the subsequent memory test is called the *retention interval*.

The various basic memory procedures are typically divided into short-term-memory (STM) and long-term-memory (LTM) paradigms with reference to the length of the retention interval. For example, a procedure called the Peterson technique is classified as an STM paradigm. In this procedure, a subject is presented with an item such as a nonsense syllable (e.g., xiq), asked to count backward by threes for a brief period of time (e.g., 3 to 18 seconds), and finally asked to recall the nonsense syllable that had originally been presented. It is assumed that one is studying short-term memory because the retention interval in this particular procedure is a matter of a very few seconds. If the retention interval is measured in terms of hours, days, or even weeks, the procedure is called a long-term-memory (LTM) paradigm.

It is also typical to divide memory paradigms into *recognition* and *recall* procedures. As the names imply, a recognition paradigm simply requires you to recognize from a list of potential items, the specific items that you had memorized (e.g., a multiple-choice test is a recognition procedure). Alternatively, a recall procedure requires you to generate the previously memorized material without any prompting (e.g., an essay examination is a recall procedure). Generally speaking, recognition memory tasks are easier than recall tasks.

It might be noted that the division of these procedures into the categories described above is not arbitrary. Experimental psychologists interested in human memory suspect, for example, that different mental processes underlie STM and LTM. If they are correct in this assumption, you can understand why it might be important for them to differentiate between the procedures used to measure short-term memory and long-term memory.

It is one thing to remember something previously learned and another to learn the material in the first place. Procedures used to measure *human learning* are typically divided into at least two general categories. Some procedures are designed to measure *associative learning* and others are assumed to measure *concept learning*. A frequently used associative-learning procedure involves the presentation of a list (e.g., 12 items) of paired-associate nonsense syllables. For example, one item on the list might be the pair *xig-noj*. The *xig* syllable is called the *stimulus syllable* and the *noj* syllable is called the *response syllable*. When the list is first presented, the subject sees the stimulus syllable and is required to answer with the correct response syllable. After a number of times through the list, subjects eventually learn all the pairs. The number of errors made during the learning of the list is assumed to be a measure of associative learning.

Procedures measuring concept learning differ from those that test associative learning in that they typically require the subject to solve a problem instead of learning item-by-item associations. An example of a concept-learning procedure would be finding the solution to an anagram puzzle. As you perhaps know, in this task the subject is presented with an anagram (e.g., ptcoenc) and asked to unscramble the letters to make a word. The correct answer in this case is the word "concept." Subjects usually improve with practice, and the time spent in solving the anagram is taken as a measure of the *concept-learning process*.

As indicated earlier, the student confronted with a research problem involving human learning and/or memory has a variety of procedures from which to choose. Perhaps the most comprehensive discussion of the various methods—their advantages and disadvantages and existing data—is presented by Puff (1982).

Comparative Learning Paradigms   It is not unusual, for various practical or theoretical reasons, for a behavioral scientist to study learning and memory processes in animals lower on the phylogenetic scale than humans (e.g., rats, pigeons, and monkeys are often used). Recall again the problem of memory function before and after surgical treatment. At some point, a proper approach to this problem could require the direct manipulation of surgical procedures in order to determine which of their elements are responsible for the memory deficits (e.g., you might want to administer more or less anesthetic). Obviously, not many patients would volunteer for such treatment. Hence, behavioral scientists often use animals other than humans in this type of research. Ethical problems not-withstanding (see Appendix B), the assumption is that the results obtained with the animals will generalize to some extent to humans.

Most procedures used in the comparative study of learning and memory fall into one of two categories called *instrumental conditioning paradigms* and *classical conditioning paradigms*. You might, for instance, train a hungry rat to run through a maze in order to obtain food in a goal box at the end of the maze; this is one example of a standard instrumental conditioning procedure. The primary characteristic of instrumental procedures is that they require the animal to learn an appropriate sequence of responses in order to obtain a reward (or avoid a negative event). Learning in the case of the maze procedure is usually measured in terms of the number of errors the animal makes prior to learning the correct route to the food and also in terms of the time required to traverse the maze.

A standard classical conditioning procedure consists of repeatedly pairing a neutral stimulus such as a tone or light (the conditional stimulus) with another motivationally significant stimulus such as the presentation of food to a hungry animal (the unconditional stimulus). The presentation of the food will usually elicit responses such as salivation or chewing movements (the unconditioned responses). If, after a number of pairings of the neutral stimulus and the food, the neutral stimulus acquires the ability to elicit food-related responses, we assume that the animal has "associated" the two stimuli. That is, the animal has "learned" that the neutral stimulus signals the delivery of food. Classical conditioning procedures are differentiated from instrumental conditioning procedures in one important respect: in the latter, the occurrence of the reward (e.g., the food) depends upon the animal making the appropriate response (e.g., running through the maze). In the former, the animal is not required to make any particular response for the food (unconditioned stimulus) to be presented.

These descriptions of basic instrumental and classical conditioning procedures are very much oversimplified, but they should give you some idea of the paradigms that are often used to study learning and memory in those "white rats" that have become synonymous with experimental psychology laboratories. For a further discussion of these paradigms, you can consult descriptions provided by Donahoe and Wessells (1980) and Fantino and Logan (1979). The latter contains a unique chapter on paradigms used to study learning in invertebrates.

Psychophysical Paradigms   A considerable amount of behavioral research is concerned with questions about human sensory abilities. How sensitive is your hearing under various conditions? What is the minimal amount of light that you can detect? Is it easier to detect increases or decreases in room temperature? What temperature is most comfortable for a person working in an office? A person recovering from surgery? A person playing handball? If you find yourself in the position of asking such questions or interpreting answers that other people have offered, you should know that there are a number of standard procedures that have been developed over the years to deal specifically with questions about these sensory and perceptual processes. The oldest of these were first discussed by the German physicist Gustav Fechner well over a hundred years ago. Since that time, they have been collectively referred to as the *psychophysical methods*. The term "psychophysical" refers to the notion that these procedures are concerned with measuring the changes in "psychological" perceptions that are produced by variations in "physical" energy. Examples of the specific procedures used to measure your sensitivity to various types of physical energy are the *method of limits,* the *method of constant stimuli,* and the *method of average error.* There are also several other more recent methods used to study sensory and perceptual skills. In order to illustrate the circumstances that require you to make use of these specialized procedures, we shall briefly describe the rationale behind the use of two of them.

Assume for the moment that you have a friend who works in a factory that manufactures cardboard boxes. The corrugating machine in the factory is extremely noisy and your friend notices that he has problems hearing after work. In fact, he is worried that, with repeated exposure to this noise, there may be permanent damage to his hearing. To help your friend, you turn to the special measurement procedures called psychophysical methods. How should you proceed to measure the sensitivity of your friend's hearing before and after exposure to the noisy factory? We shall use this example to illustrate some basic characteristics of this measurement methodology. You should keep in mind that the basic reasoning and procedures used in the context of this example will apply in a wide variety of situations involving other questions and sensory modalities.

The first step in answering questions like the one posed above is to obtain a measurement of your friend's *absolute threshold* prior to working in the noisy environment. The term "absolute threshold" refers to the minimum amount of the physical stimulus energy that the individual can detect. In this case, we are considering the *loudness threshold,* which means that we want to know the minimum *intensity* of sound energy that is detectable.

With a bit of engineering, we should be able to construct a sound source that permits us to vary the intensity of a given tone from levels well above the typical absolute threshold to levels well below it. Using this sound source, we can obtain an estimate of a particular individual's absolute threshold by systematically increasing the intensity of the tone from below-threshold values until the person reports hearing it, and, conversely, by systematically decreasing the intensity of the tone from above-threshold values in small increments until the person can no longer hear it. Given an adequate number of increasing and decreasing test procedures, we would be able to obtain a reasonably accurate measurement of the minimum amount of sound energy that the person can detect (i.e., the loudness threshold). In fact, the procedure just described (and variations on it) is the psychophysical method called the *method of limits,* mentioned earlier.

Assume, next, for purposes of discussion, that this method-of-limits procedure revealed that the minimum intensity of sound that your subject could detect was estimated to be 10 decibels (db). (Engineers measure sound energy on a scale called a decibel scale.) So the absolute threshold before working in the noisy factory was 10 db. Next, assume that your friend works in the noisy factory for one week and returns to have the loudness threshold measured again. Using the same basic procedure of increasing and decreasing sound intensity, you determine that his loudness threshold is now 15 db. In other words, it would appear that his hearing is *less* sensitive after a week of exposure to noise from the corrugating machine. A sound must now be much louder in order for him to detect it.

Based on measurements obtained with the method of limits, you might conclude that the noisy factory had damaged the subject's hearing. There is, however, an alternative interpretation of the measurements that often arises when you use the basic psychophysical methods. In order to understand this alternative interpretation, you must put yourself in the place of the person whose hearing is being measured. You are seated in a room listening for a sound through a pair of earphones. A tone is presented and you are asked if you hear it. You say no, and you are quite sure that you did not hear anything (it was well below threshold). Another tone is presented and you are asked if you hear it. Again you say no, and you know definitely that you did not hear anything. Another tone is presented. This time you think you hear something but you are not quite sure. Should you answer yes or no? You think about it a minute and figure that it is not a matter of life and death, so you say yes. Note, however, that if you had been feeling a little bit more conservative, you could just as easily have decided to say no. In other words, there are two factors on any given trial that will determine whether you say yes or no. One is the actual *sensitivity* of your ear and the other is your *response criterion;* this second factor is more difficult to describe. It involves how careful or careless you are in making up your mind on those fuzzy trials where you are not particularly sure if you heard the tone or not. If you tend to be a very conservative, careful person, you will wait until you are absolutely sure you are hearing that tone every time it is presented. One consequence of this conservative approach is that you will appear to be less sensitive (i.e., have a higher loudness threshold) than someone who is not as conservative and careful. Alternatively, if you are more careless about such matters, you will be willing to claim that you heard the tone when another person might hesitate. One consequence of this careless attitude is that you will be mistakenly thought to have very sensitive hearing. You detect tones others might find questionable. You can see that the response criterion can make the same "ear" appear more or less sensitive, depending upon how careful or careless the hearer is about making responses.

If we now return to the case of your friend, you will recall that his loudness threshold measured 10 db before he worked in the factory and 15 db after he worked there for a week. Now, however, you also know that there are two possible reasons for this difference that are not recognized by our method-of-limits procedure. One is that your friend's ear really is less *sensitive* to sound energy. The alternative explanation is that the noise did not damage his ear; instead, your friend simply decided to be more careful and conservative in making responses during the second test (after a week in the factory). This shift to a more conservative attitude made it appear that his hearing had become worse! In the vernacular of people who use psychophysical methods, this problem is called a *shift in response criterion*.

The moral of this story is that you can use the basic psychophysical methods to measure sensory capacities in many different situations, but you will occasionally wonder if you are measuring the sensitivity of the sensory system or a shift in response criterion. There is a way to resolve this dilemma. It is called *signal-detection methodology* and its advantage is that it permits you to measure changes in both sensitivity and in response criterion. Having come this far in our discussion, it would be a shame not to expose you to at least the rudiments of the signal-detection methods.

With a signal-detection approach, your first task would be to obtain an estimate of your friend's loudness threshold. Recall that our observations using the method of limits indicated a loudness threshold of 10 db. This 10 db tone can then be adopted for use in the signal-detection task. The next stage involves a large number of trials in which your friend is asked to decide whether the tone was presented or not. Prior to starting the procedure, he has been told that the tone would be present on only half of these trials and that the specific trials on which the tone was present would be randomly determined.

You should note that this procedure presents only one stimulus intensity (10 db), and that the stimulus is not presented on every trial. Your friend must report whether or not the tone was present on each trial.

If you think about it for a moment, you will realize that your friend's responses in this procedure will fall into one of four possible categories. On any particular trial, he can (1) say yes *correctly* when the stimulus is presented; (2) say yes *incorrectly* when the stimulus is *not* presented; (3) say no *correctly* when the stimulus is *not* presented; or (4) say no *incorrectly* when the stimulus is presented. In the vernacular of signal-detection methodology, these four possible outcomes are called respectively (1) a *hit*, (2) a *false alarm*, (3) a *correct rejection*, and (4) a *miss*. These four outcomes are presented schematically in Figure 3.2.

Returning now to your friend (who has not yet been exposed to the noisy factory), assume that you conducted 100 trials with the tone present on half of the trials. The hypothetical results obtained before the subject was exposed to the noisy factory conditions are presented in Figure 3.3. As the data in this figure indicate, your friend's hit rate was 50 percent when the stimulus was present (he

Subject's response

		Yes	No
	Present	Hit	Miss
Stimulus condition	Absent	False alarm	Correct rejection

Figure 3.2 Four different categories of response possible in a signal-detection procedure.

Subject's response

		Yes	No
		Yes	No
Stimulus condition	Present	(Hit) 0.50	(Miss) 0.50
	Absent	(False alarm) 0.30	(Correct rejection) 0.70

Figure 3.3 Proportion of responses in each category as measured *before* working in a noisy factory.

correctly detected 25 of the 50 tones presented); by definition, he missed on 50 percent of the stimuli presented. Note also the false-alarm rate. The data indicate that your friend claimed to hear the tone on 30 percent of the trials when it was not actually presented; by definition, he correctly rejected the stimulus when it was not presented on 70 percent of the trials.

Assume, next, that your friend worked for a week in the noisy factory and returned to be tested again. Once again, 100 trials were conducted with the 10 db tone present on half. The hypothetical results obtained on this second test are presented in Figure 3.4.

Note first that your friend's hit rate was again found to be 50 percent, which is the same as that observed before he worked in the factory. Of more interest, the false-alarm rate is now 10 percent, which represents a substantial decrease from the 30 percent false-alarm rate observed on the test conducted prior to working in the factory. What do the data in Figures 3.3 and 3.4, taken together, tell us about the effects on your friend's sensory functions? They suggest that

Subject's response

		Yes	No
Stimulus condition	Present	(Hit) 0.50	(Miss) 0.50
	Absent	(False alarm) 0.10	(Correct rejection) 0.90

Figure 3.4 Proportion of responses in each category as measured *after* working in a noisy factory.

his sensitivity to the tone (loudness threshold) was essentially the same before and after working in the factory. The evidence for this is the identical hit rate (50 percent) revealed during both test sessions. It would appear, instead, that the main effect of working in the factory was a change in your friend's *response criterion*. It seems that his week of work in the factory has turned him into a more careful and conservative individual. During the first test, he was careless enough to produce a 30 percent false-alarm rate; one week later, he has exhibited a more cautious 10 percent false-alarm rate.

We can now compare the results from the signal-detection method to those we got earlier using only the method of limits. Recall that the method of limits measured a threshold of 10 db prior to working in the factory and a threshold of 15 db after working in the factory. Looking now at the results obtained with the signal-detection method, we see that the higher threshold (15 db) obtained after working in the factory is best interpreted as a more cautious response criterion, not a change in the subject's sensitivity. The essential point is that the two factors, sensitivity and response criterion, cannot be separated when one is using the method of limits *alone*. You would thus do well to use a signal-detection procedure in this situation. In other situations where there is no reason to suspect that a subject might shift response criterion or where false-alarm rates are very low, the basic psychophysical methods like the method of limits will serve you very well.

To summarize briefly, the hit rate obtained when using a signal detection procedure provides us with an estimate of the subject's sensitivity. The higher the hit rate at any given stimulus intensity, the more sensitive the subject—given a constant false-alarm rate. The higher the false-alarm rate given a constant hit rate, the less strict is the subject's response criterion.

You should also note that, for the sake of clarity, the hypothetical example used to illustrate the basic properties of the signal-detection procedure has been oversimplified. In actual practice, a condition such as working in the noisy factory seldom produces a change in the rate of false alarms without also changing the hit rate to some extent. As you might expect, these two measures tend to covary. Also, a researcher using a signal-detection procedure would employ a number of different stimulus intensities to assess a subject's performance (e.g., 8, 9, 10, and 11 db tones). Similarly, a number of different probabilities (30, 40, 50, 60, and 70 percent) would be employed at each intensity level to obtain independent estimates of the subject's sensitivity and response criteria. However, no matter how elaborate the procedure became, the basic reasoning illustrated in the simple example just discussed would remain the same. For the reader interested in a more extensive account of signal-detection methodology, D'Amato's (1970) description is particularly lucid.

The preceding discussion of *paradigm measurements* barely scratches the surface. It should be evident to you that all these specialized procedures for measuring phenomena such as learning, memory, and sensory thresholds are essentially *operational definitions*. In the same sense that "pornography" can be operationally defined as the presence or absence of frontal nudity, "feminism" can be defined as a score on a Likert attitude scale, and depression can be defined as a score on the Beck Depression Inventory, a loudness threshold can be defined as the hit rate measured with a signal-detection procedure. All these measurement procedures provide us with reliable, repeatable operational definitions of mental processes.

DESCRIPTIVE STATISTICS

Once you have used any of the measurement procedures described above, you will find yourself with a set of numbers. In the final section of this chapter, we will consider some of the calculations that are used to summarize or describe such data. These calculations are called *descriptive statistics;* their purpose is to make the data you obtain with your measurement procedures more intelligible.

When I started planning this section, I decided to record every descriptive statistic that I encountered over a period of one week. I began the list one morning at 7 o'clock. Each day an average of a million people will wake up in a hospital in the United States. Eleven percent of all U.S. citizens are over 65 years of age. Privately run hospitals charge an average of 14.3 percent more per case than do nonprofit hospitals. Seventy-five percent of the people who contract Acquired Immune Deficiency Syndrome (AIDS) are active homosexual males. Alcohol-related motor vehicle crashes cause an average of 25,000 deaths per year in the United States. The average annual income in Laos is $95 per year, making Laos one of the poorest countries in the world. I quit recording descriptive statistics at 9 o'clock that same morning. The purpose of the one-week plan had been to impress you with the amount and variety of statistical description that bombards us every day. As it turned out, the information I recorded during just two hours seemed sufficient.

In the following discussion, we shall offer a very brief overview of the most basic ways in which data are summarized or described. You will undoubtedly be familiar with some of these concepts and calculations while others will be new to you. In either case, it is important to understand them all and to think about the ways in which they are used and misused both in science and in our everyday lives. If, after reading this basic introduction, you are interested in a more complete treatment of the topic, any basic statistics book in the behavioral sciences will be a good place to start (e.g., McCall, 1980; Edwards, 1985).

The Frequency Distribution

On a normal summer day, it is not unusual for a hundred people to enter Backstreet Imports, the video arcade first described in Chapter 2. Suppose each time someone entered the arcade you flipped a nickel; if it came up heads, you would record the amount of time this particular customer stayed in the arcade. If it came up tails, you would ignore the customer and wait for another flip that gave you a head. With this sampling procedure, every customer would have an equal chance (0.5 to be exact) of being included in your sample.

Given records on 20 customers, a number of questions come to mind. What was the longest stay in the arcade? What was the shortest stay? What was the average stay? and so on. One way to answer these questions would be to display the data in Table 3.4. With only 20 numbers, it is perhaps a forgivable sin to work with this unorganized mass of information; however, with 10,000 numbers it would be a useless exercise. One of the first and most useful ways to summarize and describe any set of measurements is to present it in graphic form, so that its major characteristics are instantly obvious. The data in Table 3.4 are most appropriately presented as a *frequency distribution*. Table 3.5 presents the frequency distribution in a tabular format, and Figure 3.5 presents these same data in a graphic format typically called a *frequency polygon*. The frequency polygon makes some of the general characteristics of the data from Table 3.4 obvious at a glance.

Several points should be made about the frequency polygon as a device for representing data graphically. First, the horizontal axis of the graph can be called either the *X* axis or the *abscissa;* the vertical axis is called either the *Y* axis or *ordinate*. The number and size of the categories you decide to have in any frequency distribution is a matter of judgment. In Figure 3.5 we have divided the total range of measurements into 9 categories of 10 minutes each. It would also be possible to divide the total range in 18 five-minute categories or 90 one-minute categories. The basic rule of thumb is to choose a category size that will make

Table 3.4   THE DURATION OF EACH VISIT TO A VIDEO ARCADE BY 20 CUSTOMERS RANDOMLY SELECTED DURING ONE DAY OF BUSINESS IN THE ARCADE

Customer	Duration of visit to arcade (min)
A	42
B	55
C	18
D	12
E	13
F	72
G	6
H	64
I	21
J	30
K	21
L	28
M	34
N	26
O	32
P	40
Q	23
R	39
S	41
T	3

Table 3.5   FREQUENCY DISTRIBUTION OF
MEASUREMENTS FROM TABLE 3.4 USING
10-MINUTE CATEGORIES

Duration of visit to arcade (min)	Frequency of people in each category
0–10	2
11–20	3
21–30	6
31–40	4
41–50	2
51–60	1
61–70	1
71–80	1
81–90	0
	$N = 20$

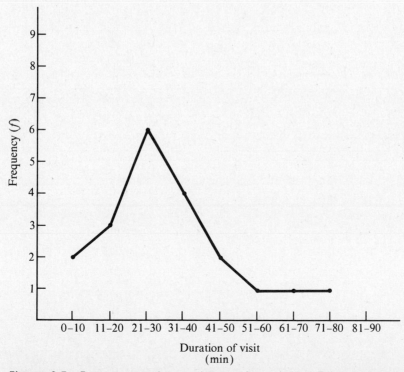

Figure 3.5   Frequency polygon of scores from data in Table 3.5 using 10-minute categories along the abscissa and frequency of measurements in each category on the ordinate. See text for an explanation of these terms.

it easy to see the general shape of the distribution and identify major character-istics like the range of scores, the most frequently occurring measurement, and so on. With reference to the data in Table 3.4, it would have been a mistake to use a much larger number of small categories along the X axis. For example, 90 one-minute categories would not provide you with a very clear picture of the general manner in which the scores are distributed.

Not all frequency polygons look like Figure 3.5. They can have several basic shapes, each of which has special properties. Figure 3.6 shows four basic types of frequency polygons and the names that are usually used to describe them. They are (1) symmetrical, (2) positively skewed, (3) negatively skewed, and (4) multimodal. Note that these examples are hypothetical and the curves have been "smoothed" to make the general shape of each type more obvious.

Panel 1 of Figure 3.6 is a symmetrical distribution in the sense that all the measurements tend to be organized symmetrically around the most frequently observed value in the distribution. Panel 2 is a *positively skewed distribution* in the sense that there are a relatively large number of scores that occur at the

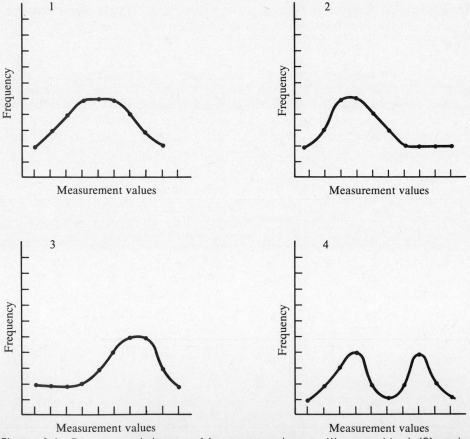

Figure 3.6 Four general shapes of frequency polygons: (1) symmetrical, (2) posi-tively skewed, (3) negatively skewed, and (4) multimodal (bimodal).

higher values on the abscissa. This causes the distribution to be asymmetrical, with a longer slope toward the higher values. When the same slope occurs in the direction of the lower values on the abscissa, the frequency polygon is the *negatively skewed distribution* seen in panel 3 of Figure 3.6. Finally, when there is more than one peak, we call it a multimodal distribution. Panel 4 of Figure 3.6 has two *peak* frequencies, hence it is specifically called a *bimodal distribution*.

Generally speaking, it does not make much sense to categorize the shape of a particular frequency distribution when it is based on very few measurements. If, for example, you measured the intelligence of 20 people, a frequency distribution of only 20 scores would probably be some bizarre shape with many "peaks" and "valleys." If, however, you measured the intelligence of 10,000 people, the frequency distribution would probably approximate the shape of the symmetrical distribution seen in panel 1 of Figure 3.6. Indeed, psychologists assume that many psychological traits like intelligence are symmetrically distributed around some average value in the population and that the frequency distribution has a "bell-like" shape. This special bell-shaped symmetrical frequency distribution is called a *normal distribution*. Although it goes beyond the scope of the present discussion to consider this mathematical abstraction, you might note that statisticians take a special interest in frequency distributions that approximate the shape of a normal distribution because of their special statistical properties (see Nunnally, 1970, pp. 35–39).

You will also want to know that the terminology used to describe frequency polygons can also be applied to other types of graphs. For example, in Figure 3.7, Fenz and Epstein (1967) have plotted some interesting changes in heart rate exhibited by novice and experienced parachutists as they progress through the events that lead up to the jump. The heart-rate measure is arranged along the *ordinate* and each particular event leading up to the jump is arranged along the *abscissa*. A single glance at the graph provides a substantial amount of information. The heart rate increases for both groups of jumpers as the events progress toward the jump at the final altitude. The increase is larger for novices and reaches a maximum level earlier in the jump sequence for the experienced jumpers. In both groups there is an immediate drop in heart rate upon landing, and the drop is much larger for the novices.

The basic point to be made by this discussion is that any collection of measurements can be effectively communicated by means of a table and/or graph that imposes some organization on the data. The effective presentation of data in either tabular or graphic form is largely a matter of judgment and practice. A properly drawn frequency polygon (or any other graph) should permit the reader to see instantly the general characteristics of the data. Once this "general picture" is constructed, it is possible to proceed with a more detailed discussion of the measurements portrayed in the graph.

Measures of Central Tendency

Any collection of measurements will have one value that is "most typical" or "most representative" of the group as a whole. Statisticians refer to this value as the measure of *central tendency*. Three such measures are most frequently

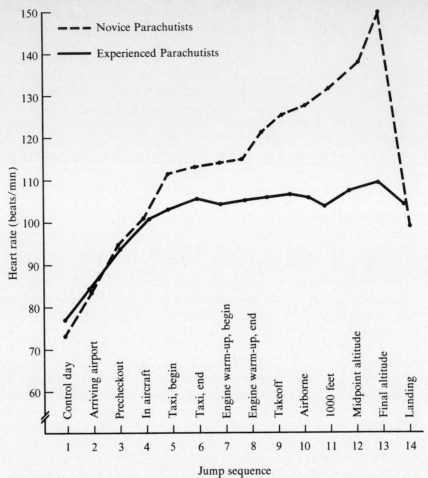

Figure 3.7 Heart rate of experienced and novice parachutists as a function of the sequence of events leading up to and following a jump. Reprinted with permission of Elsevier Science Publishing Co., Inc., from (article by) Fenz, W., and Epstein, S., Gradients of physiological arousal of experienced and novice parachutists as a function of an approaching jump, *Psychosomatic Medicine, 29,* pp. 33–51. Copyright 1967 by The American Psychosomatic Society, Inc.

employed. These are the *mean, median,* and *mode.* We will consider each of these with reference to the 20 measurements listed in Table 3.4.

The mean of a set of values is the sum of all the values divided by the total number of measurements. Equation 3.1 defines the procedure for calculating the mean of a set of numbers.

$$X = \frac{\sum_{i=1}^{n} X_i}{N} \tag{3.1}$$

As the equation indicates, the $(\overline{X})$ is obtained by adding all the values (X_i), from the first value $(i = 1)$ to the last value (n_{th}), and dividing this sum by the total number of measurements (N). If you do these calculations for the 20 values in Table 3.4, you should obtain a mean of 31 minutes.

The median of a set of measurements is the middle value in a list of values ordered for the lowest to the highest. If the list contains an even number of values, you must calculate the number that falls halfway between the *two* middle values in the ordered list. The median of the numbers listed in Table 3.4 is the number that falls halfway between the two values ranked tenth and eleventh in the list. The value ranked tenth is 28, the value ranked eleventh is 30; the median is, therefore, 29 minutes.

Finally, the last measure of central tendency we will consider is the *mode*. It is the easiest of the three to calculate and is defined simply as *the most frequently occurring value in the set of measurements*. In Table 3.4, the most frequently observed value is 21 minutes. You should note that you can have more than one mode for a set of measurements. For example, if a list of measurements has two different values that occur with the same high frequency, you would say that the distribution of scores is *bimodal* and list two modes for this distribution (see panel 4, Figure 3.6).

Measures of Variability

Two distributions can have exactly the same mean or average value, but this measure of central tendency does not tell us anything about the way in which the other values are dispersed around this central value. Hence, a measure of the amount of dispersion around the mean would provide us with some additional descriptive information. Your first thought might be to suggest that a measure of the dispersion could be obtained by simply subtracting the largest value in the distribution from the smallest value. This calculation would provide us with a descriptive statistic called the *range*. With reference to the measurements in Table 3.4, the range would be 69 (72 − 3 = 69). While the range does provide us with some additional information about the dispersion of values in our distribution, it is not the most informative measure of dispersion or variability. This point is demonstrated in Table 3.6, which contains two sets of data. These have identical means and ranges, but the manner in which the scores are dispersed around the means is very different.

Look next at Figure 3.8, which presents two different frequency polygons each based on the scores from Table 3.6. Panel 1 is a plot of the scores from set A of Table 3.6; panel 2 is a plot of the scores from set B. It is obvious that these two distributions differ in the way the scores are dispersed around their respective means, but the *range* does not describe this difference for us. The data in panel 1 are more concentrated around the central value; in 2 they are more widely spread across the entire range. We obviously need another descriptive statistic to quantify this difference in dispersion.

One way to obtain an index of dispersion or variability that makes use of *all the values* in a distribution is to calculate a descriptive statistic called the

Table 3.6　TWO HYPOTHETICAL SETS OF IQ SCORES
WITH TEN SCORES IN EACH SET

Set A[a]		Set B[a]	
Subjects	IQ score	Subjects	IQ score
A	109	A[1]	122
B	103	B[1]	121
C	111	C[1]	107
D	107	D[1]	107
E	117	E[1]	100
F	109	F[1]	96
G	122	G[1]	81
H	81	H[1]	119
I	98	I[1]	120
J	98	J[1]	82
Σ =	1055	Σ =	1055
$\overline{X}$ =	105.5	$\overline{X}$ =	105.5
Range =	41	Range =	41

[a] These two sets of scores have identical means and ranges, but the manner in which the scores are dispersed around their respective means is very different (see Figure 3.8 for an illustration of the different dispersion characteristics in each distribution).

variance. In commonsense terms, the variance is essentially an estimate of how much each score deviates from the mean of all scores in the distribution. The critical part of the calculational procedure involves subtracting each score from the mean. If the sum of these absolute differences from the mean is small, it follows that most values are clustered close to the mean score in the distribution. This commonsense description is translated into mathematical terms in equation 3.2.

$$\text{Variance} = \frac{\sum_{i=1}^{n} (X_i - X)^2}{N-1} \tag{3.2}$$

Hence, the variance is defined as the sum of squared deviations around the mean divided by the total number of scores in the distribution minus 1. Now we can apply this formula to the data first presented in Table 3.4. This procedure is illustrated in Table 3.7. In this table, each value is subtracted from the mean value and then squared. According to equation 3.2, the sum of these squared deviations is divided by $N-1$ to give you a variance of 330.74.

　　The method used to calculate the variance in Table 3.7 makes it easy to visualize the way in which the variance formula quantifies the dispersion or variability of values around the mean. You may, however, find it easier to use the computational formula illustrated in Table 3.8 as an alternative method of computing the variance for a set of scores. In Table 3.8, each value is simply squared and the sum of the squared values is plugged into equation 3.3.

Table 3.7   AN EXAMPLE OF CALCULATING THE VARIANCE OF A SET OF DATA USING EQUATION 3.2

Customer	Duration of visit to arcade (X)	X − X̄	(X − X̄)²
A	42	11	121
B	55	24	576
C	18	− 13	169
D	12	− 19	361
E	13	− 18	324
F	72	41	1681
G	6	− 25	625
H	64	33	1089
I	21	− 10	100
J	30	− 1	1
K	21	− 10	100
L	28	− 3	9
M	34	+ 3	9
N	26	− 5	25
O	32	+ 1	1
P	40	+ 9	81
Q	23	− 8	64
R	39	+ 8	64
S	41	+ 10	100
T	3	− 28	784

$N = 20$ $\Sigma X_i = 620$ $\Sigma(X - \bar{X})^2 = 6284$

$\bar{X} = 31$

$$\text{Variance} = \frac{\sum_{i=1}^{n} (X_i - X)^2}{N-1}$$

$$\text{Variance} = \frac{6284}{20-1} = 330.74$$

Now that you understand how the variance of a set of values is calculated, you should turn your attention back to the two sets of intelligence scores presented in Table 3.6. You will recall that these two sets of scores had identical means and ranges but, as the graphs in Figure 3.8 indicate, the dispersion of scores in the two distributions is very different. If the variance is a sensitive measure of differences in dispersion, we should get very different results when we calculate the variance for each set of scores in Table 3.6. In fact, the astute reader will be able to guess which set of scores will have the smallest variance before doing the calculations. To test your understanding, do these two calculations using one of the methods described earlier.

Table 3.8   A CONVENIENT COMPUTATIONAL EQUATION THAT CAN BE USED TO
CALCULATE THE VARIANCE OF A SET OF SCORES

Customer	Duration of visit (X_i)	$\overline{X}_i^2$
A	42	1764
B	55	3025
C	18	324
D	12	144
E	13	169
F	72	5184
G	6	36
H	64	4096
I	21	441
J	30	900
K	21	441
L	28	784
M	34	1156
N	26	676
O	32	1024
P	40	1600
Q	23	529
R	39	1521
S	41	1681
T	3	9

$$\Sigma X_i = 620 \qquad\qquad \Sigma \overline{X}_i^2 = 25504$$

$$\text{Variance} = \frac{N\sum_{i=1}^{n}X^2{}_i - (\sum_{i=1}^{n}X_i)^2}{N(N-1)} \qquad (3.3)$$

$$\text{Variance} = \frac{(20)(25504) - (620)^2}{20(20-1)} = 330.74$$

Finally, there is a third measure of dispersion or variability that is very often used instead of the variance. Called the *standard deviation,* it is very simply the *square root of the variance.* This close mathematical relative of the variance has a number of useful properties, particularly when you can assume that a set of scores approximates the special symmetrical distribution called the *normal distribution* mentioned earlier (p. 75). An elaboration of this point would, however, take us beyond the scope of the present discussion. It is sufficient in the present context for you to understand and be able to calculate the three basic measures of dispersion we have discussed in the preceding paragraphs: the range, the variance, and the standard deviation.

Panel 1

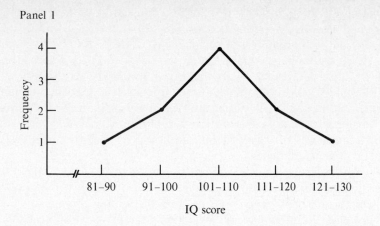

Panel 2

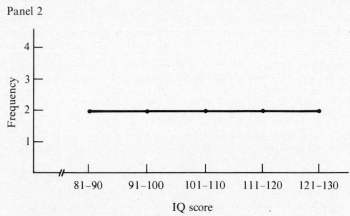

Figure 3.8 Two frequency polygons based upon the data in Table 3.6. Each polygon has the same mean and range, but you can see that the manner in which the scores are dispersed around the mean is quite different.

Descriptive Statistics and Scales of Measurement

Suppose you were given 15 bottles of wine and asked to rank order these wines in terms of their "sweetness." After tasting the 15 bottles, you arrange them in order from left to right on a shelf. The first bottle on the left is the "sweetest," and so on down the line. Assuming you can still function at this point, we now ask you to calculate the mean or "average sweetness" of these wines. The problem is obvious. With an ordinal scale of sweetness, we cannot be sure that the difference in sweetness between successive bottles of wine is equal. You can see that under these conditions it makes no sense to think about an average or mean sweetness.

The moral of this story is that one must always consider the scale of measurement before computing descriptive statistics. The mean is not an appropriate statistic with nominal or ordinal measurements for the reasons described above. It is, however, permissible to use the *median* as a measure of central tendency with ordinal data. The median is simply that value (bottle of wine) that falls in the middle of a rank-ordered set of measurements. The median makes no particular assumption about equal intervals between ranks. The general rule of thumb in these matters is that you cannot meaningfully talk about a mean (or any of the measures of dispersion based upon the mean) unless the data are at least interval measurements.

This general rule seems easy enough as stated. However, you can encounter some gray areas. Suppose, for example, that you were given 15 bottles of wine and asked to rate each on a scale of 1 to 10, with 10 being very sweet and 1 being very dry. You now have a "sweetness rating" written on each bottle. Do we still have an ordinal scale, or has this rating procedure produced an interval scale of measurement? Is the *difference* in sweetness between two bottles of wine rated 8 and 9 the same as the *difference* in sweetness between two bottles rated 6 and 7? Probably not, but it is not unusual to find examples in which data based on such rating procedures are treated as if they had interval properties. If you decide that an interval scale of measurement has been achieved with the rating procedure, it is, of course, permissible to calculate a *mean* sweetness rating. If not, you should use a median or mode as a measure of central tendency.

Descriptive Statistics and Errors of Omission

In the first part of our discussion of descriptive statistics. we stated that the average income in Laos is $95 per year. You probably accepted that statement as an accurate indication of the money earned by a "typical" citizen of Laos. Now that you have read the preceding discussion, your reaction to this statement should be more critical. If there is one lesson to be learned, it is that *no single descriptive statistic can provide a complete and accurate picture of the data*. As a consumer of statistical information on a daily basis, you should never again be content with descriptions based on a single descriptive statistic. If your boss tells you that the average salary in your office is $22,000 per year, if you read that Wade Boggs has a lifetime batting average of .353, if a magazine claims that North American males have sexual relations on the average of three times per week, or if I tell you that the average income in Laos is $95 per year, you should treat each of these statements with suspicion. The statistic might be accurate, but it does not tell the whole story.

To illustrate the more general point, suppose your income is $24,000 per year and your boss tells you that the average income in your office is $22,000 per year. Should you feel pleased, or should you ask the boss a few more questions? It might be interesting to know the median salary in your office; if the mean and median differ substantially, you can infer a skewed distribution around the mean. It would also be informative to know the variance around the mean salary. If the variance is small, you will be more pleased to make $24,000 per year than if the variance is large. In short, it pays to be persistent when one is consuming statistical information. If this brief discussion does not convince you, try reading a marvelous little book called *How to Lie with Statistics* (Huff, 1973).

CHAPTER EXERCISES

3.1. Listed below are ten different ways in which you might be measured at some point in your life. Can you indicate which scale of measurement best describes each of these measurement procedures?

1. The number of nonsense syllables that you recall on a long-term-memory test.
2. The score you made on an intelligence test when you were in seventh grade.
3. The third-place ribbon a judge awarded your recipe in a cooking contest.
4. Your seating assignment in a nonsmoking section during a commercial airline flight.
5. Your surname.
6. A loudness threshold in decibels that your audiologist measured using the method of limits.
7. The color of your hair.
8. Your height at age 13.
9. Your attitudes toward childbirth as measured with a Likert scale.
10. The amount of time it takes for you to solve the anagram CHMIFEIS.

3.2. In the preceding chapter, we considered various special procedures used to measure mental processes. Experience suggests that few of you will ever have the opportunity or need to use a signal-detection procedure, although you may have it *applied* to you! It is, however, somewhat more likely that you will want or need to measure people's attitudes. Psychologists, business managers, sociologists, environmentalists, and even mothers-in-law occasionally become involved in attitude surveys on various topics. As indicated earlier, generating "good" questions for an attitude scale is perhaps the most difficult part of the task.

In order to sharpen your skills in this area, consider eight statements taken from a Likert scale developed by two nurses (Cronenwett & Newark, 1974). This scale was used to measure the attitudes toward their wives and newborn infants of fathers who had been present in the delivery room. The fathers were asked to respond to each statement using categories of the Likert scale ranging from "strongly agree" to "strongly disagree."

Look at each of these statements and (1) determine if it is a positively worded statement or negatively worded statement, (2) give it a score from 0 to 6 based upon the extent to which it meets the criteria in Table 3.1 (p. 54), and, finally, (3) make up six statements of your own, with three positively worded statements and three negatively worded statements, relevant to this topic.

1. My wife was beautiful in childbirth.
2. My wife would have had a lot harder time in labor without me.
3. Childbearing is women's work.
4. I really felt close to my wife during labor.
5. I often felt that I was in the way.

6. I helped my wife to feel comfortable during contractions.

7. I was the person who helped my wife most during labor.

8. I didn't know what to do to help my wife.

On a scale of 1 to 10, what is your general opinion of this scale developed by Cronenwett and Newark?

3.3. Suppose that you used the Beck Depression Inventory to measure the level of depression exhibited by a sample of 30 university students. This would give you a list of 30 scores. As you sat there looking at these 30 numbers, various questions would probably come to your mind: What is the most typical depression score in this list? Are most of the scores very similar or do they vary over a wide range? Essentially, you are asking for a description of this list of scores in terms of various summarizing characteristics. To test your understanding of the descriptive statistics discussed in the third section of this chapter, make up a list of 30 scores ranging from 0 to 60. Assume that these are the scores you obtained from 30 students, plot these data in a frequency distribution, and calculate all the descriptive statistics that you think are necessary to give an interested reader a complete description of your data.

CHAPTER 4

ASKING QUESTIONS ABOUT BEHAVIOR

The noisy bruxist first described in Chapter 2 has served us very well thus far. His problem has helped us to discuss the operational-definition rule, the distortion rule, sampling procedures, and scales of measurement. And here he comes again, this time to test your creative ability in asking questions and proposing hypotheses.

When bruxism was first described, what questions came to your mind? Was the guy hungry? Was he anxious? Did he have an overbite? Perhaps the most bizarre suggestion I ever heard was made by a young woman whose uncle was a bruxist. Apparently her uncle's main claim to fame was that he could stick his tongue out, curl the protruding tip upward, and touch the end of his nose. She theorized that his oversized tongue could also be the cause of his problem. Now put your tongue back in your mouth and see if you can top that hypothesis!

The important point is that people naturally tend to ask questions about interesting phenomena. For the scientist, that is a critical stage of scientific inquiry. Most of the questions that arise in the scientist's mind will identify some factor suspected to be a cause of the phenomenon.

A question about the bruxist's hunger identifies *hunger* as a factor that is suspected as a possible cause. The same can be said about questions identifying anxiety and an overbite as possible causal factors. If you simply turn each of these questions into declarative statements, you have stated a *hypothesis* about this phenomenon. In the case of the question about the overbite, the declarative form would simply be: *An overbite is a factor that can cause bruxism.* We could similarly note a *hunger hypothesis,* an *anxiety hypothesis,* or even a *large-tongue hypothesis.* As these examples illustrate, a *hypothesis is a tentative explanation for a phenomenon.*

We may call this activity *asking questions,* though scientists are more likely to describe the same process as *hypothesis formation.* This chapter will consider the process of asking questions—or forming hypotheses—in more detail. It is divided into two basic sections. First we shall consider some of the characteristics of scientific hypotheses. They must, if they are to be valid, conform to special rules. Once you understand these rules, we can turn to the somewhat more interesting task of examining hypothesis formation as a creative process.

Asking important questions is probably one of the most difficult parts of a scientist's work and perhaps the least understood aspect of scientific inquiry. History suggests that some scientists have a natural ability to ask exciting, important, interesting questions, and these generally become the leaders in their fields. Although we do not understand the nature of their special talents, we shall consider some possibilities in the second part of this chapter.

CHARACTERISTICS OF HYPOTHESES

As defined earlier, a hypothesis is a tentative explanation for a phenomenon; it identifies one or more factors suspected to cause the phenomenon. Hypotheses differ in several very important ways. Below, we shall consider three basic ways in which hypotheses may be classified—that is, according to whether they are (1) formal or informal; (2) testable or untestable; and (3) hypotheses or theories.

Formal vs. Informal Hypotheses

The hypotheses you propose will vary in the degree to which you formally state a particular relationship between bruxism and some causal factor. At one extreme you might simply have a hunch that people tend to grind their teeth when they are anxious. Or, as suggested earlier, you might have a hunch that people with a severe overbite or malocclusion tend to grind their teeth. The somewhat vague statement that there might be a relationship between these factors and bruxism can be thought of as an *informal* hypothesis because it does not specify the exact nature of the causal connection.

Alternatively, you might want to make a more definite formal statement. For example: "An overbite is a necessary and sufficient condition for the development of bruxism." This hypothesis suggests that an overbite is a *necessary condition* in the causal relationship. It implies that bruxism will never be observed unless an overbite is present. This hypothesis also suggests that the overbite is a *sufficient condition,* meaning that bruxism will always develop when the condition called an overbite is present.

The two examples described above fall at opposite ends of a continuum. At one extreme, there are hypotheses that state formal causal relationships; at the other, there are those best described as loosely stated hunches. A formal hypothesis can be defined as *a tentative specification of the necessary and/or sufficient conditions for the occurrence of a particular phenomenon.* An informal hypothesis can be defined as *a tentative specification of the condition or set of conditions suspected to have some influence on a phenomenon.*

Formal hypotheses can often be stated in quantitative or mathematical terms. One can suggest that an overbite is a necessary and sufficient condition for bruxism and also specify an exact mathematical relationship between the amount of overbite and the intensity of the grinding behavior. Other versions of formal hypotheses might state that the overbite is necessary but not sufficient as a cause of bruxism—or that it is sufficient but not necessary. The former implies that the overbite must be present for bruxism to occur, but the presence of the overbite does not guarantee that the condition will develop. As you can see, the exact nature of the causal relationship specified by a formal hypothesis can vary considerably, but in each case the type of causal relationship is precisely specified.

In practice, it is accurate to say that formal hypotheses are relatively rare in the context of behavioral research. It is very unusual to find examples in which a behavioral scientist is willing to state a hypothesis in terms of the necessary and sufficient conditions required to produce an effect. Instead, we are content to suggest that a particular factor will probably have some influence on the phenomenon under observation. This is very different from a statement specifying that some factor is necessary, sufficient, or both.

There are probably several reasons for the popularity of a more informal approach to hypotheses. First, most scientists realize that we have never really agreed about the meaning of the term "causation." The view adopted in the preceding discussion is just one of many possible interpretations of causation in science. It comes close to what is called an *essentialist* view of causality. This view assumes, among other things, that one can eventually discover some minimal necessary and sufficient (i.e., essential) cause for any phenomenon. But this may not be a realistic assumption upon which to base a definition of causality. Can you imagine, for example, ever finding a single necessary and sufficient causal factor for phenomena as complex as cancer or mental illness? A lengthy discussion of the various views of causality in science goes beyond the scope of this book. The important point, however, is that there is much disagreement over the exact meaning of the term; therefore, scientists avoid the issue by adopting less formal hypotheses. For the reader interested in pursuing these arguments in more detail, Cook and Campbell (1979) have published one of the most succinct and readable overviews.

There is a second reason for the paucity of formal hypotheses in the behavioral sciences: since most of the phenomena they study are incredibly complex, we realize that they are probably influenced by a wide variety of conditions. Take human depression as just one example. This form of mental illness is probably influenced by a large number of very different conditions, ranging from exposure to stressful environmental conditions to changes in brain chemistry due to dietary habits. To propose, therefore, that there is some single necessary and sufficient condition for the development of depression seems naive. One feels much more comfortable with informal statements such as: "I suspect that prolonged exposure to stressful conditions might have some influence on the development and maintenance of human depression.''

Finally, a third reason for favoring informal statements is our recognition that the methods used to test many hypotheses in the behavioral sciences are often of questionable validity. Even if one were willing to make a formal statement to the effect that X was a necessary and sufficient condition for the observation of effect Y, we often lack strategies required to test the causal relationship adequately. Indeed, much of the discussion in the following chapters attempts to explain why these strategies are fallible. The basic point is, once again, that one feels more comfortable with informal hypotheses in situations where methods are not available to test formal statements adequately.

Testable vs. Untestable Hypotheses

Almost every question you ask about a phenomenon can be converted into a hypothesis. However, you should realize that not all hypotheses are immediately and easily testable. Consider, for example, the hypothesis that an overbite causes bruxism. This hypothesis is testable. We can arrange conditions in which we compare people with overbites to people with normal occlusions. If we observe bruxism in the people with overbites and fail to see the condition in people who do not have overbites, we have tested and tentatively confirmed our hypothesis. (You will discover in later chapters that this is not the best strategy for testing this particular hypothesis, but it serves our present purpose.)

Consider next the hypothesis that *anxiety* leads to bruxism. This is not immediately testable because the suspected causal factor (anxiety) is not operationally defined. Until the term *is* operationally defined, we cannot arrange conditions in which anxious people are compared to nonanxious people to determine if the anxious people develop bruxism. If we want to convert this hypothesis to a testable statement, we must find some operation that discriminates between anxious and nonanxious people. One possibility would be to measure corticosteroid levels and define anxious people as those with high levels of this stress-related substance. Given this operational definition, we can now restate the hypothesis in a testable, operationally valid form: *People with high corticosteroid levels will develop bruxism.* It should be obvious that we can now sort people into the conditions necessary to confirm or reject the statement.

The essential point is that the causal factors identified by a hypothesis must be *operationally valid*. If they are not, the hypothesis is not testable. This rule holds for any hypothesis. The rule is, however, particularly important when behavioral scientists speculate about the causal influence of *mental states* such as anxiety, frustration, depression, fear, anger, and so on.

A second problem often arises when you attempt to make a particular hypothesis operationally valid. It is very easy to find yourself trapped in a circular causal statement that is untestable by definition. Once again, the hypothesis that anxiety causes bruxism provides a good example.

As indicated earlier, many students find this idea very appealing. If they are asked what they mean by the term "anxiety" (i.e., how they would define it operationally), many will suggest that anxiety can be defined in terms of the intensity of the grinding behavior. The more intense the grinding, the more anxious the individual is assumed to be. Although this makes the term "anxiety" operationally valid, the original hypothesis is now circular. Taken to its logical conclusion, the hypothesis that *people grind their teeth because they are anxious* can now be stated in its operationally valid (but logically circular) form as *people grind their teeth because people grind their teeth*.

It is clearly necessary to avoid circularity when you define terms in your hypothesis operationally. Although the preceding example makes this point in a very direct manner, it is surprising how frequently people fall into this circular trap. In order to test your own skills in this area, consider the following example. We hypothesize that our friends LOP and JET (from Chapter 2) spend a great deal of time playing video games because they are *addicted*. Turn this hypothesis into an operationally valid hypothesis that is not circular yet is testable.

A simple *testability rule* seems like an appropriate way to summarize the two basic points made in this section. When you are forming a hypothesis (formal or informal), you should keep the following rule in mind: *All hypotheses must be operationally valid and must avoid circularity.* If hypotheses meet these criteria, you will find that it is possible to devise procedures that will permit you to confirm or reject them (i.e., they will be testable).

Hypotheses vs. Theories

I have a friend who is approaching retirement age. He is a bright, interesting fellow in good health who worries that he will be bored with retirement. Consequently, he thinks he might buy a business franchise of some sort that he could operate during those later years. He would like the franchise to be both interesting and profitable. At the present time, he has contacted three different franchise operations and is analyzing the characteristics of each.

First, there is a travel agency. It is a turnkey operation (i.e., a business in which you invest a flat sum of money and the company provides you with all the necessary equipment, connections, employee training, and so on). The total investment for the first year of the operation is $75,000. If the agency survives and does an average amount of business, the projected profit per year after five years of operation is about $60,000. Past performance records on this franchise indicate that about five out of ten survive and earn this level of profit.

The second option is a popular fast-food restaurant. Again, it is a turnkey operation, but in this case they want a $250,000 investment for the first year of operation. The projected net profit for this franchise after five years is $100,000 a year; the survival record is excellent—about 80 percent at the projected profit level.

The third option is a small local candy manufacturing operation. The current owner is willing to train the new operator, and the one present employee would plan to stay with the company. The owner wants $22,000 for the business, and it has a projected profit of about $20,000 a year based upon figures available from past years. There is, however, considerable danger of failure, since my friend does not know much about the wholesale candy business.

This situation is interesting partly because it is an excellent example of one in which a person is confronted with a risky decision. If we include the possibility of not buying anything, four options are available. In considering these businesses, my friend thought of several important questions. Should the different survival rates of these three options be an important factor in his decision? Is the amount of money to be made the most important factor, or is the extent to which he finds the business interesting more important? Are there factors other than the risk, the money, and his interest that might influence the decision?

As indicated throughout this chapter, every question you generate about such a phenomenon (in this case risky decision making) can be turned into a hypothesis by converting it into an operationally valid declarative statement. For example, I might state the hypothesis, "My friend will choose the franchise that has the highest probability of success." This identifies *probability of success* as a causal factor in his risky decision behavior. I also realize, however, that stating a single hypothesis in this situation leaves something to be desired. I am sure that this one risky decision will be influenced by a number of different factors operating simultaneously. My friend has a conservative personality, there is a large amount of money at risk, and so on.

This example shows why scientists are often not content to ask single questions that identify single causal factors about behavioral phenomena. More frequently, they form a variety of hypotheses that identify and predict the effects of a number of factors. Although there is a great deal of rhetoric about the nature of *scientific theory* (cf. Marx, 1963), the preceding example illustrates the simplest and most accurate definition. Specifically, *a scientific theory can be defined as a collection of hypotheses about a phenomenon organized into a logically consistent conceptual framework.* As such, a *theory* falls on a continuum that has a single hypothesis at one end and a larger collection of related hypotheses at the other end. The theory is more elaborate in that it specifies a number of different causal factors and the nature of any relationships suspected to exist among these causal factors.

Given the preceding definition of a scientific theory, it should not surprise you to learn that theories can differ in much the same way that single hypotheses differ. Some theories are very precise and formal in their specification of causal relationships, while others are less formal both in specifying the nature of causal relationships and in specifying relationships that exist among the various causal elements in the theory.

Let us consider a relatively informal theory that could emerge from our analysis of the risky decision behavior described earlier. These essential elements (causal factors) are outlined in Table 4.1. First, two personality characteristics are specified as important: (1) general anxiety level and (2) ego strength. Both factors can be defined operationally as scores on an appropriate personality test to measure these traits (see Chapter 3, pp. 59–62). Second, a number of situational factors are specified as important. These are operationally defined as (1)

Table 4.1   A RUDIMENTARY, INFORMAL THEORY OF RISKY DECISION-MAKING BEHAVIOR (SEE TEXT FOR DEFINITIONS OF TERMS)

Personality factors
1. Anxiety state
2. Ego strength

Situational factors
1. Amount of money to be gained
2. Amount of money to be lost
3. Chance of success
4. Chance of failure

First-order predictions
1. As anxiety state increases, attractiveness of low risk options increases if all other factors remain constant.
2. As ego strength increases, attractiveness of high risk options increases if all other factors remain constant.
3. As amount of money to be gained increases, attractiveness of options increases if all other factors remain constant.
4. And so on.

Second-order predictions
1. High level of anxiety will increase the emphasis placed on chances of success and failure and decrease the emphasis placed on money gained or lost.
2. High level of ego strength will increase the emphasis placed on money gained or lost and decrease the emphasis placed on risk of success or failure.
3. And so on.

the probability of success, (2) the probability of failure, (3) the amount of money to be made, and (4) the amount of money to be lost. Note also that Table 4.1 specifies both first- and second-order predictions. The first-order predictions state the manner in which any single factor influences the attractiveness of any given option. For example, as the chances of success increase—all other factors remaining constant—an option is predicted to increase in attractiveness. The second-order predictions are hypotheses that attempt to predict the manner in which the various single causal factors *combine* to influence risky decision making. One second-order prediction suggests that more weight should be given to the effects of the money to be gained or lost when the individual is high on the ego-strength measure. This is one example of what is meant by specifying the nature of the relationships among the various causal variables in the theory. Later, in Chapter 6, we shall consider some strategies for answering questions about the combined effects of two or more causal factors. These methods are called *factorial experiments;* you might make a mental note to come back to the present example to test your understanding of them in this context.

     The theory outlined in Table 4.1 is not intended as a serious effort to theorize about risk taking as a behavioral phenomenon. Instead, it should be viewed as a simple effort to illustrate how one might begin to construct a scientific theory and to demonstrate that this process is really very similar to the task of forming a hypothesis. If, in fact, you find questions about making risky decisions of some interest, you might read Atkinson's (1957, 1964) classic discussion of risk taking. His material is an interesting and appropriate introduction to the topic and Atkinson's approach to theory construction is a model from which many can learn.

The rudimentary theory outlined in Table 4.1 also helps to illustrate several other basic points about scientific theory. First, theories, like hypotheses, vary in the degree to which they are testable. To the extent that the various terms used in Table 4.1 can be operationally defined, the theory is testable. If we had used concepts that could not be operationally defined, the theory and the various predictions it makes could not be tested. Second, scientific theories vary in terms of their *generality*. "Generality" refers to the number and variety of phenomena a theory seeks to explain. Some theories have a considerable amount of generality and attempt to discuss the causal factors associated with a wide variety of behavioral phenomena. Other theories tend to focus on a very narrow range of situations. For example, Atkinson's (1964) theory of risk taking is narrowly focused. He attempts to predict risky decisions and specifies, in addition, that he deals only with those decisions where skill is involved in the outcome. In other words, his theory should not be applied where the outcome is determined by chance factors (e.g., certain gambling situations). Hence, one might consider Atkinson's theory of risk-taking behavior to be of limited generality. We have argued elsewhere (Dunham, 1977) that behavioral scientists have tended, over the past fifty years, to develop theories that make relatively precise and formal predictions but do so in a very limited or narrow domain. The theory outlined in Table 4.1 might be considered an example of this type of "miniature theory," since it deals only with risk-taking phenomena and a limited number of causal variables.

Finally, you might ask yourself why anyone would go to the trouble of constructing an elaborate theory about risk taking. Although some scientists (e.g., Sidman, 1960) have argued that theorizing is a superfluous activity, others (e.g., Marx, 1963) have argued effectively that theories serve at least two important functions in science. Marx calls these (1) the tool function and (2) the goal function.

The *tool function* is the capacity of a theory to suggest causal relationships that might not otherwise receive consideration. For example, the rudimentary thoughts about the nature of the risk-taking process expressed in Table 4.1 should serve as a *tool* to stimulate your thinking about this phenomenon. If you examine, for example, the list of situational factors in Table 4.1, it should prompt thoughts of other factors that might be involved in this process of decision making. You may notice that we have ignored the potential importance of the *social status* associated with each business option. (Some businesses are perceived as more attractive than others in terms of their social status—e.g., an art gallery as compared to a fast-food outlet.) The point is that a theory often opens up new ways of thinking about a phenomenon that might not otherwise develop.

The *goal function* of a scientific theory is a bit more difficult to explain. One favorite example for illustrating this is crude but perhaps effective. Go back in history and imagine yourself as a scientist observing two curious phenomena: a piece of metal that is deteriorating by a process we now call "rusting" and a piece of wood that is deteriorating by a process we now call "burning." Your initial efforts to construct a theory would probably consist of a "miniature theory of rusting" and a "miniature theory of burning." Each of these miniature theories would list a number of suspected causal factors and any suspected interactions between these causal factors, much as we did in Table 4.1. As you might imagine, if scientists had a separate "miniature theory" for every observable phenomenon in nature, the catalogue of scientific theories would be incredibly large—in fact, as large as the number of observable phenomena. Therefore, one of the goals of the scientist who believes in developing theories is to subsume as many different phenonena under one theory as possible. This is essentially the goal function of theory as Marx (1963) has discussed it. For example, once you recognized that the same basic causal factors were operating to make metal rust and wood burn, you might formulate a single, more general theory that subsumed both of these observable phenomena under a single theoretical process called *oxidation*. The example is crude, but the essential point to be made is that theory serves to organize many different observable phenomena within a single framework. Hence, theory serves as both a tool and a goal for the scientist.

ASKING QUESTIONS AS A CREATIVE PROCESS

Neurotransmitters and Split Brains

One night in 1921, the scientist Otto Loewi had a dream in which he asked an interesting question. He wondered if the vagus nerve (which, among other things, stimulates the heart muscle) might secrete a chemical substance that inhibits muscular contractions of the heart. In 1921 this question (or hypothesis) would have seemed absurd to experts in the field of neurophysiology. The prevailing belief for the preceding fifty years had been that any connection between a nerve fiber and muscle tissue was "electrical" in nature. It was impossible to think that a chemical was involved. The effect of a nerve impulse on a muscle was assumed to be far too rapid for a chemical process to be operating. Loewi, however, proceeded against all odds to arrange a simple but elegant experiment to determine if a chemical substance was released at the junction of the nerve and muscle. The results of his experiment clearly demonstrated that a chemical inhibitor was released by the vagus nerve, just as his dream had predicted. Loewi's question and the experiment that it generated are now recognized as the beginning of an incredibly important and productive period of modern research concerned with the role of chemical transmitters in the nervous system (Kuffler & Nicholls, 1976, p. 147). These transmitter substances are suspected to control such complex processes as sleep, depression, and certain types of mental illness.

Consider also Ronald Myers, who, over thirty years ago, began his doctoral research at the University of Chicago. At that time it was common knowledge that a cat could be trained to discriminate between two visual stimuli (e.g., a square and a circle) simply by associating food with one visual stimulus and no food with the other. Furthermore, it was not surprising to anyone that the cat could learn the same discrimination if you put a patch over its left eye. If, afterwards, you moved the patch to the right eye and tested the same cat, it still managed to make the correct discrimination and find the food. Myers also knew that the cat's brain, like all mammallian brains, is divided into two symmetrical halves or hemispheres. Each hemisphere is an anatomical mirror image of the other, and the two halves are connected by a large bundle of nerve fibers called the *corpus callosum*.

In 1951, Myers and his adviser Roger Sperry asked a simple but interesting question. Specifically, they wondered if they could teach the discrimination described above to *only half* of the cat's brain. They did a number of clever experiments demonstrating that the answer to their question was yes. They found that a discrimination could be taught to half of the cat's brain while the other half learned nothing. A cat that could perform perfectly well with stimuli received by the left half of the brain was unable to perform the task when the same stimuli were delivered to the right half of the brain. Apparently the two halves of a mammalian brain can function independently in a learning task.

The question asked by Myers and Sperry and the experiments that followed are now generally recognized as the beginning of a very exciting and productive period of contemporary research. These experiments make use of the split-brain procedure and other related techniques to identify various specialized functions in each brain hemisphere. There has been a literal explosion of research in this area over the past thirty years. It is now generally recognized, for example, that the left half of the human brain is involved in the control of speech and most language skills, whereas the right hemisphere is primarily involved with spatial tasks such as finding your way around a building or reading a map. If you are interested in further information, Springer and Deutsch (1981) have published a very readable overview of this extensive literature.

The important point of this example is that the questions asked by Myers and Sperry were to some extent inconsistent with prevailing ideas about the organization and function of the brain. From the early 1900s, the most popular view of brain function was that one hemisphere (usually the left) was *dominant* over the other. The subordinate hemisphere (usually the right) was assumed not to have any particular specialized functions of its own. You can see that the question asked by Myers and Sperry challenged this notion of *cerebral dominance*. Their question implied that each half of the brain might be able to function independently, and their research eventually discovered that each has apparently evolved its own specialized functions.

Although some might argue with the historical details, the message to be appreciated in these two stories is the same. Specifically, some scientists manage to ask questions that have tremendous impact on the scientific community while the questions of others seem to attract very little attention. History tells us that Loewi, Myers, and Sperry posed some real "blockbusters." Once their questions had been asked and a few answers were forthcoming, research interest in them exploded.

As you might suspect, questions of the sort that came to Loewi in a dream are very rare in any scientific discipline. Thousands of scientists toil at their jobs every day of the week. Each of them is asking questions and trying to arrange experiments to answer them. You might consider many of these questions interesting and clever, but the historical record seems to indicate that very few produce a major change in the thoughts and activities of other scientists. Indeed, many efforts are published in obscure journals and go virtually unnoticed.

The fact that most questions are unlikely to have a major impact upon the scientific community does not mean that they are useless. I recently read, for example, an experiment concerned with a question that most students find very interesting. We know that people are reasonably good at identifying the emotional expressions that appear on another person's face (e.g., anger, fear, happiness). This is obviously an adaptive social communication skill. Is this skill a specialized function of either the left or right hemisphere of the brain? The scientists who wondered about this hypothesized that the right hemisphere of the brain would play a major role in processing this type of information. They developed a clever procedure to answer the question, and the hypothesis was confirmed. In this context, however, the discovery that the right hemisphere plays a major role in discriminating different facial expressions is not the important point. It is that this particular question and experiment will, in all probability, not have the massive impact on the scientific community that Loewi's question or the one asked by Myers and Sperry did. Instead, a substantial number of scientists who are interested in this area of research will read the article and file it away as one more interesting validation of the basic idea that the two halves of the brain have evolved different specialized functions. It simply provides additional confirmation of an existing or prevailing view of nature, and this confirmation is important but not revolutionary in its impact. Most questions asked by scientists fall into a category that might be thought of as confirming and extending the prevailing views about nature, and these extensions permit us to predict and understand an increasing number and variety of phenomena.

Paradigm Shifts

The preceding thoughts are to a large extent congruent with the view expressed by T. S. Kuhn (1962) in his influential book concerning progress in science and the development of scientific revolutions. Kuhn argues that most sciences at any given time exist in a state that he calls a *paradigm*. Loosely defined, a paradigm consists of a set of assumptions about nature that fit the existing data reasonably well yet also manage to generate a large number of unanswered questions which will keep the scientific community busy. One might say that neuroscientists interested in brain function now subscribe to a paradigm which assumes that chemical transmitters play a major role in brain function; many in this scientific community are asking questions that extend and confirm this view in various ways.

Kuhn also argues that science progresses primarily in terms of spurts or "revolutions," each of which essentially consists of a major shift in paradigms.

When a paradigm changes, traditional assumptions and traditional methods are challenged by a new and interesting alternative. This challenge disrupts the existing paradigm and generates a new one in its place. Kuhn documents these arguments with an impressive array of examples from the history of science.

If Kuhn's analysis is correct, you can see that the activity I call *asking questions* is of fundamental importance to the development of the paradigm shifts or scientific revolutions that he has described. A question of the sort asked by Loewi can potentially be a more important determinant of scientific progress than any single experiment or observation reported in a century of later work. If you accept this view of science and the way in which it progresses (for alternative arguments you might like to consult Manicas & Secord, 1983, or Gholson & Barker, 1985) you will want to think about the creative process that produces these revolutionary questions. It would appear that very few individuals have what it takes to generate such questions; almost by definition, we do not really understand how the process works. It is, however, interesting to speculate.

Hypothesis Myopia

Kuhn's basic thoughts about how paradigm shifts originate in the mind of the scientist are encapsulated in the following paragraph:

> Any new interpretation of nature, whether a discovery or a theory, emerges first in the mind of one or a few individuals. It is they who first learn to see science and the world differently, and their ability to make the transition is facilitated by two circumstances that are not common to most other members of their profession. Invariably, their attention has been intensely concentrated upon the crisis-provoking problems; usually in addition, they are men so young or so new to the crisis-ridden field that practice has committed them less deeply than most of their contemporaries to the world view and rules determined by the old paradigm. How are they able, what must they do, to convert the entire profession or the relevant professional subgroup to their way of seeing science and the world? (p. 143)

There are a number of interesting thoughts about the creative process in the preceding paragraph. First, Kuhn recognizes that relatively few individuals ask the really important questions in any science, and he then notes that two factors tend to characterize them. First, they apparently have the ability to find and focus their attention on phenomena that do not fit the prevailing views or ideas about nature (i.e., the "crisis-provoking problems"). In any science, there is a gradual accumulation of observations one might call "puzzling" in the sense that they do not quite fit the prevailing assumptions. Sperry (1964) states, for example, that he was disturbed by reports of medical cases in which surgeons had severed the corpus callosum and noticed that these patients seemed to behave normally in all respects afterward. These observations were "puzzling" since they implied that the corpus collosum served no function. As Sperry says, "Exactly what purpose the corpus callosum served became more and more of a mystery" (p. 42).

If Kuhn's analysis is correct, individuals who ask revolutionary questions are working in fields where the number of puzzling observations is reaching a crisis point for the science. They have both the ability to recognize the crisis and the creative talent necessary to ask questions that, once answered, will resolve the crisis (i.e., offer an alternative view that subsumes both the existing knowledge and the "puzzling cases").

You might also note that Kuhn's analysis of the creative process permits the somewhat less creative scientific minds to play a significant role. Specifically, it is those scientists who manage to uncover "puzzling" cases that will eventually create a crisis for the existing view. Their work slowly sets the stage for the next major crisis and consequent revolution in thinking.

This leads us to Kuhn's second major point in the preceding quotation: individuals asking the revolutionary questions are usually "young" or "new to the crisis-ridden field." I have a colleague who is so convinced of this that he plans to stop doing research at the age of 45 and spend his remaining years teaching and doing administrative work. Of course, it is possible that age and experience do not always prevent the scientist from asking revolutionary questions. Indeed, the historical record reveals examples of important contributions made by both young and old scientists. The basic problem is that the longer and more often you have thought about the world from a certain point of view, the harder it becomes to escape these assumptions and see the world in a different perspective. The astute reader will realize that this point is directly related to the topic discussed in Chapter 2. In that chapter, we discussed the distortion rule and several examples in which personal beliefs and assumptions managed to distort the subject's observations of the world. Such distortions are not the exclusive domain of the aged. Young scientists can also be blinded by their assumptions and beliefs. It does not matter so much how old you are, but it *does* matter how firmly you are committed to your assumptions.

Bachrach (1981) has an interesting term to describe the problem of being misled or "blinded" by our assumptions; he calls it *hypothesis myopia*. His argument, like Kuhn's, is that once you have implicitly accepted some assumption about the events you observe in nature, you may find it impossible to ask a question that does not reflect this assumption. It is perhaps instructive to conclude our discussion of this important point with a few contemporary examples of hypothesis myopia. One of my favorite examples of this problem comes from an interesting book titled *Beautiful Swimmers* (Warner, 1976). This example calls for a brief digression if it is to be appreciated fully.

In recent years, biologists have discovered that many aquatic organisms make use of chemical communication systems. The most extensively studied animals in this respect are some of the marine crustaceans—in particular, crabs, lobsters, and shrimp. One of the most frequently asked questions is whether or not these animals release a chemical signal (i.e., a sex pheromone) that serves to attract a mate. In most species, mating is restricted to a brief period immediately after the female molts, when her new shell is still soft. The biologists who are most familiar with the life history, anatomy, and physiology of these animals have for the past fifty years always started from the assumption that it is the female who releases the sex pheromone and attracts the male. Over the years, the results of research on this question have been inconsistent (cf. Dunham, 1978).

Given this information, consider now the "Chesapeake Bay watermen" who earn a living fishing for crabs by baiting large traps placed on the bottom of the bay. The watermen like to catch crabs during the period immediately after they molt, when the shell is still soft. These soft-shelled crabs command a high price from East Coast restaurants. If you ask a waterman how to catch a soft-shelled female crab, he will tell you to bait the trap with large *males* called "Jimmies." They have observed that these males will attract the female crabs, called "peelers," which are just ready to molt.

It would appear that, over the past fifty years, biologists could have learned something from the watermen, who would never have baited their traps with attractive Jimmies if they had been blinded by the same assumptions that influenced biologists. The different assumptions held by biologists and watermen restricted the thinking of each to a very different set of hypotheses about the crab's behavior. The biologists' hypothesis myopia may explain some of the inconsistent results that have been obtained from research on this problem.

The watermen have one additional insight into the crab's sex life that might be of some value in generating new and interesting questions. According to them, the males make good bait for females only during the early spring months. Although this might seem a puzzling observation to a biologist, the watermen understand it fully. According to one old-timer, "Old crabs is just more horny in the spring. It's a long wait they had" (Warner, 1976, p. 140).

For a second example of hypothesis myopia, you should go back and read the quotation from Kuhn's discussion of the topic (p. 96). It is ironic that the quotation itself offers us a prime example of the manner in which our implicit assumptions influence our predictions about nature. Specifically, Kuhn's selection of nouns implies that the only scientists who might ask revolutionary questions are *males* (e.g., "They are men so young or so new to the crisis. . ."). His predictions about the origins of scientific revolutions are biased by sexist assumptions concerning the nature of scientific progress. Indeed, it might be argued in general that our social conditioning as males or females can to some extent influence the questions we will ask about nature.

Contemporary anthropologists have provided some of the most pertinent information on this issue. Leavitt, Sykes, and Weatherford (1975) compared the observations of male and female anthropologists studying primitive cultures and found overwhelming evidence for *androcentrism,* the tendency for male observers to ask questions that reflect the assumption of male superiority in the culture and to portray cultural institutions as male-dominated. One student, after reading the evidence gathered by Leavitt and co-workers, may have put the problem in its proper perspective. She argues succinctly that "the mere presentation of the different perspectives of women anthropologists regarding these cultures does not, however, serve to refute the male evidence. Perhaps women anthropologists are guilty of the mirror image of androcentrism."

In other words, we cannot escape our social conditioning as a source of hypothesis myopia. It does, however, seem clear that the increasing number of females coming into traditionally male-dominated sciences will inevitably provoke some new and interesting questions from their special perspective.

In summary, it is perhaps impossible to understand completely the complex creative process that generates those revolutionary questions in a scientific discipline. However, one message emerges from the preceding discussion. In asking questions about nature, the scientist must constantly ferret out the implicit assumptions that constrain creative thinking and try to transcend them. It is easy to say but apparently almost impossible to do.

CHAPTER EXERCISES

4.1. Listed below are three behavioral phenomena that you might find interesting. List any questions you have about each of these phenomena and convert them to hypotheses (declarative statements) that are operationally valid and avoid circularity:

1. A friend who works in a rape crisis center reports that rape victims often experience a period of severe depression after their trauma. Ask some questions about the factors that might affect the development and severity of these depressive reactions and convert these questions into operationally valid hypotheses.

2. It is commonly observed that elderly people sometimes have difficulty remembering whether they ate lunch or took their medicine during the day, but they can easily recall events from their youth. Ask some questions about the factors that might influence this memory defect and convert these questions into operationally valid hypotheses.

3. Diabetics must assume a major role in the treatment and control of their own disease. They are often required to follow a strict dietary regimen, administer insulin to themselves at prescribed dosages, and perform urine sugar tests accurately. Surprisingly, up to 75 percent of treated diabetics often fail to comply with their physician's instructions on these matters (Surwit, Feinglas, & Scovern, 1982). The consequence of such failures can be serious. For example, diabetics are twice as likely to experience heart disease and stroke and 25 times more likely to suffer from blindness than are members of the general population (Davidson, 1981). Ask some questions about the factors that you think might influence a diabetic's tendency to monitor diet and follow a prescribed schedule of insulin injections and convert these questions into operationally valid hypotheses.

4.2. In the preceding chapter we described the rudiments of what might be called a *theory* of risk-taking behavior. It identified several factors that might influence such behavior and specified the manner in which these factors interacted when operating together. Can you develop a rudimentary theory of this type that is concerned with any one of the three phenomena described in Exercise 4.1?

4.3. In the preceding chapter we made several rather extensive references to T. S. Kuhn's book *The Structure of Scientific Revolutions*. If you have serious plans to pursue a career as a scientist, you should try to find this book in the library and spend a few evenings reading it. Not everyone agrees with his analysis of how science progresses, but it is perhaps one of the most influential views on the matter.

CHAPTER 5

A SIMPLE ANALYTIC EXPERIMENT

In his fascinating book *The Mind of a Mnemonist,* the Soviet psychiatrist A. R. Luria describes a man called S. As the title of the book implies, S. was one of those rare individuals with a perfect memory. Fifteen years after S. had memorized a long list of meaningless numbers, Luria casually inquired if he still remembered them. Although this man had not seen or thought about these numbers for fifteen years, he recalled the list without error.

The conductor Arturo Toscanini was another person with an incredible memory. Apparently he memorized each note for every instrument in some 250 symphonic works. Stories about his phenomenal memory are well known among his admirers. One such episode is described by George Marek (1975). Just before a concert in St. Louis, a musician informed Toscanini that his bassoon had a broken key. Toscanini reflected on the matter for a moment and told the musician not to worry, since the particular note would not occur in this concert program.

Although these examples suggest that the capacity of the human brain to store information is almost without limit, the other side of the coin suggests that memory is also easily destroyed or distorted. For example, Milner and associates (1968, 1974) have observed that removing certain parts of the brain during brain surgery can have very dramatic effects on memory. In one of her cases (Milner, 1968), a patient with epilepsy displayed an excellent memory prior to a surgical procedure that removed parts of his temporal lobe. After he recovered from the procedure, he could still remember events from his past; he knew his relatives by name, he remembered where he lived, he recalled where he grew up, and so on. He was, however, completely unable to retain any *new information*. If, for example, you introduced yourself and then left the room for a few moments, he would greet you as a complete stranger when you returned. Once the patient had left the hospital, he moved to a new home. He could remember his old address very well but was never able to learn and remember the new one. Apparently the surgery destroyed the patient's ability to transfer immediate experiences into longer-term memory. This particular set of symptoms is often called *Milner's syndrome* in recognition of her extensive research on the problem, and it demonstrates how fragile the process of remembering can be.

Yet another example of memory loss comes from research suggesting that a convulsive seizure disrupts memory for events immediately preceding the seizure. This phenomenon is called *retrograde amnesia,* because the effects of the seizure are retrograde, or work backward in time to affect previously learned events. Depressive mental patients treated by electroconvulsive shock suffer these retrograde effects on memory, as do animals used in studies of electroconvulsive shock (e.g., Spevak & Suboski, 1969).

As the preceding examples indicate, the study of human memory covers a wide range of fascinating phenomena. In this chapter, we shall use one simple question about human memory to illustrate a particular strategy that can be used to answer it and other questions. We call this strategy an *analytic experiment,* and it is perhaps the best method available for answering those questions to which it can be applied. Feinstein and Horowitz (1982), for example, refer to the analytic experiment as the "gold standard" of scientific research methods because it has fewer defects than most.

We shall also keep this first example of an analytic experiment as simple as possible so that you can understand its logic and structure. More complex variations will be discussed in Chapter 6. In order to understand the complex examples, you must have a solid understanding of the simple case.

ASKING THE QUESTION

As noted above, it has been established that a severe physical insult like an electroconvulsive shock can disrupt memory for events immediately preceding it. Is it also possible that a severe "emotional or mental shock" will cause retrograde amnesic effects? If, for example, you were casually strolling down the street and suddenly encountered a dismembered body lying on the sidewalk, would your memory for the events immediately preceding this one be disrupted?

FORMING A HYPOTHESIS

Two hypotheses intuitively follow from the preceding question. First, it is possible that a severe emotional shock will disrupt memory for preceding events much like a severe physical insult to the brain, but to a lesser degree. Alternatively, you might hypothesize that memory for events associated with an intensely emotional experience might actually be enhanced by it. You can take your choice or devise yet other questions and hypotheses. For reasons you will discover later, we shall hypothesize that an emotional shock will disrupt memory in much the same manner as will a physical insult to the brain. We can state the hypothesis as follows: "An emotional shock will disrupt memory for events that occur within 15 seconds prior to its occurrence."

How do we test this hypothesis?

THE LOGIC OF THE ANALYTIC EXPERIMENT

The basic logic of the analytic experiment as a research strategy is very simple. Essentially, the scientist arranges to observe the phenomenon (in this case memory) under two sets of conditions which are identical in all respects except one. The exception is that factor identified by the hypothesis as a *causal* factor. With reference to the retrograde amnesia phenomenon, we want to arrange two sets of conditions that are identical in all respects except that an "emotional shock factor" will be *present* in one set of conditions and *absent* in the other set of conditions. If emotional shock does cause retrograde amnesia, this contrast between the two sets of conditions should be informative. We should observe a disruption of memory in the one set of conditions but not in the other. The basic architecture of this research strategy is illustrated in Figure 5.1.

As indicated in Figure 5.1, we begin the experiment with 20 people (subjects), 10 of whom are observed under a set of conditions that includes the emotional shock designated as "condition X." The other 10 are observed under the set of conditions that excludes emotional shock, hence the label "condition −X." Conditions A, B, C, D, and E are identical for both groups of subjects.

The essential point is that there is only one condition that differentiates these two groups: the presence or absence of an emotional shock. If we observe a difference in the memory of these two groups, it seems reasonable to conclude that the differences will have been caused by the emotional shock factor.

DEVISING AN EXPERIMENTAL PROCEDURE

Thus far we have (1) identified a phenomenon, (2) asked a question about it, (3) formed a hypothesis, and (4) selected a strategy called an analytic experiment to test this hypothesis. The next task is to convert the basic logic and architecture of the analytic experiment into an actual experimental procedure that specifies exactly what will happen to the subjects.

There are many details to consider in arranging an experiment, but most of the decisions you must make will fall into four categories: (1) you will have to operationally define the terms in your hypothesis, (2) you will have to make some important decisions about selecting subjects, (3) you will have to decide how to

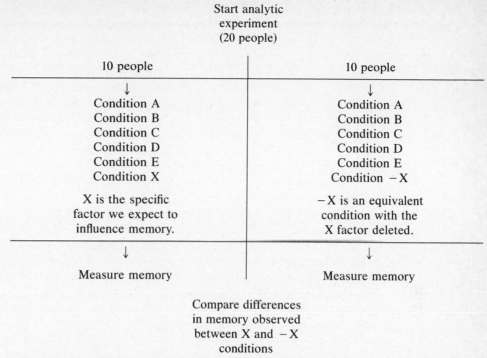

Figure 5.1   The logic and architecture of a simple analytic experiment to examine the effects of factor X on memory. See text for explanation of terms.

assign subjects to the different treatment conditions, and (4) you will have to arrange a variety of mechanical details concerning the observation and measurement of the subjects' behavior. It is instructive to consider each of these tasks in somewhat more detail.

Defining Terms Operationally

Our informal hypothesis specifies that an "emotional shock" will disrupt memory for immediately preceding events. In the language of operationism, there are at least four basic questions to be asked at this point: (1) how to define "emotional shock," (2) how to define "memory disruption," (3) how to define "events," and (4) how to define "immediately precede"?

In short, your task is a difficult one. You must devise a procedure and operationally define the terms of your hypothesis in a manner that meets the logical requirements of the analytical experiment in Figure 5.1. You might like to pause for a second and test your own creative skills.

Imagine for a moment that you have volunteered to be a subject in this memory experiment. You arrive at the laboratory at 1 o'clock in the afternoon and we go through all the procedures required by the code of ethics (see Appendix

B). According to my instructions, you will then see a travel film and be asked to remember as much of the information in this film as you can. You will see only one of two possible versions of the ten-minute film. In version A, the last minute of the film takes place in an open-air market in which the narrator is discussing the prices of several items. A crowd of people is gathered around one particular table and the camera is focused on a craftsman weaving straw hats. The film ends with this scene. Version B of the film is identical in all respects to version A except for the final 15 seconds, in which the camera again focuses on a craftsman seated at the table. However, instead of a person weaving a basket, the viewer sees a full-screen view of a severely mutilated human body slumped in a chair. This final scene in version B is obviously intended to provide an unexpected emotional shock. Version A contains all of the same elements as B without the emotional shock.

Immediately after you have viewed the film, I will ask you to answer ten questions about the prices of market items that were mentioned during the one-minute period immediately preceding the final 15-second scene in the film. Can you remember these prices? Do people who were exposed to the emotional shock remember the prices less well than the people who were not?

This basic procedure (although many details are omitted) accomplishes the two main goals stated earlier. It keeps the logic of the analytic experiment intact and provides publicly reproducible operational definitions for all the important terms in the hypothesis. "Emotional shock" is defined as the final 15-second scene in version B of the film; "memory" is defined in terms of the number of correct answers on the ten-question test; "events" refers to the list of prices mentioned during the last minute of the film; and "immediately precede" is operationally defined as the 1-minute period that immediately precedes the final 15-second scene in the film.

You will probably agree that this procedure permits us to translate our hypothesis into an operationally valid form that is repeatable without danger of confusion by any interested party. Indeed, the operationally valid version of the hypothesis can be stated as follows:

> An unexpected 15-second scene that portrays a mutilated body at the end of a ten-minute travel film will disrupt a person's memory of the price of ten items listed in the film during a one-minute period immediately preceding the final scene.

Clearly other, more imaginative procedures for operationally defining these terms and testing the hypothesis could be developed. Each new procedure you create will, of course, lead to different operational definitions of the important terms in the hypothesis. The points to appreciate are these: (1) any experimental procedure you devise must provide operational definitions of the terms in the hypothesis and (2) the procedure must also meet the logical requirements of the analytic experiment. Within these limits, devising experimental procedures is a great test of your creative powers and one of the most interesting aspects of scientific research.

Selecting Subjects

Figure 5.1 indicates that we plan to use 20 subjects to conduct this simple analytic experiment. Where do psychologists obtain these subjects? The behavioral science journals concerned with human learning and memory point to the answer very clearly. In several recent issues of a psychology journal called *Human Memory and Cognition,* every experiment employed college students as subjects. This practice is understandable when you realize that most research is conducted in a university setting, where students are readily available in large numbers. Although it is convenient, however, the use of college students as subjects can be costly in other respects. To illustrate, suppose that we enlisted 20 students as subjects for our experiment concerned with the disruptive effects of emotional shock. Assume also that we completed the experiment and found that the results supported our hypothesis. It would seem reasonable, at this point, to ask about the generality of these results. Would we obtain the same results if we had used young children as subjects? Would we have obtained the same results if we had used a group of construction workers? Would our hypothesis have been confirmed by a group of elderly females? In short, the process of selecting subjects to participate in an experiment is very important, and the sample of subjects will determine the extent to which our conclusions can be generalized.

The moral of the preceding story is simple to understand but surprisingly difficult to implement. You must make two basic decisions when you select subjects for any experiment. First, you must define the population of subjects to which you want your results to apply. That population will most likely be too large to let you include every member in your experiment. This leads to the second decision. You must select a smaller representative sample from the population and choose a method of doing so. If this problem sounds familiar, it should. In Chapter 2, when we were discussing the ways in which our observations can be distorted, we considered the characteristics of various sampling procedures. You will recall from that discussion that we wanted to estimate the number of mothers in North America who gave birth during the past year and decided to breast-feed their children. In that example, it was argued that the best procedure to use was a *random sampling procedure* (see Chapter 2, p. 29). Any other method of sampling suffered from bias and distortion. Exactly the same concerns about sampling procedures are relevant in the present context. When you must select a group of subjects to participate in your experiment and you want your results to be representative of a larger population, a random sampling procedure is your best strategy.

Some of the issues mentioned in Chapter 2 are also relevant to the present discussion. The process of conducting an analytic experiment consists essentially of *observing and measuring* the phenomenon once again but under a different set of conditions. Hence, all the issues discussed in Chapters 2 and 3 (observation, description, measurement) are again relevant in the context of the analytic experiment.

To summarize briefly, the two decisions we face when selecting subjects is to (1) define the population from which we wish to sample and (2) decide on a sampling procedure. The first decision will determine how widely we can generalize our results; the second will determine the extent to which we can be confident that our sample is representative of the larger population. Both decisions affect what Campbell and Stanley (1966) have called the "external validity" of our experiment. An experiment is assumed to have *external validity* to the extent that the same results would also be obtained with subjects other than those used in the experiment. We shall discuss this concept in more detail in Chapter 7.

How, then, should we actually proceed to select the 20 subjects we need? In theory, it would be nice to think that we could randomly sample 20 individuals from the entire population of North America and assume our results would generalize to this large population. In practice, this is next to impossible. Instead, we will follow the more typically used method of asking for volunteers from the introductory psychology course. This is obviously a very specialized sample and hardly meets the standards of a *random* sampling procedure. In fact, one would have serious questions about the external validity of the results obtained in this way. In its defense, on the other hand, we do not really know if anything interesting or systematic will come from this first experiment. Hence, the convenience of using a readily available population might be justified for practical reasons. If our initial results look promising, we can always start the process over again and place more emphasis upon the external validity and generality of our procedures.

Assigning Subjects to Treatments

We now have 20 volunteers for our memory experiment. Some are males, some are females; some are bright, some are not so bright; some are motivated, some are lazy; and so on. The logic of our analytic experiment as illustrated in Figure 5.1 demands that we divide these subjects into two groups with 10 in each group. One group will be assigned to the set of treatment conditions that includes an emotional shock and the other will be assigned to an identical set of conditions without an emotional shock. How shall we proceed?

One of the *worst* ways to proceed would be to take the first 10 individuals who arrived at the laboratory and assign them to the "no emotional shock" condition. At first thought, this might seem to be a reasonable approach. Why would it be a serious mistake? The problem with assigning people on this basis is that it almost guarantees a difference between the two groups. It is very likely that the first 10 subjects to volunteer and arrive at the laboratory will be more highly motivated than the last 10. These highly motivated subjects would be likely to do better on the memory task.

This example shows that certain methods of assigning subjects to treatment conditions can bias the results of the experiment. There are, of course, many sources of bias other than the "motivational" differences described in this specific example. If, for example, all the intelligent students happen to be assigned to the "no shock" treatment condition and you then observe a disruption of memory in the "shock" group, you will not know if the shock group's poor performance was caused by the treatment or by the accidental assignment of the less intelligent subjects to this group.

The logic of the simple analytic experiment requires you to assign subjects to treatments in a manner that renders the two groups *equivalent*. One of the most effective methods of doing this is to use a random assignment procedure. It will not guarantee equivalence, but it is perhaps the most effective means of avoiding nonequivalent groups with respect to a wide variety of variables.

A *random assignment procedure* is any method in which each subject has an equal probability of being assigned to any treatment condition in the experiment. Suppose that we put the 20 names of our volunteers in a box, mixed them up, and drew each name from the box one at a time. If every other draw were assigned to a different treatment condition, each person would have an equal probability of being assigned to each treatment condition. Thus we have met the requirements of a *random assignment procedure*. Of course there is still some small chance that this method will assign all the intelligent subjects to the same treatment condition, but mathematicians who examine these matters tell us that the probability of bias given a reasonably large number of subjects is very small (assuming truly random assignment).

You might note that behavioral scientists are often very careless about using random assignment procedures in their experiments. It is not unusual, for example, simply to assign every other subject who arrives at the laboratory to a different treatment condition. This procedure assumes that nature (and public transportation schedules) has served to randomize order of appearance in the laboratory. There is a fundamental error in this thinking, and the use of these nonrandom procedures will very likely build a bias into the experiment before it even begins. Nature has incredibly devious ways of delivering subjects to a laboratory in a nonrandom sequence.

Finally, with reference to subject assignment procedures, we shall digress briefly to note that there are at least two ways to guarantee that one group in our memory experiment is not "smarter" than the other group. First, we could simply expose *all 20* subjects to *both* treatment conditions and test their memories after exposure to each. Alternatively, we could measure the intelligence of all 20 subjects prior to assigning them to treatment conditions. They could then be assigned to two groups of 10 subjects each that were *matched* in terms of their scores on our IQ test measurements. In both these procedures we manage to guarantee that the groups are equivalent in terms of intelligence and that one group will not enjoy any advantage over the other group. The first procedure is called, appropriately enough, a *within-subjects* experiment; the second is called a *matched-subjects* experiment. You will encounter both these methods frequently in behavioral research. We shall discuss both these options in subsequent chapters, and you will discover that they do indeed eliminate the small chance of bias present in a random assignment procedure. However, they introduce other, more subtle sources of bias that perhaps offset their apparent advantages.

Mechanical Details

You should now understand the basic logic of the analytic experiment, know how to select subjects, and be able to assign them to treatment conditions in a way that preserves this logic. Perhaps more importantly, you are now aware of some of the problems that can arise if you deviate from certain basic procedures when using this strategy. Obviously there are many other decisions you will be required to make when you actually arrange the experimental procedure. How long should the travel film be? What time of day will you conduct the experiment? Will you show the film to one subject at a time or to the entire group? Will you ask the questions at the end of the film or put them in the form of a written questionnaire? Will the experiment be conducted by a male or a female? Will the experimenter have any knowledge of the hypothesis? Will you tell the subjects the true purpose of the experiment or will you deceive them in some way? Will the 20 subjects make up a large enough sample or will you use more than 20? Will you read the instructions aloud or give the subjects written ones? Will you permit the subjects to ask you questions during the experiment or insist on silence throughout?

We could continue the list, but the point has been made. For lack of a better term, decisions of the sort listed above may be called the *mechanical details* of the experimental procedure.

If you refer back to Figure 5.1, you will realize that the various factors listed as conditions A, B, C, and so on are essentially these mechanical details. Condition A, for example, might refer to the sex of the experimenter, condition B to the time of day, condition C to the length of the travel film, and so on down the list. It is important to note that the logic of the experiment requires that each decision about its mechanical details be made for both groups of subjects. If you decide that a male will conduct the experiment, the same male must be used with both groups. The reasons for this parallel treatment should be obvious: if two different experimenters were used in the two different groups, you would not be able to tell whether the differences between the two groups were caused by the emotional shock or the difference in experimenters.

Are there any particular rules to be followed in making these decisions about mechanical details? Clearly, many of the decisions are largely arbitrary and determined by practical problems, ethical considerations, and available equipment and facilities. You should note, however, that these arbitrary decisions can be very important and should not be taken lightly. The sex of the experimenter might, for example, seem at first glance to be very unimportant. It has been established, however, that male and female experimenters will interact with subjects in very different ways. Male experimenters, for example, are more friendly to and tend to smile more at female subjects (cf. Rosenthal, 1967). It is possible to use a male experimenter in one analytic experiment and later discover that you do not obtain the same results when you use a female experimenter. Hence, decisions of this kind should always be made with the awareness that the results of the procedure will be valid only for that particular set of conditions (e.g., male experimenters). The astute reader will realize that we are once again talking about the issue of *external validity*.

To summarize briefly, we have considered some of the basic decisions that you must make when you devise an experimental procedure to fit the logical requirements of the design illustrated in Figure 5.1. These include devising operational definitions for the basic concepts in your hypotheses, selecting a population of subjects, selecting a method of sampling this population, deciding on a method of assigning subjects to treatment conditions, and making some decisions about the many details in the experimental procedure. Given this background, we should now be able to add some information to the simple experiment illustrated in Figure 5.1. Figure 5.2 is a more detailed illustration of our experiment, letting you see some of the additional information inserted into the appropriate places.

RELEVANT TERMINOLOGY

Now that you understand the basic logic and structure of the analytic experiment, we will consider some of the terms that are traditionally used to describe the

Start analytic experiment—
20 subjects from
introductory psychology course
(should use random sample from a defined population)

Random assignment (10 subjects)	Random assignment (10 subjects)
A. Male experimenter	A. Male experimenter
B. Written instructions	B. Written instructions
C. 10-minute travel film	C. 10-minute travel film
D. 1 o'clock testing	D. 1 o'clock testing
E. Group test session	E. Group test session
X. 15-second final scene, version A—mutilated body seated in a chair ("emotional shock")	−X. 15-second final scene, version B—craftsperson weaving a basket seated in a chair ("no emotional shock")

↓	↓
Measure memory (10 questions)	Measure memory (10 questions)

Compare differences
in memory observed
between X and −X
conditions

Figure 5.2 The logic and architecture of a simple analytic experiment to examine the effects of emotional shock on memory for prior events. See text for explanation of terms.

various elements of its structure. Be forewarned that you will need to know these terms. We shall make extensive use of them in future discussion of more complex variations and throughout the remainder of the book.

Independent Variables

In a simple analytic experiment, the factor which your hypothesis (or question) identifies as a causal agent is called an *independent variable*. It is typically the one factor that is contrasted across the experiment's different treatment conditions. In our memory experiment, the independent variable is the emotional shock treatment. The hypothesis suggested that such shock might be a causal agent in the disruption of memory. In this experiment we contrasted the *presence* and *absence* of shock in the two treatment conditions. Please note than an alternate procedure might have contrasted two different *levels* of emotional shock, such as a *mild* vs. a *severe* one. We would still call the emotional shock treatment an independent variable.

Dependent Variables

In an analytic experiment, the *dependent variable* is the factor that is predicted to change or vary with the presence and absence of the independent variable. In the context of our memory experiment, we are measuring *the number of questions that the subject can correctly answer about the film*. We expect to see fewer correct answers after the version of the film containing the emotional shock (independent variable present) than after the other version (independent variable absent). Hence our measure of the subject's memory is our dependent variable.

Note that it is not uncommon, during an experiment, to measure additional factors that you think might be influenced by the independent variable even if those additional factors have not been directly specified in the hypothesis. We might measure, for example, the subject's heart rate during the film to see if the emotional shock produced a strong physiological response. Although there is nothing in the hypothesis about memory specifying that we should measure heart rate during the experiment, this measure could be added to the list of dependent variables. There is, in fact, no limit to the number of dependent variables a scientist might choose to measure in any particular experiment, and the more measures taken, the more informative and understandable the results of the experiment are likely to be.

Controlled Variables

The concept of a controlled variable is easy to understand in the context of a simple analytic experiment. It will become more difficult as we discuss more complex experimental designs and procedures. Basically, a *controlled variable* is any factor that is held constant across all treatment conditions. In the context of our memory experiment, factors such as the time of day, the sex of the experimenter, and the length of the travel film are all controlled variables. The length of the film, for example, is held constant at ten minutes in both treatment conditions.

Several points should be noted about controlled variables. First, the controlled variable is in a very real sense the earmark of the analytic experiment. All variables must be held constant except the independent variable you have identified as a causal agent. If any one of the controlled variables is permitted to *covary* with the independent variable, the logic of the design is destroyed. If, for example, we showed a *one-hour film* in the emotional shock condition and a *ten-minute film* in the other treatment condition, we would not be able to decide whether a disruption in memory was caused by the emotional shock or the *longer* film. These two factors covary in the procedure. The film length must be a controlled variable in order to maintain the logical properties of the experiment.

A second point about the concept of a controlled variable is that it extends beyond the simple operation of holding a variable (such as the length of the film) at a constant value across treatment conditions. Recall, for example, our previous discussion of assigning subjects randomly to different treatment conditions. The purpose of this was to reduce the chance of including all the "smart" subjects in one treatment group. In effect, the random assignment is an attempt to control *all* those variables that differentiate subjects (e.g., intelligence, hair color, sex, etc.). With random assignment of subjects, we assume that factors like hair color and intelligence are equivalent (held constant) across different treatment conditions. For now, you should remember that the basic purpose of "controlling" a variable is always the same: to prevent it from covarying with the independent variable. But the exact method of accomplishing this varies from one situation to another.

Confounded Variables

If the controlled variable is the earmark of an analytic experiment, the *confounded variable* is the Achilles heel. Defined very simply, a *confounded variable* is any factor in the experiment that covaries with the independent variable across different treatment conditions. We have already discussed a number of potential confounded variables in the context of our memory experiment. The use of a one-hour film in the emotional shock treatment condition and a ten-minute film in the other condition was one such example. Less obvious, perhaps, is the case in which the experimenter uses a nonrandom subject-assignment procedure. If a nonrandom procedure is used—for example, if all females are assigned to one treatment condition and all males to the other—the sex of the subjects would be confounded with the independent variable. Hence, one danger of nonrandom subject-assignment procedures is that they increase the chance that a confounded variable will spoil the experiment.

One cannot stress enough the importance of a confounded variable. Any claim that a scientist makes about the results of a simple analytic experiment can be invalidated if you discover a confounded variable in the experiment. The examples used thus far are all relatively obvious cases. Few scientists would be so inept as to actually use two different lengths of film in the memory experiment that we have been discussing. On the other hand, it is not unusual to find examples of confounded variables in the scientific literature. Practical problems often make it difficult to control all the relevant variables that might covary with the independent variable.

In subsequent chapters we shall discuss a number of research strategies that deviate in some important respects from the logic of the analytic experiment. Each deviation from this logic introduces problems that make the new strategy less desirable than the analytic experiment. You will find that the problem most often met when you deviate from the basic analytic experiment is an increased chance that a confounded variable will contaminate the procedure. Once again, it is vital that you understand this basic concept.

Now that you have been introduced to a number of basic terms, we shall again update Figure 5.2. Figure 5.3 places the appropriate labels on the various

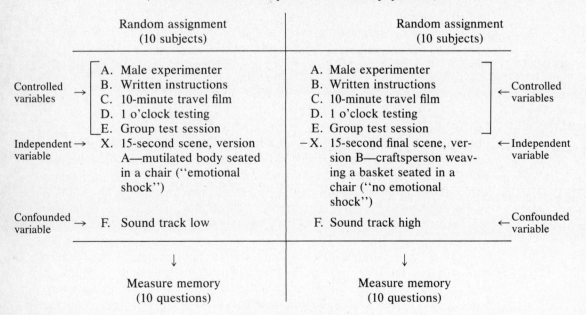

Figure 5.3 The logic and architecture of a simple analytic experiment to examine the effects of emotional shock on memory for prior events. Various elements of the experiment are labeled with appropriate terminology. See text for explanation of terms.

elements of the design. Note that we have added a *confounded variable* designated as *sound track low* and *sound track high* in the two different treatment conditions. This is to illustrate the manner in which a variable that should be controlled can covary with the independent variable.

Bivalent and Multivalent Architecture

Figure 5.1 makes it very easy to see the logic of the simple analytic experiment in terms of two treatment conditions administered to two different groups of subjects. One group is exposed to severe emotional shock; the other is not. In referring to this architecture, it makes sense to say that the independent variable is manipulated at two levels or two values: the presence and the absence of emotional shock. Plutchik (1983, p. 85) refers to all such cases as *bivalent* (two-valued) experiments. The term has useful descriptive properties and we shall use it in all subsequent discussions.

It is often desirable to compare more than two levels or values of the independent variable in the same experiment. In the context of our memory experiment, for example, you might want to extend the bivalent architecture illustrated in Figure 5.1 to an experiment that compares *three* different levels of the independent variable: (1) no emotional shock, (2) mild emotional shock, and (3) severe emotional shock. Assuming that you can devise another ten-minute film with a mild emotional shock condition, the architecture of the three-level experiment is illustrated in Figure 5.4. As you can see, the same basic logic applies to the two-level bivalent case (Figure 5.1) and the three-level case (Figure 5.4). All factors are held constant except the one factor identified by the hypothesis (emotional shock). If we find that a different degree of memory disruption occurs at each level of emotional shock, we have further confirmation of our hypothesis. Plutchik (1983, p. 38) calls any experiment that manipulates more than two levels of the independent variable in the same experiment a *multivalent* (many-valued) experiment. All the terms that you have learned with reference to the elements of the experimental design extend appropriately to the multivalent experiment (e.g., independent variable, controlled variable, dependent variable, etc.)

Between-Subjects and Within-Subjects Architecture

Returning once again to the simple bivalent analytic experiment illustrated in Figure 5.1, you will note that each treatment condition in this experiment is administered to a different set of subjects (ten in each condition). Note that this basic procedure produces a *between-subjects* design. Alternatively, when every subject is exposed to all the treatment conditions, the procedure defines a *within-subjects* design. It is possible to have both between-subjects and within-subjects bivalent and multivalent experiments; within-subjects designs have some special problems best discussed at a later time.

Finally, although memorizing terminology is not much fun, make sure that

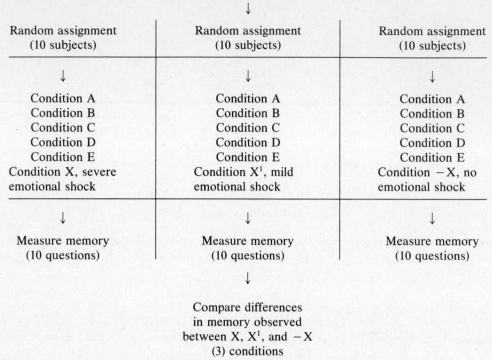

30 subjects
randomly sampled
from a defined population

↓

Random assignment (10 subjects)	Random assignment (10 subjects)	Random assignment (10 subjects)
↓	↓	↓
Condition A Condition B Condition C Condition D Condition E Condition X, severe emotional shock	Condition A Condition B Condition C Condition D Condition E Condition X^1, mild emotional shock	Condition A Condition B Condition C Condition D Condition E Condition $-X$, no emotional shock
↓	↓	↓
Measure memory (10 questions)	Measure memory (10 questions)	Measure memory (10 questions)

↓

Compare differences
in memory observed
between X, X^1, and $-X$
(3) conditions

Figure 5.4 The logic and architecture of a simple analytic experiment to examine the effects of *three* levels of emotional shock on memory for prior events.

you understand and can use the terms introduced in the last few paragraphs. You will encounter them frequently in the pages that follow.

ANALYZING THE RESULTS

Imagine for the moment that we enlisted some subjects and conducted the bivalent between-subjects experiment illustrated in Figure 5.2. After the experiment, we would have a measure of each subject's memory. It would consist of a score from 0 to 10 that tells us how many of the ten questions about the film each subject answered correctly. Our prediction was that subjects exposed to emotional shock will remember less than subjects not exposed to emotional shock. If nature was very cooperative and our hunch about memory was correct, the experiment might produce the data presented in Table 5.1. As these data indicate, every subject in the emotional shock condition had a memory score of less than 5 out of a possible 10, and every subject in the other group had a memory score

Table 5.1 HYPOTHETICAL RESULTS OF
AN EXPERIMENT DESIGNED TO MEASURE
THE EFFECTS OF EMOTIONAL SHOCK
UPON MEMORY

"Emotional shock" condition[a]		"No emotional shock" condition[a]	
S-1	2	S-1	7
S-2	1	S-2	8
S-3	3	S-3	7
S-4	4	S-4	8
S-5	3	S-5	9
S-6	3	S-6	7
S-7	2	S-7	6
S-8	3	S-8	7
S-9	4	S-9	6
S-10	1	S-10	8
Σ	19	Σ	67
$\overline{X}$	1.9	$\overline{X}$	6.7

[a] There was no overlap in the scores obtained in
the two conditions.

greater than 5 out of a possible 10. The average shock in the emotional shock
condition is 1.9; that in the other is 6.7. Having read Chapter 3, you will also
realize that there are several other *descriptive statistics* that can be calculated to
help describe these two sets of scores and that these data can be plotted as two
frequency distributions. The distributions for both groups of subjects can be
plotted on the same axes. We have done this in Figure 5.5 and, as you can see,
the two distributions do not overlap.

Any scientist would consider these results to support our hypothesis very
convincingly. First, we have adhered very closely to the logic of the analytic
design and avoided any confounded variables. The only difference between the
two treatment conditions is the presence of emotional shock in one of them. If
there is a difference in memory, it seems reasonable to attribute it to the emotional
shock treatment. Second, it does not seem likely that this perfect arrangement
of scores in favor of our hypothesis would have occurred purely by chance.
Imagine having a deck of 20 cards composed of 10 black cards (emotional shock)
and 10 white ones (no emotional shock). You shuffle them and deal one at a time
from the top of the deck. Suppose this process produced 10 consecutive black
cards followed by 10 white cards. Even if you are not familiar with the funda-
mentals of probability theory, experience should tell you that this particular
chance outcome would be very rare. The analogy is not perfect, but it does make
the point. Specifically, scientists are always afraid that differences between treatment conditions like those in Table 5.1 might have occurred by chance. If such
differences are *unlikely* to have occurred by chance, they accept the data as a
tentative confirmation of their experimental hypothesis (i.e., they assume that

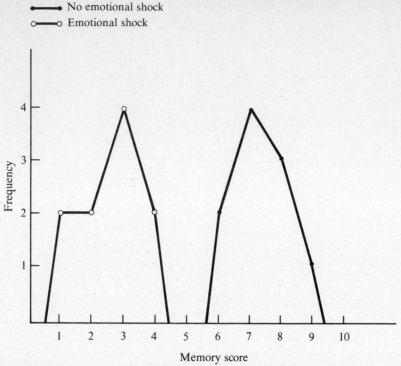

Figure 5.5   Frequency distribution of memory scores in emotional shock condition (10Ss) and no emotional shock condition (10Ss).

the independent variable produced the observed differences). If, however, a particular difference is likely to have occurred by chance, they are hesitant to accept it as a "true" difference. When they suspect that chance has produced the difference, they reject their experimental hypothesis and temporarily accept the notion that no "true" difference has been produced by the independent variable. The latter decision is called *accepting the null hypothesis*. The term "null hypothesis" refers to the assumption that the difference observed between these two sets of measurements is very likely to have been produced by chance variation.

After the data have been collected in an experiment, it is possible to estimate the exact probability that any particular difference between your treatment conditions is a product of chance variation. These calculations vary with the characteristics of the data under consideration. Taken together, however, the methods used to estimate the probability of a chance result are called *inferential statistics*. For example, if we wanted to estimate the probability that the differences in Table 5.1 occurred by chance, there are several methods we could use. One that is particularly easy to understand and calculate is the Mann-Whitney *U* Test (cf. Siegel, 1956, p. 116).

To summarize the preceding information briefly, *descriptive statistics* are calculations that help us summarize and describe various characteristics of a set of measurements (see Chapter 3). Alternatively, *inferential statistics* are methods for calculating the probability that any particular difference in two or more sets of numbers might be expected to occur by chance alone. It is, for example, conventional to accept your experimental hypothesis as confirmed when an inferential statistic estimates the probability of a difference occurring by chance to be less than 5 chances in 100 ($P<.05$). If, for example, you apply a Mann-Whitney *U* Test to the data in Table 5.1, it will estimate the probability of these differences occurring by chance alone to be *less than* 5 chances in 100 ($P<.05$). Under these conditions, we are prepared to accept our experimental hypothesis, which suggested that an emotional shock would disrupt memory performance, and to reject the *null hypothesis*.

Look next at another set of hypothetical results in Table 5.2. It is again the case that more forgetting occurred in the emotional shock condition. If you look at the actual numbers in Table 5.2, it seems possible that these differences could have been produced by chance variation. In fact, if you think back to our analogy with the black and white cards, it seems *very likely* that chance played a role in producing the differences observed in Table 5.2.

The results illustrated in Figure 5.2 are more typical than those observed

Table 5.2   HYPOTHETICAL RESULTS
OF AN EXPERIMENT DESIGNED TO
MEASURE THE EFFECTS OF EMOTIONAL
SHOCK UPON MEMORY

"Emotional shock" condition[a]		"No emotional shock" condition[a]	
S-1	2	S-1	7
S-2	3	S-2	6
S-3	1	S-3	8
S-4	1	S-4	7
S-5	4	S-5	3
S-6	9	S-6	2
S-7	7	S-7	1
S-8	8	S-8	4
S-9	1	S-9	9
S-10	5	S-10	5
Σ	41	Σ	52
$\overline{X}$	4.1	$\overline{X}$	5.2

[a] There is a difference between the average memory scores in the two treatment conditions, but there is also considerable overlap in the two sets of scores.

in Table 5.1. Precisely because it is rare, in behavioral experiments, to obtain the consistent differences obtained in Table 5.1, inferential statistics are almost always applied to the data. However, since we promised (in Chapter 1) that we would not elaborate on inferential statistics, we shall end the discussion at this point and refer the reader interested in more detailed examples to Appendix D.

THREE SIMPLE ANALYTIC EXPERIMENTS

You are about to discover that our hypothetical experiment concerned with the effects of emotional shock on memory is not so hypothetical. Indeed, the same question was asked by two psychologists from the University of Washington (Loftus & Burns, 1982). They conducted three experiments designed to determine if a severe emotional shock would produce retrograde amnesia. The details of these experiments differ considerably from those of our hypothetical example, but the basic logic and architecture of their experimental designs approximate those of the analytic experiment we have been discussing.

These experiments have been reprinted for your convenience with brief comments inserted throughout; these comments should be helpful if you are not used to reading articles in scientific journals.

After you have read the journal article, go on to the chapter exercises, which should test your grasp of the material in this chapter and your ability to apply it to a real-world example. Good luck and read with a critical eye!

Note to Reader

Not all journals that publish the results of behavioral research use the same format. The article reprinted on the following pages uses the format suggested by the American Psychological Association in their *APA Publication Manual.* This format is widely used in the social sciences and health professions, so you will encounter it frequently. Each article is preceded by a short title; then an *abstract* or summary of the main contents of the article is presented. This particular abstract summarizes the results of three experiments included in the publication.

MENTAL SHOCK CAN PRODUCE RETROGRADE AMNESIA

ELIZABETH F. LOFTUS AND TERRENCE E. BURNS

University of Washington, Seattle, Washington 98195

Abstract

Subjects in three experiments saw a short film of a mentally shocking event in which a young boy is violently shot in the face. Compared to other subjects who saw a nonviolent version of the same film, those who saw the mentally shocking version showed poorer retention of the details of the film. Retention was poorer whether measured by recognition or recall. Furthermore, impaired memory occurred only when the event was mentally upsetting and not when it was merely unexpected but not upsetting. These results suggest that mentally shocking episodes may disrupt the lingering processing necessary for full storage of information in memory.

Note to Reader

The next section of the report, headed "Introduction," generally reviews any existing research that seems to be directly relevant to the research that is reported in the article. It must also state the rationale or purpose of the research to be reported. Loftus and Burns briefly discuss previous research demonstrating that physical injury can cause retrograde amnesia. They also note research reported by Tulv-

Loftus, E., and Burns, T., 1982. Mental shock can produce retrograde amnesia. *Memory and Cognition, 10,* 318–323.

ing (1969) which demonstrates that an unusual word presented in a
list of common words will cause forgetting of words that immediately
precede this unusual word. Then they state their rationale for doing
the research and, finally, their hypothesis. The hypothesis is informally
stated in the last paragraph of the introduction.

Retrograde amnesia refers to the loss of memory for events that occur
prior to some critical incident, such as a head injury, electroconvulsive stimulation, or the administration of a variety of drugs. The size of the memory deficit
typically varies with the temporal interval between the earlier event and the
critical incident. A leading interpretation of these results is that memory traces
consolidate with the passage of time, and that a critical incident, such as an
injury to the brain, can disrupt the process of consolidation (Deutsch & Deutsch,
1966). Other interpretations are also possible: for example, that the critical
incident affects retrieval, rather than storage, of information in memory (Cotman & McGaugh, 1980), or that it affects semantic or context encoding
processes in some way (see Sten, 1981, for a review of these theories).

Nearly all of the work on retrograde amnesia with humans has involved
an actual insult to the brain, whether by accidental injury (Goldberg, Antin,
Bilder, Gerstman, Hughes, & Mattis, 1981; Russell & Nathan, 1946; Whitty &
Zangwill, 1977) or by deliberate administration of drugs, electroconvulsive
therapy (Squire, 1975), or other intervention. One exception to this rule is a
phenomenon that resembles retrograde amnesia that has been produced
under laboratory conditions using memory for lists of common words. The
critical incident in this case was the presentation of an unusual word, typically
the name of a famous person, such as Columbus, Freud, or Aristotle (Tulving,
1969). In this research, and in studies that were stimulated by it (e.g., Saufley
& Winograd, 1970; Schulz, 1971), significant decrements in recall of items that
precede a critical name have been consistently observed. These results are
generally interpreted as providing support for some version of the consolidation
hypothesis (Tulving, 1969). Of course, it should be kept in mind that the resemblance between the retrograde effects observed in these studies and the
retrograde effects that have been associated with physical insult to the brain
in no way indicates that a common mechanism lies at the heart of the two
retrograde effects.

The phenomenon of retrograde amnesia is of great theoretical importance, and to advance our understanding of it, we must find ways of producing
the phenomenon in laboratory settings that more naturally mirror the information processing demands of real-life situations. We describe here three
experiments, involving 566 subjects, that demonstrate retrograde amnesia in
human beings who are exposed to mentally, but not physically, shocking
experiences that are realistic in nature. A major goal of this work was to
demonstrate the existence of retrograde effects with highly realistic material.
Once [they were] achieved, we explored some characteristics of the retrograde effect obtained with these materials.

EXPERIMENT 1

Note to Reader

The next major section of the report describes the *method* used to do the research. There are three major parts to the method section: (1) subjects, (2) materials, and (3) design and procedure. These are self-explanatory for the most part. You might note, however, that this is an incredibly large number of subjects to use in a human memory experiment. It is more common to encounter between 10 and 20 subjects per treatment condition. You will also note that the subjects are not randomly sampled from a defined population and the authors did not specify how the subjects were assigned to treatment conditions. One hopes that a random procedure was used. We should also mention that you will seldom find the experimental design identified by name. Usually, you have to extract the logic and architecture of the design from the general description of the design and procedure.

Method

Subjects.   The subjects were 266 students at the University of Washington. They participated in small groups, and this participation satisfied a course requirement. They were told that they were free to leave the experiment at any time and still receive full credit but none of them chose to do so.

Materials.   Subjects viewed a film of a bank robbery lasting approximately 2.25 min. The film is part of a training program designed to instruct employees on how to react in the event of a robbery. The film clip was taken from *3:57 Friday Afternoon,* produced by the Idaho First National Bank in 1977. The robbery portrayed in the film is the type that occurs most frequently, in which a lone individual holds up a single teller. After robbing the teller, the robber walks quickly out of the bank. The teller shouts that she has just been robbed, and two male employees chase the robber into a parking lot where two young boys are playing. In the violent version of the film, as the robber runs toward a getaway car, he turns and fires a shot toward the two men in pursuit. The shot hits one of the boys in the face and he falls to the ground bleeding, his hands clutching his face. In the nonviolent version, the events are identical until just prior to the shooting, when the film flashes back to the inside of the bank, where the manager is informing the employees and customers about what has happened and asking everyone to stay calm. The two endings are approximately 15 sec in length.

Design and Procedure.   The film was shown using a .75 in. video cassette player, with 115 subjects viewing the violent version and 111 viewing the nonviolent version. Immediately after viewing the film, they answered a set of 25 multiple-choice and fill-in-the-blank questions. After each question, they indicated their confidence in their answers by choosing a number from 1 (indicating "guessing") to 5 (indicating "very sure"). The last question was critical. It asked the number on the football jersey of one of the young boys who was playing in the parking lot and it required the subject to fill in the blank with the answer. The correct number was 17; it could be seen for a total of 2 sec, and specifically from 4 sec to 2 sec prior to the critical incident (the shooting in the violent case, the return to the bank in the nonviolent case). A still shot from the videotape, showing the boy and the number 17 just prior to the critical incident, is shown in Figure 1.

Included on the questionnaire were two personal questions, one referring to the interest level and the other asking about how upsetting the viewing of the videotape was for the subject. These two questions were answered on a scale from 1 (indicating "least interesting" or "least upsetting") to 5 (indicating "most interesting" or "most upsetting"). The experiment lasted approximately 30 min.

Note to Reader

The next major section of the report is headed "Results." There are two points to be made in this context. First, the basic results are

Figure 1   Reprinted by permission of Loftus, E., and Burns, T., 1982. Mental shock can produce retrograde amnesia. *Memory and Cognition, 10,* 318–323. Copyright 1982.

presented in Table 1, which indicates the percentage of subjects providing the correct answer to each of the questions on the memory test in the violent and the nonviolent film treatments. Second, the results on the critical question that immediately precedes the mental shock are subjected to an *inferential statistical analysis* to determine the likelihood that the differences in the two treatment conditions are due to chance. Only 4.3 percent of the subjects in the mental shock condition correctly remembered the information whereas 27.9 percent in the nonviolent treatment condition remembered it. The inferential statistic called a X^2 (chi square) indicated that there was less than one chance in a thousand ($P < .001$) that this difference would occur by chance factors alone.

Results

The results for the critical item were dramatic: Subjects were far less likely to recall the number on the boy's jersey when its appearance preceded the eruption of violence than when it did not. Only 4.3% of the subjects correctly recalled the number in the violent condition, whereas 27.9% recalled it in the nonviolent condition [$X^2(1) = 21.72$, $P < .001$]. Subjects were marginally more

Table 1   Percent Correct (PC) and Mean Confidence Ratings (CR) in Experiment 1

Item	Violent		Nonviolent	
	PC	CR	PC	CR
Day of week	91.3	4.47	85.6	4.59
Time of day	73.0	4.50	75.7	4.68
Color robber's hair	98.3	4.42	99.1	4.49
Robber moustache?	88.7	4.17	89.2	4.19
Color robber's eyes	62.6	2.18	82.0	2.31
Robber glasses?	93.0	4.51	93.7	4.63
Robber's clothes	79.1	4.39	82.0	4.32
Robber's shirt	16.5	2.84	25.2	2.93
Note to teller	91.3	4.56	94.6	4.81
Teller putout money	91.3	4.58	93.7	4.66
Robber's words	80.9	3.66	86.5	3.93
Alarm button	93.0	4.62	91.9	4.64
Robber's expression	63.5	3.18	76.6	3.63
Number employees	94.8	4.68	99.1	4.78
First man out	78.3	3.50	81.1	3.48
Direction out bank	86.1	4.34	91.9	4.37
Number on jersey	4.3	1.41	27.9	1.69

NOTE: The last item was the critical item.

confident in their answers to this item in the nonviolent than in the violent condition [1.69 vs. 1.41; $t(224) = 1.79$, $P < .07$].

In analyzing the results, we also considered performance on the filler items, but we confined our analysis to those items on the questionnaire that could only be answered with information presented in the identical portion of the film, that is, the time prior to the critical incident. Thus, an item such as "What was the color of the carpeting in the bank?" was excluded from this analysis, since the carpeting could be seen again in the nonviolent version when the scene returned to the inside of the bank. Subjects who viewed the nonviolent version would obviously have an advantage on this item, which we wished to avoid. There were 16 filler items that could be answered only with information presented in the identical portion of the film, and 14 of them were answered correctly more often when subjects had viewed the nonviolent rather than the violent version ($P < .05$, by a sign test). A brief description of these items and performance on them for the two groups of subjects is shown in Table 1. They are listed in the order in which subjects answered them, which approximates the order in which information about them was presented in the film. It should be kept in mind that most of these items referred to information that was presented several times during the film, and over extended periods of time at that. For example, the question "What was the color of the robber's eyes?" or "How many men chased the robber?" could be answered with information obtained at multiple points in time during the film. However, the critical item about the number on the boy's football jersey appeared only once and for a brief period of time. Thus, although it appears as if responding to the item that occurred immediately before the critical incident was affected much more than responding to those items that occurred earlier in the film (suggesting a temporally graded effect), this cannot be conclusively assumed because of the noncomparability of the items.

Table 1 also contains confidence ratings for each item. It can be seen that for 14 of 16 filler items, as well as the critical item, subjects who viewed the nonviolent version were more confident of their answers.

Finally, as expected, subjects found the experiment to be far more upsetting in the violent condition than in the nonviolent condition [3.30 vs. 1.77; $t(224) = 10.68$, $P < .001$], and they rated it as significantly more interesting [3.77 vs. 3.50; $t(224) = 2.11$, $P < .03$].

Note to Reader

The final section of a typical report is headed "Discussion." It generally summarizes the results of the experiment and interprets these results in terms of the existing literature on the topic or related topics. In this particular report three experiments are reported, so the discussion after each experiment is very brief. After all three experiments have been described, a somewhat longer discussion section headed "General Discussion" is presented.

Discussion

In Experiment 1, we found that subjects who viewed a violent version of an event were less able than control subjects to remember details that occurred prior to the eruption of the violence. It is impossible to disentangle whether this impairment in memory was because of a failure to store the pertinent information or because of an inability to retrieve it later. Experiment 2 was conducted, in part, to address this question.

EXPERIMENT 2

Note to Reader

In Experiments 2 and 3, the same basic format is employed as used in Experiment 1. Descriptions of the *method* are abbreviated as much as possible to eliminate redundant details.

The primary purpose of this experiment was to determine whether exposure to the violent film segment would produce retrograde amnesia with a recognition task, as it did with a recall task in Experiment 1. However, it had as a secondary purpose to assess the viability of an alternate explanation for the effects obtained in the first study.

Experiment 2 was essentially a replication of Experiment 1 with two important modifications. First, the critical item was tested with a recognition test question rather than a recall test question. Subjects were asked to designate the number on the football jersey by choosing one of four alternatives: 10, 13, 1, and 17. The rationale for this modification was that if retrograde amnesia is caused by a failure of initial registration or encoding of the event into memory, then detrimental effects of mental shock should be apparent when subjects are tested via recognition as well as recall. On the other hand, if retrograde amnesia is caused by a breakdown of the retrieval of adequately stored information, then detrimental effects might not appear when subjects are tested via recognition, because recognition minimizes the need for retrieval.

A second change in this experiment was the addition of a third version of the event. It could be argued that the results depended upon the particular nonviolent version that we created. It happened that the version we used terminated the "parking lot" episode of the plot and presented the subject with a new "back in the bank" episode. In contrast, the violent version continued in the parking lot. It is possible that details from different episodes within an overall story may simply interfere with each other less. To explore this possibility, we created a third version of the film, in which, in place of the shooting scene, a police car arrives in the parking lot and some conversation follows. It was identical in length to the other two endings.

Method

Subjects were 180 students who participated in this study as a filler activity in conjunction with another, unrelated experiment. Because of time constraints, subjects first saw one of three versions of the film (violent, nonviolent-bank, and nonviolent-police) and then engaged in a short unrelated activity. Finally, they answered the critical item about the number on the football jersey. As indicated earlier, they responded to a four-alternative forced-choice recognition item.

Results

As in Experiment 1, subjects were far less likely to remember the number on the football jersey when its appearance preceded an eruption of violence than when it did not. Only 28% of the subjects responded correctly in the violent condition, whereas 55% and 52% of the subjects responded correctly in the nonviolent-bank and nonviolent-police conditions, respectively. The smaller of these two figures, 52%, is significantly different from the violent-film group's performance of 28% by a wide margin [$X^2(1) = 6.81$, $P < .01$]. It should be kept in mind that the four-alternative forced-choice test item yields 25% correct recognition by chance alone. Thus, the performance of those who viewed the violent version did not exceed chance level, whereas the performance of those who viewed the nonviolent versions was considerably better than chance.

Discussion

Experiment 2 demonstrates that the viewing of a violent event affects not only the recall of information but recognition as well. Some investigators might contend that this result argues against retrieval failure as an explanation of the retrograde effect. For example, Detterman and Ellis (1972) have specifically stated that "failure to demonstrate retrograde amnesia using a recognition task would ... [seem] to argue for retrieval failure as the origin of retrograde amnesia" (p. 315). However, this conclusion assumes that recognition involves little or no retrieval whatsoever, and this assumption is certainly controversial. (See Baddeley, 1976, for a discussion of this aspect of recall vs. recognition.) Certainly there was much more relevant retrieval information for the critical to-be-remembered detail without even suggestive evidence for any attenuation of the major effect observed in Experiment 1.

A rather conservative interpretation of the results of Experiment 2 is that the retrograde effect in the violent condition is sufficiently strong that it appears not to matter whether the subject is tested via recall or recognition, suggesting we have a profound effect, indeed. Of course, it is possible that there is some aspect of the violent version, other than its sheer violence, that is responsible for the impairment in memory. For example, one could argue that the violent version of the event may have been quite unexpected, and perhaps any unexpected change whether violent or not would produce a similar retrograde amnesia for the critical item. To test this possibility, a third experiment was conducted.

EXPERIMENT 3

Experiment 3 used three groups of subjects. One group of 55 subjects saw the violent version that had been shown in previous experiments, and a second group of 53 subjects saw the nonviolent-bank version. A third group of 52 subjects saw a new version containing an unexpected, but nonviolent, ending. In this version, the scene shifts at the critical moment, just prior to the shooting scene in the violent version, to a completely different film clip showing two people at a distance walking along the beach. This ending, like the other two, was approximately 15 sec in length.

In all other ways, the experiment was identical to the previous one: subjects saw the event, engaged in a 10-min filler activity, and then answered the critical question about the number on the football jersey. Again, their memory was measured via their response to a four-alternative forced-choice item.

As in the other experiments, subjects were far less likely to remember the number on the football jersey when its appearance preceded an eruption of violence than when it did not. Only 24% of the subjects responded correctly in the violent condition, whereas 47% and 50% of the subjects responded correctly in the nonviolent-bank and nonviolent-beach conditions, respectively. The smaller of these two figures, 47%, is significantly different from the violent group's performance of 24% by a wide margin ($P < .01$), whereas the two larger percentages obviously do not differ from each other.

In summary, this experiment showed that an unexpected event that is nonviolent in nature does not produce a similar retrograde effect for the critical item. Of course, it could be argued that the particular film segment we used had little action and few specific events to be encoded. A segment that was unexpected and unusual but more similar to the other conditions of information content might have produced a very different pattern of results. We cannot rule out this possibility.

GENERAL DISCUSSION

Note to Reader

In the general discussion, the authors interpret the results of all three experiments in terms of their implications for existing views of the memory process and retrograde amnesia. You will note that they speculate about the relationship of their findings to those reported by other scientists. They also discuss possible relationships between these data and other phenomena they suspect involve similar processes. Finally, they suggest that these results have important practical implications for eyewitness testimony in courtroom proceedings. In cases involving a severe emotional shock to the witness, it is possible that the memory of such a witness should not be trusted.

Taken together, these experiments provide support for the theory that exposure to mentally shocking events can cause retrograde amnesia for other events that occur a short period of time earlier. These effects occur whether retrograde amnesia is tested via recognition or recall. A promising explanation for these memory deficits is that mental shock disrupts the lingering processing necessary for full storage of information in memory. This idea resembles the formulation advanced long ago by Muller and Pilzecker (1900), who suggested that environmental stimuli initiate neural activity that endures for some length of time beyond the actual stimulus presentation. If this activity is left uninterrupted, an increasingly secure memory trace will be established. However, if the activity is interrupted, the memory trace will not be securely established.

Our results showed that impairment in memory occurred not only for an item seen immediately prior to the critical incident, but also for items occurring nearly 2 min earlier. Although this may seem to challenge the consolidation explanation, it can be accounted for by assuming that there are two consolidation processes, one for short-term traces and another for long-term traces (Deutsch & Deutsch, 1966). Presumably, exposure to violence disrupts not only short-term consolidation but also long-term consolidation.

Another way to discuss the encoding deficit is in terms of level of processing of input items. Detterman (1975), after observing retrograde effects in recognition as well as recall of verbal materials, suggests that "the effect of the critical item is to change a subject's level of processing" (p. 627). In other words, items before the critical item might be processed differently. It is difficult to see why the items before the critical event should be processed differently by subjects who are treated identically. Perhaps the implicit assumption is that processing extends through time to the critical event, but it then becomes difficult to distinguish this notion from the more typical one of consolidation.

We do not mean to suggest that other theories of amnesia cannot explain the present results. For example, it may be that some form of the context encoding theories (see Stern, 1981) may be developed to accommodate these findings. It may be that subjects witnessing the shocking event are in a different emotional state at the time of retrieval and that state-dependent retrieval effects are operating. It is also possible that the mental shock has other effects that we have not measured here, such as the reconstruction or alternation of previously stored memory. For example, viewing the shooting of a young boy may cause a reconstruction of previously stored information about the robber (e.g., he is now a killer as well as a mere robber). The present materials do not, unfortunately, permit a test of this idea.

Whether the final explanation for the damaging effects of observing mentally shocking episodes is a cognitive one, an emotional one, or some combination, these results shed light on the speculation that certain substances released in affective states—for example, neurotransmitters such as norepinephrine—might have the effect of promoting memory storage (Kety, 1972). In a similar vein other researchers have talked about the selection value of permanently retaining biologically crucial but unexpected events (Brown & Kulik, 1977). The argument seems to be that it is possible that certain environmental presentations that are important for survival may produce an affective state that may "serve concurrently to reinforce and consolidate new and significant sensory patterns in the neocortex" (Kety, 1972, p. 73). If this hypothesis is correct, why do we and others (Clifford & Hollin, 1981; Clifford & Scott, 1978) show results indicating poorer retention for the details of mentally shocking events? It is entirely possible that memory for some aspect of the violent event (for example, the shooting incident in the film) is better consolidated or reinforced. This enhancement may be partially or solely responsible for the poorer retention of other details (such as the number on the football jersey). A test of this idea would necessarily involve a comparison of memory for the identical item when it appeared in a context in which it was shocking vs. nonshocking, something that was not possible within the constraints of the present stimulus materials. On the other hand, it may be that norepinephrine or other substances, when injected alone, can promote memory storage, but cannot when released within the context of a particularly stressful event.

As we noted earlier, the superficial resemblance between the retrograde effects produced with and without physical insult to the brain do not necessarily indicate that the same mechanism is at work. In fact, there is at least one important difference: With clinical amnesia produced with electroconvulsive shock, drugs, anoxia, concussion, or disease, at the "eye of the storm" there is nothing. However, in the studies utilizing jolting material, the critical event itself is well recovered (Schacter & Tulving, 1981; Kinsbourne, Note 1). It may well be, then, that our effects are more accurately described as *von Restorff* effects (see Wallace, 1965), situations in which an "outstanding" item is embedded within a list of otherwise homogeneous material. Invariably that item is well recalled. Although researchers have come to expect this memory enhancement for the critical item, the impact on surrounding items has been relatively unpredictable. Sometimes memory for surrounding items is enhanced (e.g., Jones & Jones, 1942), sometimes it is impaired (Jenkins & Postman, 1948), and sometimes any spread of effects is only temporarily observed (Brown & Oxman, 1978). Smith and Stearns (1949) once tried to make sense of the disparate results by suggesting that the effect would depend upon the particular use that was made of the unusual item. Even then, however, they raised their hands in despair and concluded that what use a person makes of the unusual item "seems to result from factors quite difficult to specify" (Smith & Sterns, 1949, p. 381). It was no wonder that Wallace (1965) was led to conclude that no definite conclusions could be reached as to the influence of an unusual item on surrounding material.

Whatever the theoretical explanation for the observed memory impairment, the results have important practical implications. They suggest that witnesses to emotionally traumatic events, such as crimes, accidents, or fires, may be less able to recall key events that occurred prior to the eruption of the trauma. In many crime situations, for example, there is often a period of observation prior to an act of violence during which information is available. Many lay persons believe that these observations are free from the deleterious effects of mental shock. In fact, even judges have been known to express the belief that the reliability of witnesses' memories is increased in the case of violent crimes (see cases cited by Wall, 1965; Woocher, 1977). The present research suggests otherwise.

One caution about these results is in order. In all three experiments, we have used only a single upsetting event, and we have shown that, in each case, memory for a peripheral detail is impaired. We have excluded some possible explanations for this robust result. Therefore, a needed step for future research is to further study the effects of upsetting events on memory in order to isolate the precise reason for memory impairment.

REFERENCE NOTE

1. Kinsbourne, M. Personal communication, 1981.

REFERENCES

Note to Reader

The final section of the report lists all references used in the report so that readers can consult them if they wish. You might note that the most recent version of the *APA Publication Manual* (1983), the third edition, shows a number of changes in style since the Loftus and Burns article was published. It is now appropriate to place the date for an article or book reference immediately following the author's name.

Baddeley, A. D. *The psychology of memory.* New York: Basic Books, 1976.

Brown, A. S., & Oxman, M. Learning through participation: Effects of involvement and anticipation of involvement. *American Journal of Psychology,* 1978, 91, 161–172.

Brown, R., & Kulik, J. Flashbulb memories. *Cognition,* 1977, 5, 73–99.

Clifford, B. R., & Hollin, C. R. Effects of the type of incident and the number of perpetrators on eyewitness memory. *Journal of Applied Psychology,* 1981, 66, 364–370.

Clifford, B. R. , & Scott, J. Individual and situational factors in eyewitness testimony. *Journal of Applied Psychology,* 1978, 63, 352–359.

Cotman, C. W., & McGaugh, J. L. *Behavioral neuroscience, an introduction.* New York: Academic Press, 1980.

Detterman, D. K. The von Restorff effect and induced amnesia: Production by manip-ulation of sound intensity. *Journal of Experimental Psychology: Human Learning and Memory,* 1975, 1, 614–628.

Detterman, D. K., & Ellis, N. R. Determinants of induced amnesia in short-term memory. *Journal of Experimental Psychology,* 1972, 95, 308–316.

Deutsch, J. A., & Deutsch, D. *Physiological psychology.* Homewood, Ill: Dorsey, 1966.

Goldberg, E., Antin, S. P., Bilder, R. M., Jr., Gerstman, L. J., Hughes, J. E. O., & Mattis, S. Retrograde amnesia: Possible role of mesencephalic reticular activation in long-term memory. *Science,* 1981, 213, 1392–1394.

Jenkins, W. O., & Postman, L. Isolation and spread of effect in serial learning. *American Journal of Psychology,* 1948, 61, 214–221.

Jones, F. N., & Jones, M. H. Vividness as a factor in learning lists of nonsense syllables. *American Journal of Psychology,* 1942, 55, 96–101.

Kety, S. S. Brain catecholamines, affective states, and memory. In J. L. McGaugh (Ed.), *The chemistry of mood, motivation, and memory.* New York: Plenum, 1972.

Muller, G. E., & Pilzecker, A. Experimentalle beitrage zur lehre vom gedachtnis. *Zeitschrift fur Psychologie,* 1900, 1, 1–300.

Russell, W. R., & Nathan, P. Traumatic amnesia. *Brain,* 1946, 69, 280–300.

Saufley, W. H., & Winograd, E. Retrograde amnesia and priority instructions in free recall. *Journal of Experimental Psychology,* 1970, 85, 150–152.

Schacter, D. L., & Tulving, E. Amnesia and memory research. In L. S. Cermak (Ed.), *Human memory and amnesia.* Hillsdale, N.J.: Erlbaum, 1981.

Schulz, L. S. Effects of high-priority events on recall and recognition of other events. *Journal of Verbal Learning and Behavior,* 1971, 10, 322–330.

Smith, M. H., & Sterns, E. G. The influence of isolation on the learning of surrounding materials. *American Journal of Psychology,* 1949, 62, 369–381.

Squire, L. R., Slater, P. C., & Chace, P. M. Retrograde amnesia: Temporal gradient in very long-term memory following electroconvulsive therapy. *Science,* 1975, 187, 77–79.

Stern, L. D. A review of theories of human amnesia. *Memory & Cognition,* 1981, 9, 247–262.

Tulving, E. Retrograde amnesia in free recall. *Science,* 1969, 164, 88–90.

Wall, P. M. *Eyewitness identification in criminal cases.* Springfield, Ill: Thomas, 1965.

Wallace, W. P. Review of the historical, empirical, and theoretical status of the von Restorff phenomenon. *Psychological Bulletin,* 1965, 63, 410–424.

Whitty, C. W. M., & Zangwill, O. L. *Amnesia* (2nd edition). London: Butterworths, 1977.

Woocher, F. D. Did your eyes deceive you?: Expert psychological testimony on the unreliability of eyewitness identification. *Stanford Law Review,* 1977, 29, 969–1031.

CHAPTER EXERCISES

5.1. In the three experiments reported by Loftus and Burns, the label that best describes the logic and architecture of the experimental design used in each experiment is

Experiment 1:
Experiment 2:
Experiment 3:

5.2. Describe the independent variable in each of the three experiments reported by Loftus and Burns.

Experiment 1:
Experiment 2:
Experiment 3:

5.3. Loftus and Burns measured several different variables that they suspected might be influenced by their independent variable. List each dependent variable in each of the three experiments and discuss the reason for making each of these measurements. Also identify the scale of measurement that best describes each of the dependent variables.

5.4. In arranging the mechanical details of their experiments, Loftus and Burns described a number of different variables that would be considered controlled variables in the logic and architecture of their experiments. Describe as many different controlled variables as you can identify in each of the three experiments.

5.5. In discussing the results of Experiment 2, Loftus and Burns identify a variable they suspect to be confounded with their independent variable. What is the confounded variable and how does the logic of the third experiment deal with this confounding?

5.6. Give one example of a descriptive statistic that was used in dealing with the results of the first experiment reported by Loftus and Burns. Explain how it was calculated and what characteristic of the data it describes (e.g., central tendency, variability, etc.).

5.7. Explain in your own words what it means to accept an experimental hypothesis and reject a null hypothesis in the first experiment reported by Loftus and Burns.

5.8. If you were unable to do Exercises 5.1 through 5.6, you do not understand the basic material in Chapter 5. You should go back and read it again before proceeding to the next chapter.

CHAPTER 6

MORE COMPLICATED ANALYTIC EXPERIMENTS

Think back to the previous chapter and the ten-minute travel film that we used in our hypothetical memory experiment. We were interested in the effects of an emotional shock upon the ability to remember information presented at the end of the film. Specifically, the memory test required that the subject recall prices of some products for sale in an open-air market.

To introduce you to the material in the present chapter, we shall use this same basic travel film (the version without the mutilated body) and ask yet a second question about human memory. Two different sensory systems are at work when you "watch" a travel film. Some of the information is visual and some is auditory. The price on a handwoven basket for sale in the market could either be *seen* on a price tag or *heard* from the vendor. Is our memory for visual information better or worse than our memory for auditory information?

With some clever camera work and a little bit of film editing, we should be able to produce two versions of our travel film that differ in only one respect. In the *auditory version* of the film, each vendor will mention the price as part of an oral description of the product. In the *visual version* of the film, the auditory information will be deleted and a brief visual image of the price tag will be substituted. At the end of the film, we can ask each subject ten questions about the prices of various products to test memory for this information.

With this example, we shall not go into the particulars of forming a hypothesis, defining terms operationally, and the mechanical details of the experiment. To refresh your memory, however, Figure 6.1 presents the basic logic and architecture of an experiment designed to answer this question about memory (see panel 1). Figure 6.1 also compares this experiment to the one concerned with the effects of emotional shock, discussed in Chapter 5 (see panel 2). You should know, at this point, that both experiments are best described as *bivalent, between-subject analytic experiments*. We also assume that you can identify all important elements in the experiments, such as the independent, dependent, and controlled variables.

Assume for a moment that we actually conducted these two experiments and obtained the results presented in Figure 6.2. The results in panel 1 of Figure 6.2 tell us that the subjects recalled the visual information better than they recalled the auditory information. The results in panel 2 of Figure 6.2 are consistent with the data reported by Loftus and Burns (1982). They tell us that an emotional shock disrupts memory for preceding events. At this point in the discussion, it is clear that we have answered *two* questions about human memory by using two different bivalent analytic experiments.

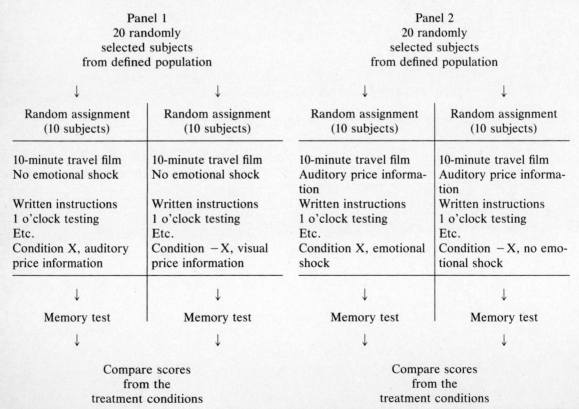

Figure 6.1 Two bivalent, between-subjects analytic experiments, each designed to answer one question about human memory.

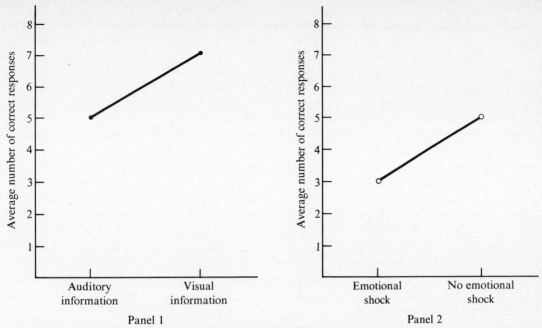

Figure 6.2 Hypothetical results of the two bivalent memory experiments. Panel 1 compares average number of items recalled under auditory and visual treatment; Panel 2 compares average number of items recalled under the two treatment conditions.

Consider now a third, related question about memory. Does the disruptive effect of an emotional shock upon memory occur with both auditory and visual information?

The results of the two hypothetical experiments in Figure 6.1 tell us (1) that auditory information is not remembered as well as visual information and (2) that emotional shock disrupts memory. They do not, however, tell us whether the disruptive effects of emotional shock will be equivalent for both auditory and visual information. The primary purpose of the present chapter is to show you how to extend the logic of the simple bivalent analytic experiment into a more complicated architecture that will answer all *three* questions about memory in a *single* experiment. This more complicated architecture is called a *factorial experiment*. You will discover that the factorial experiment is an incredibly efficient device for answering questions that would otherwise require a less efficient and less effective series of bivalent or multivalent analytic experiments.

A SIMPLE ANALYTIC FACTORIAL EXPERIMENT

Asking a Question

The majority of behavioral phenomena will be influenced (caused) by a wide variety of conditions. Hence, many of the questions that arise about any particular phenomenon will identify more than one factor as a "causal agent." If, for example, we ask whether emotional shock disrupts memory for both auditory and visual information, we have identified two factors that might be involved in the process of forgetting: emotional shock and sensory modality.

Forming a Hypothesis

Once again, a question usually identifies the factors suspected to act as causal agents. If you convert the question to a declarative statement, you have a hypothesis. This hypothesis can be stated with varying degrees of formality with reference to the nature of the suspected causal relationship. When dealing with two possible causal variables, a formal hypothesis might state, for example, that *an overbite is a necessary condition for the development of bruxism, and that a combination of the overbite with a high level of anxiety forms the necessary and sufficient conditions for the development of bruxism.* This formal prediction is particularly interesting in that it suggests that an overbite is necessary but not sufficient when it occurs alone. Anxiety must also be present for bruxism to develop. The factorial experiment provides a unique method for identifying causal relationships in which a phenomenon occurs only when a particular combination of independent variables act together simultaneously.

With reference to our experiment concerned with the combined effects of emotional shock and sensory modality, it is perhaps best at this point to keep the hypothesis informal, in the interrogative form: *Does emotional shock disrupt memory for both auditory and visual information?* Given the state of our knowledge about these processes, it would seem somehow presumptuous to make predictions about necessary and sufficient causal relationships in this context.

Designing the Factorial Experiment

Designing a factorial experiment is a three-stage process. First, any time the question under consideration identifies more than one suspected causal factor (e.g., the overbite plus anxiety), you must identify each of the causal factors in the question. Our question about memory identified *two* possible causal factors: (1) the emotional shock and (2) the sensory modality involved in learning the information. Once you have identified the causal factors, the second step requires you to decide how many *levels* of each factor you want to consider in your experiment. In our hypothetical memory experiment, we will keep things simple and consider just two levels of each of the two causal factors: (1) emotional shock vs. no emotional shock and (2) auditory vs. visual memory information. You should realize, of course, that it is possible to design experiments with several levels of each factor (e.g., severe emotional shock, mild emotional shock, and no emotional shock).

Thus far we have (1) identified two factors suspected to influence memory and (2) decided to investigate two levels of each factor. The third step in designing the experiment is to determine how many combinations of each of the factors at each level are possible. Continuing with our memory example, we can combine the emotional shock treatment with the auditory condition and with the visual condition. We can also combine the condition that has no emotional shock with the auditory condition and the visual condition. Thus there are four possible combinations of treatment conditions in our memory experiment. These four combinations are illustrated in Figure 6.3 as (1) emotional shock plus auditory information, (2) emotional shock plus visual information, (3) no emotional shock plus auditory information, and (4) no emotional shock plus visual information.

Once you have defined these four possible treatment combinations, you are ready to select a sample of subjects and randomly assign them to the treatment conditions illustrated in Figure 6.3. With the various subjects assigned to each of the treatment combinations, you can proceed to arrange the details of the procedure and complete your experiment.

You should now be able to see that the factorial design makes use of the same basic logic we used in the simple analytic experiment. As indicated in Figure 6.4, all conditions are held constant (controlled variables) in each of the treatment groups except the particular combination of treatment conditions that the experimenter wants to contrast (the independent variables). Memory performance is compared across all four possible combinations of treatment in the design. In fact, it is instructive, at this point, to note that you can make the same basic comparisons between treatment conditions in Figure 6.4 as we made with the two bivalent experiments described at the beginning of the chapter (Figure 6.1). Specifically, in Figure 6.4 you can compare the memory performance in condition X_1 to that in condition $-X_1$. This comparison is essentially the same as that in the original bivalent experiment in which we compared the effects of emotional shock and no emotional shock upon memory (note that the information

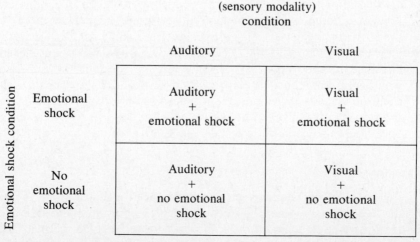

Figure 6.3 A contingency table that defines the four possible treatment combinations resulting from two treatment factors, each at two levels.

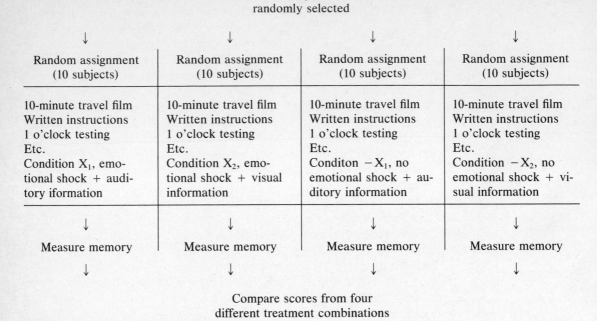

Figure 6.4 The logic and architecture of a factorial design with two different independent variables each at two levels of treatment.

was auditory in both groups). Similarly, in Figure 6.4, if you compare condition $-X_1$ to condition $-X_2$, you essentially have a bivalent experiment that compares memory performance for auditory vs. visual information (note that there is no emotional shock in either of these treatment groups). Hence, the two original bivalent experiments that answered our two original questions about memory remain as components of the factorial design.

Are the effects of emotional shock the same for both auditory and visual information? This was the question our two original bivalent experiments could not answer, and you will soon discover that the factorial experiment can give you this information. The real beauty of the factorial experiment is that it answers both our original questions about memory and also gives us an answer to this third question. However, before we continue, we shall digress briefly and introduce you to some basic terms.

Relevant Terminology

Fortunately, all the terms introduced in Chapter 5 also apply to the elements of the factorial experiment. The two variables you manipulated as causal agent in the hypothetical memory experiment illustrated in Figure 6.4 are called *independent variables* (note that the term "factors" is used interchangeably with the term "independent variables" in discussing factorial experiments). The measure of memory performance used in the procedure is the *dependent variable*. Finally, the variables held constant across the different treatment conditions are called *controlled variables*.

Conventional usage describes the memory experiment we have been discussing in the present chapter as a *2 × 2 factorial* design. Each numeral refers to a different independent variable, and the numeral itself describes the number of levels of that variable used in the experiment. Hence, the memory experiment in Figure 6.4 is a two (emotional shock vs. no emotional shock) by two (auditory vs. visual information) design. Using the same terminology, a 2 × 3 factorial experiment would have two levels of one independent variable and three levels of a second independent variable to form six possible treatment combinations (groups) in the experiment. Similarly, a 2 × 2 × 2 factorial experiment would have three independent variables each at two levels. How many treatment combinations would occur in the 2 × 2 × 2 architecture? To further test your understanding, look at one additional modification of our hypothetical memory experiment illustrated in Figure 6.5 and see if you can label it correctly.

Finally, in all the examples of factorial experiments described thus far, a separate group of subjects is assigned to each of the treatment combinations. If

	Information (sensory modality) condition	
	Auditory	Visual
No emotional shock	Auditory + no emotional shock	Visual + no emotional shock
Mild emotional shock	Auditory + mild emotional shock	Visual + mild emotional shock
Severe emotional shock	Auditory + severe emotional shock	Visual + severe emotional shock

(The left-hand axis is labeled: Emotional shock treatment condition)

Figure 6.5 A factorial design to test your skills with the terminology. What is the appropriate name for this design, what are the independent variables, and how many levels are there for each independent variable?

you glance back to Figure 6.4, you will note that the experiment started with a sample of 40 subjects. Ten subjects were then randomly assigned to each of the four treatment combinations. As such, each of the examples would be called *between-subjects factorial experiments*. Note that it is also possible to employ factorial designs in which each subject is exposed to all the treatment combinations in some predetermined order. These are appropriately called *within-subject factorial experiments*. Similarly, it is possible to use a between-subjects procedure for some treatment combinations and a within-subjects procedure for other treatment combinations in the same factorial experiment. This procedure is appropriately called a *mixed between- and within-subject factorial experiment*. Each of these variations on the basic *between-subjects* factorial experiment raises some special problems that can be discussed more efficiently in subsequent chapters. For the time being, you should know that these variations exist and memorize the appropriate terminology.

ANALYZING THE RESULTS

Combined Effects

Assume for the moment that we actually conducted the 2×2 factorial experiment illustrated in Figure 6.4 and obtained the results plotted in Figure 6.6. When you look at the graphed results of a factorial experiment, it is a useful tactic to first ask yourself questions about the effects of just one independent variable (e.g., emotional shock) and then proceed to consider the *combined effects* of both independent variables. With reference to Figure 6.6, first examine the effects of emotional shock upon memory. If you look at the filled circles, you will note that emotional shock disrupted memory somewhat. The score under emotional shock is 3, as compared to 5 in the condition in which no emotional shock was used. Note, however, that the filled circles compare the effects of the presence and absence of emotional shock when the material to be remembered was auditory. If you examine the open circles in Figure 6.6 next and ask about the effects of emotional shock, you will observe a very different story. Specifically, memory is equally good in both the presence and absence of emotional shock (a score of 7 in both cases).

The hypothetical results in Figure 6.6 have been concocted to illustrate the usefulness of the factorial experiment. If, after reading the Loftus and Burns experiment in Chapter 5, you had been asked about the effects of emotional shock on memory, your answer would have been to say that emotional shock disrupts memory. If, after reading the results of the two bivalent experiments plotted in Figure 6.2, you had been asked about the effects of emotional shock on memory, your answer would again have been that emotional shock disrupts memory. However, now that you have completed the factorial experiment and obtained the results plotted in Figure 6.6, if you were asked about the effects of emotional shock on memory, your answer must be modified. Specifically, you must say: *The effects of emotional shock on memory depend on the sensory*

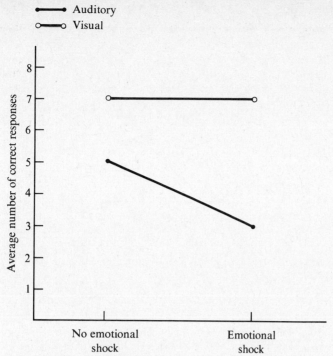

Figure 6.6 Hypothetical results of a 2 x 2 factorial experiment concerned with the effects of emotional shock and sensory modality upon memory. The data indicate that the two variables *interact* in their effects upon memory.

modality used to store the information. Emotional shock disrupts memory for auditory information, but it has no effect on memory for visual information.

The essential point made by this hypothetical example is that *the effects of one independent variable (emotional shock) are different at different levels of the other independent variable (auditory vs. visual).* When the effects of one independent variable are different at the different levels of the other independent variable, we say that an *interaction* has occurred in our factorial experiment.

To fully appreciate the meaning of the term "interaction," it is worthwhile to examine some data in which *no* interaction occurs between the independent variables. To this end, imagine that we again conduct our hypothetical 2 × 2 factorial memory experiment, and this time we obtain the results illustrated in Figure 6.7. Once again, look at the graph and ask yourself a question about the effects of emotional shock on memory. If you look first at the filled circles, it is obvious that the emotional shock treatment disrupted memory (an average score of 3 as compared to 5 in the condition without emotional shock). The filled circles represent performance when the material to be remembered was auditory. If you look next at the open circles, it is also obvious that emotional shock disrupts memory performance (a score of 5 as compared to a score of 7 without emotional shock).

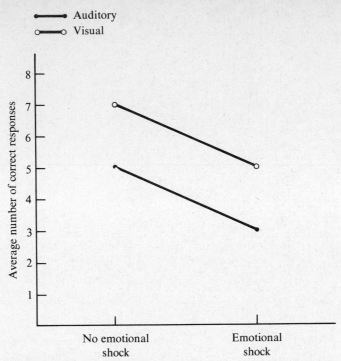

Figure 6.7 Hypothetical results of a 2 x 2 factorial experiment concerned with the effects of emotional shock and sensory modality upon memory. The data indicate that the two variables are *additive* in their effects upon memory.

The essential point illustrated by the data in Figure 6.7 is that emotional shock disrupts memory and it does so to an equivalent degree in both the auditory and visual conditions. When the effects of one independent variable (emotional shock) are essentially equivalent at both levels of another independent variable (auditory vs. visual), we say that the combined effects of the two independent variables are *additive*.

To summarize briefly, the two independent variables in a 2×2 factorial experiment can have two different types of combined effect on memory: they can interact or they can be additive. Figures 6.6 and 6.7 provide one example from each of these two possible categories. The real value of the factorial design is particularly obvious in the case of an *interaction*. As the data in Figure 6.6 show, an interaction typically requires us to modify the conclusions that we would have reached if we had conducted two separate bivalent experiments with two independent variables.

Main Effects

In the preceding paragraphs, we have described how to interpret the combined effects of two independent variables in a factorial design. We considered these examples of combined effects first because they demonstrate the value of the factorial design when compared to a series of bivalent experiments. It is also possible, however, to extract information from a factorial design about the effects of each independent variable considered alone. Referring again to the results of the memory experiment illustrated in Figure 6.7, we can ask the following questions: (1) what are the effects of the emotional shock (ignoring the auditory and visual conditions) and (2) what are the effects of the auditory and visual conditions (ignoring the effects of the emotional shock condition)? To answer the first question, you simply sum the scores obtained in the emotional shock condition across both the auditory and visual conditions (5 + 3 = 8), and compare this sum to the sum of scores across the auditory and visual conditions in the case of "no emotional shock" (7 + 5 = 12). Hence, you can see that the *main effect* of the emotional shock variable (ignoring or summing across auditory and visual conditions) is a net loss of memory performance under emotional shock.

To answer the second question, we simply sum the scores obtained under visual conditions across both levels of the emotional shock condition (7 + 5 = 12), and compare this to the sum of scores across the two levels of emotional shock in the auditory condition (5 + 3 = 8). Thus, the main effect of the sensory modality independent variable is that memory suffers a net loss when the material to be remembered was presented in the auditory modality.

Please note that you will feel comfortable speaking exclusively about the *main effects* of the independent variables only when the combined effects are additive. When there is an interaction, it is difficult to discuss the main effects without qualifying your statement by describing the interaction. The main effects alone will not provide a complete description of the results when an interaction is present.

Statistical Issues

You will note that we have judiciously avoided any mention of statistical matters in discussing the results of the factorial experiments described in the preceding pages. You should know, however, that the basic rationale for computing these statistics is essentially the same as that used in the simpler examples discussed in Chapter 5 and Appendix D. The computations are, of course, more involved. You should be content at this point to examine the results of any factorial experiment, identify all the independent variables, describe the main effects, and interpret the combined effects. Indeed, if you want to test your skills, you might examine yet a third set of hypothetical results in Figure 6.8. Can you identify the independent variables and describe both main effects and combined effects?

SIMPLE VS. COMPLEX ANALYTIC EXPERIMENTS

The "Gold Standard"

In Chapter 5 we considered simple bivalent and multivalent analytic experiments. In the present chapter we have discussed more complicated analytic experiments in which the scientist manipulates more than one independent variable in a single

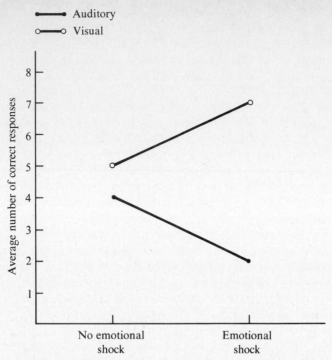

Figure 6.8 Hypothetical results of a 2 x 2 factorial experiment concerned with the effects of emotional shock and sensory modality upon memory. Describe these results in terms of the main effects and combined effects of the two independent variables.

experiment. I hope you understand that the logic underlying both the simple and complex analytic experiments is the same. The more complex experiments simply have a more elaborate structure based upon this same basic logic.

You should also appreciate that these basic experimental designs (analytic experiments) are the most potent and effective procedures available to a scientist who wishes to explore causal relationships in nature. I am particularly taken with the metaphor used by Feinstein and Horowitz (1982) to describe the analytic experiment. They refer to these procedures as the "gold standard" of scientific research methods. I like this metaphor for two basic reasons. First, over the long haul, history tells us that holding gold has been among the most reliable ways to maintain accumulated wealth. A friend who is an economist tells me that an ounce of gold purchases about the same amount of most commodities today as it did several hundred years ago—obviously a better record than that of paper currency! The analytic experiment is much the same in my opinion. In the long run, it is perhaps the best single procedure we can use to explore the various causal relationships we suspect might operate in nature. There are, as you will discover shortly, alternatives to the analytic experiment. Like paper currency, however, their purchasing power is less stable.

The second alternative aspect of the gold-standard metaphor is that one must assess the purchasing power of gold over a long period of time—not on a daily basis. On any given day (as commodity dealers know), gold can fail miserably. Once again, the same can be said of the analytic experiment. In spite of our best efforts to apply the logic of the analytic experiment to a particular situation, on any given day unsuspected and undetected confounded variables can seriously undermine the validity of the procedure. The history of science tells us, however, that eventually such problems are detected and new information gradually accumulates to make nature more understandable and predictable. The moral of this story is simple. The analytic experiment is perhaps the best method available for the development and maintenance of the "scientific wealth" we call knowledge.

If you think about the material discussed in the past two chapters for a moment, you will realize that I have provided you with several examples of analytic experiments that vary from simple bivalent experiments to complex examples with two or more independent variables. In all of this discussion, however, I have not *explicitly* listed those factors that uniquely describe the analytic experiment as a procedure. There are, of course, many pitfalls associated with any attempt to reduce such a complex entity to a set of identifying features. Nevertheless, I would suggest that there are perhaps three characteristics in any experiment that would qualify it, in the strictest sense, as an analytic experiment. These characteristics are (1) random selection of subjects from a defined population, (2) random assignment of subjects to different treatment conditions, and (3) concurrent contrast and control of the relevant variables. It is perhaps worthwhile to review each of these characteristics briefly before we proceed to the next chapter and consider some *deviations* from these characteristics.

Random Selection of Subjects

Scientists should always specify the population to which they hope their observations will generalize. Once that population has been defined and if the entire population cannot be included in an experiment, a sample must be selected. While there are many ways to select a sample of subjects from the population, you now realize that a *random sampling procedure* must be used in order for the experiment to qualify as an analytic experiment (see Chapter 2, p. 29).

Random Assignment of Subjects to Treatments

Scientists can assign a sample of subjects to different treatment conditions in many ways. In the preceding discussion, we have limited our analysis to the *between-subject* designs in which each subject has an equal probability of being assigned to each treatment condition in the experiment. This *random assignment* of subjects to treatments is a second identifying feature of the analytic experiment (see p. 29).

Concurrent Contrast and Control of Relevant Variables

In an analytic experiment, the scientist *contrasts* different levels of the suspected causal variable and *concurrently* holds constant the influence of all other variables in the situation. This concurrent contrast and control of the relevant variables is the earmark of the analytic experiment. Unless all factors except the one (or several) to be contrasted are controlled, claims for the causal influence of the contrasted variable are tenuous.

As you become more familiar with research in the social sciences, you will discover that it is difficult to find pure examples of this gold standard called the analytic experiment. Most research deviates from these three basic criteria in one respect or another, and the deviations are often unavoidable. This is, however, a story to be told in subsequent chapters. For now, you must understand the logic and architecture of analytic experiments.

AN ACTUAL FACTORIAL EXPERIMENT

To complete the discussion of the material in this chapter, we have reprinted with their permission a research report by Tomlinson, Hicks, and Pellegrini (1978). The article was chosen partly because it deviates from the theme of memory research used throughout the chapter and partly because it deviates slightly from the basic architecture of the experiment we have been using as an example. Hence, your understanding of the concepts we have been discussing will be tested in a context that is slightly different from our well-worn examples. How well can you generalize the principles that you have learned?

When you have read the article, the Chapter Exercises that follow will once again help you test your understanding of the material.

ATTRIBUTIONS OF FEMALE COLLEGE STUDENTS TO VARIATIONS IN PUPIL SIZE

NANCY TOMLINSON, ROBERT A. HICKS, AND ROBERT J. PELLEGRINI

San Jose State University, San Jose, California 95192

Abstract

Ratings were obtained from 246 female college students to the full-face photographs of a male and female peer. For each model, the photographs had been retouched to provide a continuum of pupil sizes (i.e., small, moderately large, and large). Consistent with a limited literature, a significant inverse linear trend was observed between pupil size and the positiveness of the like-sex ratings. The relationship between pupil size and the positiveness of the cross-sex ratings was an unanticipated inverted U-shaped curve. The significance of these data for the pupil size-nonverbal communication literature was discussed.

As a consequence of recent reviews of the pupillometric literature, Hess (1975b) and Janisse (1977) have reached dissimilar conclusions concerning the role of pupil size in nonverbal communication. Largely on the basis of his own research (also see Hess, 1975a, and Hess & Goodwin, 1974, for reviews), Hess has concluded that pupil size is important in nonverbal communication in that it appears to act as an innate releaser for certain prosocial behaviors (e.g., sexual interest). In contrast, Janisse concluded that, at best, pupil size is a trivial variable in the nonverbal communication process.

Perhaps the most striking feature of these conclusions is that they are based on what can charitably be described as a weak and very limited data base. At this time, it seems premature to classify pupil size as an innate releaser or to dismiss it as a relatively meaningless variable. In fact, a fair bit of research seems to be indicated before any reliable conclusions can be drawn concerning the role of pupil size in the nonverbal communication process. For example, not one study has been published that measured effective responses to more than two pupil sizes. That is, the relationship between a continuum of pupil sizes and affective ratings has yet to be established.

The purpose of this research was to measure the attributions of female college students to photographs of a male and a female peer in which the pupils had been retouched to provide a 3-point continuum of pupil size. We

Tomlinson, N., Hicks, R. A., and Pellegrini, R. J. 1978. Attributions of female college students to variations in pupil size. *Bulletin of the Psychonomic Society, 12,* 477–478.

selected females as subjects because limited previous research has shown that women tend to rate increases in pupil size in photos of men and women in opposite directions, that is, more positively for men and less positively for women (see Hess & Goodwin, 1974). Since these relationships between like- and cross-sexed stimulus persons has not been as clearly established (or as adequately studied) in men, it was thought that the responses of a sample of women would provide the most sensitive first test of the relationship in question.

METHOD

Subjects

A group of 246 female college students, who were enrolled in classes that were primarily of interest to women, were the subjects for this study. These subjects were tested in groups during the class periods.

Materials and Procedure

The photographs of the male and female stimulus persons were selected in the following manner. First, from a commercial photographer, we obtained a large number of full-face photos of persons who appeared to fall within the age range that is typical of most college undergraduates. From this group, we selected the photos of 10 males and 10 females that seemed to us to be moderately attractive. Next, a 35-mm slide of each photograph was prepared. These slides were shown to a group of 35 judges, who rated each photograph for attractiveness on a 7-point graphic scale. The male and female photographs that were rated nearest the midpoint of the scale with the least variance were selected as the stimulus persons. Next, each of these photos was retouched so that, for each person, three identical photos were created that varied only in pupil size. The area of the iris covered by the small, moderately large (medium), and large pupils were 6%, 29%, and 46%, respectively. Finally, for each of the resulting six photographs, a 35-mm slide was prepared, and these slides were shown to our subjects.

The rating scales used were identical with those used by Hicks, Reaney, and Hill (1967) in a similar study. Essentially, these were two 5-point graphic scales bounded by sets of bipolar adjectives (i.e., pleasant-unpleasant and warm-cold).

The subjects were handed six sets of rating scales and then were asked to rate each photograph on both of the 5-point scales as these were projected onto a screen at the front of the room. Each slide was projected for a 30-sec period, and a 30-sec interslide interval was used. The order of presentation was randomized for each.

To obtain a score for each person for each slide, the person's two ratings for a given slide were summed, and thus six scores were derived for each subject.

RESULTS AND DISCUSSION

The summed rating data for each stimulus person by pupil size photograph are summarized in Table 1.

First, these data were analyzed using an analysis of variance (ANOVA). The results of this ANOVA revealed significant main effects for both sex of model [$F(1,490) = 162.9$, $P < .001$] and pupil size [$F(2,980) = 16.05$, $P < .001$]. Further, the Sex of Model by Pupil Size interaction was also significant [$F(2,980) = 11.58$, $P < .001$].

The significant main effect for sex of model was unexpected, since we had thought that we had equated these photographs for attractiveness during the preexperimental procedures used in selecting the final two stimulus persons. Apparently, when given a two-choice option, as was the case here, subjects will select one as more attractive, and this will be reflected in the overall mean ratings.

Both the significant pupil size main effect and the Sex of Model by Pupil Size interaction were anticipated. However, the difference in the pattern of the female and male pupil size mean do not conform to the inverse and direct relationships for like- and cross-sex ratings that were mentioned earlier. To further elaborate the functions indicated by the sets of means given in Table 1, trend analyses were computed from the male and female model data. This analysis of the female model data revealed a significant linear trend [$F(1,490) = 26.83$, $P < .001$]. As a result of a separate analysis of the male model data, a significant quadratic trend was obtained [$F(1,490) = 25.10$, $P < .001$]. The linear trend observed when females rate pupil sizes in other females lends reliability to the results of an earlier study (i.e., Hicks et al., 1967) that observed a similar trend using only two pupil sizes. The significant inverted U-shaped trend that characterized the cross-sex ratings obtained in this study may help to clarify inconsistencies in the literature. As Janisse's (1977) recent review carefully documents, the few studies that have considered cross-sex responsiveness to a small-large pupil dichotomy reported either a direct relationship between pupil size and positiveness of response or no relationship at all. Given the reliability of our data, then, either of these results could be obtained with a dichotomous manipulation of pupil size, depending, of course, on the size

Table 1   Means and Standard Deviations of the Summed Ratings for the Six Photographs

Sex of Model	Pupil size					
	Small		Medium		Large	
	Mean	SD	Mean	SD	Mean	SD
Female	7.7	1.7	7.2	2.0	6.8	2.0
Male	5.4	2.1	5.9	1.9	5.2	2.0

of the large pupil used. However, since previous studies have failed to report the percent of iris covered by the pupils used, we cannot determine the validity of this possibility.

Finally, we wish to point out certain reservations we have concerning the generalizability of these findings. We did not use male subjects for the reasons given earlier. Clearly, the relationships we have reported here may only apply to females. Further, as mentioned, we were surprised by the significant (and substantial) main effect for sex of model. Although we have rationalized this is an artifact of the procedure used, this may not be the case at all. Perhaps, the functions we have observed here were not the result of cross- and like-sex ratings but, rather, were primarily the result of rating relatively more attractive and less attractive models. We are currently testing for this possibility.

REFERENCES

Hess, E. H. The role of the pupil size in communication. *Scientific American,* 1975, *233,* 110–119. (a)

Hess, E. H. *The tell-tale eye.* New York: Van Nostrand Reinhold, 1975. (b)

Hess, E. H. & Goodwin, E. The present state of pupillometrics. In M. P. Janisse (Ed.), *Pupillary dynamics and behavior.* New York: Plenum, 1974.

Hicks, R. A., Reaney, T., & Hill, L. Effects of pupil size and facial angle on preference for photographs of a young woman. *Perceptual and Motor Skills,* 1967, *24,* 388–390.

Janisse, M. P. *Pupillometry: The psychology of the pupillary response.* Washington, D.C.: Hemisphere, 1977.

(Received for publication September 19, 1978)

CHAPTER EXERCISES

In the experiment reported by Tomlinson and co-workers:

6.1. What are the independent variables?

6.2. What is (are) the dependent variables?

6.3. Can you list some of the more important controlled variables?

6.4. What is the best term to describe the experimental design used?

6.5. Can you describe the main effects of each of the independent variables and the combined effects of the independent variables?

CHAPTER 7

ANALYTIC EXPERIMENTS: EXTERNAL AND ECOLOGICAL VALIDITY

Visintainer, Volpicelli, and Seligman, three psychologists from the University of Pennsylvania, published an interesting experiment in the journal *Science* several years ago (1981). It was designed to test the hypothesis that psychological stress causes cancer. In this experiment, 93 healthy adult male rats were injected with a preparation of Walker 256 tumor cells which, under normal conditions, will induce tumor growth in about 50 percent of the recipient rats. Twenty-four hours after the tumor preparation was injected, the rats were randomly assigned to three different treatment groups. In the group called the "escapable shock condition," each rat was placed in a chamber with a grid floor and a lever protruding through one wall. At random intervals, 60 mild electric shocks were delivered through the grid floor. Each shock lasted for 60 seconds unless the animal pressed the lever to terminate it; hence, the term "escapable" shock condition.

In a second group, called the "inescapable shock condition," each rat also received 60 electric shocks. These rats could not, however, terminate or control the shocks. Each rat in this inescapable shock group received the shocks in a pattern matched or "yoked" to one of his counterparts in the escapable shock group. The essential point is that the rats in the inescapable shock condition had to take the shocks as they came; there was no way to control when the shocks began or when they terminated. Finally, the third group of rats were placed in the chamber for the same period of time but did not receive any shocks. This group was aptly called the "no shock condition." All three groups were treated the same in all other respects during the experiment.

With reference to this experiment, note that existing research has demonstrated that stress is produced by the shock treatments described above and that the inescapable shock condition is a particularly effective method for producing stress. In other words, the inescapable shock condition is a widely accepted operational definition of stress.

The primary question of interest in the experiment was whether or not these three different treatment conditions would have any effect on the development of cancer in those rats that were exposed to the Walker 256 tumor cells. Figure 7.1 describes the basic logic, architecture, and results of the experiment. As the data indicate, 54 percent of the no shock group rejected the tumor preparation. This was the expected rate of rejection for this dosage of Walker 256 cells. Note, however, that only 27 percent of the high-stress animals (inescapable shock condition) managed to reject the tumor preparation. Seventy-three percent of these stressed animals developed palpable tumors during the 30-day period following the injection. Finally, 63 percent of the animals in the less stressful escapable shock condition rejected the tumor preparation. The data, therefore,

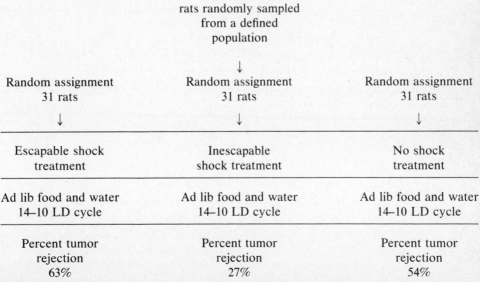

Figure 7.1 Logic and architecture of the experiment concerned with the effects of stress upon rejection of Walter 256 reduced tremors (Visintainer, Volpicelli, and Seligman, 1982). The design is best described as a between-subjects multivalent analytic experiment (see Chapter 5, Figure 5.4).

support the hypothesis that a psychological variable like stress can play an important role in the development of malignant tumors. As you might imagine, this experiment generated a substantial amount of interest. You might like to consult Cunningham (1985) for a more complete discussion of the topic.

INTERNAL VS. EXTERNAL VALIDITY

You will recognize the experiment described above as a between-subjects multivalent analytic design. The independent variable is the three levels of stress treatment operationally defined as no shock, escapable shock, and inescapable shock. The dependent variable is the percentage of rats able to reject the effects of the Walker 256 tumor preparation. Rats were randomly assigned to treatment conditions, and variables such as the food and water supply were held constant across the three groups. As such, the experiment meets all the basic criteria of an analytic experiment as outlined in Chapter 5 (p. 113).

When you have met the criteria of an analytic experiment and can find no reason to suspect a confounded variable, you may assume that the experiment has *internal validity*. This term, initially suggested by Campbell and Stanley (1963), means you can logically conclude that any differences observed in the treatment groups were produced by the independent variable. Of course, if you discover one or more confounded variables in your experiment, the internal logic is disrupted and the validity of any causal claim is questionable. *The confounded variable is the main threat to the internal validity of an analytic experiment.*

Thus far, we have been primarily concerned with the internal validity of experiments. The present chapter will examine an equally important concept called *external validity* which was briefly mentioned in Chapter 5 (p. 108). Basically, an experiment has external validity if we can expect to observe the same results over a wider range of conditions than those specifically used in the original experiment. To what extent can the claims made about stress and cancer by Visintainer and his colleagues be generalized beyond the specific conditions of their experiment? Will these claims generalize to humans? Will they generalize to other stressful experiences, or are these results unique to the specific set of conditions used in this experiment? If these results are confined to the specific conditions in this experiment, we can conclude that the experiment has internal validity but lacks external validity. You will probably agree that external validity is a very important concept, particularly for the consumer of scientific information. If this particular experiment with laboratory rats has external validity, the results will have important implications for your personal life-style; you might, that is, want to reduce the amount of stress in your life. If the experiment lacks external validity, you will be less concerned about these data.

In the next few pages we will deal with the difficult problem of assessing the external validity of an experiment. A lot of attention has been given to this issue over the years (cf. Berkowitz & Donnerstein, 1982; Mook, 1983; Ostrom, 1984); you should be forewarned that there is no generally accepted procedure for precisely measuring external validity. Despite these problems, I will, in the following discussion, describe an approach to the issue that should help you come to your own conclusions about the external validity of the research you encounter.

In my opinion, there are four important factors to consider when you assess the external validity of any particular experiment. These are (1) the population from which the sample of subjects used in the experiment was selected, (2) the operational definitions used in the experiment, (3) the parameter values of the variables that were manipulated and held constant in the experiment, and (4) any demand characteristics that might be operating in the experimental procedure. Some of these terms are probably foreign to you at present. You will become familiar with them as we discuss each in the order mentioned.

Population Selection and External Validity

When Visintainer et al. decided to use laboratory rats for their experiment, they made an important decision with reference to external validity. Most students consider the use of laboratory rats a serious threat to the external validity of psychological research. They feel that any results obtained with rats will have very little application to human beings. In one sense, this is a valid criticism. If you do research with a population of laboratory rats, any attempt to generalize your results directly to a human population will always be questionable. Similarly, if you do research with human males, the generalization to females must be made with caution; or if you do research with Caucasians, the generalization to Orientals will be questionable. In theory, you must use caution in any attempt to generalize your results beyond the population from which you have selected subjects and, unfortunately, there is no ruler to measure the size of the chance you take when you claim that your results will generalize.

In actual practice, scientists seem to use a somewhat subjective "rubber ruler" to judge external validity. I call this ruler "the principle of converging evidence." Basically, scientists interested in the results reported by Visintainer et al. will ask themselves whether or not the laboratory rat is a "unique" animal. Does, for example, the available evidence indicate that rats are similar to humans in their feeding habits, sleeping habits, physiological functions, and behavior? Does the available evidence suggest that rats are similar to other animals (including humans) in their physiological and behavioral responses to stress? Does the available evidence indicate that the cancers we find in rats are similar to those we see in other animals, including humans? To answer these questions, the scientist must have access to a wide range of relevant information about the phenomena under consideration. If, taken together, all the relevant evidence converges on the conclusion that the laboratory rat is not a unique organism when it comes to matters of stress and cancer, the scientist will tentatively assume that the results of the experiment of Visintainer et al. have considerable external validity. In other words, rats are not the only organisms that should eliminate stress from their lives!

The principle of converging evidence can be defined as follows: *Confidence in the external validity of results obtained with a particular population of subjects and particular experimental conditions is increased to the extent that the available relevant information indicates that these conditions are not unique.*

One additional point should be made about the principle of converging evidence before we turn our attention to the next issue. There are instances in which this principle will lead you to the conclusion that a particular subject population is somewhat unique or specialized. In such cases the external validity of the experiment will be questioned, and you will be hesitant to generalize these results to other subject populations. Does the fact that a particular experiment lacks external validity mean that the experiment is worthless? I would argue that the answer to this question is no.

Each properly designed, internally valid experiment provides us with a piece of information about nature; and, as I indicated in Chapter 4 (pp. 93–99), it is very difficult to know when a particular experiment will have substantial impact on the way we think about nature. A scientist may know in advance that experiments concerned with cancer in insects will have questionable external validity (i.e., insects will be considered a unique and specialized population in this context). If, however, excessive concern about external validity prevented the scientist from doing this research, some novel and potentially important information about the causes of cancer might go undiscovered.

The conclusion you should extract from the preceding example is important. It is always a bonus to know that an experiment has external validity, *but* external validity should not always be an obsessive concern for either the scientist or the consumer of scientific information. Instead, the importance that you place on external validity should depend to some extent upon the purpose of the research. If you work in a government laboratory that tests substances for carcinogenic properties, you should take the concept of external validity very seriously. You will want to know if your results are widely generalizable. If, however, your purpose is to search for the basic mechanisms that cause various forms of cancer, you should, in my opinion, be less concerned about external validity. Indeed, one might argue that an excessive concern with external validity can impede the discovery of important new information. It will be more productive to search wherever your fertile creative mind takes you. The secrets of cancer may lurk in places not charted on the map that leads to external validity.

Sampling Subjects   The preceding discussion explains the implications of deciding upon a *population* of subjects to use in your research. Once this general population (e.g., laboratory rats, college students, etc.) has been selected, you will have to select a sample of subjects to be used in the experiment. The problems encountered when selecting a sample from the population have already been discussed at length in Chapter 2 (pp. 26–31) and noted again briefly in Chapter 5 (p. 109). From those discussions, you will recall that the most appropriate method for obtaining a sample that is representative of the more general population is to use a *random* sampling procedure (i.e., one in which every member of the population has an equal chance of being included in the sample).

The problems associated with obtaining a sample of subjects also have implications for the external validity of your experiment. Specifically, you can generalize your results to the population from which you have drawn a sample only if the sample is representative of that population (i.e., a random sample). Stated positively, this means that a random sampling procedure increases confidence in claims about the external validity of your results.

Although the typical deviations from random selection of subjects (e.g., convenience sampling) threaten the external validity of an experiment, once again this deviation does not render the experiment worthless. In actual practice, most scientists do not worry too much about this problem in the early stages of a research program. They assume that they can employ more rigorous and systematic sampling procedures if they obtain initial results that are sufficiently interesting to justify further research.

Operational Definitions and External Validity

You may remember our extensive discussion of the *operational definition rule* in Chapter 2, where we argued at length over definitions of the term "pornography." Visintainer et al., in their experiment, also had to struggle over the question of how to define the term "stress" operationally. (Clearly, to conduct an experiment concerned with the effects of stress on the development of cancer, one must develop an acceptable operational definition of stress.) As you know, the definition they decided to use was the presentation of uncontrollable, unpredictable electric shocks to the rats. Once again, this choice has implications for the external validity of their experiment. Often, when people claim that an experiment is artificial and/or lacks generality, they make specific reference to the operational definitions used by the experimenter. In the case of the experiment of Visintainer et al., the claim might be that their definition of stress is very unusual and has little to do with stress in the real world. As such, the external validity of the results obtained with this definition would be considered questionable.

Scientists ask themselves the same question. Should we take this operational definition of stress seriously? Does it have external validity? In my opinion, the answer will again depend upon a principle of converging evidence. Other stress research will be considered, and a wide variety of other operational definitions of stress will be examined. Before making any decisions, scientists will want to know if the definition of stress as inescapable shock (1) has unique properties that are unrelated to other operational definitions of stress or (2) has properties that are very similar to various other operational definitions of stress. If it has similar properties, they will feel more comfortable about the external validity of this cancer experiment. If it appears to be an unusual and unique manipulation, they will question its external validity.

The preceding point can be elucidated by reference to the hypothetical conditions outlined in Figure 7.2. Four potential operational definitions of stress are listed. Of these four, the lines drawn in the figure suggest that three definitions (exposure to overcrowding, exposure to inescapable shock, and exposure to sensory deprivation) have a similar effect on several phenomena thought to be

Operational definitions of stress	Phenomena associated with stress

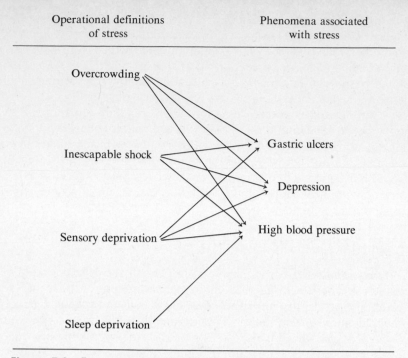

Figure 7.2 Four operational definitions of stress, three of which have similar properties in terms of their effects upon phenomena associated with stress. One operational definition (sleep deprivation) appears to be unique in that it does not affect all three stress-related phenomena.

associated with stress (gastric ulcers, depression, and high blood pressure). Note also that one definition, sleep deprivation, appears to be associated only with the high blood pressure condition. The principle of converging evidence would suggest that sleep deprivation is a somewhat unique and unusual operational definition, but that inescapable shock has properties similar to several other operational definitions. Given this converging evidence, scientists would be more suspicious of the external validity of the sleep deprivation operation than they would be of the other three.

Once again, a warning note should be sounded. Research that employs "unique" or "unusual" operational definitions might sacrifice external validity in the short term, but this does not mean that the research is worthless. In fact, one can argue that the more different operations used to define stress, the greater our chances of gaining a complete understanding of the concept. With reference to Figure 7.2, it would, in fact, be interesting to discover that sleep deprivation has "unique" properties that differentiate it from other definitions of stress. A complete understanding of stress will emerge only when a wide variety of definitions have been thoroughly investigated.

Parameter Values and External Validity

You will recall that two of the basic elements in the architecture of the analytic experiment are the independent variables and the controlled variables. When you are arranging the details of an experiment, you will select certain values for each of these variables. For example, Visintainer and his colleagues decided to use a light-dark cycle of 14 and 10 hours as a controlled variable in their experiment. The values you select for each variable in your experiment are called the *parameter values* of the experiment. You will find that it is not uncommon to question the external validity of an experiment because of the parameter values that have been selected. If people feel that you have selected atypical or unusual parameter values for either your independent or controlled variables, they will be more likely to question the generality of the results you obtain in the experiment.

To illustrate the problem, there is a growing body of research suggesting that certain food additives (e.g., artificial coloring and preservative substances) can cause emotional problems in some children (cf. Weiss, 1982; Feingold, 1975). Although the data relevant to this question are inconsistent, people who hear about this research are obviously concerned. They almost always ask the same questions about the research: What substances were used in this research? How much of the substance was necessary to induce the adverse effects? Essentially, they are asking about the parameter values of the independent variables. Implicit in their question is the hope that the adverse effects of these substances are observed only with very high, unusual dosages. If the research uses extremely high dosages to produce the emotional effects, people will question its external validity and not worry about those particular food additives. In short, the use of extreme or unique parameter values for your independent variable can often lead to questions about the external validity of your experiment.

The parameter values of the *controlled variables* in any particular experiment will also be considered in making judgments about its external validity. If, for example, an experiment concerned with the effects of a food additive on behavior administered the substance immediately before bedtime each night, the time at which the substance was administered to all subjects would be a controlled variable. It is also possible that any results obtained in the experiment would be observed only when this controlled condition was a part of the experiment. For example, the substance might not have the same deleterious effects if it were ingested with regular meals. In this example, we are questioning the external validity of the experiment in terms of the parameter value of a specific controlled variable. Although people inquire less often about the parameter values of controlled variables, these values can also be viewed as a threat to external validity if they are unusual.

Again, the use of extreme or unusual parameter values in an experiment does not necessarily diminish its importance. On the contrary, discovering that a particular food additive has certain effects on behavior only when it is ingested before bedtime might provide important clues about the nature of this phenomenon. The same argument can be made for using extreme dosages of the substance, in spite of the fact that these dosages are seldom encountered under normal conditions.

Demand Characteristics and External Validity

An old experiment reported by Berkowitz and LePage (1967) describes the behavior of college students who have been asked to shock each other under two different conditions. In one condition, students were asked to administer shocks to another person in a laboratory environment containing several objects typically associated with violence (e.g., a shotgun and a revolver were lying on a nearby table). In the control condition, the students were asked to administer shocks to a person in a laboratory environment that did not contain any objects associated with violence (e.g., a tennis racket replaced the shotgun and revolver). Although the experiment was more elaborate than this brief description implies, these two conditions constituted the important factors used to determine whether or not people will behave more aggressively in the presence of stimuli associated with violence.

The results of the experiment supported the hypothesis proposed by Berkowitz and LePage. Those students exposed to the weapons behaved more aggressively by delivering more shocks. From these results, Berkowitz and LePage argued that aggressive behavior in general is triggered by the presence of objects related to violence.

This experiment has attracted considerable interest during the past two decades (cf. Page & Scheidt, 1971; Berkowitz, 1971; Berkowitz & Donnerstein, 1982). Most of this attention has *not* been directed at the hypothesis originally proposed by Berkowitz and his associates. Instead, the discussion has centered upon an alternative interpretation of their results. Specifically, it has been suggested that the students who participated in this experiment (1) were eager to please the experimenter and (2) had guessed the nature of the hypothesis and therefore behaved in a manner that complied with that hypothesis. In essence, this alternative explanation suggests that subjects exposed to the weapons condition assumed that the experimenter wanted them to be aggressive and deliver more shocks, so they did. Although Berkowitz and LePage (1967, p. 206) recognized this possibility, they argued that it could not account for their results.

This particular case has never really been resolved, despite a great deal of discussion. The important point in the present context is that any experimental procedure using human subjects can suffer from this problem. We know that the most common attitude encountered in human subjects is a desire to do what is expected of them, to please the experimenter, and to appear in all respects "normal." (If you are skeptical see Carlsmith, Ellsworth, & Aronson, 1976, for an excellent discussion of the evidence on this point.) Of course, there is also a small minority who come to the experiment with a belligerent, defensive attitude and attempt to do exactly the opposite of what they think is expected of them. In most contemporary psychology laboratories, the latter attitude is affectionately referred to as the "screw-you phenomenon."

The subject's attitude in any experiment can become a problem when the procedures contain subtle cues that inform the subject of the experimenter's expectations. Even if every precaution is taken to eliminate such cues, experience suggests that people will impose their own ideas on the situation, so that the experimenter is left wondering why the subjects are behaving in such a bizarre fashion.

When these subtle cues interact with the subjects' attitudes, you find yourself in a situation similar to the one encountered by Berkowitz and LePage. Are the results in the experiment produced by some genuine effect of the weapons upon aggressive behavior, or do they indicate that the subjects guessed the hypothesis and were trying to comply with it to please the experimenter? This problem is so ubiquitous in psychological research that it has acquired a label of its own. The subtle cues in a research procedure that influence a subject to behave in a certain way are called *demand characteristics*. In the Berkowitz and Lepage experiment, it has been argued that the weapons in the laboratory were not simply stimuli associated with violence but were also demand characteristics that informed the subjects how they were expected to behave if they wished to please the experimenter.

If you think about these problems for a moment, you will realize that demand characteristics can threaten both the *external* and the *internal* validity of the experiment. To illustrate the point, consider again the results obtained by Berkowitz and LePage. Will their claim that the weapons caused the aggressive behavior *generalize* beyond the specific conditions of this experiment? If you ignore, for the moment, questions about subject population, operational definitions, and parameter values and consider only the problem of demand characteristics, you would probably answer no, they will not generalize. If a subject behaved aggressively in order to comply with the experimenter's wishes, it would seem foolhardy to argue that weapons in general will provoke aggressive behavior. If the results are produced by the demand characteristics, they are clearly specific to those experimental situations in which demand characteristics are operating. Hence, demand characteristics are a serious threat to the external validity of an experiment.

Consider also the related problem of demand characteristics and the internal validity of the experiment. Berkowitz and LePage would like to claim that objects associated with violence provoke aggressive behavior. Their claim is based on the observation that subjects in the weapons condition were more aggressive. This claim is suspect because the behavior could also have been caused by the demand characteristics in the situation. Was it the weapons per se that caused the effect, or was it the demand characteristics? Until this confounding of the two factors is eliminated, the internal validity of the experiment is questionable.

The important message to be extracted from the preceding discussion is that demand characteristics can pose a threat to both the internal and external validity of analytic experiments. You should not underestimate the importance of this problem in psychological research and social science in general. People have a powerful need to find "messages" in an experimental procedure and an equally strong desire to comply with these messages. Orne and Evans (1965) reported, for example, that college students were willing to handle poisonous snakes or to throw nitric acid into a person's face on instruction from an experimenter. The students invariably assumed that these activities were safe because they were part of an experiment, and they wanted to comply with the wishes of the experimenter.

For a more thorough analysis of this many-faceted and important problem, the interested reader should consult recent discussions by Mook (1983), Henschel (1980), and Berkowitz and Donnerstein (1982).

ECOLOGICAL VALIDITY

You may recall that we briefly considered the concept of ecological validity in Chapter 5 (p. 108) when we were discussing the mechanical details of arranging an experimental procedure. In that context, ecological validity was defined as a measure of the degree to which an experiment examines a phenomenon in its natural context.

Ecological validity is related to external validity and is just as difficult to measure precisely. In this final section of the chapter, I want to discuss the concept of ecological validity in a little more detail so that you understand the implications of this concept and its relationship to external validity.

First, consider the experiment by Visintainer, Volpicelli, and Seligman (1981) which was used to introduce the present chapter. In considering the *external validity* of this experiment, you now realize that you can ask the generality of the results with reference to the subjects used, the operational definitions employed, the parameter values selected, and—if relevant—the demand characteristics of the experimental procedure. In considering the *ecological validity* of this same experiment, the question is somewhat different. We now want to ask whether the results can be generalized specifically to the natural environments in which stress and cancer phenomena are typically observed.

Past experience tells me that students often judge this experiment by Visintainer et al. to be lacking in ecological validity. The electric shock, the rats, and the injection of tumor cells are all viewed as contrived, artificial versions of stress and cancer phenomena. They feel that these conditions have little to do with stress or cancer as they occur in the natural situations of everyday life. If you think about these judgments, you will realize that ecological validity is actually a specific version of external validity. Both are concerned with the generality of results obtained in an experiment. When judging the external validity of an experiment, we are concerned with the extent to which these results generalize to a wide variety of conditions. In judging the ecological validity, we are concerned with the extent to which these results will generalize to a *specific* set of conditions that are of particular importance to us (i.e., the natural states in which stress and cancer are typically observed). You can make judgments about ecological validity along the same dimensions as you make judgments about external validity (e.g., subjects used, operational definitions employed, etc.). It should also be obvious that such judgments are as difficult or more difficult to make than judgments of external validity. Judgments of ecological validity tend to be somewhat subjective. What one person sees as natural, eco-logically valid conditions, another person might not. Ask 20 people what they consider to be a typical, naturally occurring stressful situation, and chances are that each one will give you a different answer. Hence, these same 20 people might have considerable difficulty agreeing on the ecological validity of any single operational definition of stress that might be employed in psychological research.

Although strong arguments are being made in the contemporary literature for research with more ecological validity (e.g., Neisser, 1982), there are dangers associated with the trend. Some of nature's most interesting secrets may be hidden away in conditions that almost everyone would consider highly artificial and lacking in ecological validity. It would be a shame to miss some of these secrets in the exclusive pursuit of subjects, operational definitions, and parameter values considered relevant and ecologically valid.

CONCLUDING COMMENT

At this point, you should be able to read any analytic experiment and make reasonable judgments about its external and ecological validity. My guess is that no single experiment will every satisfy you in this respect; there will always be some concern about the generality of the results. Perhaps the most optimistic view of this particular dilemma is to assume that the problem will correct itself if you give it enough time. Experiments similar to the one reported by Visintainer and his colleagues will continue to be developed and each new variation will provide yet another test of the internal, external, and ecological validity of those that precede it. You are free to pass judgment at any time on any particular experiment, but the best adjudicator will be additional research and experimen-tation. Given enough time, science is a self-corrective process. Unfortunately, the public often requires definitive answers to difficult questions on unreasonably short notice.

On the following pages, I have reprinted an article that contains a number of features relevant to the concepts introduced in the present chapter. Once again, you should read the article, dissect the logic and architecture of the experiment, and—in the exercises at the end of the chapter—make some judg-ments about its internal, external, and ecological validity. If you have understood these concepts, you should find the article interesting and have no difficulty with the questions.

You will note that the style of this article differs from the style of those reprinted at the ends of Chapters 5 and 6. As you have perhaps discovered, different journals have different styles. The articles at the ends of Chapters 5 and 6 are in the style recommended by the American Psychological Association. The article that follows is published in the journal *Science* and is in the style recom-mended by the American Association for the Advancement of Science.

INDUCED HEARING DEFICIT GENERATES EXPERIMENTAL PARANOIA

Abstract

The development of paranoid reactions was investigated in normal people experiencing a temporary loss of hearing. In a social setting, subjects made partially deaf by hypnotic suggestion, but kept unaware of the source of their deafness, became more paranoid as indicated on a variety of assessment measures. The results support a hypothesized cognitive-social mechanism for the clinically observed relationship between paranoia and deafness in the elderly.

Clinical observation has uncovered a relationship between deafness and psychopathology (1-3). In particular, when deafness occurs later in life and the hearing loss is relatively gradual, paranoid reactions are often observed (4-14). Delusions of persecution and other paranoid symptoms, first noted by Kraepelin (6) in 1915, seem especially prevalent among the hard-of-hearing elderly (7-9). Audiometric assessment of hospitalized, elderly patients (with age and other selection factors controlled statistically) has revealed a significantly greater degree of deafness among those diagnosed as paranoid than among those with affective disorders (10-12).

Maher (15) suggested that one process by which deafness may lead to paranoid reactions involves an initial lack of awareness of the hearing defect by the person, as well as by interacting others. Paranoid thinking then emerges as a cognitive attempt to explain the perceptual anomaly (16) of not being able to hear what people in one's presence are apparently saying. Judging them to be whispering, one may ask, "about what?" or "why me?" Denial by others that they are whispering may be interpreted by the hard-of-hearing person as a lie since it is so clearly discrepant with observed evidence. Frustration and anger over such injustices may gradually result in a more profound expression of hostility.

Observers, without access to the perceptual data base of the person experiencing the hearing disorder, judge these responses to be bizarre instances of thought pathology. As a consequence, others may exclude the hard-of-hearing person, whose suspiciousness and delusions about their alleged plots become upsetting (17). Over time, social relationships deteriorate, and the individual experiences both isolation and loss of the corrective social

Zimbardo, P., Andersen, S., Kebat, L. 1981. Induced hearing deficit generates experimental paranoia. *Science, 212,* 1529–1530. Copyright 1981 by the American Association for the Advancement of Science.

feedback essential for modifying false beliefs (18, 19). Within a self-validating, autistic system, delusions of persecution go unchecked (20). As such, they eventually become resistant to contrary information from any external source (21). In this analysis, paranoia is sometimes an end product of an initially rational search to explain perceptual discontinuity, in this case, being deaf without knowing it.

We now report an experimental investigation of the development of paranoid reactions in normal subjects with a temporary, functional loss of hearing. Across a variety of assessment measures, including standard personality tests, self-reports, and judgments of their behavior by others in the situations, these subjects became significantly more paranoid than did subjects in two control conditions. The effect was transient and limited to the test environment [by the specificity of the instructions, by extensive postexperimental interviews (debriefing procedures), and by the healthy "premorbid" status of each participant]. Nevertheless, qualitative observations and objective data offer support for the role of deafness-without-awareness as a causal factor in triggering paranoid reactions. Although the subjects were young and had normal hearing, these results have obvious bearing on possible cognitive-social mechanisms by which deafness may eventuate in paranoia among the middle-aged and elderly.

Participants were 18 college males selected from large introductory classes. In the selection process, each student (i) demonstrated that he was highly hypnotizable according to the Harvard Group Scale of Hypnotic Susceptibility (22) and the Stanford Scale of Hypnotic Susceptibility, form C (23); (ii) evidenced posthypnotically induced amnesia; (iii) passed a test of hypnotically induced partial deafness; (iv) scored within the normal range on measures of psychopathology; and (v) attended at least one of two hypnosis training sessions before the experiment.

Six participants were randomly assigned to the experimental treatment in which partial deafness, without awareness of its source, was hypnotically induced. The remaining participants were randomly assigned to one of two control groups. In one of these groups, partial deafness with awareness of its source was induced to demonstrate the importance of the knowledge that one's difficulty in understanding others is caused by deafness. In the other control group, a posthypnotic suggestion unrelated to deafness was experienced (a compulsion to scratch an itchy ear) along with amnesia for it, to establish whether merely carrying out a posthypnotic suggestion with amnesia might be sufficient to yield the predicted results. Taken together, these two groups provide controls for experimental demand characteristics, subject selection traits (hypnotic susceptibility), and the rational basis for the experienced sensory anomaly (24).

During group training sessions, each subject was instructed in self-hypnosis and completed consent and medical history forms, a number of Minnesota Multiphasic Personality Inventory (MMPI) scales (25), and our clinically derived paranoia scale (26). In the experimental session, subjects were hypnotized, after which they listened through earphones to deep relaxation music and then heard taped instructions for one of the three treatments. The use of coded tapes randomly selected in advance by one of the researchers (L.K.) made it possible for the hypnotist (P.Z.), experimenter (S.A.), observers, and confederates to be ignorant of the treatment assignment of the subjects. All subjects were given the suggestion to begin experiencing the changed state when they saw the posthypnotic cue ("FOCUS") projected on a viewing screen in the laboratory. In order to make the task socially realistic and to conceal the purpose of the experiment, each subject was led to believe he was participating, along with two others (who were confederates), in a study of the effects of hypnotic training procedures on creative problem solving. Because of the hearing defect that subjects were to experience, all instructions and tasks were projected automatically by timed slides, the first of which was the posthypnotic cue. While working on a preliminary anagram task, the two confederates engaged in a well-rehearsed, standard conversation designed to establish their commonality, to offer test probes for the subject's deafness, and to provide verbal content that might be misperceived as antagonistic. They recalled a party they had both attended, laughed at an incident mentioned, made a funny face, and eventually decided to work together, finally asking the subject if he also wanted to work with them.

The instructions had previously suggested that group effort on such tasks is usually superior to solitary responding. The subject's behavior was videotaped, observed directly by two judges from behind a one-way mirror, and scored independently by the confederates immediately after the session. After this conversation, the three participants were asked to develop stories about pairs of people in ambiguous relationships [Thematic Apperception Test (TAT)]. On the first task, they had the option of working together or of working alone. Thus, interdependence among confederates and the subject was created [important in the natural etiology of paranoia (17, 19, 21)], which centered around developing a common creative solution. On the second TAT task, participants had to work alone.

After these tasks were completed, each confederate was instructed by the slides to go to a different laboratory room while the subject stayed in the room to complete evaluation forms, including the MMPI and others. Extensive debriefing followed (27), and to remove any tension or confusion, each subject was rehypnotized by the experimenter and told to recall all the events experienced during the session. Subjects were reevaluated in a 1-month follow-up.

Major results are summarized in Table 1, which presents group means and one-tailed t-test values derived from a single a priori planned comparison that contrasted the experimental group with the two control groups taken together (28). This analysis followed standard analysis of variance tests. As predicted, the experience of being partially deaf, without being aware of its source, created significant changes in cognitive, emotional, and behavioral functioning. Compare with the control groups, subjects in the deafness-without-awareness treatment became more paranoid, as shown on an MMPI paranoia scale of Horn (25, p. 283) and on our clinically derived paranoia scale (26). Experimental subjects also had significantly elevated scores on the MMPI

Table 1   Mean Scores on Dependent Measures Distinguishing Experimental From Control Subjects

| | Treatment | | | | |
| | | Control | | | |
Dependent measures	Deafness without awareness (N=6)	Deafness with awareness (N=6)	Posthypnotic suggestion (N=6)	t(15)	P
Paranoia measures*					
MMPI-Paranoia	1.50	.33	−.17	1.838	<.05
MMPI-Grandiosity	1.33	−.83	−1.00	1.922	<.05
Paranoia clinical interview form	.30	−.09	−.28	3.667	<.005
TAT					
Affective evaluation	83.35	16.65	33.50	2.858	<.01
Self-assessed creativity	42.83	68.33	73.33	3.436	<.005
Self-rated feelings					
Creative	34.17	55.83	65.83	2.493	<.05
Confused	73.33	39.17	35.00	2.521	<.05
Relaxed	43.33	81.67	78.33	2.855	<.01
Agitated	73.33	14.17	15.33	6.586	<.001
Irritated	70.00	25.00	7.00	6.000	<.001
Friendly	26.67	53.33	56.67	2.195	<.05
Hostile	38.33	13.33	13.33	1.047	<.05
Judges' ratings					
Confused	40.83	27.08	17.67	1.470	<.10
Relaxed	34.17	54.59	65.42	2.839	<.01
Agitated	51.25	24.59	13.75	3.107	<.005
Irritated	45.84	18.92	11.25	3.299	<.005
Friendly	23.34	48.34	65.00	3.385	<.005
Hostile	18.75	5.00	1.67	2.220	<.05

* These measures were taken before and after the experimental session; reported means represent difference scores (after minus before).

grandiosity scale of Watson and Klett (25, p. 287)—one aspect of paranoid thinking. Experimental subjects perceived themselves as more irritated, agitated, hostile, and unfriendly than control subjects did and were perceived as such by confederates ignorant of the treatment. When invited to work with confederates on the TAT task, only one of six experimental subjects elected to do so; in contrast, 9 of 12 control subjects preferred to affiliate ($z=4.32$, $P < .001$).

The TAT stories generated by the subjects were assessed in two ways. Subjects' own ratings of the creativity of their stories indicated that experimental subjects judged their stories to be significantly less creative than did subjects in either of the control groups. Second, the stories were scored (reliably by two judges) for the extent to which subjects evaluated TAT characters. An evaluative-judgmental outlook toward other people is a hallmark of paranoia. The experimental subjects used significantly more evaluative language, both positive and negative (for example, right-wrong, good-bad)($t = 2.86$, $P < .01$) than controls did. In addition, they differed significantly ($z = 5.00$, $P < .001$) from the controls in their greater use of positive evaluative language. Experimental subjects reported feeling no more suspicious than did control subjects. These last two findings weaken the possible criticism that the results were based simply on anger induced by the experimental manipulation.

Both groups experiencing a hearing deficit reported, as expected, that their hearing was not keen, but reported no other sensory difficulties. Those who were partially deaf without being aware of the source of the deafness did experience greater confusion, which is likely to have motivated an active search for an appropriate explanation. Over time, however, if their delusional systems were allowed to become more coherent and systematized, the paranoid reaction would be less likely to involve confusion. Ultimately, there is so much confidence in the proposed paranoid explanatory system that alternative scenarios are rejected.

Despite the artificiality of our laboratory procedure, functionally analogous predicaments occur in everyday life. People's hearing does deteriorate without their realizing it. Indeed, the onset of deafness among the elderly is sometimes actively denied because recognizing a hearing deficit may be tantamount to acknowledging a greater defect—old age. Perhaps self-deception about one's hearing deficit may even be sufficient, in some circumstances, to yield a similar response, namely, a search for a more personally acceptable alternative that finds fault in others rather than in oneself. When there is no social or cultural support for the chosen explanation and the actor is relatively powerless, others may judge him or her to be irrational and suffering from a mental disorder. Although our subjects were young and had normal hearing, these findings have obvious bearing on a possible cognitive social mechanism by which deafness may lead to paranoia among the middle-aged and elderly.

PHILIP G. ZIMBARDO

SUSAN M. ANDERSEN*

Department of Psychology,
Stanford University
Stanford, California 94305

LOREN G. KABAT

Health Sciences Center,
State University of New York,
Stony Brook, New York 11794

* Present address: Department of Psychology, University of California, Santa Barbara 93106.

REFERENCES AND NOTES

1. B. Prizker, *Schweiz. Med. Wochenschr.* 7, 165 (1938).
2. F. Houston and A. B. Royse, *J. Ment. Sci,* 100, 990 (1954).
3. M. Vernon, *J. Speech Hear, Res.,* 12, 541 (1969).
4. K. Z. Altschuler, *Am. J. Psychiatry,* 127, 11 and 1521 (1971).
5. Personal communication from J. D. Rainer (14 July 1980), who has studied the psychiatric effects of deafness for the past 25 years at the New York State Psychiatric Institute.
6. E. Kraepelin, *Psychiatrie,* 8, 1441 (1915).
7. D. W. K. Kay, *Br. J. Hosp. Med.,* 8, 369 (1972).
8. F. Post, *Persistent Persecutory States of the Elderly* (Pergamon, London, 1966).
9. H. A. McClelland, M. Roth, H. Neubauer, R. F. Garside, *Excerpta Med. Int. Cong. Ser.* 4, 2935 (1968).
10. A. F. Cooper, R. F. Garside, D. W. K. Kay, *Br. J. Psychiatry* 129, 532 (1976).
11. A. F. Cooper, A. R. Curry, D. W. K. Kay, R. F. Garside, M. Roth, *Lancet* 1974-II 7885 (1974).
12. A. F. Cooper and R. Porter, *J. Psychiatry* 129, 216 (1976).
13. A. F. Cooper, *Br. J. Psychiatry* 129, 216 (1976).
14. D. W. K. Kay, A. F. Cooper, R. F. Garside, M. Roth, ibid. 129, 207 (1976).
15. B. Maher, in *Thought and Feeling,* H. London and R. E. Nisbett, Eds. (Aldine, Chicago, 1974), pp. 85–103.
16. G. Reed, *The Psychology of Anomalous Experience* (Houghton Mifflin, Boston, 1974).
17. E. M. Lemert, *Sociometry* 25, 2 (1962).
18. L. Festinger, *Hum. Relat.* 7, 117 (1962).
19. N. A. Cameron, in *Comprehensive Textbook of Psychiatry,* A. M. Freedman and H. I. Kaplan, Eds. (Williams & Wilkins, Baltimore, 1967), pp. 665–675.
20. A. Beck, in *Thought and Feeling.* H. London and R. E. Nisbett, Eds. (Aldine, Chicago, 1974), pp. 127–140.
21. W. W. Meisner, *The Paranoid Process* (Jason Aronson, New York, 1978).
22. R. E. Shor and E. C. Orne, *Harvard Group Scale of Hypnotic Susceptibility, Form a* A (Consulting Psychologists Press, Palo Alto, Calif., 1962).
23. A. M. Weitzenhoffer and E. R. Hilgard, *Stanford Hypnotic Susceptibility Scale, Form C* (consulting Psychologists Press, Palo Alto, Calif., 1962).
24. A fuller presentation of procedures is available by request.
25. W. G. Dahlstrom, G. S. Welsh, L. F. Dahlstrom, *An MMPI Handbook,* vol. 2, *Research Application* (Univ. of Minnesota Press, Minneapolis, 1975).
26. We derived this scale specially for this study; it consisted of 15 self-declarative statements responded to on 7-point rating scales. The scale was drawn from a clinical study of paranoia (14).
27. L. Ross, M. R. Lepper, M. Hubbard, *J. Pers. Soc. Psychol.* 35, 817 (1977).
28. W. L. Hays, *Statistics for Psychologists* (Holt, Rinehart & Winston, New York, 1965), p. 465.
29. This report is dedicated to Neal E. Miller as part of a commemoration by his former students of his inspired science teaching. We wish to acknowledge the expert and reliable research assistance of Harry Coin, Dave Willer, Bob Sick, James Glanzer, Jill Fonaas, Laurie Plautz, Lisa Carrol, and Sarah Garlan. We thank Joan Linsenmeier and David Rosenham for critical editing of the manuscript.

CHAPTER EXERCISES

7.1. Which of the following labels best describes the experiment reported by Zimbardo et al.?

1. A within-subjects bivalent analytic experiment
2. A between-subjects bivalent analytic experiment
3. A within-subjects multivalent analytic experiment
4. A between-subjects multivalent analytic experiment.
5. A between-subjects 2 × 2 factorial analytic experiment.

7.2. Describe the dependent variable(s) in the experiment reported by Zimbardo et al.

7.3. Describe some of the variables that were controlled in the experiment reported by Zimbardo et al.

7.4. Are there any confounded variables which, in your opinion, threaten the internal validity of the experiment reported by Zimbardo et al?

7.5. What is (are) the independent variable(s) in the experiment reported by Zimbardo et al.?

7.6. Describe any concerns you have about the external and/or ecological validity of the experiment reported by Zimbardo et al. and organize your discussion under the headings (1) subject selection, (2) operational definitions, (3) parameter values, (4) demand characteristics.

7.7. Zimbardo et al. claim that the two control groups used in the experiment allowed them to determine whether demand characteristics were operating in their experimental procedure. If, in fact, such demand characteristics were operating, how would the results obtained with these control groups be different from those actually obtained in the experiment?

CHAPTER 8

QUASI-ANALYTIC EXPERIMENTS: WITHIN-SUBJECTS PROCEDURES

Several years ago, I saw some incredible film footage of the assassination of Anwar Sadat, the president of Egypt. If you happened to see this film, you will recall that terrorists killed Sadat during a public ceremony. Dozens of government officials were also killed or seriously wounded by fragmentation grenades and machine-gun fire. In one scene, just after the main attack, the camera focused on an injured official lying amid the rubble. He was speaking calmly to a soldier who was applying a tourniquet to the bloody stump of the official's left arm. The film sequence did not seem real; even though the man's arm had been torn from his body, he was not in any obvious pain.

That film was a dramatic illustration of the extent to which our perception of pain can be blocked under severe physical and psychological stress. Psychologists, neuroscientists, and health professionals have recently developed an interest in this phenomenon, and they now realize that it is possible to modify pain sensitivity through exposure to stressful conditions much less extreme than those described above. The phenomenon is called *stress-induced analgesia*. (For examples, see Hayes, Bennet, Newlon, & Mayer, 1978; Willer, Dehen, & Cambier, 1981.)

Most of the research on stress-induced analgesia has been conducted with laboratory animals rather than humans. A typical experiment might involve the random assignment of 40 laboratory rats to two treatment conditions. In one treatment condition, 20 of the rats are exposed to some type of stress treatment; their sensitivity to pain is then measured. In the other treatment condition, the remaining 20 rats are treated identically but not exposed to the stress condition. If the former group reveal a higher pain threshold (i.e., are less sensitive to pain), it is concluded that stress has induced an analgesic condition.

RANDOM ASSIGNMENT PROCEDURES

The procedure described above is a simple bivalent between-subjects analytic experiment. You will recall that one important characteristic of the analytic experiment is the *random assignment* of subjects to the different treatment conditions—*and* that "random assignment" refers to any procedure guaranteeing that each subject has an equal probability of being assigned to *either* treatment condition.

Note that this random assignment feature of the analytic experiment is a marvelous device. When you conduct an analytic experiment like the one described above, perhaps your single biggest worry is whether the two experimental groups will differ in some way other than the "stress" and "no stress" treatments. It would be disastrous, for example, if all those rats that happen to be highly sensitive to pain were accidentally assigned to the no-stress treatment condition of your experiment, or if all the "fat and lazy" rats were accidentally assigned to the stress treatment. Random assignment to treatments is the strategy used to prevent such problems. In theory, any truly random method for assigning the rats to the two groups will distribute the "sensitive" rats and the "fat and lazy" rats equally across the two groups. In this way the random assignment procedure helps the scientist control a number of variables in the experiment. Some of these we recognize as important sources of potential error (e.g., differences in pain sensitivity), while others might not seem important. In either case, random assignment helps us to control these variables.

Given the importance of the random assignment feature to the logic of analytic experiments, it should be evident that any deviation from this procedure can lead to serious problems. For this reason, I will call any experimental procedure that deviates from random assignment a *quasi-analytic experiment*. In this chapter we will consider a basic deviation from random assignment called a *within-subjects treatment procedure*. As you will discover, there are several variations on the within-subjects treatment method, some of which pose more problems for the scientist than others.

WITHIN-SUBJECTS TREATMENT PROCEDURES

A Bivalent Within-Subjects Case

Imagine for a moment that you are an experimental psychologist interested in stress-induced analgesia, and you are somewhat surprised to discover that most of the experimentation published thus far has used laboratory rats. In particular, you feel that some of the results obtained with laboratory animals might not generalize to humans. Consequently, you decide to design an experiment that examines stress-induced analgesia in humans. This will require, at the minimum, (1) a situation that will induce stress in humans, (2) a procedure for measuring a person's sensitivity to painful stimulation, and (3) people who are willing to expose themselves to these procedures. The first two of these problems may be easier to solve than the third. Stop for a moment and test your creative skills. Can you devise an appropriate experiment using human subjects?

You will probably agree that it is not easy to find workable procedures to solve these problems. People are not generally willing to expose themselves to stress and pain. My own (somewhat less than inventive) suggestion is that we organize our experiment with a group of ten people who are about to start flying lessons at a small airport just outside the city of Halifax, Nova Scotia. Three females and seven males are enrolled in this flying class and none have had any previous flight experience. The aircraft they will fly is relatively new. It is called an "ultralight" because it is very small and can carry only one person—the pilot. In fact, these aircraft are little more than hang-gliders with small engines and propellers attached. Instructors associated with this flight training course claim that 5 hours of flight training in the two-seated trainer and 20 hours of ground school (plus a fee of $450) will suffice to let a person solo in an ultralight.

The point is that we are talking about an activity that is stress-inducing! Looking down from a thousand feet with a kite and motor strapped to their backs should prove stressful for even the most daring individuals. Consequently, I think you will accept this as an operational definition of stress.

We now need a method that will permit us to measure sensitivity to pain. I do not have much experience in this domain, but a student who is now investigating pain perception at McGill University in Montreal described a device to me that might be of some use. This gadget looks like a miniature vise into which the subject inserts a finger. The jaws of the vise come together on the finger with a predetermined pressure. At moderate pressure levels, a person experiences no *initial* pain, but, as time passes, the subject will begin to feel discomfort. Eventually, the procedure becomes painful enough for the subject to request relief. The amount of time that elapses between the application of the vise and the subject's request to remove it is a measure of the person's ability to tolerate pain. This would seem to be a workable measure (operational definition) of pain sensitivity. I thought that it was a particularly clever method, because most people would not have any fear of the procedure once it was explained. Painful procedures involving heat or electric shock would certainly prove less popular among volunteer subjects.

If we can assume, for the moment, that the ten people enrolled in the ultralight flight training course will agree to participate in our experiment, the next question we must address concerns the experimental design. At first glance, our old friend the bivalent between-subjects analytic experiment would seem to be the obvious choice. We could randomly assign the ten student pilots to two groups, with five subjects exposed to the stress condition and five subjects exposed to the no-stress condition. The five stress subjects would be informed that they will take their solo flight that day, and we could measure pain sensitivity with our viselike gadget one hour before flight time. The five no-stress subjects would be treated identically in all respects except that they would not be given their solo flight instructions that day. Our experimental hypothesis is that the stress group will, on the average, tolerate more pain (i.e., have a higher pain threshold). If the data support this hypothesis, the discovery would extend the generality of the stress-induced analgesia phenomenon to an experimental situation involving human subjects.

As you consider this bivalent analytic experiment, several features might concern you. First, it is distressing to note that there are only five subjects in each of these two treatment conditions. People obviously vary in the degree to which they can tolerate pain, and a few subjects with very high pain tolerance might be "randomly" assigned to the stress treatment condition. Similarly, there are three females in the original sample of ten subjects. Even if we use random assignment procedures, with this small number of subjects there is a reasonably good chance that all three will be assigned to one particular treatment group. This would also be a source of bias in the experiment.

The point is that random assignment of subjects to treatment conditions will not always be the best approach. In this particular case, there are a very small number of subjects to divide into the two treatment conditions, and the probability of some bias occurring during random assignment is uncomfortably high. In fact, one of the most common reasons for deviating from the random assignment procedure is the limited availability of subjects.

One obvious solution to this problem is to use, instead, a within-subjects experimental design in which all subjects are exposed to both treatment conditions. By using all ten subjects in both the stress and no-stress conditions, we eliminate any chance that an accidental difference between the two groups will contaminate the results (e.g., all the pain-sensitive or all the female subjects in one group). By using a within-subjects procedure, we also increase the number of measurements we can make in each of the treatment conditions from five to ten. Hence, this within-subjects deviation from our original between-subjects bivalent experiment would appear to be a tactical improvement.

Order Effects

The moral of the story is that the within-subjects procedure can solve problems such as too few subjects and too few measurements. However, whenever you are tempted to use a within-subjects procedure (or find yourself reading about one), you should immediately worry about a basic problem that usually arises. Specifically, you should be concerned about the *order* in which the treatments are administered to the subjects.

To illustrate the potential problems associated with order of treatments in within-subjects experiments, suppose that we conduct our experiment concerned with stress-induced analgesia by first measuring the pain sensitivity of all ten flight training subjects on a day when they do *not* expect to make their first solo flight (i.e., the no-stress condition). Next, we repeat our measurement of all ten subjects on a day when they have been told to expect the solo flight (i.e., the stress condition). Assume that the results of this within-subjects experimental procedure are those illustrated in Figure 8.1. These data would appear to confirm our hypothesis on stress-induced analgesia—or do they?

If you think about these results for a minute, you will realize that the higher tolerance for pain under the stress condition might not have anything to do with the stress treatment. Instead, we could be measuring a "practice effect" in which people have a higher tolerance for pain merely because this is the *second time* that we have tested them. In other words, they may have learned to tolerate more pain by going through the measurement procedure twice. The *order* in which the treatments were administered is *confounded* with the difference in treatment conditions. Therefore, we cannot know whether the stress condition itself or the order in which the treatment conditions were administered has caused the differences plotted in Figure 8.1.

Whether you are a consumer of scientific information or a scientist designing an experiment, the use of a within-subjects treatment procedure should immediately cause a warning signal to flash in your brain, saying "beware of con-

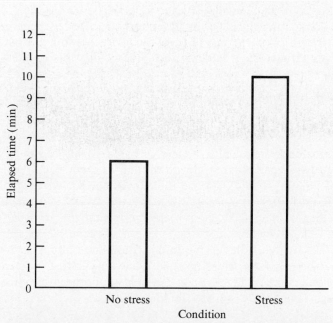

Figure 8.1 Results of a hypothetical experiment concerned with the effects of stress upon sensitivity to pain as measured in terms of the length of time a subject will tolerate a painful pressure stimulus. The basic design is a bivalent within-subjects experiment. Subjects under stress tolerate pain for a longer period of time (i.e., are less sensitive to pain).

founded order effects.'' They are the Achilles heel of this particular quasi-analytic experiment.

Counterbalancing

There are, of course, methods of dealing with the problem of confounded order effects in some within-subjects quasi-analytic experiments. In the case of the bivalent experiment we have been using as an example, perhaps the simplest solution is illustrated in panel 1 of Figure 8.2. Once again, we begin the experiment with ten subjects, each of whom will be exposed to both the stress and no-stress treatments. As indicated in panel 1 of Figure 8.2, five of the subjects will be exposed to the no-stress condition first and the stress condition second. The other five will be exposed in the reverse order. The basic logic behind splitting the subjects into two groups and reversing the order of treatment is that any effect of order of treatment will be *balanced* equally across the stress and no-stress conditions. This basic logic, which can also be employed in more complex within-subjects experiments, is called *counterbalancing*. Counterbalancing procedures are essentially attempts to *control* or hold constant the order-of-treatment effects that would otherwise be confounded across different levels of the independent variable. Any *order* effects (e.g., practice effects, fatigue effects, etc.) are assumed to contribute equally to each level of the independent variable (e.g., stress and no-stress treatments) when counterbalancing has been employed.

Panels 2 and 3 of Figure 8.2 provide a further illustration of the logic underlying counterbalancing. Panel 2 presents one possible outcome of a within-subjects experiment that employed counterbalancing. As the data indicate, an average pain tolerance of six minutes was obtained under the no-stress treatment regardless of whether that treatment was administered first or second in the sequence of treatments. Similarly, the stress condition increased the pain tolerance to ten minutes regardless of whether it was measured first or second. Hence we would conclude from the data in panel 2 that the *order* in which subjects were exposed to the treatments made no difference in their sensitivity to pain, and that the stress condition did increase their tolerance for pain. Panel 3 of Figure 8.2 tells us quite a different story. In this case, the results of our counterbalanced experiment suggest that subjects tolerate more pain the *second* time they are measured, whether they are under stress or not! Hence, this second hypothetical experiment tells us that order of treatment has a large effect on our measure of pain tolerance and that the stress treatment has no effect. Obviously, the results of the hypothetical experiment in panel 2 would support our hypothesis on stress-induced analgesia and the results of the hypothetical experiment in panel 3 would not support it.

Factorial Analysis of Order Effects

The astute reader will have thought back to the factorial designs discussed in Chapter 6 and realized that the data obtained in these bivalent within-subjects experiments with treatment order counterbalanced can be logically analyzed as

Panel 1

10 subjects	5 subjects → randomly assigned	→	First measure under no stress	→	Second measure under stress
	5 subjects → randomly assigned	→	First measure under stress	→	Second measure under no stress

Panel 2

10 subjects	5 subjects → randomly assigned	→	First measure under no stress = 6	→	Second measure under stress = 10
	5 subjects → randomly assigned	→	First measure under stress = 10	→	Second measure under no stress = 6

Panel 3

10 subjects	5 subjects → randomly assigned	→	First measure under no stress = 6	→	Second measure under stress = 10
	5 subjects → randomly assigned	→	First measure under stress = 6	→	Second measure under no stress = 10

Figure 8.2   Panel 1 illustrates a method of using a within-subjects treatment procedure in which order-of-treatment effects are counterbalanced; panel 2 illustrates the results of an experiment in which the effects of stress are the same regardless of the order in which subjects are exposed to treatment; panel 3 illustrates the results of an experiment in which the order of treatment determines the results obtained and stress has no effect.

mixed factorial designs. In a mixed factorial design (Chapter 6, p. 140), we would view the stress and no-stress treatments as a within-subjects independent variable with two levels; we would also view the two treatment orders as a second independent variable that is a between-subjects variable (five subjects in each of the two different treatment orders). Before looking at Figure 8.3, see if you can plot the results from panel 3 of Figure 8.2 in the form of a 2 × 2 factorial graph. If you need some help doing this, look at Figure 8.3, where the results from panel 2 of Figure 8.2 have been plotted as a factorial graph.

Once you decide you want to analyze the results of a within-subjects counterbalanced design as a factorial, you have essentially made the order of treatments an independent variable in the logic of your experiment. You can discuss its effects on pain tolerance in exactly the same manner as you would discuss the effects of the stress and no-stress treatments. Of course, one of the major advantages of using the counterbalancing technique is that it enables you to

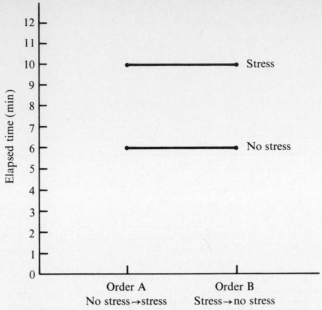

Figure 8.3   A factorial plot of the data from panel 2 of Figure 8.2. There are two levels of the stress variable (stress and no stress) and two levels of the treatment order variable (order A and order B). A main effect is produced by the stress variable; no main effect is produced by the order-of-treatment variable. The combined effects are obviously additive.

determine from your data whether treatment order did have an effect and to interpret the nature of that order effect when it occurs (i.e., does it interact with the stress/no-stress treatments or is it additive?).

VARIATIONS ON WITHIN-SUBJECTS TREATMENT PROCEDURES

Obviously you will encounter within-subjects experiments that are more complex than the simple bivalent examples described above. In these more complex cases, the basic problem is the same. You must avoid confounding treatment order with your independent variables. The solutions to the more complicated cases differ, but the underlying principle stays the same.

Consider first a more complex version of the basic example discussed in the preceding paragraphs. We are still interested in studying the effects of stress on pain tolerance, and in this case we have a drug (D) that will induce stress. Assume that we have six subjects who are willing to expose themselves to this drug and a placebo (P), which has absolutely no pharmacological properties. We expect the drug to increase tolerance for pain.

Given the small number of subjects, we decide to use a within-subjects procedure, with each subject exposed to the drug (D) *twice* and the placebo (P) *twice* during the experiment. Two exposures to each treatment condition obviously gives us more information than just one exposure. We now face the inevitable task of deciding on the treatment sequence. We know that each subject will receive four treatments, two with the D and two with the P. We also suspect that there will be a gradual linear increase in each subject's pain tolerance over the four treatment sessions (whether they receive any drug or not). Which sequence of treatments should be used with the various subjects?

You probably realize at this point that it would be an unpardonable error to use a treatment sequence such as P,P,D,D over the four sessions with all subjects. If there were a linear increase in pain tolerance, this would surely bias the results in favor of observing more pain tolerance under the drug conditions. Using the P,P,D,D sequence, the drug is administered during sessions 3 and 4 when pain tolerance is at its highest levels. Your tendency will probably be to adopt a variation on the approach used in the previous, simpler example. The obvious extension of that solution to the present example would be to split the six subjects into two groups, with three subjects receiving the treatment sequence P,P,D,D and the other three the treatment sequence D,D,P,P. In this way, the advantage gained by the drug treatment in the first three subjects would be counterbalanced by the advantage gained by the placebo in the other three subjects. Analysis of the data as a factorial design with drug vs. placebo as one independent variable and the two treatment orders as the second independent variable would tell you if the counterbalancing was effective.

This counterbalancing solution is a reasonable approach to this specific example, but it is by no means the only possible approach. Problems that arise in quasi-analytic experiments usually have several possible solutions; common sense will often dictate the use of one solution over another. In this case, an alternative solution will permit you to expose all six subjects in the experiment to the same treatment sequence rather than split them into two groups, each of which is exposed to a different sequence. As indicated earlier, it would be a mistake to expose all six to the sequence P,P,D,D or the sequence D,D,P,P. These would bias the results in favor of either drug or placebo respectively. Consider, however, the sequences P,D,D,P or D,P,P,D. If, in fact, you know that the subjects increase their level of pain tolerance in a linear fashion over the four sessions of the experiment, either of these sequences will distribute this linear practice effect equally to the two treatment conditions, D and P.

If you do not immediately see why either the P,D,D,P or D,P,P,D sequence would be an effective counterbalancing technique to use with all six subjects in the experiment, consult Figure 8.4. The graph in this figure presents the suspected linear change in pain tolerance that occurs over the four consecutive sessions (whether the subjects are treated with a drug or not). The treatment sequences listed below the graph are intended to demonstrate how all but one of these sequences (P,D,D,P) will bias the results. The P,D,D,P sequence distributes the changes in pain tolerance over sessions equally to the D and P treatment conditions. If you feel that you understand the principle at this point, you might test yourself by constructing your own version of Figure 8.4 for a within-subjects experiment in which you had six subjects, each of whom would be exposed to 16 consecutive treatment sessions. The drug should be administered for 8 of the sessions and the placebo for the other 8. Is there a sequence that would counterbalance a linear increase in pain tolerance over these 16 consecutive sessions? At this point you should be familiar with at least two solutions to this specific problem.

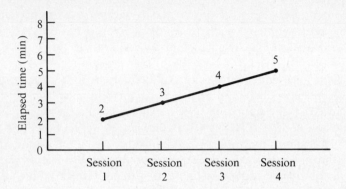

Select the treatment sequence(s) from the list below which will distribute this "practice" effect equally across the two treatment conditions drug (D) and placebo (P) in a within-subjects design.

Session 1	Session 2	Session 3	Session 4	
D(2)	D(3)	P(4)	P(5)	Drug = 5 Placebo = 9
P(2)	P(3)	D(4)	D(5)	Drug = 9 Placebo = 5
P(2)	D(3)	P(4)	D(5)	Drug = 8 Placebo = 6
P(2)	D(3)	D(4)	P(5)	Drug = 7 Placebo = 7

Figure 8.4 The graph at the top illustrates the practice effects you might expect with repeated measurement of the subject's tolerance of pain. Each session, the subject "learns" to tolerate an additional minute without any difference in treatment over the four sessions. The figure above illustrates four different sequences of treatment (drug and placebo). The only appropriate sequence will counterbalance the practice effects in the figure equally across both drug and placebo conditions. The sequence P, D, D, P obviously accomplishes this task.

Randomization

The preceding discussion has implied that any problem with order of treatment in a within-subjects experiment can easily be solved using a variation on the counterbalancing principle. This is not, however, the whole story. In fact, it is often impossible to know in advance if there will actually be a systematic change in behavior during the repeated measurements in an experiment and/or to know the exact nature of that change. We do not really know at this point, for example, if pain tolerance will change each time we use our vise gadget on a subject; if it does change, we cannot know for sure if the change will take the form of a linear increase. The linear increase illustrated in Figure 8.4 is simply a guess.

Suppose, instead of the linear increase plotted in Figure 8.4, a person's pain tolerance changed over the course of the four sessions in a *curvilinear* fashion (an increase in pain tolerance during the middle two sessions followed by a decline during the last session). It would be disastrous to have selected the treatment sequence P,D,D,P if, in fact, the change in pain tolerance over repeated sessions is curvilinear. This would bias the results in favor of the drug condition. If you do not follow this reasoning, take a pencil and plot another, curvilinear line on the graph in Figure 8.4. Then examine the treatment sequences below to determine which of these sequences would, in the case of a curvilinear change, distribute the effects equally to both treatment conditions.

The point is that there are changes other than linear practice effects that can occur in within-subjects treatment procedures; perhaps more importantly, we usually have no basis for knowing the actual nature of the change. It could be linear or curvilinear, or it might be something totally unpredictable that happens during the experiment. How, then, does one select an appropriate counterbalancing sequence of treatments?

The answer is that you do not attempt to counterbalance treatment effects unless you have some basis for knowing the nature of the change that is occurring over the repeated measurements in the experiment. Instead, you use a principle called *randomization of treatment order*. "Randomization" refers to any procedure in which you have let chance alone determine the sequence of treatments and in which each of the possible treatment sequences has an equal chance of being selected. For example, in the case we have been discussing, you might put four slips of paper in a hat, with two slips labeled D and two slips labeled P. When the first subject arrives for your experiment, you decide on the treatment sequence for that subject by drawing one slip at a time. If four draws generate the sequence D,P,D,P, you use this treatment sequence with the first subject. The procedure of drawing slips from the hat is then repeated for each of the remaining five subjects in the experiment.

Common sense will tell you that if you randomize the order of treatments for each subject in your experiment, any effects of treatment order (linear, curvilinear, or unpredictable) should be equally distributed to each of the treatment conditions in the experiment once you have summed your data across all of the different subjects.

Figure 8.5 is designed to illustrate the manner in which the randomization procedure works in theory. This figure presents a randomized treatment order for six subjects, each of whom will be exposed to a drug treatment twice and a placebo treatment twice. The graph in Figure 8.5 presents one possible example of a nonlinear change in the subjects' ability to tolerate pain on each successive measurement. In theory, when you randomize the treatment order for each subject, any bias in one particular subject will be canceled by a different bias for another subject.

To summarize briefly, randomization of treatment order represents an alternative method for controlling order-of-treatment effects in within-subjects experiments. This procedure can be used when you do not know the nature of the progressive changes occurring during the repeated measurements. It should also be obvious that adoption of the randomization solution means that you have given up the opportunity to conduct the factorial analysis of the data discussed earlier. As you can imagine, it is not always easy to choose between the randomization and counterbalancing tactic or among various approaches to counterbal-

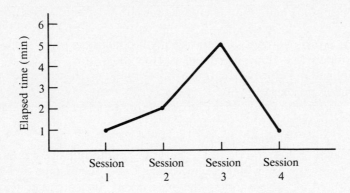

Randomized Treatment Sequences

	Session 1	Session 2	Session 3	Session 4
Subject #1	P	P	D	D
Subject #2	P	D	P	D
Subject #3	P	D	D	P
Subject #4	P	P	D	D
Subject #5	D	P	D	P
Subject #6	D	P	P	D

Note: Subject #3 is biased in favor of the drug.
   Subject #6 is biased in favor of the placebo.
   Etc.

Figure 8.5 The graph indicates that there are changes in the subject's pain tolerance over four sessions of repeated measurement. The nature of these changes is usually unknown to the scientist, so counterbalancing is inappropriate. Listed below the graph are the treatment sequences produced by randomization (pulling them out of a hat). As you can see, with each subject there is a bias in favor of the drug or placebo, but scanned across all subjects, the bias is eliminated.

ancing when the latter is the method of choice. It would be counterproductive, at this point, to attempt a description of all the alternative choices you might encounter in both simple and complex within-subjects quasi-analytic experiments. The preceding discussion and examples should, however, provide you with an understanding of the *principles* of counterbalancing and randomization from which you can extrapolate to specific situations.

TIME-SERIES DESIGNS

To complete our discussion of within-subjects procedures, I want you to consider the case history of someone you can remember as "Time-Series Joe." Joe is a university student who has always had an intense, irrational fear of hypodermic injections. For as long as he can remember, the mere thought of an injection was sufficient to trigger an anxiety attack. Surprisingly, Joe had managed to live with this phobia without major complications until he developed a very serious infection that required a number of antibiotic injections. During this treatment, he had an extremely severe anxiety attack and fainted. For a period of two years after that, Joe's mental health deteriorated. Events other than injections began to cause anxiety attacks, and eventually he developed several different phobias so severe that he could not attend classes.

Joe is a real person, and his case history is not unusual as phobias go. I invented his name and some of the details, but the patient just described is similar to a man described by Gatchel (1977) in an experiment published by the *Journal of Consulting and Clinical Psychology.* Joe was the only subject in this experiment; I selected it as a typical example of yet another type of within-subjects quasi-analytic experiment called a *time-series design.* As you will discover, the deviation from an analytic experiment is even more pronounced in time-series designs than in the within-subjects examples that have been discussed thus far. The problems that can arise are, therefore, more extreme.

In the experiment reported by Gatchel (1977), Joe agreed to serve as a subject to determine if a particular type of therapy called *biofeedback training* could be used to eliminate the anxiety attacks. All versions of the biofeedback training procedure involve equipment that lets an individual monitor some aspect of his or her physiological state. For example, with a small amount of engineering, an electrocardiograph, and a signal light, you can get immediate feedback about any change in your heart rate. Similar feedback can be provided for other physiological states such as respiration rate, blood pressure, and muscle activity. It is reasonably well established that practice with this feedback procedure will permit an individual to acquire some degree of control over these various physiological states, although the exact mechanisms by which such control is achieved are still not well understood.

The theoretical ideas behind the use of biofeedback training as a therapeutic technique are relatively simple. It is assumed that if you can learn to control the physiological changes underlying emotional states like anxiety (i.e., increases in heart rate and blood pressure), you will also be able to control the emotional state per se. Gatchel's experiment with Joe as a subject was designed to test this basic hypothesis. He introduced a biofeedback procedure to train Joe to reduce his heart rate and hoped, in turn, to reduce the frequency of Joe's anxiety attacks.

The basic architecture of Gatchel's experiment is divided into three phases. During an initial *pretreatment baseline phase,* no biofeedback training was used and Joe was required to keep a diary of his anxiety attacks for a period of 14 days. During this period, Joe rated each anxiety attack on a scale of 1 to 5, with 5 being a very severe attack. Following the pretreatment baseline phase, biofeedback training was introduced and Joe learned to control his heart rate over a period of 14 consecutive days, using one-hour training sessions in the laboratory each day. Joe also continued to monitor the frequency and rate the severity of his anxiety attacks. Next, the biofeedback training was terminated and Joe continued to monitor his anxiety attacks for a 14-day *posttreatment baseline period.*

The results of this quasi-analytic experiment were very straightforward. Joe did learn to decelerate his heart rate during the biofeedback training by an average of 7.6 beats per minute. As predicted, he also reduced the frequency and severity of his anxiety attacks to manageable levels. Joe maintained this control throughout the posttreatment baseline period; when he was checked six months later, his anxiety problems were still under control.

Gatchel's experiment is one example of a within-subjects quasi-analytic experiment typically called a *time-series* design; it illustrates the basic logic used in all variations on the theme. Essentially, a measurement is taken under a pretreatment condition, a treatment is then introduced, and any changes occurring thereafter are assumed to be caused by the treatment. Subsequent removal of the treatment (posttreatment baseline) is often used to determine how permanent the changes are.

The logic of the time-series design deviates in two very basic ways from the logic of an analytic experiment: (1) subjects are not randomly assigned to treatment conditions and (2) the attempt to control and manipulate relevant variables is not *simultaneous,* but *sequential* over time. The attempt to control and manipulate variables sequentially is a particularly dangerous practice. Any other factor that happens to change at the same time as the treatment is introduced will be confounded with the treatment condition. Figure 8.6 illustrates this potential problem in the case of Gatchel's experiment. In this figure, the boxes below each phase of treatment contain just a few of the variables in Joe's life that might also change coincidentally with the introduction of the biofeedback training. Any change in one of these variables would therefore be confounded with the biofeedback treatment, and we could not determine which change in Joe's life actually caused the reduction in anxiety attacks. The posttreatment baseline data do not help us solve this dilemma. They simply tell us that whatever variable caused the change in the anxiety attacks produced a relatively permanent change.

As noted earlier, the time-series design is a frequently encountered variation on the within-subjects quasi-analytic experiment. In this particular example, it is applied to only one subject. Even if Gatchel had used a hundred subjects like Joe, two troublesome characteristics would remain. First, the treatment procedure is *sequential;* a treatment condition is introduced after a period of baseline

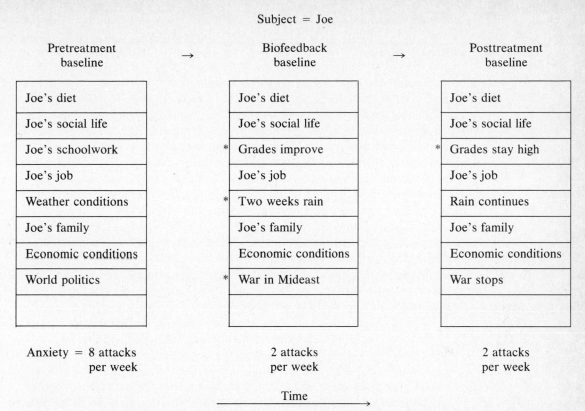

Subject = Joe

Pretreatment baseline		Biofeedback baseline		Posttreatment baseline
	$\rightarrow$		$\rightarrow$	

Pretreatment baseline	Biofeedback baseline	Posttreatment baseline
Joe's diet	Joe's diet	Joe's diet
Joe's social life	Joe's social life	Joe's social life
Joe's schoolwork	* Grades improve	* Grades stay high
Joe's job	Joe's job	Joe's job
Weather conditions	* Two weeks rain	Rain continues
Joe's family	Joe's family	Joe's family
Economic conditions	Economic conditions	Economic conditions
World politics	* War in Mideast	War stops

Anxiety = 8 attacks per week	2 attacks per week	2 attacks per week

Time →

Figure 8.6 Three phases of a simple time-series design. During the pretreatment baseline phase, 8 anxiety attacks per week are observed; during biofeedback treatment, 2 attacks per week occur; and during posttreatment baseline, 2 attacks per week occur. The boxes below each phase of the design indicate some of the variables that might also change coincidentally when biofeedback treatment is initiated. If the variables marked with an asterisk change, they are logically confounded with the biofeedback treatment.

measurements. As such, any other factors that vary over the course of time (and there are obviously a great many, not the least of which is Joe's age) are likely to be confounded with the independent variable (i.e., the introduction of the biofeedback training). You will recall that the analytic experiment avoids this sequential problem for the most part by *concurrently* contrasting and holding constant the relevant variables in the experiment. That is one of the distinguishing features of the analytic experiment as described in Chapter 5. You might also recall that most of the within-subjects quasi-analytic experiments discussed in the present chapter also manage to avoid this problem by *counterbalancing* any changes that occur over time (in spite of the fact that any particular subject is exposed to various treatments sequentially). The time-series design fails to use either of these safeguards and, therefore, runs a high risk of being contaminated by one of those extraneous variables that might be changing at the same time the treatment is introduced.

Note that it is not unusual to find quasi-analytic time-series designs in which there is even less opportunity to control potential confounded variables than in the Gatchel experiment. Some data discussed by Nathan (1983) provide a more extreme example of this lack of control. Nathan points out that there are a number of statistics suggesting that drunk driving is one of the major causes of death among young people in North America. This has prompted some to argue that the legal drinking age should be increased to prevent teenage drinking. They assume that an increase in the legal drinking age would reduce the number of traffic fatalities and injuries. In Michigan, two changes in the legal drinking age have been legislated. There, the drinking age was lowered from 21 to 18 in 1972. In 1978, the legal age was again raised to 21. If you measure the number of alcohol-related traffic accidents in Michigan before and after the 1972 change in the legal drinking age and do the same before and after the 1978 change, you have the makings of a time-series design. In this case it would be called a *multiple time-series* in that two changes were introduced sequentially and measurements were taken before and after each change. Note also that you are actually making your measurements long after the actual changes were introduced by examining the historical records of traffic accidents during the relevant period. As you might imagine, this approach to the time-series design is particularly dangerous, because it is very difficult to know what other changes might have taken place in 1972 and 1978 that were confounded with the changes in the legal drinking age.

Wagenaar (1982) actually did the analysis described above, with some very interesting results. He found that a lowering of the drinking age to 18 in 1972 increased the percentage of alcohol-related traffic accidents from 15 to 25 percent. In 1978, when the drinking age was raised again—you guessed it—there was a significant reduction in alcohol-related traffic accidents.

Data from time-series experiments like the one reported by Wagenaar can be seductive. It is impossible to hold all important variables constant while you introduce a change in the legal drinking age; hence the probability that some confounded variable will contaminate the results should be very high. Note, however, that raising the age lowered the accident rate and lowering the age raised the accident rate. It would seem unlikely that the same confounded variable was causing the accident rate to vary in both directions just at the time when the changes were introduced. Or is it?

No matter how convincing the data seem to be, you should always look for possible alternative explanations (confounded variables) in time-series designs. It so happens, for example, that there was a substantial increase in the availability of alcoholic beverages across the entire state of Michigan in 1972; this, unfortunately, coincides perfectly with the lowering of the drinking age. Which factor caused the increase in alcohol-related accidents? Similarly, in 1978, when the drinking age was again raised and accidents decreased, there was also a serious energy crisis. Long lines at gas stations, a shortage of gasoline, and a lot less driving in 1978 might offer an interesting alternative explanation for the decline in traffic accidents that year.

Both Joe and his anxiety attacks and the legal drinking age in Michigan are interesting and important phenomena to psychologists, social scientists, and health professionals; both offer some typical examples of the quasi-analytic experiment called a time-series design. Given the problems with confounded variables that the time-series design can encounter, you might be asking yourself, at this point, why anyone would bother to use it. The answer is obvious if you think about it. Try to design a simple bivalent between-subjects analytic experiment (or the sort described in Chapter 5) that will answer either of the questions raised in the experiments reported by Gatchel or Wagenaar. Now I grant you that it is reasonably easy to *describe* the logic and architecture of such experiments. The point is, however, that it would be impossible to implement this logic and collect the data. Can you imagine, for example, randomly assigning half the young adults in Michigan to a legal-drinking-age treatment of 18 and the other half to a drinking age of 21? Even if this operation were possible, can you conceive of the problems you would encounter in enforcing the two different age limits? The point is simple. There are a large number of important questions that scientists would like to answer about the world. In many cases, however—as you will discover—it is impossible to use the best available tool: the analytic experiment. Indeed, sometimes the scientist has no choice but to use a less than adequate experimental design—like the-time series designs described above—and risk contamination from confounded variables. When this situation does arise, it is important to understand the high risk of confounded variables and be appropriately cautious in your interpretation of the results obtained. Very often the media reports of these results do not make the distinction and do not employ the necessary caution. Certainly, Gatchel (1977) and Wagenaar (1982) understand the problems described in the preceding pages and both are very cautious about stating any definite conclusions based upon time-series procedures. For example, Gatchel (1977) suggests that his arguments are only convincing to the extent that they are considered in conjunction with other research on biofeedback procedures using more rigorous experimental designs (e.g., Gatchel & Proctor, 1976).

This concludes our discussion of the first category of quasi-analytic experiments called *within-subjects treatment procedures*. You should now understand that there are several variations on these and that each variation introduces some new problems that can, if ignored, make these designs much less effective than the analytic designs discussed in Chapters 5 and 6. In closing the discussion, it should perhaps be said that the within-subjects deviation from the analytic experiment is by no means the most serious one that you will encounter. Some of the procedures to be discussed in subsequent chapters have more severe problems associated with them. To the extent that you can manage to control for the effects of treatment order in many within-subjects designs, your experiment will approximate the "gold standard" described in Chapters 5 and 6. Indeed, some might argue that a properly arranged within-subjects experiment should actually be included in the special class that I have called analytic experiments.

Before turning your attention to a new class of quasi-analytic experiment in the next chapter, read the research paper reprinted on the following pages and once again test your understanding of the concepts that have been discussed in this and the preceding chapters. This paper, by Maurer and Young (1983), is concerned with the ability of newborn infants to discriminate between natural and distorted arrangements of human facial features. For most of the present century, psychologists assumed that the newborn infant enters the world with a very limited ability to perceive it accurately. Research concerned with the sensory and perceptual skills of newborn infants during the past ten or fifteen years has, however, challenged this traditional assumption (see Bower, 1982). The newborn infant apparently arrives with some impressive skills, and the ability to discriminate the difference between a natural arrangement and a distorted set of facial features might be one of these. The experiment reported by Maurer and Young (1983) speaks to this question.

NEWBORN'S FOLLOWING OF NATURAL AND DISTORTED ARRANGEMENTS OF FACIAL FEATURES*

DAPHNE MAURER AND ROSEMARY E. YOUNG

McMaster University

Goren, Sarty, and Wu (1975) reported that newborns have an unlearned preference for a proper face-like stimulus. This conclusion was based on the finding that newborns followed a naturally arranged schematic face farther than either of two scrambled arrangements, both of which they followed farther than a featureless oval. In contrast, other studies have shown that infants younger than 2 months do not fixate a stationary schematic face with the features arranged naturally longer than they fixate ones in which the features are scrambled (Fantz, 1961, 1967; Maurer & Barera, 1981). Nor do they fixate a novel arrangement longer than one to which they have been habituated (Maurer & Barrera, 1981).

The discrepancy between the literature on infants' fixations and the results obtained by Goren et al. is difficult to explain. Perhaps their procedure is more sensitive than measuring visual fixations on stationary stimuli. That might be the case if newborns respond better to moving than to stationary stimuli or if they can regulate their head- and eye-turning better than their fixations.

Alternatively, the results of Goren et al. might not be reliable. In their study the experimenter held the baby on her lap, facing her. With one hand the experimenter supported the infant's head and with the other hand, she presented the stimuli. She also noted how far the baby turned his head and eyes by looking at a protractor placed over the baby's abdomen. When we experimented with this technique, we found it difficult not to see the stimulus and not to influence the baby by moving, especially since the experimenter must shift toward the side to judge accurately the baby's turning. Therefore, it seemed possible that in the study of Goren et al. the experimenter was at least sometimes able to identify the stimuli and thus to influence the baby. We designed a procedure which avoids these problems and attempted to replicate the results of Goren et al.

The subjects were 40 healthy, full-term newborns (at least 38 weeks ges-

* We would like to thank Mary Stire, Anne Lees, and Adrienne Richardson who helped to collect and analyze these data. This research was supported by Canadian National Science and Engineering Research Grant A9797. Correspondence and requests for reprints should be sent to Daphne Maurer, Department of Psychology, McMaster University, Hamilton, Ontario, Canada L8S 4K1.

Maurer, D., & Young, R. 1983. Newborn's following of natural and distorted arrangements of facial features. *Infant Behavior and Development, 6,* 127–131.

189

tation and 2500 grams at birth) between 12 hours and 5 days old. An additional 46 babies were not included because of a procedural error ($n=10$) or because they fell asleep before completing the procedure ($n=36$).

The infant sat in an infant seat angled at approximately 30° and with a protractor attached to the top. One experimenter stood behind a blind at the infant's feet and held up the stimuli, which had been arranged face down in front of her. She began a trial in which she judged the infant's head to be centered and his eyes to be on the stimulus 20 cm from his face. Then she moved the stimulus slowly in an arc of 90° either to the left or right. This experimenter, who could not identify the stimuli, judged how far the infant moved his eyes. A second experimenter, who could see the stimuli, stood behind the infant and judged how far the infant moved his head.

The four stimuli were similar to those used by Goren et al.: white oval shapes with the features of a face arranged naturally (Stimulus A in Figure 1), moderately scrambled (B), or thoroughly scrambled (C), and a blank grey oval equated in luminance to the other stimuli (see Figure 1). Each stimulus

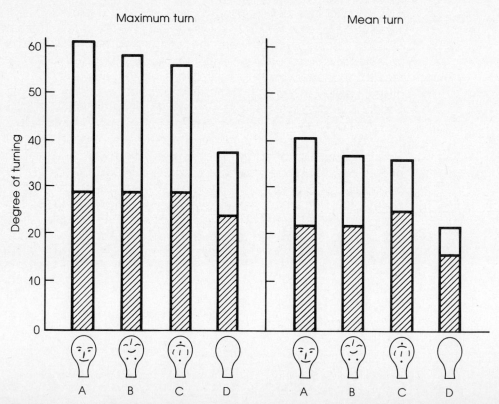

Figure 1 The mean amount of following of the four stimuli with head (shaded bars) and with eyes (unshaded bars). The left panel shows the data for the maximum scores; the right panel, the data for the mean scores. Reprinted, with permission of D. Maurer and R. Young, from Newborn's following of natural and distorted arrangements of facial features. *Infant Behavior and Development,* Vol. 6, pp. 127–131, copyright 1983.

was about life-size (17 by 26 cm) and was attached to a stick. The order of presentation was random, as was the side on which testing began with each stimulus. As in the experiment of Goren et al., an infant was tested seven times with a stimulus moving toward one side, and then seven times with it moving toward the other side, except that testing on a side stopped as soon as the infant had moved his head and eyes on three trials.

All subjects followed each of the stimuli on at least one trial. The scoring for the first analysis was identical to that used by Goren et al. For each stimulus and measure (head-turning or eye-turning) we added the infant's largest turns to the left and to the right. Thus, the maximum possible score for a stimulus on each measure was 180. Figure 1 shows the score for each stimulus averaged across the 40 infants.

Friedman two-way analyses of variance on the maximum scores showed the stimulus affected how far the infants followed with their eyes, $X^2(3) = 42.76$, $P < .001$, and tended to affect how far they moved their heads, $X^2(3) = 7.70$, $P < .06$.[1] We then used Wilcoxon tests of matched pairs, adjusted by Ryan's (1960) procedure, to determine which stimuli the newborns followed differently with their eyes. These tests showed that the infants followed the blank less far than the other stimuli (all P's $< a'$, a' set by Ryan's procedure with = .05), but there were no significant differences in how far the infants followed the different arrangements of the facial features (all P's $> a'$).

The first analysis ignored what infants did on trials on which they did not make the largest turn: An infant could receive the same score for two stimuli even though he followed one on every trial but followed the other on only one trial. Therefore, we analyzed the mean response to each stimulus. For each stimulus and measure we calculated an infant's mean response on the first three right-side trials (regardless of whether or not he had turned) and added it to his mean response on the first three left-side trials (see Figure 1).

Friedman two-way analyses of variance on the mean scores showed that the stimuli affect how far the infants followed both with their eyes, $X^2(3) = 41.69$, $P < .001$, and with their heads, $X^2(3) = 14.20$, $P < .01$. Wilcoxon tests of matched pairs showed that the infants followed the blank less far than the other stimuli with both head and eyes (all P's $< a'$, a' set by Ryan's procedure with $a = .05$. In addition, with their eyes they followed the natural arrangement farther than the thoroughly scrambled arrangement, $T(40) = 216$, $P = .009$, $a' = .0125$.

The results show that the newborns in this study, like those studies by Goren et al., followed the blank less far than any of the patterned stimuli. They could have done so on the basis of differences in patterning, in intensity (the blank was grey while the patterned stimuli was black and white), or in contrast, all of which are cues other investigators have reported that newborns can use to make discriminations (cf. Fantz, 1963; Hershenson, 1964; Rose, Katz, Birke & Rossman, 1977).

Goren et al. also reported that with both head and eyes newborns

---

[1] Like Goren et al., we used nonparametric statistics because the measure, degrees of turning, is not distributed normally.

followed the natural arrangement of facial features farther than either scrambled arrangement. We did not find such a general preference. Using the analysis of Goren et al. there was no evidence for a preference in either eye- or head-turning. Using what we suspected might be a more sensitive variable, mean turn to each stimulus, we found a difference between the natural arrangement and only one of the scrambled arrangements. Moreover, newborns showed this difference only in their eye-turning and not in their head-turning. These results support the claim by Goren et al. that eye-turning is a sensitive measure of newborns' discriminative capacity, but contradict their assertions that head-turning is also a sensitive measure and that newborns have a general preference for natural to unnatural arrangements. Instead newborns may simply prefer some arrangements to others—because in the region they process the contour density is optimal, the elements form an interesting pattern, etc.

Several procedural differences between our study and that of Goren et al. could have led to the discrepancy in results. Our infants were slightly older, but it is unlikely that infants at birth would follow a natural facial arrangement farther than all others yet lose some of that ability within a few days. The fact that our infants sat in an infant seat rather than with the head supported on the experimenter's lap is likely to be a more important procedural difference. It could be argued that newborn infants sitting in an infant seat are not able to control their head or eye movements sufficiently well to demonstrate the discriminations they can make, especially since the absolute level of following was much lower in this study than in that of Goren et al. However, the infants in this study controlled their following well enough to demonstrate the discrimination of the blank from each of the three patterned stimuli, and two of the patterned stimuli from each other. Alternatively, sitting in an infant seat may be critical to the difference between the two studies because it minimizes the possibility of physically influencing the baby's turning, as well as the possibility of observer bias.

This study suggests that eye-turning is a more sensitive index of newborns' discriminative capacity than either head-turning or fixation. Infants showed they could discriminate between two arrangements of facial features in how far they followed them with their eyes, but not with their heads. And using fixation as a measure, no one has demonstrated that infants younger than 2 months can discriminate between such arrangements (Maurer & Barrera, 1981). Eye-turning may be more sensitive than fixation because newborns attend more to moving than to stationary stimuli (Fantz, 1967). In addition, newborns' eye-turning consists of repeated localization of a stimulus which has moved into peripheral vision (Kremenitzer, Vaughn, Kurtzberg & Dowling, 1979), an ability well developed at birth (Harris & MacFarlane, 1974; Lewis, Maurer, & Kay, 1978). In contrast, head-turning is not well regulated at birth and newborns appear to have difficulty voluntarily maintaining fixation on a stimulus (Brown, 1961; Guernsey, 1929; Ling, 1942; Peiper, 1963). It would be interesting to use eye-turning to study other discriminative capacities in newborns.

REFERENCES

Brown, C. The development of visual capacity in the infant and young child. *Cerebral Palsy Bulletin, 1961, 3,* 364–372.

Fantz, R. The origins of form perception. *Scientific American,* 1961, *204,* 66–72.

Fantz, R. Pattern vision in newborn infants. *Science,* 1963, *140,* 296–297.

Fantz, R. Visual perception and experience in early infancy: A look at the hidden side of behavior development. In H. Stevenson, E. Hess, & H. Rheingold (Eds.), *Early Behavior: Comparative and developmental approaches.* New York: Wiley, 1967.

Goren, C., Sarty, M. & Wu, P. Visual following and pattern discrimination of face-like stimuli by newborn infants. *Pediatrics,* 1975, *56,* 544–549.

Guernsey, M. A quantitative study of the eye reflexes in infants. *Psychological Bulletin,* 1929, 26, 160–161.

Harris, P., & MacFarlane, A. The growth of the effective visual field from birth to seven weeks. *Journal of Experimental Child Psychology,* 1974, *18,* 340–348.

Hershenson, M. Visual discrimination in the human newborn. *Journal of Comparative and Physiological Psychology,* 1964, *58,* 270–276.

Kremenitzer, J., Vaughn, H., Jurtzberg, D., & Dowling, K. Smooth pursuit eye movements in the newborn infant. *Child Development,* 1979, *50,* 442–448.

Lewis, T., Maurer, D., & Kay, D. Newborns' central vision: Whole or hole? *Journal of Experimental Child Psychology,* 1978, *26,* 193–203.

Ling, B. A genetic study of sustained visual fixation and associated behavior in the human infant from birth to six months. *Journal of Genetic Psychology,* 1942, *62,* 227–277.

Maurer, D., & Barrera, M. Infants' perception of natural and distorted arrangements of a schematic face. *Child Development,* 1981, *52,* 196–202.

Peiper, A. *Cerebral functioning in infancy and childhood.* New York: Consultants Bureau, 1963.

Rose, S., Katz, P., Burke, M., & Rossman, E. Visual following in newborns: Role of figure-ground contrast and configurational detail. *Perceptual and Motor Skills,* 1977, *45,* 515–522.

Ryan, T. Significance tests for multiple comparison of proportions, variances, and other statistics. *Psychological Bulletin,* 1960, *57,* 318–328.

CHAPTER EXERCISES

8.1. Which of the labels listed below best describes the logic and architecture of the experimental design used by Maurer and Young?

1. A between-subjects bivalent analytic experiment
2. A between-subjects multivalent analytic experiment
3. A between-subjects multivalent quasi-analytic experiment
4. A within-subjects multivalent quasi-analytic experiment
5. A within-subjects quasi-analytic 2 × 5 factorial experiment

8.2. Describe the independent variable(s) in the experiment reported by Maurer and Young.

8.3. Two basic dependent variables were measured in the experiment by Maurer and Young. Describe these two dependent variables and the various different ways in which the experimenters decided to present these measurements.

8.4. In the introduction to their paper, Maurer and Young refer to some earlier research on the same problem reported by Goren, Sarty, and Wu (1975). Maurer and Young suggest that there may have been a confounded variable in the experiment reported by Goren et al. Describe the confounded variable that Maurer and Young suggested and discuss how it might have caused the infants in the Goren et al. experiment to react differently to the different stimulus conditions.

8.5. If you answered exercise 8.1 correctly, you know that the experiment reported by Maurer and Jones is a within-subjects multivalent quasi-analytic experiment. You should also know that the order of treatments must be controlled in some manner to prevent treatment order from being confounded with the independent variable. Describe how Maurer and Young managed to prevent this confounding. What other approaches could they have used to control treatment order, and why might you prefer one method over the others in this particular experiment?

8.6. If you are really ambitious, you might like to go back to Chapter 6 and review the experiment reprinted at the end of that chapter (i.e., Tomlinson, Hicks & Pellegrini, 1978). You now realize that this 2 × 3 factorial design is a within-subjects experiment and that these authors also had to control for the effects of treatment order in their experiment. Describe how Tomlinson et al. managed to prevent a confounding of treatment order and their independent variables in this factorial experiment, then ask yourself how you might have arranged this same experiment so that treatment order would be confounded with the independent variables.

CHAPTER 9

QUASI-ANALYTIC EXPERIMENTS: EX POST FACTO DESIGNS

In Chapter 7 we examined an experiment in which Visintainer, Volpicelli, and Seligman (1981) discovered that rats exposed to stressful stimulation were less resistant to cancer. You will recall that we were primarily concerned with the *external validity* of their discovery, or the extent to which their results with laboratory rats would generalize to people and the kinds of stress that we experience.

You might find it instructive, as an introduction to the topics in the present chapter, to pause for a moment to see if you can think of an analytic experiment that would answer this same question using humans as subjects instead of laboratory rats. I think you will find that it is impossible to design such an experiment. If your design meets all the logical requirements of an analytic experiment, it will not meet the ethical requirements for human experimentation outlined in Appendix B of this text. It would be unthinkable to randomly assign a sample of subjects to two treatment conditions and expose one group to a carcinogenic agent and severe stress. Put very simply, you cannot design an analytic experiment in this case because you cannot randomly assign people to the treatment conditions and expose them to danger.

Given the preceding dilemma and assuming that you want to pursue the matter, there are two possible solutions. Solution 1 involves finding a group of people who have a lot of stress in their lives (e.g., air traffic controllers). Once you have found them, you can measure the incidence of cancer in this group over the next ten years and compare it to a group of people with very little stress in their lives (e.g., department store clerks). Solution 2 involves finding a group of people with cancer and searching back in time to determine how many of them, as compared to a group that is free of cancer, have been exposed to stress during the preceding ten years.

Both solutions escape the ethical problems produced by randomly assigning people to stress and carcinogenic treatments. Solution 1 simply measures the incidence of cancer in people whose lives are already stressful. You have not added any stress. Solution 2 simply measures the amount of stress people have experienced prior to developing cancer. It does not expose them to stress or carcinogenic agents. The basic logic and architecture of these two solutions are illustrated in Figure 9.1, and they would appear at first glance to approximate a bivalent analytic experiment. They are not, however, to be confused with bivalent analytic experiments. Both these experimental designs deviate in very important ways from analytic experiments. As indicated in Figure 9.1, these quasi-analytic experiments are called *prospective ex post facto* and *retrospective ex post facto* designs. In the present chapter, we will discuss these two frequently encountered designs with particular reference to (1) the circumstances in which one might use them, (2) the manner in which they deviate from analytic experiments, (3) the unfortunate consequences of these deviations, and (4) some possible solutions to these unfortunate consequences.

PROSPECTIVE EX POST FACTO DESIGNS

The label "ex post facto" refers to the selection of subjects who have already been exposed to particular treatments or who already exhibit particular characteristics. They are, so to speak, selected for these properties *after the fact*. This is the earmark of all ex post facto designs and the most fundamental way in which they differ from analytic experiments.

The term "prospective" means that the procedure searches *forward in time* to see if the subjects belonging to the ex post facto groups develop cancer.

In scientific research, an incredible number of questions arise that force us to abandon the analytic experiment in favor of a prospective ex post facto design. The reasons for adopting this particular design fall into two general categories. First, as was illustrated by the preceding example, ethics often prevent us from randomly assigning subjects to certain treatment conditions. Although there is a great deal of interest in the properties of stress, we simply cannot do experiments in which we expose subjects to long-term, severe levels of stress. In a similar vein, consider the plight of a psychologist interested in the psychological effects of exposure to various drugs, of a death in the family, or of violent crimes like

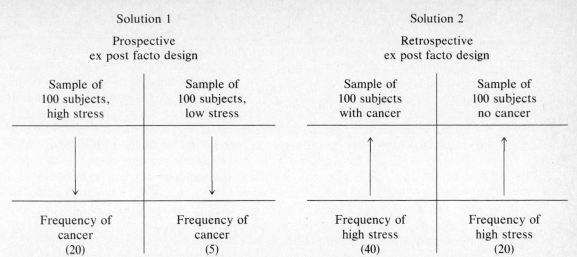

Figure 9.1 Two ex post facto designs to determine if stress had any effects upon the development of cancer.

rape. Consider also the plight of the medical scientist who must determine if a particular substance causes a particular disease. Do high levels of cholesterol in the diet cause heart disease? Does the use of certain drugs during childbirth have any effect upon the infant's survival and subsequent development? These questions provide some indication of the wide range of cases in which ethical considerations would prevent us from using random assignment procedures and force us to deviate from the "gold standard" called the analytic experiment. The list could easily be extended to other areas of research, but the essential point is that ethical considerations, more frequently than any other single factor, force us to abandon the advantages of the analytic experiment.

The second general reason for adopting a prospective ex post facto design is that organisms often come equipped with some particular characteristic that we wish to investigate as a treatment condition. In such cases, we really do not have any choice but to select groups of organisms that have the characteristic and compare them to groups that do not. Some common examples in psychological research are characteristics such as age, sex, intelligence, and various personality traits. If you want to investigate the effects of age on risk-taking behavior, you have no choice but to select different age groups (ex post facto) and compare their tendency to take risks. You obviously cannot randomly assign people to different *ages* any more than you could assign them to male and female, black and white, or schizophrenic and normal treatment conditions. These variables are often called *organismic* variables (Dunham, 1977) in the sense that they are measurable characteristics of organisms that cannot be easily changed or manipulated. When organismic variables are used as independent variables in scientific research, they also force us to use ex post facto designs similar to those illustrated in Figure 9.1.

Problems with Prospective Ex Post Facto Designs

The major problems with prospective ex post facto designs arise from our inability to assign these subjects randomly to the different treatment conditions in an experiment. This drawback produces a major deviation from the logic of the analytic experiment, and the consequences can be serious. The two most common problems can best be explained by reference to our stress and cancer example.

Many people have great stress in their daily lives. There are also some who go through life without much stress. Suppose that you could divide the entire world into these two categories and observe each group during the next ten years. This would provide extensive data about the incidence of cancer in these two populations (high- vs. low-stress). Suppose also that these data indicated that there was a much higher rate of cancer in the high-stress group. Would it be safe to conclude that a high level of stress contributes to the development of cancer? I think not. These two different populations of people might also differ in some other way that contributed to the development of cancer, and this large ex post facto experiment does not eliminate the possibility. For example, it is possible (even likely) that there is a much higher incidence of smoking in the high-stress group and that smoking is the causal factor. You should recognize this problem as our old nemesis, the confounded variable. If the two populations differ in ways other than the high- and low-stress characteristic, these differences represent confounded variables, and any claim that one factor is causal is questionable.

In reality, we would not be able to conduct the ex post facto experiment described above. It would obviously be impossible to divide the entire world into these two categories. Instead, we would have to settle for a smaller sample of people selected from each category. We could then follow these people forward in time and observe the incidence of cancer in each group. Once again, suppose that we observed a much higher incidence of cancer in a small, high-stress *sample* of 100. The use of smaller samples does not solve the original problem, and it may create yet another source of bias in the experiment. Specifically, we must be very careful about the procedure we use to select the high- and low-stress samples from the larger population. In practice, convenience often dictates how people select their samples in this type of experiment. In this particular example, it might be convenient to select a particular occupation known to have a lot of stress associated with it and ask 100 people from that occupation to participate as your high-stress group. I suspect that most people would agree that air traffic controllers would constitute a valid high-stress group. For your low-stress sample, you might decide to select a group of 100 department store clerks.

The *convenient* sampling procedures often found in ex post facto research should always be viewed with suspicion. In our example, the convenient access to air traffic controllers could bias the sample in the direction of finding cancer for reasons other than their high level of stress. Air traffic controllers, unlike department store clerks, are constantly exposed to the radiation from video display terminals. If the output from these video displays was a health hazard, your convenient sampling procedure would have biased the results in favor of finding an increased incidence of cancer in the high-stress group. The other side of the coin is also true. If, somehow, your procedure for selecting low-stress subjects biased the sample in the direction of finding less cancer for reasons that have nothing to do with stress, your results are again contaminated.

I am sure you recall, from Chapter 2, that the best way to avoid introducing bias in selecting your small sample from each of these large populations is to use a completely *random* sampling procedure in which all the individuals in each population have an equal chance to participate. Unfortunately, these conditions are seldom observed in ex post facto research. The really demoralizing point, however, is that the use of a completely random sampling procedure to select the 100 people in each group would still not solve the original problem. The *entire* population of high- and low-stress individuals can still differ in important ways that will continue to be confounded in your smaller samples.

The preceding discussion describes the two most common problems with prospective ex post facto experiments; Figure 9.2 has been designed to summarize these problems for you. Panel 1 consists of our original prospective ex post facto design concerned with the effects of stress on the development of cancer. At the top of the panel, you find the two large populations of people; one with high and the other with low levels of stress. From these two large populations, you *conveniently* define and isolate 100 high-stress people by selecting air traffic controllers from the local airport. Similarly, you select 100 department store clerks for your low-stress sample. You follow these people forward in time for ten years and measure the incidence of cancer in both groups. The results indicate that there were 20 cases of cancer in the high-stress group and 5 in the low-stress group. Now, note in particular the list of other variables that characterize these two samples. The 100 high-stress people have an average age of 35, live in a large city, and are married. They share these characteristics in common with the low-stress group. In the language of analytic experiments, we would say that these are controlled variables. However, the four other characteristics listed represent *confounded* differences that might exist between the high- and low-stress samples. Three of these variables were probably confounded in the original large population of high-stress individuals. These include high rates of smoking, high-fat diets, and a high level of prescription drug usage in the high-stress group; each of these factors rates low in the low-stress group. The difference in rate of cancer is as likely to have been produced by these confounded differences as by differences in stress level. The fourth characteristic is exposure to video display terminals. The unusually large difference in such exposure is also a confounded difference between the two samples, but in this case the confounding was produced by the *convenient* sampling of air traffic controllers for the high-stress sample. All four of these confounded variables pose a threat to the internal validity of the experiment and render questionable any claim that high stress contributes to the development of cancer.

Alternatively, panel 2 of Figure 9.2 illustrates how effective it would be to do the experiment as a bivalent analytic experiment. In this case, we begin with a large general population and randomly select 200 individuals from it. We then randomly sort our selected subjects into two treatment groups of 100 each. One of these groups is exposed to some diabolical high-stress treatment for a period

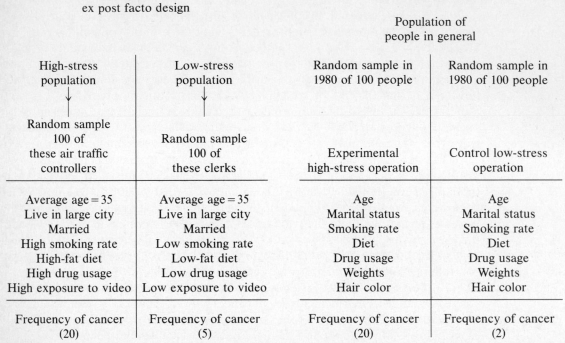

Panel 1 Prospective ex post facto design		Panel 2 Bivalent analytic design
		Population of people in general
High-stress population ↓	Low-stress population ↓	Random sample in 1980 of 100 people	Random sample in 1980 of 100 people
Random sample 100 of these air traffic controllers	Random sample 100 of these clerks	Experimental high-stress operation	Control low-stress operation
Average age = 35 Live in large city Married High smoking rate High-fat diet High drug usage High exposure to video	Average age = 35 Live in large city Married Low smoking rate Low-fat diet Low drug usage Low exposure to video	Age Marital status Smoking rate Diet Drug usage Weights Hair color	Age Marital status Smoking rate Diet Drug usage Weights Hair color
Frequency of cancer (20)	Frequency of cancer (5)	Frequency of cancer (20)	Frequency of cancer (2)

Figure 9.2 Comparison of prospective ex post facto and bivalent analytic designs in terms of the confounded variable likely to occur in each case.

of several years while the other lives a relatively stress-free life. Now look at the list of characteristics in each of these groups. The random assignment of subjects to treatment conditions should effectively equate the groups with reference to almost any characteristic. Random assignment should distribute drug usage patterns, diets, smoking—and a variety of other factors we have not even considered—equally across both treatment conditions. Perhaps now you can appreciate the importance of the random assignment feature of analytic experiments. It is our best defense against the nefarious confounded variable. It would, however, be unethical to conduct this analytic experiment.

Several other aspects of the prospective ex post facto design are also potential sources of error and bias. In terms of measuring the frequency of cancer, this design assumes that it is equally easy to detect and measure the dependent variable in each of the treatment conditions of the experiment. One might, for example, be concerned that members of the high-stress group would see a physician more frequently for various minor ailments than those in the low-stress group. This difference would increase the likelihood of detecting cancer in the high-stress group. This one example, of many possible, suggests that it is very important to arrange the measurement procedures in the prospective experiment in a manner that eliminates any possibility of this problem. This form of bias occurs frequently enough to have acquired its own label: Feinstein (1977) calls it *detection bias*.

The ex post facto design also assumes that we can accurately identify the members of each treatment group, and this is not always easy to do. In some cases it may be necessary to consult the "historical record" to identify a particular group. If we wanted, for example, to compare the academic performance of children with a history of sleeping disorders to that of children who have not had such problems, it would be necessary to interview parents to obtain the information. Correct identification of the two groups assumes that the parents have an accurate memory of the child's behavior *and* that they would be honest with you about their children's problems. Both assumptions are dubious.

Up to this point, we have focused on problems that threaten the *internal validity* of the ex post facto experiment. There can also be difficulties with their *external validity*. One threat arises when you select samples from the larger populations. In our stress and cancer example, any deviation from a random sampling procedure will produce a "special" sample of high- and low-stress people. The selection of air traffic controllers as the high-stress group illustrates the problem. One would be less likely to generalize from results obtained with this "special" group than to generalize from a random sample of all high-stress occupations. Threats to external validity also arise when we depend on volunteer subjects. People living under very high levels of stress are less likely to volunteer. They would not want the extra hassle added to their already stressful lives. This could eliminate very high-stress people from the sample and once again limit the generality of the results. Finally, prospective ex post facto experiments often take place over extended periods of time. Again, it seems reasonable to suggest that a certain type of subject may drop out of the experiment before it is completed. If all of the dropouts happen to be from the extreme levels of stress, once again the generality of the results would be limited. Please note that these threats to external validity posed by sampling problems are not unique to the ex post facto experiment. They can also occur in analytic experiments.

To summarize briefly, the most fundamental problem with the prospective ex post facto design is that we are likely to acquire confounded variables when we select our subject populations according to some characteristic such as high and low stress. The other problems described above arise to varying degrees depending upon the specific research problem under consideration. The reader interested in a more detailed analysis of some of these issues will do well to consult excellent discussions by Feinstein (1971a, 1971b).

Matching as a Solution

If the primary problem of prospective ex post facto designs is the selection of confounded variables along with our independent variables (high- vs. low-stress groups), one solution has perhaps already occurred to you. Why not eliminate the confounded differences between the high- and low-stress groups by *matching* the subjects in the two groups so that they do not differ on any characteristic other than high and low stress? This method should be as effective as random assignment for *controlling* differences between groups that would otherwise be confounded.

In theory, matching subjects can be a solution to the problem of confounded variables. In practice, it is seldom a completely satisfactory solution. In order to understand the matching solution and its particular difficulties, consider once again our stress and cancer example. The four confounded variables in the prospective ex post facto design illustrated in Figure 9.2 are (1) smoking rate, (2) fat in the diet, (3) prescription drug usage, and (4) exposure to video display terminals. If we wanted to use the matching solution to control these confounded variables, two basic approaches are used most frequently.

One approach is called *subject-for-subject* matching. In this case, for each person selected in the high-stress group, we would search for a person in the low-stress population who was a good match. For example, if one high-stress person smoked two packs of cigarettes a day, then one low-stress person should also smoke two packs a day. The second basic approach is *distribution-for-distribution* matching. In this case, if the high-stress *group* smokes an *average* of two packs of cigarettes a day, we would select a group of low-stress people who matched this average. In addition, we would also try to match the two groups in terms of other distributional characteristics, such as variability (see Chapter 3).

The *subject-for-subject* matching procedure is obviously a very precise method of matching subjects. Unfortunately, it has several drawbacks. First, it is often difficult to find a match for everyone, particularly the extreme cases in the sample. If we find one person who smokes eight packs of cigarettes a day in the high-stress sample, it will probably be very difficult to find a match in the low-stress sample. This means that we will have to drop the eight-pack smoker from the high-stress sample, and when we selectively drop subjects in this way we limit the generality (i.e., external validity) of the final results. This problem is exacerbated if you try to match *subject for subject* on more than one variable. Can you imagine the problems you would encounter trying to match a low-stress subject to a high-stress subject who smoked eight packs of cigarettes each day, took medication for hypertension, and was a vegetarian? The search would be difficult indeed. The task becomes impossible when you multiply the problem by a large number of subjects, each of whom must be matched on a large number of potentially confounded variables. In such cases, you inevitably drop many subjects selectively from your samples and restrict the external validity of the results.

As a practical alternative, matching *distribution to distribution* would seem to be very appealing. It does alleviate the problems described above to some extent. It is definitely easier to match the two groups in terms of the average number of cigarettes they smoke. Once again, however, when you start to match on the basis of several different averages, the task become difficult and subjects must be selectively dropped. It can also be impossible to match the groups on certain variables. Can you imagine, for example, trying to find 100 low-stress people who have as much exposure to video display terminals as your 100 air traffic controllers?

Finally, even if you find that your matching procedure does manage the task without dropping too many subjects from the samples, you will still be haunted by the possibility that you have missed some of the confounded variables created when the two groups were formed. All things considered, it is clear that matching can help with the problem of confounded variables in the prospective ex post facto experiment, but it should never be considered an adequate substitute for the random assignment feature of the analytic experiment.

Measuring Variables as a Solution

Another approach to the problem of confounded variables in ex post facto designs is to search for these variable and simply measure them to see if they are actually confounded. This solution does not rid the experiment of confounded variables, but it does either confirm or deny their presence in a particular experiment. A recent experiment reported by Singer and Fagan (1984) illustrates the properties of this approach very well.

Early in the first year after birth, some infants fail to gain weight at normal rates. When an infant's weight gain (relative to height) falls below the third percentile of normal growth curves, pediatricians call the condition *failure to thrive* (Barbero & McKay, 1969) and express concern about the child's development. Singer and Fagan suspected that the failure-to-thrive condition might also have some effect on the child's mental development, so they designed a prospective ex post facto experiment that compared the mental development of 36 failure-to-thrive infants to a group exhibiting normal growth rates. They followed these infants forward in time for three years after the diagnosis and measured mental development with several tasks and standardized tests (e.g., Bayley Mental Scale of Infant Development; Stanford-Binet Intelligence Scale). Suffice it to say that at 3 years of age, the mental development of the failure-to-thrive infants lagged significantly behind that of the normal-growth group. Apparently early evidence of failure to thrive predicts later problems with mental development.

If you understand the basic weaknesses of prospective ex post facto designs, you must be asking yourself at this point if there are any other differences between these two groups of children that might be the cause of the slower rate of mental development in the failure-to-thrive group. Singer and Fagan were aware of this problem, but they did not make any elaborate efforts to match the two groups on variables that might have been confounded. Instead of matching, they attempted to measure directly other differences between the two groups they thought might be important. Of the various factors measured, two did emerge as important: (1) the failure-to-thrive infants were more often placed in the care of someone other than the mother during the first few years and (2) the parents of failure-to-thrive infants had less education than parents of normal-growth children. Both these characteristics were, therefore, confounded with the independent variable in this study. By measuring these variables, Singer and Fagan were able to determine that they were confounded. A number of the other characteristics they measured did not differ across the two groups.

The important point is that progress can be made by searching for and measuring confounded variables in an ex post facto experiment. The confounded variables discovered by Singer and Fagan are important discoveries suggesting some *potential* causes of retarded mental development. The suggestion that a change of caretakers during early infancy might have adverse effects on mental development is particularly interesting and controversial; it certainly deserves additional attention.

It must be recognized that measuring other variables does not eliminate them as confounded variables in the experiment. It simply tells us that they are confounded. Nor do such measurements guarantee that the experimenter has discovered *all possible* confounded variables in the ex post facto design. I would not be surprised, for example, to find that, in the failure-to-thrive group, the incidence of breast-feeding was lower, the parents were younger, and the average income of the parents was lower. These variables were not measured by Singer and Fagan, hence we do not know if they were confounded in this experiment.

We shall return to the technique of measuring potential confounded variables later, in Chapter 11, when we discuss the logic of multivariate methods. For now, it should be clear that the measurement of confounded variables is a worthwhile solution, but again, it can never completely substitute for the random-assignment feature of the analytic experiment.

The Relative Risk Ratio as a Dependent Variable

The prospective ex post facto experiment is encountered so often in medical research concerned with the causes of disease that a special calculation is often used to describe the results. It is called a *relative risk ratio;* the simple arithmetic involved is illustrated in Figure 9.3. Assume that you conducted the prospective ex post facto experiment concerned with stress and cancer depicted in panel 1 and obtained the results indicated: 20 cases of cancer in the high-stress group and 5 cases in the low-stress group. Panel 2 casts these results into a 2 × 2 contingency table, which makes it easy to see that the two important ratios are 20/100 in the high-stress group and 5/100 in the low-stress group. When we divide the lower ratio by the higher ratio, we obtain a relative risk ratio of 4, indicating that the incidence of cancer was four times higher in the high-stress group.

Although it is common practice to report such data in terms of the relative risk ratio, you should be distressed when you read accounts of ex post facto research reporting only this ratio as the dependent variable. This calculation is intended to facilitate communication of the data; instead, it hides important information. Suppose, for example, that you read a report describing the incidence of toxic shock syndrome as five times higher in females who use tampons during their menstrual cycle. This relative risk ratio could be based on either of the two sets of hypothetical data in Figure 9.4. If the relative risk ratio was based on data obtained in Panel 1, you would perhaps be concerned about the use of tampons. Of the 1000 tampon users, 250 developed the disease: therefore, the *absolute risk* is quite high. Alternatively, if the relative risk ratio was based on

Panel 1	Panel 2
Prospective ex post facto design	Contingency table for prospective ex post facto data and risk-ratio calculations

Panel 1

Prospective
ex post facto design

100 subjects, high-stress group	100 subjects, low-stress group

↓ ↓

Frequency of cancer = 20	Frequency of cancer = 5

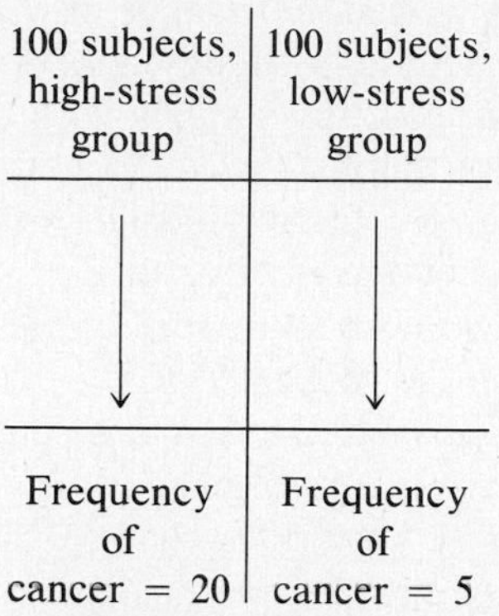

Panel 2

Contingency table for
prospective ex post facto data
and risk-ratio calculations

	High stress	Low stress	
Cancer cases	20	5	25
No cancer cases	80	95	175
Totals	100	100	200

$$\text{Relative risk ratio} = \frac{20}{100} \div \frac{5}{100}$$

Relative risk ratio = 4

Figure 9.3 Calculating the relative risk ratio from the results of a prospective ex post facto design.

the data in Panel 2, you might be less concerned about tampon use. Only 5 out of 1000 tampon users developed the disease, hence the *absolute risk* is quite low.

The relative risk ratio is an unfortunate calculation precisely because it hides valuable information about the absolute risk factor. The more general point is that numerical manipulations of the dependent variable in any experiment should be made with care. They should facilitate communication and not hide potentially important characteristics of the data.

Panel 1

	Tampon users	Nonusers
Toxic shock syndrome	250	50
No toxic shock syndrome	750	950
	1000	1000

Relative risk ratio = 5

Panel 2

	Tampon users	Nonusers
Toxic shock syndrome	5	1
No toxic shock syndrome	995	999
	1000	1000

Relative risk ratio = 5

Figure 9.4 Two hypothetical sets of data based on 1000 subjects. Both sets have the same relative risk ratio. The absolute risk of disease is, however, much higher in Table 1.

RETROSPECTIVE EX POST FACTO DESIGNS

If you refer back to Figure 9.1 (p. 197), you will recall that solution 2 to the ethical dilemma posed by studying the effects of stress on cancer was also an ex post facto solution. In that solution, we identified 100 people with cancer (after the fact) and contrasted them with 100 people without cancer. The primary difference between the two solutions is that solution 2 starts with the *effect* and follows the group backward in time to search for a *cause*. It is for this reason that solution 2 is called a *retrospective* ex post facto design. The retrospective design has problems similar to those found in prospective designs, but they are more insidious and difficult to deal with. These extra difficulties are usually associated with searching *backward* in time for causes.

If the problems with ex post facto designs are made worse by the adoption of a retrospective approach, why would anyone ever choose the retrospective solution over the prospective solution? The answer is that a wide variety of practical problems often force the use of a retrospective design. In many cases, a prospective ex post facto design involves long and expensive procedures. This is particularly true in the case of medical research intended to find the causes of various diseases. Our hypothetical stress and cancer example is reasonably realistic in this respect. It would probably be necessary to follow a sample of high- and low-stress people forward in time for several years in order to obtain information to be meaningful. The difficulty is compounded when the disease occurs with a very low frequency in the population. Psychologists interested in a syndrome like multiple personality would be required to follow extremely large samples of people forward over long periods of time in order to observe any cases of this rare psychosis. Hence, the psychologist interested in this problem would be well advised to adopt a retrospective ex post facto design in which an already dignosed group is followed backward in time to search for possible causal factors. The number of people involved is smaller, the time taken to do the experiment is shorter, and the retrospective approach is much cheaper. Although I do not have actual figures on the matter, I would not be surprised to find that at least 75 percent of all ex post facto experiments published in the existing literature are retrospective designs.

Problems with Retrospective Ex Post Facto Designs

There is a large population of people in the world with some form of cancer. There is also a large population (fortunately much larger) without the disease. Once again, our problems begin when we divide the world into these two groups to compare them. Suppose, for example, that we conducted a massive retrospective experiment in which everyone in the population with cancer was included in one group and everyone who did not have cancer was included in the other. Assume also that, one by one, we searched back through the history of each individual in these two populations and measured the amount of stress in their lives. If the level of stress in the cancer population was much higher than that in the noncancer population, you might be tempted to accept the conclusion that stress contributed to the development of cancer. Once again, however, a thorough search of the history of the cancer and noncancer groups would very likely reveal some characteristics in addition to stress that differentiated the two groups. The process of retrospectively splitting the world into two groups on the basis of some particular characteristic has increased the probability of confounded variables.

You should also note, in parallel with the problems described for prospective designs, that we are seldom able to do a retrospective experiment in which we examine the entire population of people with cancer and compare it to the entire population without the disease. Instead, we would select a much smaller sample of people from each of these two categories and search back through the history of the individuals in these samples. Once again, you must select the samples appropriately, or serious problems can arise. As you know, the best approach would be to select a random sample from the cancer population and another random sample for the noncancer population. As you might imagine, random sampling seldom occurs in retrospective research. Indeed, scientists often have the ''diseased'' group selected for them in the form of individuals seeking treatment. With reference to our stress and cancer study, any sampling procedure used to select 100 cancer patients that also favors the selection of high-stress individuals will contaminate the experiment. This unfortunate procedure would suggest that the high-stress condition is a cause of cancer, when in fact the large number of high-stress people in the cancer group is an artifact of the biased sampling procedure.

This problem with sampling bias is surprisingly common. The most interesting recent case I can recall involved a number of retrospective ex post facto experiments designed to search for the cause of toxic shock syndrome. This disease, mentioned earlier, is a serious infection observed most commonly in menstruating women. It occurs with a very low frequency in the general population. According to Hulka (1982), there are about 9 cases per 100,000 population per year.

The initial detection of an outbreak of toxic shock syndrome in the 1970s provoked considerable interest from the mass media. Early speculation suggested that the use of tampons during menstruation might be a causal factor. Curiously, this speculation persisted in spite of the fact that the initial report of the disease included three males among the seven diagnosed cases (Todd et al., 1978). Following the initial report, a number of retrospective ex post facto studies were conducted using a relatively small sample of cases that had been referred to medical scientists from various sources. To make a long and complicated story short, the data from these retrospective experiments suggested that the risk of toxic shock was much higher among tampon users (in some cases risk ratios of 18 were reported).

Should you accept the implications of these data and assume that tampons are a causal factor in the development of toxic shock syndrome? The economic implications for the manufacturers of tampons are substantial, and the health implications for users of the product are potentially a matter of life and death. The answer remains unclear. Of the many problems that characterize retrospective ex post facto experiments, one is particularly relevant in the present context. The sample of patients with toxic shock syndrome selected for participation in these retrospective experiments was probably biased in favor of females who use tampons. There are a number of ways in which this sampling bias could have occurred, but the most likely explanation is that the physicians who referred their toxic shock cases to the medical scientists had been *sensitized* by media reports to selectively look for toxic shock when they were dealing with female patients who used tampons. This bias was made worse by the fact that toxic shock symptoms are not always easy to differentiate from other types of infection. Put very simply, the possible scenario is that media reports influenced family physicians to look particularly hard for the tampon–toxic shock combination in their patients; hence the sample of patients eventually referred to the scientists had this bias built into it. The arguments as to whether or not this is the correct interpretation of the data have not, to my knowledge, ever been settled. The reader interested in the entire story is referred to an excellent systematic account of these and other methodological problems associated with the toxic shock research by Harvey, Horwitz, and Feinstein (1982). Indeed, this account should be required reading for anyone who wants to develop a thorough understanding of retrospective ex post facto designs and their potential problems.

Another source of bias in retrospective designs in parallel with the prospective approach is the threat of *detection bias*. The retrospective design assumes that, as you search back in time, it is equally easy to detect the presence of the suspected causal factor with the cancer and noncancer groups. Detection bias should not be underestimated; it can develop in very subtle ways. In our stress and cancer example, think for a moment about the problems associated with measuring the presence or absence of stress in the history of subjects in each of these two groups. If you decide to interview all subjects about the stressful events in their lives during the past five years, I suspect you will bias your results in favor of finding more stress in the antecedent lives of cancer patients. There is good reason to suspect that any cancer patient will have been thinking a great deal about the potential causes of his or her disease and will be highly motivated to discover them. Alternatively, noncancer control subjects have considerably less reason to remember and report stressful events. Hence, the list of stressful events obtained from an interview with a cancer patient will probably be longer and more elaborate than the list from the noncancer control subject. The problem is even more severe if you decide to use the formal health records of cancer patients who have already died of the disease. These health records would probably be more complete than those of a noncancer control subject. Once again, detection bias would favor the discovery of stressful events in the health records of the cancer group. Detection bias can be insidious in retrospective ex post facto research, where you are forced to search backward in time for events over which you have no control.

Finally, it should be noted that the retrospective ex post facto design suffers from all the threats to *external validity* that were described in our discussion of prospective designs. The primary problem in this regard is that random sampling procedures can seldom be used to select subjects from the larger populations.

Solutions to Retrospective Design Problems

The major problems with retrospective ex post facto designs are the confounded variables that can be produced when you divide people into the different groups of interest (cancer vs. noncancer patients) and/or when you take samples of these different populations for your experiment. The solutions available to you in the retrospective design are essentially the same as those in the prospective design. You can try to match the subjects using the various matching procedures I have described, or you can try to measure other characteristics in the populations to see if they differ in any way other than the one you have defined. These solutions are no more or less effective with retrospective designs than they were with prospective designs, but they are much more difficult to employ in most retrospective ex post facto experiments.

Consider how difficult it would be to match two samples taken from a population of cancer subjects and another of noncancer subjects. You would have to search back in time to measure every characteristic that you wanted to match. Their diets, history of drug usage, smoking habits, and many other characteristics would presumably be important and potentially confounded. Note, however, that their memory of these events, or any other source of information about these events from their past lives, will inevitably lack reliability. Given the difficult and questionable sources of such information and the problems associated with obtaining a precise match, it is difficult to place much faith in this solution in the context of retrospective designs.

The same arguments obviously apply to any attempt to measure potential confounded variables in the cancer and noncancer groups. Accurate sources of such information will be difficult to find largely because you must search some type of historical record to obtain them. In short, confounded variables continue to be the primary weakness in retrospective ex post facto designs and solutions are much less likely to be realized.

The Relative Odds Ratio as a Dependent Variable

As was the case in prospective ex post facto designs, it is not uncommon to see the dependent measure in these designs expressed as a ratio statistic. Figure 9.5 illustrates a hypothetical retrospective ex post facto design in panel 1 and the manner in which the ratio statistic is calculated in panel 2. Note that exactly the same contingency table is used in both prospective (Figure 9.3) and retrospective (Figure 9.5) examples. The calculations are, however, necessarily different. The ratios used to calculate the relative risk ratio, if applied to the data in panel 2, would be 20/25 divided by 80/175. These comparisons are obviously meaningless. They would imply that the absolute risk of cancer in both the high- and low-stress groups is incredibly high. In fact, these high absolute risks are inflated precisely because we selected half the total number of subjects because they had cancer! The appropriate calculation from the contingency table is 20/5 divided by 80/95. Statistical reasoning (which need not be elaborated upon in the present context) has demonstrated that this calculation is a good estimate of the relative

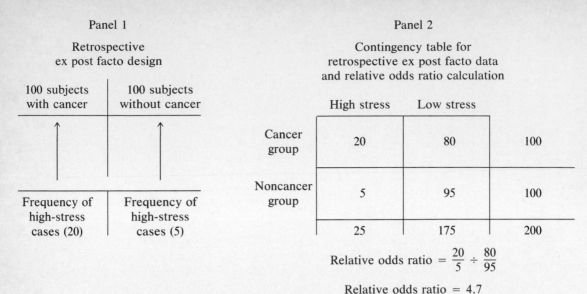

Figure 9.5   Calculating the odds ratio with data from a retrospective ex post facto design.

risk ratio obtained from prospective data. In order to differentiate the two statistics, the ratio calculated from retrospective data is typically called the *relative odds ratio*. I might also note, in conclusion, that the statistical reasoning that lets us decide that the relative odds ratio is a good estimate of the relative risk ratio *also* makes the dubious assumption that we used a random sampling procedure to obtain our subjects from the cancer and noncancer populations.

Perhaps the most important point is that the relative odds ratio hides information from us in the same way that the relative risk ratio does; hence, you should remember to inquire about the absolute risk levels observed in the experiment and to avoid exclusive use of these ratio statistics.

EX POST FACTO RESEARCH AS A NECESSARY EVIL

It should be clear from the preceding discussion that anyone who wishes to make causal arguments from either major type of ex post facto design will find it frustrating. Although the analytic experiment carries no guarantee when it comes to confounded variables, I will place my money on it every time in comparison to ex post facto deviations. On the other hand, I think you can now see that an incredible amount of scientific research could not be done if we did not use quasi-analytic experiments. Perhaps the most appropriate approach is to employ the best tools available for the job but also to be aware of the threats to internal and external validity associated with them.

Consider, for example, a short article in the magazine *Science News,* claiming that women who use contraceptive foams as a method of birth control are twice as likely to bear children with birth defects. As I read the magazine article, my thinking proceeded in the following manner: (1) I first doubted if the claim was based on an analytic experiment (ethics would not permit it) and (2) I then concluded that it must be an ex post facto design of some type, and a retrospective ex post facto design seemed the most likely candidate. It would take too long to observe (forward in time) women who used spermicidal foam and count birth defects in their offspring. It would be much faster and cheaper to select women who had children with birth defects and search backward in time to compare birth control methods. When you encounter such claims, I hope your thinking will proceed in a similar manner and that you will systematically ask questions about likely confounded variables, sampling bias, detection bias, absolute risk, and so on.

In case you are interested, the study of contraceptive foam was, in fact, a retrospective ex post facto design (see Jick et al., 1981) and it does suffer from some of the usual ailments. If you think that you need practice in diagnosing these ailments and would like to test your understanding of the concepts discussed in the preceding paragraphs, I have reprinted portions of an experiment reported by Jacobs and Charles (1980) on the following pages. This particular experiment suggests (appropriate to our overused example) that stressful events in the lives of young children might contribute to the development of cancer. If you can answer the questions about this experiment in the Chapter Exercises, you have a reasonably good understanding of the important concepts in this chapter.

LIFE EVENTS AND THE OCCURRENCE OF CANCER IN CHILDREN

THEODORE J. JACOBS, MD, AND EDWARD CHARLES, MA

Abstract

Over a two-year period the families of twenty-five children with cancer and of a comparison group of children brought to a general pediatric clinic were studied by means of the Holmes-Rahe Life Schedule of Recent Events and by personal interviews. Results obtained by use of the Holmes-Rahe questionnaire revealed significant differences between the patient and control groups. Histories obtained from families in both groups also revealed that in the cancer group certain important life events were found to have occurred with greater frequency in the year prior to the onset of the disease. The relevance of these findings to previous work done in the field and to some current theories concerning the relationship of genetic, viral, endocrine, and psychological factors in the development of cancer are discussed.

It is over twenty years ago that Greene and Miller (1), in a pioneering study, investigated the role of emotional and psychological factors in the development of leukemia in children and adolescents. This study extended and expanded prior work done by Greene and his associates on the relationship of such factors to the onset of leukemia and lymphoma in adults (2–4).

The study of the pediatric age group, consistent with the earlier findings, suggested that experience of separation and loss played a role as one of the multiple conditions determining the development of leukemia in children. Of the thirty-three patients with lymphocytic and myelogenous leukemia investigated, thirty-one were said to have experienced one or more losses or separations in the two-year period prior to the onset of their illness, with half of these experiences occurring in the six months prior to that time. These events, which included such experiences as a change of residence or school, the death of a parent, and separation or threat of separation from grandparents, often involved as well "a separation, loss, or change for the mother, father or other members of the family." A subsequent investigation by Greene and Swisher (5) of the monozygotic twins discordant for leukemia lent weight to the idea that major psychological stress may constitute one of the precipitating factors in the onset of the manifest symptoms of leukemia.

Since that time a number of studies (6–10) have investigated the relationship of life change experiences, Including real or threatened loss, to the onset of a variety of disease states. Despite the potential significance of Greene's work to the field of pediatric cancer, however, there has been no systematic study that has attempted to carry forward the investigation of the relationship of psychological factors to the occurrence of cancer In children. Nonetheless, a considerable amount of anecdotal material, based primarily on individual case records, has suggested that the kind of life experiences reported by Greene in his group of patients are not infrequently met with in the recent history of children and adolescents with cancer. It was because the senior author, quite by chance, came across such instances in the course of obtaining the social and family histories of pediatric cancer patients, that we decided to undertake this study.

METHOD

Utilizing a questionnaire (The Holmes and Rahe Schedule of Recent Events), a semistructured interview schedule, and an open-ended format, one or both parents of twenty-five children and adolescents with cancer were interviewed over a two-year period. An equal number of youngsters who were brought to a medical facility for a variety of physical complaints served as a comparison group. The children with malignancies were diagnosed as having either leukemia, a lymphoma, or other form of cancer, and were being treated on one of the two pediatric services associated with the Albert Einstein College of Medicine.

Neoplastic diseases of several kinds were included for two reasons. The first was a practical one. The number of cancer patients seen on the pediatric services in any one year is not large and it would have required several more years of study to accumulate a sufficient number of cases of any one kind. The authors also felt that the inclusion of neoplasms of several kinds would be of interest from the point of view of the setting in which they arose. As it turned out, the majority of cases were diagnosed as having leukemia, with lymphomas being the next most frequently encountered group.

The comparison group, which was matched for sex, age, and socioeconomic background, was drawn from children who were brought to the general pediatric clinic. The great majority of these children suffered from minor ailments such as sore throats or upper respiratory infections, although some more serious conditions, e.g., asthma, were also diagnosed. There was no effort on the part of the researchers to select the children on the basis of their diagnoses or the seriousness of their complaints. The only criteria used were that the comparison group be matched in the parameters mentioned and that they be brought by their families to see a physician. A group of children who were considered to be physically ill were chosen for comparison rather than normal, healthy children because research in recent years has shown that life changes such as those cited by Greene in relation to leukemia are likely to precede the onset of a variety of illnesses In children (11–13).

The semistructured interview schedule included a detailed medical history of the patient and his family; a history of the mother's pregnancy and delivery; a developmental history of the child, including personality characteristics and psychological symptoms; a history of exposure to known carcinogens; information on the quality of the child's relationship to family and friends prior to the onset of the illness; a history of psychological symptoms in other members of the family; questions pertaining to assessment of the marriage and the parents' relations to each other, their own parents, and children; a history of the illness, including its onset, course, and treatment; and, finally, an exploration of life changes within the family one year prior to the apparent onset of the disease.

For the last purpose, the Holmes and Rahe Life Schedule of Recent Events was included (14,15). The use, in this way, of a standardized instrument, whose forty-three items have been assigned a weighted value, measured in life change units, allowed for some quantification of the data obtained and for a more meaningful comparison between the two groups. The fact that the Holmes and Rahe Scale includes a broad spectrum of questions pertaining to events that have involved the entire family, as well as the child, made it suitable for our purposes.

To obtain a more thorough picture of the family's experience in the two years prior to the onset of the disease, more extensive, open-ended interviewing was also undertaken. The material thus obtained provided some insight into the quality of life and coping styles of the child and his family as well as providing information on experiences and social supports not touched on in the Life Events Scale. Although not all of this material could be quantified, as in the Holmes and Rahe weighted scoring system, the clinical data thus obtained supplemented and enriched our understanding of the recent experiences of the families that we studied.

RESULTS

Patient and Comparison Group Characteristics

The patient group ranged in age from three to seventeen years with a mean age of 9.5 years (see Table 1). There were fifteen cases of leukemia, four of non-Hodgkin's lymphoma, and three of Hodgkin's disease. Other types of cancer diagnosed and represented by one case each were: Ewing's sarcoma, Wilms' tumor, and a sarcoma of the brain. The diagnoses and demographic characteristics of both the patient and the comparison group are shown in Table 1.

Information pertaining to several factors of importance in the study of pediatric cancer was obtained from the semi-structured interview schedule and compared for the two groups (see Table 2). There were five first born children in the patient group (20%), compared with 9 (36%) in the comparison group. Thus the high percentage of first born children reported by Greene (55%) was not confirmed in the present study. Eighty percent of the children

Table 1 Characteristics of the Child and Adolescent Sample ($N = 50$)

	Patient group (n = 25) (%)	Comparison group (n = 25) (%)
Sex		
Female	56	56
Male	44	44
Age		
1–5 years	20	24
6–10 years	44	40
11–17 years	36	36
Religion		
Catholic	68	56
Protestant	20	28
Jewish	12	16
Education		
Preschool	16	20
<8th grade	60	60
High school	24	20
Socioeconomic Class (Hollingshead Scale)		
Class I	4	4
II	12	8
III	56	60
IV	20	20
V	8	8
Symptoms and/or Diagnosis		
Leukemia	60	
Lymphoma	16	
Other cancer	12	
Upper respiratory/sore throat and fever		56
Stomach virus		16
Asthma		12
Eczema		8
Kidney disease		4
Deafness		4

in the patient group and 84% in the comparison had siblings. Some pediatric oncologists, noting the occurrence of cancer in certain later born children with older parents, have speculated about the possible significance, from a genetic point of view, of maternal age. In our study, only 8 mothers in the patient group and 6 of the comparison group mothers were over the age of thirty at the time of the birth of their children.

The incidence of known cancer in the families of the patient group was 60% as compared with 32% in the comparison group families. This included

Table 2   Characteristics of the Patient and Comparison Group on the Semistructured Interview Schedule ($N = 50$)

	Patient group ($n = 25$) (%)	Comparison group ($n = 25$) (%)
Birth order		
Only child	20	16
1st born	20	36
Later born	60	48
History of cancer in the family[a]	60	32
Planned pregnancy[a]	32	90
Somatic and/or emotional problems reported during pregnancy[a]	56	28
Difficult birth[a] (cesarean, forceps, etc.)	20	4
Frequency of illness during childhood		
Common infectious diseases	44	36
Upper respiratory and colds	60	44
Ear, eye, urinary infection[a]	24	8

[a] Statistical significance between patient and control groups with Yates correction for discontinuity, χ^2 tests, $P < 0.01$.

both the immediate and the more extended families. In one case, the older sibling of a five-year-old boy had died of Hodgkin's disease several years before the boy developed a Wilms' tumor. In two cases of children with acute lymphocytic leukemia (ALL), siblings of their fathers had died in early adolescence of leukemia. In the cases of two other children, one with Hodgkin's disease and one with ALL, the patients' own fathers had developed thyroid and lung cancer as young adults. This high incidence of cancer, both in the immediate family and in close relatives, while not unexpected, is nevertheless noteworthy.

The incidence of other known illnesses in the families of both groups was similar with the exception of heart disease, which occurred more frequently in the comparison group families. There was no difference in the reported incidence of diabetes, hypertension, asthma, or blood disorders.

Data on the pregnancies of mothers of both groups of children were obtained. In the patient group, 56% of the mothers reported either somatic or emotional problems during their pregnancies. Sixty-eight percent of the pregnancies in this group were unplanned. In the comparison group, 28% of the mothers reported similar problems, and 10% of these pregnancies were unplanned. Seventy-two percent of the mothers in the comparison group gave a history of nonproblematic pregnancies. The kinds of difficulties reported were as follows: acute viral illnesses, vaginal and kidney infections, intermittent bleeding, drug allergies, and severe depression and anxiety in some women as a consequence of family and marital problems and unplanned pregnancies.

It was not possible to pinpoint with sufficient accuracy the time during the pregnancies that these events occurred for us to comment on the temporal relationship between them and phases in the prenatal development of the hematopoietic system. Green's interesting idea that physical or emotional stress occurring at a specific time in that development could affect the blood forming elements in such a manner as to pave the way for the later development of malignant changes could not, in this study, be investigated.

No difference was found between the patient and comparison groups with regard to the common infectious diseases of childhood, nor was there any difference in the amount of immunization received or in the reaction of the children to these procedures. There were, however, six children (24%) who had a history of having had rather severe ear, eye, or urinary infections in the patient group as compared with two (8%) in the comparison group. In several instances, the mothers of children with leukemia reported that their youngsters were diagnosed as anemic by physicians several years before the apparent onset of the disease. In addition, parents of the patient group reported a higher number of colds, sore throats, and upper respiratory infections in their children than did the parents of the comparison group children.

There was a small number of children in the patient group who were said to be unusually healthy prior to their developing cancer. This was also true, however, of a number of children in the comparison group. As there was no way of documenting the minor illnesses reported in the patient group, neither their nature nor severity could be ascertained.

Life Events

Results obtained by use of the Holmes and Rahe Schedule of Recent Events revealed significant differences between the patient and the comparison groups. Each item on this scale has been assigned a weighted value that is based on extensive testing carried out in the general population. For example, "death of a spouse" is assigned a value of 100, "marital separation" a value of 65, and "son or daughter leaving home" a value of 29. In our interviews of the families of both groups of children, information was obtained about events occurring in the one year prior to the apparent onset of illness child. On many items it was also of interest to use a two-year peri onset as the basis for comparison.

Mean "Life Change Units" (LCU), i.e., total weighted score number of life events were contrasted in the two grou individual life events were compared. Use of the first me score of 197.0 for the patient group as compared wi comparison population. This is a highly significant a level of confidence and suggests that the patient grou greater number of the designated life change events a of this instrument, events of greater emotional significance than did the comparison group.

Figure 1 graphically compares the matched patient and comparison groups for each of the 25 cases. The difference in the groups is clearly seen. The actual emotional impact on the children of the events may, however, vary quite widely from child to child and is very much an individual matter. Experiences that have been assigned a low value on the scale may, for a given youngster, be of great emotional significance and vice versa. Only a study of the individual cases provides insight into such situations.

Calculation of the mean number of life events included in the scale that had actually occurred in each group showed an average of 5.7 for the patients and 2.8 for the comparison population. This indicates that the number of designated events which took place in the lives of the children with cancer in the one year prior to their becoming ill was approximately twice that of the comparison group. The number of such events experienced by individuals is considered by Holmes and Rahe to be the single most important measure by which meaningful comparisons can be made between such groups. This might

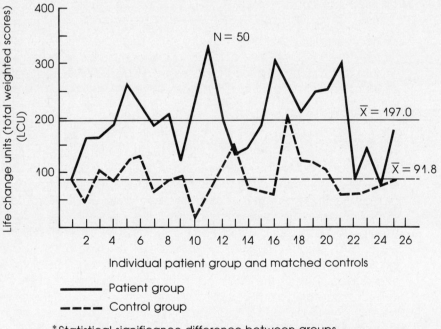

* Statistical significance difference between groups,
t-test p<.001
Correlation coefficient r = .07

Figure 1 Comparison of life change units of the individual patients and the matched controls (comparison group). Reprinted with permission of Elsevier Science Publishing Co., Inc., from Life events and the occurrence of cancer in children, by J. Jacobs and E. Charles, *Psychosomatic Medicine,* Vol. 42, pp. 11–24. Copyright 1980 by the American Psychosomatic Society, Inc.

suggest, then, that the emotional setting in which illness may develop is characterized not so much by the single stressful experience, as by the accumulative effect of a number of such experiences.

Of particular interest are some of the individual items (see Table 3). A marital separation occurred in 32% of the patients' families and, in an additional 20%, there was a loss by death of a family member (other than a parent). The average parent age in both groups was approximately 33 years, and in no case was there a report of a parent's death. In the comparison group, 12% experienced a marital separation, and 4% reported the death of a close family member.

With regard to a change of school, 56% of the youngsters in the patient group had that experience as compared to 32% in the comparison group. Other findings of interest were as follows: 60% of the patient group reported a major change in the health or behavior of a family member (not including the patient) as opposed to 24% in the comparison group. Examples of such changes were: serious illness of a parent, sibling, or grandparent; alcoholism in one of the parents or grandparents; hostility and alienation between parents and grandparents; and marital discord between parents.

Forty-eight percent of the patients' families reported a major change in their financial state (in all it was worse) as compared to 22% in the comparison families. In 32% of the patients and 12% of the comparison group a major personal injury or illness was experienced by a member of the family other than the patient. Twenty percent of the patient group also reported "a major

Table 3   Frequency of Occurrence of Individual Life Events^a ($N = 50$)

Life event	Patient group ($n = 25$) (%)	Comparison group ($n - 25$) (%)
Marital separation	32	12
Death of close family member	20	4
Change in residence	72	24
Change in schools	56	32
Change in health or behavior of a family member (other than patient or control)	60	24
Personal injury or illness (other than patient or control)	32	12
Change in the number of arguments with spouse	20	4
Major change in social activities	16	8
Wife beginning or stopping work	20	44
Son or daughter leaving home	12	20
Gain of new family member	4	12

^{a} Statistical significance between groups over all items, χ^2 test, $P < 0.001$.

change in the number of arguments with spouse," compared to 4% in the comparison group. In all instances there was an increase in such arguments. In addition, 16% of the patients' families reported a major change in social activities as compared to half that percentage in the comparison population.

There were some differences, too, on the other side of the ledger. In 44% of the comparison group there was a change in the mother's work status (most often with her beginning to work) as compared to 20% in the families of patients. Also, 20% of the comparison families reported a son or daughter leaving home and 12% reported the birth of a new child, in contrast to the patient group (12% and 4%, respectively).

A surprising 72% of the families in the patient group had moved within two years of the onset of the illness. This compared with 24% of the families in the comparison group. The figures for the one-year period prior to the apparent onset of the disease were 60% and 12%, respectively. In many instances, it is quite clear that moving was associated in a youngster with strong feelings of anxiety or depression. In others, however, there was no clear evidence that such reactions played a significant role in the child's life.

Note to Reader

The remainder of the results section of this article is devoted to a discussion of several case histories taken from patients in the cancer group. These case histories are used to make the point that children in this group did experience some major upheavals in their lives during the year preceding diagnosis.

I have also, in the interest of space, omitted the discussion section of this article. In general, Jacobs and Charles spent most of the discussion arguing that these life-stress events were, in fact, very stressful to the children and speculating about some of the resulting physiological changes that might increase the child's susceptibility to cancer.

If you are interested in this topic and want to do additional reading, I have included the reference list from the Jacobs and Charles article.

REFERENCES

1. Greene WA Jr, Miler G: Psychological factors and reticuloendothelial disease. IV. Observations on a group of children and adolescents with leukemias: an interpretation of disease development in terms of mother-child unit. *Psychosom Med* 10: 124-144, 1958.
2. Greene WA Jr: Psychological factors and reticuloendothelial disease. III. Further observations on psychological and somatic manifestations in patients with lymphomas and leukemias. Presented at the Annual Meeting, *American Psychosomatic Society*, Chicago, 1952.

3. Greene WA Jr: Psychological factors and reticuloendothelial disease. I. Preliminary observations on a group of males with lymphomas and leukemia. *Psychosom Med.* 16: 220-239, 1954.

4. Greene WA Jr, Young LE, Swisher SN, Miller G: Psychological factors and reticuloendothelial disease. II. Observations on a group of females with lymphomas and leukemias. *Psychosom Med* 18: 284-303, 1955.

5. Greene WA Jr, Swisher SN: Psychological and somatic variables associated with the development and course of monozygotic twins discordant for leukemia. Ann NY Acad Sci 164: 394-408, 1969.

6. Adler R, MacRitchie K, Engel GL: Psychologic processes and ischaemic stroke (occlusive cerebrovascular disease). I. Observations on 32 men and 35 strokes. *Psychosom Med* 31: 1-29, 1971.

7. Brown GW, Birley JLT: Crises and life changes and the onset of schizophrenia. *J Health Soc Behav* 9: 203-214, 1968.

8. DeFaire U: Life change patterns prior to death in ischaemic heart disease: a study on death-discordant twins. *J Psychosom Res* 19: 273-278, 1975.

9. Rahe RH, Bennett L, Romo M: Subjects' recent life changes and coronary heart disease in Finland. *Am J Psychiatry* 130: 1222-1226, 1973.

10. Theorell T, Rahe RH: Psychosocial factors and myocardial infarction. I. An inpatient study in Sweden. *J Psychosom Res* 15: 25-31, 1971.

11. Heisel JS: Life changes as etiologic factors in juvenile rheumatoid arthritis. *J Psychosom Res* 16: 411-420, 1972.

12. Marx MB, Garrity TF, Bowers FR: The influence of recent life experiences. *J Psychosom Res* 19: 87-98, 1975.

13. Stein SP, Charles E: Emotional factors in juvenile diabetes mellitus: A study of early life experiences of adolescent diabetics. *Am J. Psychiatry* 128: 56-60, 1971.

14. Holmes TH, Meyer M, Smith M, et al: Social stress and illness onset. *J Psychosom Res* 8: 35-44, 1964.

15. Rahe RH, Arthur RJ: Life change and illness studies: past history and future directions. *J Human Stress* March 3-15, 1978.

16. Engel GL: Studies of ulcerative colitis: the nature of the psychologic processes. *Am J Med* 19: 231-255, 1955.

17. Rabkin JG, Streuning EL: Life events, stress and illness. *Science* 194: 1013-1020, 1976.

18. Theorell T, Lind E, Floderus B: The relationship of disturbing life changes and emotions to the early development of myocardial infarctions and other serious illnesses. *Int J Epidemiol* 4: 281-292, 1975.

19. Bartrop RW, et al: Depressed lymphocyte function after bereavement. *The Lancet* 1: 834-836, 1977.

20. Locke SE: The influence of stress and emotions on immune response. *Biofeedback Self-Regulation,* 2, 1977.

21. Rogers MP, Dubey D, Reich P: The influence of the psyche and the brain on immunity. *Psychosom Med* 41: 147-164. 1979.

22. Gross SJ: Human blood groups. A substance in human endometrium and trophoblast. *Am J Obstet Gynecol* 1149-1159, 1966.

23. Holden G: Cancer and the mind—How they are connected. *Sci News* 20, June 3, 1978.

24. Klein G: The Epstein-Barr virus. In: Kaplan, AS (ed). *The Herpes Viruses.* Edited by AS Kaplan, New York, Academic Press, p. 521-55.

25. Rapp F: Ca-A *Cancer Journal for Clinicians* Vol 28, No. 6, 1978.

CHAPTER EXERCISES

9.1. Identify one of the following as the best description of the experiment reported by Jacobs and Charles (1980), and explain the basic characteristics that define this type of experiment.

1. Bivalent analytic experiment
2. Within-subjects quasi-analytic experiment
3. Retrospective ex post facto quasi-analytic experiment
4. Prospective ex post facto quasi-analytic experiment

9.2. The Jacobs and Charles experiment identifies two populations: children with cancer and children with minor illnesses. Are there differences other than the amount of stress in the lives of these two populations that could contribute to the development of cancer? If so, how does this affect the internal validity of the experiment?

9.3. Jacobs and Charles select two small samples from the two populations: children with cancer and children with minor illnesses. Is there any reason to suspect a bias toward selecting children with high-stress lives in the cancer sample or toward selecting children with low-stress lives in the noncancer sample?

9.4. Do the sampling procedures used by Jacobs and Charles lead to any problems with the external validity of the results that they obtain?

9.5. Does detection bias threaten the internal validity of the experiment reported by Jacobs and Charles?

9.6. What precautions do Jacobs and Charles take in order to deal with potential confounded variables in their experiment?

CHAPTER 10

QUASI-ANALYTIC EXPERIMENTS: BIVARIATE CORRELATION DESIGNS

I n 1978, Michael Cimino directed a film called *The Deer Hunter*. The story examined the personalities of several young men prior to their war experiences in Vietnam and their psychological adjustment after the war. If you saw this film, you know that each man was changed in some unique way by his experience in Vietnam and that these changes were psychologically destructive. The movie is a sensitive and powerful portrayal of the havoc that war can wreak upon the human mind.

The questions examined in *The Deer Hunter* are obviously of interest to psychologists. War exposes its participants to incredibly traumatic and stressful events, and some surveys (e.g., Laufer, Gallops, & Frey-Wouters, 1984) suggest that this was particularly true of the war in Vietnam. In addition to the psychological trauma produced by killing and the fear of dying, the soldier in Vietnam was frequently exposed to or participated in terrible abusive acts of violence against the enemy and civilian populations. Interviews with American soldiers who returned from Vietnam provide some indication of the abusive violence in which they participated.

It included acts against the civilian population:

According to a marine from Westchester, "The ARVN did the interrogating, they brought in a woman whose husband was a Viet Cong ... they wanted to get information out of her. They stripped her to her waist and took a … generator … and they took one wire and put it to her left breast, the other wire and put it to her right breast and they started to crank it which could produce an electrical charge." (Laufer et al., 1984, p. 68)

Violent acts against prisoners of war:

According to a veteran from Brooklyn, "The back deck of our vehicle was grated and hot air from the engine comes out and that back deck gets to be 600 degrees after a while, and you cannot stand there. It will burn through your shoes. That is where we would put our prisoners. Rope them, tie them, just throw them down there like a piece of steer, piece of cattle." (Laufer et al., 1984, p. 68)

The use of insidious, cruel weaponry:

According to a veteran from Los Angeles, "We were told not to drink water in Viet Nam unless it was prepared in our base, with ice in it because the VC sympathizers would put ground glass in the ice. They were also selling Zippo lighters, said 'Made in USA' on it, and the second time you strike it, it would blow up in your hand right in front of your face." (Laufer et al., 1984, p. 69)

And torture to extract information:

According to a veteran from Bridgeport, "One they just shot in cold blood, because he didn't give up information. Another one, they were using a couple of torture techniques … pulling a fingernail off … strap a man to a chair and take a pair of pliers and just pull his finger off and other things. Use a wire and loop it around his balls and slowly twist it … you know … they would continue until he passed out from shock or something … torture is to gradually break down a guy." (Laufer et al., 1984, p. 69)

Can men return to a normal existence in society after sustained participation in these abusive acts of violence? Or will they suffer aftereffects in the form of serious psychological disorders? The question is an important one, and very real for thousands of veterans of the Vietnam War now living in North American society. How might we attempt to answer it?

In the question just asked, the presumed causal variable is participation in acts of abusive violence, and the suspected effect is some form of psychopathology. Any attempt to answer the question will first require an operational definition of these two variables. I would suggest that violent behavior is most insidious when pain, injury, and/or death are inflicted on people who do not pose any direct, immediate threat. The incidents of abusive violence described earlier would fit this definition, and I suspect that the amount of guilt and stress associated with these violent acts is more intense than in cases justified by self-defense. For the purpose of the present discussion, I will assume that interviews with veterans will yield a count of the violent incidents in which they had participated (although I admit that there are good reasons to suspect the validity of data obtained in this manner). With reference to the psychological effects produced by exposure to such violence, any number of standardized tests could be used to index the degree of psychopathology. One such test developed specifically for this type of research is called the *Stress Scale* (Boulanger, Kadushin, & Martin, 1981). It measures some 21 different symptoms often associated with the postraumatic, psychopathological stress disorders that might be expected in war veterans.

Given these two operational definitions, it should be possible to design an experiment to determine if participation in abusive violence during war causes subsequent psychological problems. Can you think of any way in which to answer this question with an analytic design? Obviously not. As was the case with our stress and cancer example in the preceding chapter, it would be unthinkable to permit violent behavior of this sort in the laboratory. On the other hand, either prospective or retrospective ex post facto designs can be used to study this problem. In fact, you might find it instructive to explore the use of these designs in this context.

A third type of quasi-analytic design is also employed to answer questions which for various reasons cannot be subjected to the logic and architecture of the analytic experiment. I am referring to *correlation designs*. In this chapter, we will consider the simplest versions of correlation designs and some of the problems you will encounter when you use them. In Chapter 11, we will explore those more complex versions that attempt to solve some of these problems. Hence, it is important for you to master the basic concepts in this chapter as background for Chapter 11.

A BIVARIATE CORRELATION DESIGN

In its simplest form, the correlation design hardly deserves to be called a quasi-analytic experiment. Variables are neither manipulated nor controlled in any sense of these terms. A simple bivariate correlation design involves (1) the selection of a sample of subjects (e.g., the Vietnam veterans), (2) the measurement of the two variables of interest (e.g., participation in abusive violence and psychological adjustment), and (3) calculations to determine if a systematic relationship exists between these two variables (e.g., whether changes in one variable are related to changes in the other). The first two steps are essentially measurement procedures much like those discussed in Chapter 2.

To illustrate these points in more detail, consider first, panel 1 in Figure 10.1. Assume that we have randomly selected a sample of 10 veterans designated as subjects A through J at the top of panel 1. Two measurements have been taken on each subject. The first measurement (variable X) is the frequency of participation in abusive violence during the war. Subject A participated in 12 such incidents, subject B, three such incidents, and so on. The second measurement (variable Y) is the veteran's score on the Stress Scale test which operationally defines current state of mental health. Assume that the higher the score on the Stress Scale, the more severe the psychopathology. Subject A, with a score of 16, is less well adjusted than subject B, whose score was 7, and so on.

Now that we have acquired our sample of subjects and measured each of the two variables (the presumed cause and its presumed effect), we can examine these two variables to see if there is any obvious systematic relationship between them. Does a high level of participation in abusive violence tend to be associated with a high score on the Stress Scale? Do the two measures tend to covary? A casual inspection of the measures suggests that they do.

One way to obtain a better view of the extent to which these measures are related or covary is to plot a graph similar to the one seen at the bottom of panel 1 in Figure 10.1. The *X* variable (which you suspect to be causal) is usually plotted on the horizontal axis (abscissa), and the *Y* variable is plotted on the vertical axis (ordinate). For each subject in your sample, these two measures define one data point on the graph. As you can see, there is an impressive positive, linear relationship between these two variables. As the frequency of violent incidents increases, we see a corresponding increase in the level of maladjustment. Graphic representations of the relationship between two variables like those seen at the bottom of the three panels in Figure 10.1 are often used to help visualize the degree to which the variables are actually related. They are called *scatterplots*. As you will soon discover, the more "scattered" the data points, the less impressive the relationship between the two variables being plotted.

Calculating the Pearson *r*

Both casual inspection of the data in panel 1 of Figure 10.1 and the scatterplot of these data indicate a positive linear relationship between these two variables. There are several methods you can use to *quantify* the degree to which they are related or covary. The particular method you use will depend primarily on the measurement scale that describes the two variables (see Chapter 3 if you need to review the various scales of measurement). When the two variables are measured on at least an interval scale, the appropriate procedure for quantifying the relationship is called a *Pearson* r *correlation coefficient*. Although this label sounds intimidating, the arithmetic involved in calculating any simple bivariate correlation coefficient is no more difficult than that required to calculate some of the other simple descriptive statistics we discussed in Chapter 3 (e.g., the mean and variance). In fact, a correlation coefficient is just one more descriptive statistic that helps us to describe the extent to which two sets of measurements covary.

Figure 10.2 presents the data from panel 1 of Figure 10.1 in a tabular format convenient for calculating the Pearson *r*. The two variables to be correlated are listed in columns 1 and 2 of the table. In columns 3 and 4, each of the measurements has been squared, and column 5 contains the cross-product of the two measures taken on each subject. Once these columns are completed, a sum for each column is calculated and these sums provide all the values necessary to solve the equation for the Pearson *r* presented below the table. As the calculation indicates, the *r* for these data is +1.00. The plus sign indicates that it is a positive linear relationship, and the *r* value of 1.00 is, in fact, the largest value possible from this equation. It indicates that there is a *perfect* positive linear relationship between these two variables for this sample of subjects. For each unit increase in the frequency of violent incidents, there is a perfectly predictable corresponding increase in the score on the Stress Scale. This is obviously a special case.

Subjects	Frequency no. violent incidents (X)	Adjustment score (Y)
A	12	16
B	3	7
C	14	18
D	16	20
E	1	5
F	5	9
G	9	13
H	11	15
I	7	11
J	17	21
Σ	95	135

N = 10

Subjects	Frequency no. violent incidents (X)	Adjustment score (Y)
A	12	11
B	3	20
C	14	9
D	16	7
E	1	21
F	5	18
G	9	15
H	11	13
I	7	16
J	17	5
Σ	95	135

N = 10

Subjects	Frequency no. violent incidents (X)	Adjustment score (Y)
A	12	15
B	3	21
C	14	11
D	16	13
E	1	5
F	5	20
G	9	18
H	11	7
I	7	9
J	17	16
Σ	95	135

N = 10

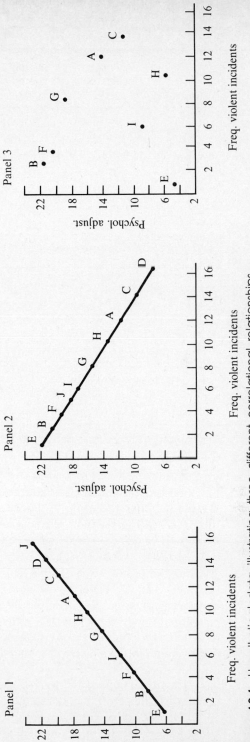

Panel 1

Panel 2

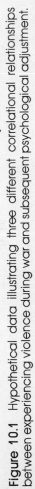

Panel 3

Figure 10.1 Hypothetical data illustrating three different correlational relationships between experiencing violence during war and subsequent psychological adjustment.

227

Subjects	(Column 1) Frequency violent incidents (X)	(Column 2) Adjustment score (Y)	(Column 3) (X²)	(Column 4) (Y²)	(Column 5) (XY)
A	12	16	144	256	192
B	3	7	9	49	21
C	14	18	196	324	252
D	16	20	256	400	320
E	1	5	1	25	5
F	5	9	25	81	45
G	9	13	81	169	117
H	11	15	121	225	165
I	7	11	49	121	77
J	17	21	289	441	357
$\overline{\Sigma} =$	$\overline{95}$	$\overline{135}$	$\overline{1171}$	$\overline{2091}$	$\overline{1551}$
$\overline{X}$	9.5	13.5			

$$\text{Pearson } r = \frac{N\Sigma XY - (\Sigma X)(\Sigma Y)}{\sqrt{[N\Sigma X^2 - (\Sigma X^2)][N\Sigma Y^2 - (\Sigma Y)^2]}} \tag{10.1}$$

$$\text{Pearson } r = \frac{19(1551) - (95)(135)}{\sqrt{[10(1171) - (95)^2][10(2091) - (135)^2]}}$$

$$\text{Pearson } r = \frac{2685}{2685} = +1.00$$

Figure 10.2 Computational procedure for computing the value of r, the Pearson product moment correlation on the hypothetical data from panel 1 of Figure 10.1.

Not many correlations will reach the maximum values of +1.00 or −1.00 (a perfect positive and negative linear relationship, respectively). Most, including the present example, will fall between an r of 0 (no linear relationship) and the maximum values of +1.00 and −1.00. To gain a better understanding of the way in which the computational formula for r works, I suggest that you return your attention for a moment to Table 10.1 and calculate the r for the hypothetical data in panels 2 and 3. Panel 2 will yield another perfect correlation, this time in the negative direction. As participation in abusive violence increases, the level of psychopathology decreases (an unlikely case!). Panel 3 is the third special case in which r is equal to zero, indicating that there is no linear relationship between the two variables, a condition that is well illustrated by the scatterplot at the bottom of panel 3.

  If you can understand the formula for computing the Pearson r at an intuitive level, it will help you to understand the basic concept of correlation that underlies all such procedures for calculating correlation coefficients. To understand this computational formula, think of yourself as subject C in Figure 10.2. As such, you participated in 14 violent incidents during the war, and your Stress Scale score was an unhealthy 18. This shows that your participation in violent incidents was 4.5 points *higher* than the *average* veteran measured in this sample of ten. It also shows that your score on the Stress Scale was 4.5 points *higher* than the *average* score of the ten veterans in this sample. Hence, both measures deviate *by the same amount* from the average scores. To the extent that we can say the same thing about every other person in the sample, these two measures must be perfectly related. On the other hand, to the extent that subjects in the sample *deviate* from the average by different amounts on each of the two measures, these two measures are not highly related. In commonsense terms, the formula for computing the Pearson *r* (and the many variations on this basic formula) is essentially computing the extent to which the deviations from the average on each measure are similar for each subject in the sample.

Statistical Inference

Suppose that we selected a sample of 100 veterans and calculated the correlation between a measure of exposure to abusive violence and Stress Scale scores and obtained a Pearson *r* of $+.5$. At this point, we have calculated a number between $+1$ and -1 that describes the degree of relationship between these two variables. There is also the possibility that this relationship could have occurred purely by chance. If, for example, our correlation for a sample of 100 was a perfect $+1$, intuition suggests that this is very unlikely to have been produced by chance alone (although there is some very small probability of such a chance outcome). Alternatively, if we observe a perfect correlation between these measures on a sample of four veterans, intuition suggests that this outcome might well have been produced by chance. For any particular sample size, the larger the correlation coefficient, the less likely that it will have occurred by chance alone.

The basic point is that the correlation coefficient simply describes the degree to which a relationship between two variables exists for a particular sample of subjects. Additional statistical tests are required to determine the probability that this particular correlation should be considered significant or should be considered the result of chance alone. As I have indicated throughout the text, we will not consider these *inferential statistics;* and for the sake of discussion, assume that the correlations obtained in the examples used in this chapter are significant and not the product of chance alone.

Shared Variance and Correlation Coefficients

Correlation coefficients are also discussed in terms of the concept of *shared variance.* To understand this concept, look at the various measures of psychological adjustment (Stress Scale scores) in Figure 10.3. When *r* is $+1.00$ or -1.00, all the variability that you observe in these Stress Scale scores (X) can be accounted for by the variability in the abusive violence measure (Y). To the extent that the *r* is less than $+1.00$ or -1.00, there will be some variability in the Stress Scale scores not accounted for by the variability in abusive violence scores. This means that these two variables share less of the total amount of variance and that some other unknown factors must account for some of the variability in the scores. The value of *r* squared (r^2) is typically used as an estimate of the proportion of the variance that is shared by the two variables in the bivariate correlation. Once again, the limiting values of *r* make the point most

	$n = +.67$	
Subjects	X Frequency of violent incidents	Y adjustment score
A	10	17
B	1	6
C	12	15
D	14	19
E	2	8
F	3	5
G	7	15
H	9	13
I	5	11
J	17	21
Σ	80	130
$\overline{X}$	8	13

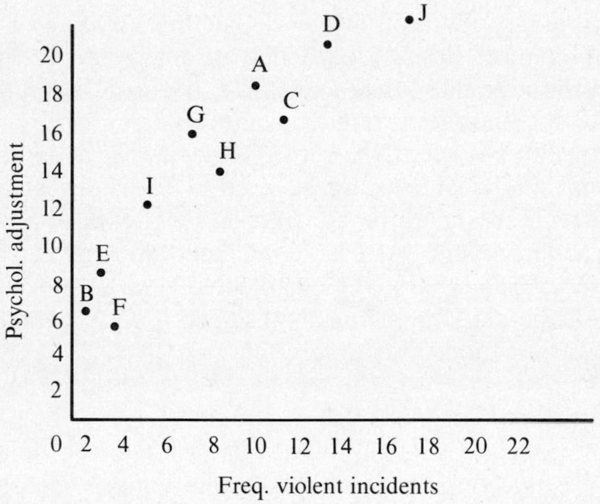

Figure 10.3 Hypothetical data and scatter plot relating frequency of exposure to abusive violence to psychological adjustment. The Pearson r for these data $= +.67$.

effectively. When $r = 0.00$, then r^2 will also equal zero. This means that none of the variability you observe in the Stress Scale scores is accounted for by the variability in the abusive violence measure. When $r = +1.00$ or -1.00 then r^2 is also 1.00, which means that 100 percent of the variance you observe in the Stress Scale scores is accounted for by the variability in the abusive violence scores.

The concept of shared variance can also be illustrated graphically with Venn diagrams, as seen in Figure 10.4. Each circle in the diagram represents 100 percent of the variability that you have observed in each of your variables X and Y. The shaded area of overlap between the two circles represents the proportion of the variability shared by the two variables. As the diagrams indicate, the amount of overlap increases as r increases.

Special Types of Correlation Analysis

The examples of correlation data described up to this point have all used two variables that are to various degrees *linearly* related, with each variable measured on at least an interval scale of measurement. If you encounter a situation in which a scatterplot of the data suggests that the variables are not *linearly* related,

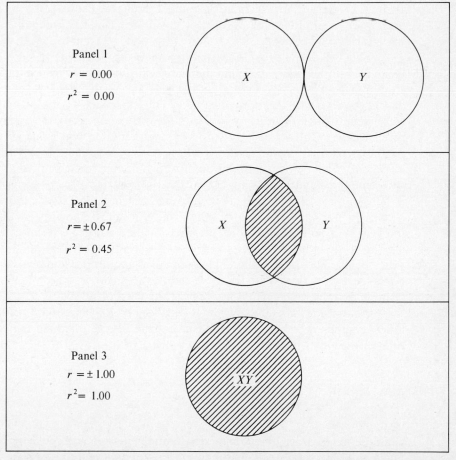

Figure 10.4 Venn diagrams in which each circle represents the total amount of variance observed for each variable. The shaded area represents the proportion of total variance shared between the two variables. The amount of shared variance increases as the correlation between the two variables increases respectively in panels 1, 2, and 3.

or if they are not measured on an interval or ratio scale of measurement, you cannot use the computational formula for the Pearson r (equation 10.1, p. 228) to calculate the correlation coefficient. Consider, for example, the correlation that every fly fisherman has observed between water temperature and number of trout caught. Early in the spring, when the water is very cold, the catches are low. As the water gradually warms up, the fishing improves. Here in Nova Scotia, the trout fishing seems to reach a peak about the middle of May. Although the water temperature continues to increase after May, the trout catch declines. Hence, the relationship between temperature and trout fishing is not *linear*. If you used a sample of 100 fishermen and plotted the size of their catches as a function of water temperature, the scatterplot would be *curvilinear*. As water temperature increases, fishing also improves—up to a point—and then begins to decline. An impressive correlation remains between the two variables, and there is a substantial amount of shared variance; but it is *curvilinear* not *linear,* and a special procedure for calculating r must then be used. Most basic statistics textbooks (e.g., Rosenthal & Rosnow, 1984) describe the procedure for calculating r for curvilinear data.

You will also encounter cases in which the variables to be correlated are measured on less than an interval scale (i.e., on nominal or ordinal scales). For example, psychologists have long suspected a correlation between handedness and certain types of learning disability. One approach to the problem has been to correlate some measure of handedness with some index of learning disability (e.g., Dean & Rothlisberg, 1983). If you decided to correlate an index of learning disability with left-handed and right-handed people, equation 10.1 for computing a Pearson r will obviously not be applicable. Even if you assume that the measure of learning disability is an interval scale, the measure of handedness is not. It is a dichotomous variable, or, in the language of Chapter 3, handedness is typically measured on a nominal scale. When one variable is nominal and the other is interval, a special version of the Pearson r called a *point-biserial correlation* (r_{pb}) is used to quantify the relationship. Once again, most basic statistics books will describe the special calculational procedures required when the variables to be correlated are measured on less than an interval scale. Perhaps the most important point is that the fundamental meaning of this descriptive statistic does not change with the method of calculating it. Regardless of that method, a bivariate correlation coefficient is basically a measure of the degree to which two variables are related (i.e., to which they covary).

INTERPRETING BIVARIATE CORRELATIONS

You can see that it was necessary to work through some of the preceding calculations in order to understand scientists when they discuss correlation coefficients. These simple correlation designs involve little more than measuring some variables in nature and doing the calculations described in the preceding section. Of course, you will encounter different calculational procedures depending on the type of data involved, but the basic interpretation of correlation coefficients is the same regardless of the computational methods employed.

Given that you understand the basic mechanics of correlation, we can now consider the most important question: How do you interpret the results of a correlation design? The answer, very simply, is that correlation results should be interpreted with great caution! If the analytic experiment is the "gold standard" for identifying causal relationships in nature, this simple bivariate design must be regarded as "fool's gold." It knowingly ignores several sacred principles of the analytic experimental design. In the correlation design, (1) subjects are not randomly assigned to different treatment conditions, (2) there is no attempt to control variables that might covary with the two variables being measured, and (3) there is no attempt to contrast different values of an independent variable while concurrently controlling other variables.

These deviations from the analytic experiment lead to two common and major problems with correlation research: (1) the third-variable problem and (2) the directionality problem.

The Third-Variable Problem

To illustrate the major and most obvious problem with a bivariate correlation design, consider once again our example of the psychological effects of wartime experiences. Suppose you decided to make a serious attempt to study this problem and you randomly selected 1000 veterans of the Vietnam War now living in North America. You contacted and interviewed each of these veterans to determine the extent to which they participated in abusive violence during the war. Once this information was collected, you administered the Stress Scale in order to obtain information about their mental health. Finally, you put this large body of data into the university computer and calculated a Pearson r to quantify the degree of relationship between participation in violence and Stress Scale scores. You will probably agree that this would represent an impressive amount of work and a substantial sample of data. Although it is highly unlikely, suppose the computer told you that the Pearson $r = +1.00$. This would be a very impressive result. With this many data points and a perfect correlation, it would be very hard *not* to believe that the veterans' wartime experience with abusive violence was causally related to their subsequent psychological adjustment. Unfortunately, even though the correlation is perfect, you may have encountered a convincing sample of the "fool's gold" mentioned earlier. There is absolutely nothing about this bivariate correlation design that prevents some other "third variable" from covarying with the two that you have measured. Hence, I would be completely justified in suggesting that some third (or fourth, or fifth, etc.) variable was the actual cause of the psychopathology in this large sample of veterans. Basically, this third variable is our old friend the confounded variable as it appears in the correlation design. It threatens any claim for a causal relationship. The correlation design is perhaps the most vulnerable to this threat of any of the quasi-analytic designs discussed thus far in the book.

The third-variable problem is illustrated in more concrete terms in Figure 10.5. The X and Y columns of the table contain the scores for participation in abusive violence and the Stress Scale respectively. The correlation between X and Y is $+1.00$. The scatterplot for the X and Y variables is plotted at the bottom

Subjects	X frequency of violent incidents	C ?	Y adjustment score
A	3	5	1
B	9	11	7
C	7	9	5
D	12	14	10
E	4	6	2
F	5	7	3
G	8	10	6
H	15	17	13
I	6	8	4
J	17	19	15

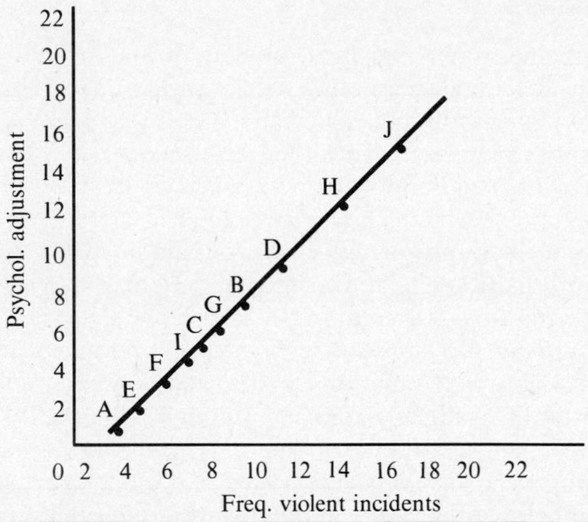

Figure 10.5 A hypothetical example of a perfect correlation between two variables (X and Y) and a third variable (C) that is confounded.

of the figure. Note also column C. This is a mysterious third variable that is also perfectly correlated with the scores on the Stress Scale (Y). It therefore follows that *both* exposure to violence and variable C predict psychological adjustment, and they do so equally well. Can you think of some actual variable that might function as the third variable (C) in this example?

One of several possible third variables that might be confounded is drug usage during the war. It is possible that soldiers exposed to high levels of abusive violence resorted to drugs as a way of dealing with their situation. If the variable C in Figure 10.5 was an index of each veteran's use of hard drugs in Vietnam, it seems reasonable to suggest that the level of drug abuse would be correlated with subsequent psychological adjustment when the soldier returned to civilian life. You may be able to think of other "third" variables that are equally problematic. The important point is that we do not know if there *are* others, and the bivariate correlation design makes no attempt to deal with this possibility.

In actual practice, the problem of confounded variables in the correlation design is every bit as prominent as the preceding hypothetical example implies. Laufer, Gallops, and Frey-Wouters (1984) conducted a large and much more elaborate correlation study of the problem we have been using as an example. They were primarily interested in the correlation between participation in abusive violence during the Vietnam War with subsequent psychological adjustment. They used a number of more sophisticated methods to measure the variables and to deal with potential third variables. Their data revealed a small but reliable correlation between participation in abusive violence and subsequent psychopathology. Although their procedures were elaborate, they did not consider drug abuse as a potential third variable in this correlation. Therein lies the problem with any correlation design. No matter how sophisticated the procedure, the probability that some third variable is confounded will always be high; and it is often a variable that we have overlooked. As you know, the random assignment of subjects to treatments in the analytic design is one form of protection against these overlooked confounded variables. Unfortunately, random assignment is not a method available to us when we are dealing with war violence and psychological adjustment as independent and dependent variables!

The Directionality Problem

Implicit in our discussion of the psychological difficulties experienced by veterans is the assumption that participation in abusive violence predicts *subsequent* psychopathology. The direction of the relationship is assumed to be similar to a causal relationship in which a cause precedes an effect. This assumption can be questioned in many correlation designs. The correlation design does not always contrast the relevant variables in the appropriate causal order; hence there is no guarantee that the "independent variable" (e.g., participation in abusive violence) precedes the "dependent" variable (e.g., psychological adjustment) in time. In many cases, it is just as legitimate to argue that the reverse is true. It is possible that the psychological problems actually *preceded* participation in abusive violence. In this case, the best predictor of participation in abusive violence during the war would be the veteran's psychological adjustment *prior to the war*. In many correlation designs, the directional claim that X causes Y is no more justified than the claim that Y causes X. This is one more reason why a correlation coefficient must be interpreted with caution. No matter how large the correlation coefficient is, it is best interpreted as an index of shared variance, not an index of the strength of a causal relationship.

There are, of course, some correlation designs that do not suffer from this directional problem. Suppose, for example, that we discovered a high negative correlation between the amount of alcohol pregnant women consume during pregnancy and their infants' scores on the widely used Brazelton Neonatal Behavioral Assessment Scale. These data would suggest that alcohol might have disruptive effects on the infant's development. The directionality problem does arise when one is discussing this correlation. It is not reasonable to suggest that the mother's alcohol consumption was influenced in some way by the infant during pregnancy. It is, however, reasonable to consider the third-variable problem. Many third variables might be correlated with alcohol consumption during pregnancy (e.g., diet and smoking), and these might also account for the negative correlation with infant development.

To summarize briefly, when you interpret the results of any correlation design, you should always think about potential third variables and the directionality problem. You should also remember that the size of the correlation coefficient is irrelevant when you are thinking about either of these problems. Both problems can occur when the correlation is small or when the correlation is perfect.

CORRELATION VS. EX POST FACTO DESIGNS

In a more general sense, correlation designs are a type of ex post facto experiment. In a correlation design, the experimenter measures the two variables of interest as they exist in nature (after the fact). Indeed, it is possible to convert correlation designs into the ex post facto designs discussed in Chapter 9. Several brief examples will help to illustrate the important relationships between these two types of quasi-analytic experiment.

Over the years, evidence has accumulated suggesting that gender differences can be measured with certain types of mental-cognitive tasks. Specifically, the data suggest that males are superior to females on tasks that require mathematical or spatial reasoning skills. The evidence on this issue indicates that the high levels of androgen, the male sex hormone, found in males during puberty may account for this difference between males and females (cf., Hier & Crowley, 1982; Kagan, 1982).

Suppose you wanted to examine this question yourself. To do so, you randomly selected 10 males and 10 females from your psychology class. You ask each of these people to look at object 1 in Figure 10.6 and match it correctly with a rotated version of the same object embedded among objects 2, 3, and 4. You keep a record of how long it takes each person to make the correct match. This is a task requiring spatial reasoning skills, and if the existing literature is correct, males should be faster than females at finding the correct object. Incidentally, the objects illustrated in Figure 10.6 have been used extensively as a spatial reasoning task in a wide variety of cognitive research (e.g., Cooper, 1975).

You will probably agree that the architecture of your experiment is correctly represented in panel 1 of Figure 10.7. The architecture looks like a bivalent analytic experiment in which you compare the performance of a group of males (A to J) to a group of females (K to T). You should realize, however, that it is not an analytic experiment. The subjects have not been randomly assigned to the two treatment conditions, male and female. Gender is an ex post facto variable,

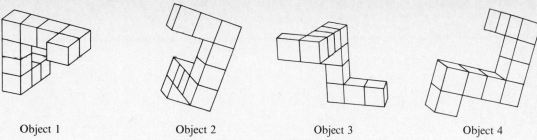

Object 1   Object 2   Object 3   Object 4

Figure 10.6   Mental rotation task. Is 2, 3, or 4 a rotated version of object 1?

and these two groups are assigned (after the fact) as males and females. In the language of Chapter 9, this design would be most appropriately identified as a *prospective ex post facto quasi-analytic experiment* and, as indicated in panel 1 of Figure 10.7, your results support the hypothesis that males are better than females at this mental rotation task. The average time for males to solve the problem was 2 seconds, as compared to 5 seconds for females. Your next step would be to use an inferential statistic to assure yourself that this difference is unlikely to have occurred by chance alone (see Appendix D for an example). Essentially, this experiment lets you compare the performance of two different groups of subjects to see if the group averages are the same or different.

Consider, next, panel 2 of Figure 10.7. These are the same data as seen in panel 1, but they are now arranged in a manner that permits you to analyze them as a correlation design. The two variables to be correlated in this case are gender (the X variable) and the solution time on the mental rotation task (the Y variable). Note that these variables have different scales of measurement. The gender variable is measured on a *nominal* scale (males vs. females), and the solution time is measured on a *ratio* scale (seconds). As noted earlier in the present chapter, different scales of measurement will require different calculational procedures to obtain a correlation coefficient. In this example, in which one variable is on a nominal and the other is on a ratio scale, the appropriate method is called a *point-biserial correlation coefficient*. The point-biserial calculations require you to assign an arbitrary number to each level of the nominal variable. In this example, we have assigned a 1 to females and a 0 to males. The numbers you choose do not matter. We could just as easily have assigned males the number 16 and females the number 15; either approach will yield the same correlation coefficient. Assigning arbitrary numbers to a dichotomous, nominal variable like gender is called *dummy coding*. Its greatest virtue (other than permitting us to calculate correlation coefficients with nominal data) is its capacity as an examination item to uncover misguided wit.

The dummy coding procedure generates the data for the X variable seen in panel 2 of Figure 10.7. I shall not burden you with the details of calculating a point-biserial correlation (see Cohen & Cohen, 1975, or Rosenthal & Rosnow, 1984, for calculational methods). Suffice it to say that this set of data yielded a point-biserial correlation between gender and solution time on the mental rotation task of $r = +.96$, which indicates a high positive relationship between a person's

Panel 1		Panel 2		
Prospective ex post facto design		Bivariate correlation design		
(10) Males	(10) Females	Males = 0 Females = 1	X sex	Y solution time
A–2	K–5	A	0	2
B–2	L–5	B	0	2
C–1	M–6	C	0	1
D–3	N–4	D	0	3
E–2	0–3	E	0	2
F–1	P–5	F	0	1
G–1	Q–4	G	0	1
H–2	R–5	H	0	2
I–3	S–6	I	0	3
J–3	T–7	J	0	3
Solution Σ = 20 Time (sec) $\overline{X}$ = 2	Solution Σ = 50 Time (sec) $\overline{X}$ = 5	K	1	5
		L	1	5
		M	1	6
		N	1	4
		O	1	3
		P	1	5
		Q	1	4
		R	1	5
		S	1	6
		T	1	7
		Σ	10	70
		$\overline{X}$	.5	3.5
		r_{pb} = +.96		

Figure 10.7 Data from a hypothetical prospective ex post facto experiment that compares males and females on a mental rotation task. Panel 1 analyzes both in the architecture of an ex post facto design. Panel 2 analyzes the same data as a correlation design using a point-biserial *r*.

sex and his/her ability to solve this mental rotation problem. As such, the correlation analysis provides support for the hypothesis in the same way that the ex post facto analysis did.

The point of the two examples illustrated in Figure 10.7 is very important. They demonstrate that you can organize data from the same basic experiment in several different ways. In this example, you can choose to organize it in a manner that permits you to compare the average performance of males to the average performance of females (panel 1). As such, it is a prospective ex post facto design. Or you can choose to organize it in a manner that permits you to calculate the degree to which the two variables are correlated (panel 2). Now ask yourself a simple question. When it comes to arguing for a causal relationship between gender and solution time in these experiments, does the organization in panel 1 make a better case for causality than the organization in panel 2? The answer is that your causal arguments do not really depend on how you choose to organize the data from this experiment. Instead, the strength of your causal argument depends on the likelihood of confounded variables and the extent to which they were controlled in your experimental procedure. In the ex post facto experiment in panel 1, you should be asking whether or not there are confounded differences between the male and female groups of the experiment and whether the experimenter attempted to control (e.g., match) for any confounded differences. In the correlation design in panel 2, you should be asking whether there is a third variable correlated with the others being measured. These are the questions relevant to the causal arguments you hope to make. The issue of causality does not change when you discuss the data in terms of the difference between group averages (panel 1) or in terms of the size of the point-biserial correlation coefficient (panel 2).

These arguments can be extended to retrospective ex post facto designs and correlation designs in which both variables are nominal (e.g., cancer vs. no cancer, smoking vs. no smoking). In this case, the appropriate correlation coefficient is called a *phi coefficient*. You can treat the data in either way: as a correlation design or as retrospective ex post facto design. Neither provides a particularly good basis for a causal argument. While it goes beyond the scope of the present text, it should be noted that this same argument can be generalized to the domain of the analytic experiment. If you are interested in pursuing the argument beyond this point, Rosenthal and Rosnow (1984, chap. 17) provide a good introduction to the topic; for students with a more advanced knowledge of statistics, Cohen and Cohen (1975) contains an excellent discussion.

To summarize briefly, correlation designs are related to ex post facto designs in several ways. Both involve "independent variables" selected after the fact; consequently both carry a high risk of confounded variables. Experimenters can often choose to organize their data as either a correlation design or an ex post facto design. The manner in which the data are organized does not alter the extent to which causal arguments are justified. The extent to which the procedures used to collect the data managed to exercise control over potential confounded variables is the critical question in the context of causal inferences.

OTHER APPLICATIONS FOR BIVARIATE CORRELATIONS

A few decades ago it was not uncommon to find examples of bivariate correlation designs in the scientific literature. In the contemporary literature, however, you will have a hard time locating a correlation design that examines the simple relationship between two variables in the manner described in the present chapter. Contemporary correlation designs have become much more complicated. I suspect that there is one major reason for this trend. Scientists realize that the simple bivariate correlation is inevitably plagued by the problem of confounded third variables. Discovering a correlation between two variables is not particularly satisfying when you realize that there could be a number of third variables participating in the relationship. It would be more satisfying to know if third variables are part of the relationship, and the extent to which the various third variables account for the variance. This has led to more complex ways to think about correlation data called *multivariate methods* or, more specifically, *multiple correlation techniques*. As you will discover in the next chapter, these techniques permit the scientist to determine the degree to which several variables participate in a correlation relationship. Hence, it is not surprising that multivariate methods are increasing in popularity.

Although bivariate correlation designs are a rare species these days, you should not think the work that you have done in the present chapter is wasted. You will discover that the bivariate correlation finds many uses as a descriptive statistic to quantify the extent to which two variables are related. A couple of brief examples should be sufficient to illustrate this point.

Behavioral research very often requires us to observe behavior and make judgments about the occurrence of particular events. Suppose, for example, you are interested in whether or not a young infant several weeks old is capable of imitating the facial expressions of its mother. If the mother smiles, does the infant smile? If the mother frowns, does the infant frown? Measuring whether or not an infant is smiling is not an easy task. The typical solution has been to use an observer who is unaware of the conditions of the experiment and ask that observer to make a judgment based on some operational definition of a smile (e.g., corners of mouth turned up and eyes open). One way to determine if this operational definition is reliable—and can be repeated in different laboratories—is to use two observers and have them independently make judgments based on the operational definition. After they have both judged the expressions of a large number of infants, a bivariate correlation can be calculated to determine the degree to which their judgments agree (i.e., are correlated). The most desirable operational definitions are those that produce a high correlation between the judgments of several observers. In this type of research, for example, one would attempt to find a definition of smiling that would produce a correlation of at least $+.9$ between the two independent observers.

Back in Chapter 3 (p. 57), I mentioned another context in which the bivariate correlation coefficient finds a valuable role as a descriptive statistic. As a part of the process involved in constructing a test to measure people's attitudes (e.g., using a Likert scale), you will recall that it was necessary to determine the extent to which an answer on any particular question was positively related to the score on the test as a whole. The statistic alluded to in that discussion was essentially a correlation coefficient. If you go back and read that section of the text again, perhaps the statistic will no longer seem so mysterious.

You will encounter various ways in which the correlation coefficient is used as a descriptive statistic without any reference to causal arguments per se. Hence, the material you have mastered in this chapter should prove valuable in this respect. Note, too, that concepts you have learned in the present chapter will generalize directly to the multiple correlation techniques to be discussed in the next chapter and should facilitate your understanding of the latter. In the meantime, to test your understanding of bivariate correlation designs with an example from the real world, I have reprinted on the following pages a short experiment reported by Siegel and Loftus (1978) that is concerned with the relationship between anxiety and memory for complex events. After reading it, complete the Chapter Exercises that follow.

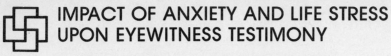

IMPACT OF ANXIETY AND LIFE STRESS UPON EYEWITNESS TESTIMONY

JUDITH M. SIEGEL AND ELIZABETH F. LOFTUS

University of Washington, Seattle, Washington 98195

Abstract

Eighty-four subjects participated in a study designed to explore the relationship between the psychological state of a witness and the witness's ability to accurately perceive and recall a complex incident. It was found that persons who are anxious and preoccupied, as measured by standard tests, performed more poorly on a test measuring eyewitness accuracy.

In France's (1909) *Penguin Island,* there is a chapter about "the dragon of Alca." It is about a frightful dragon who was supposedly ravaging the Penguin people, a group of peaceful people who ordinarily inhabited Alca in perfect tranquility. One day, the elders of the village assembled in a public place to query the villagers about the dragon. One said, "He has the claws of a lion, the wings of an eagle, and the tail of a serpent." Another said, "He has the head of a dragon, the claws of a lion, and the tail of a fish." One said he was red, another green, another blue, another yellow, and yet another, "His colour? He has no colour."

Although obviously fiction, France's story illustrates an important fact. When people witness a complex event, their recollections differ. No two people will give the identical account. Thus, it is important from both a practical and a theoretical point of view to determine those factors that best predict an individual's ability to perceive and recall complex information accurately.

Past research has looked at such witness factors as age, sex, education, intelligence, and training, but there has been little investigation of the role that anxiety and life stress play upon the ability of an eyewitness to perceive and recall accurately. There are several lines of research that suggest that these factors relate to eyewitness ability. Easterbrook (1959) showed that increased emotional arousal is associated with a reduction in the range of task-relevant cues to which an individual attends. Thus, the highly aroused individual may be prevented from encoding important information about a stimulus event. Sarason (1975) suggested that not only does the anxious individual attend to

Siegel, J., & Loftus, E. 1978. Impact of anxiety and life stress upon eyewitness testimony. *Bulletin of the Psychonomic Society, 12,* 479–480.

fewer task-relevant cues, but he or she may also become preoccupied with internal cues, such as concerns about performance or worries about other problems. It was hypothesized, therefore, that higher scores on personality measures of anxiety would be associated with lower scores on a test of eyewitness ability.

In a legal proceeding, one may wish to analyze particular eyewitnesses with an eye toward determining which witnesses are likely to report accurately. Should a connection between anxiety and eyewitness ability be observed, this factor could be used to screen witnesses. On the other hand, it is not easy to determine how anxious a given individual is; this must be done by administering a standardized test. It would be desirable to have a way of tapping anxiety indirectly, without actually testing the witness, for all too often such testing is impossible. A measure of the witness's recent life changes may provide this indirect measure. Several studies have suggested that the accumulation of undesirable life changes, or life stress, is associated with psychological problems such as anxiety and depression (Dohrenwend & Dohrenwend, 1972; Sarason, Johnson, & Siegel, in press; Vinokur & Selzer, 1975). It might be expected, then, that life stress would also be negatively related to performance on a test of eyewitness ability. The present study was aimed at determining the interrelationship among these variables.

METHOD

Eighty-four undergraduate students enrolled in introductory psychology courses participated in this study. Subjects were run in groups of three to five, and they were told that the purpose of the experiment was to assess their performance on cognitive tasks.

During the experimental session, each subject completed a self-report measure of anxiety, an eyewitness testimony task, and a scale designed to measure self-preoccupation. The anxiety measure, the Multiple Affect Adjective Checklist (MAACL) (Zuckerman & Lubin, 1965), consists of a list of 132 mood adjectives (e.g., agitated, calm, desperate). Subjects respond by endorsing the adjectives that are descriptive of the way they feel at the time the test is administered. Twenty-one of the adjectives are relevant for the scoring of the anxiety subscale of the MAACL.

The eyewitness testimony task was designed to measure the subject's ability to perceive and recall a complex event. The subjects were shown a sequence of 24 slides, at a 5-sec rate, depicting a wallet-snatching incident in a small town. The sequence opens with a young woman walking down a busy street. She meets a friend and stops to talk for a moment. As the woman continues down the street, she is approached by a man wearing a cowboy hat who bumps into her, causing her to drop her shopping bag. The man and woman both stoop to pick up some articles that have fallen out. When the woman is looking the other way, the man reaches into her shoulder bag and takes her red wallet. The woman does not notice and the two part. Soon, the victim becomes aware that her wallet is missing, at which point two other women cross the street toward her and gesture in the direction of the fleeing man.

After viewing the slides, the subjects spent about 1 min clearing their desks and writing their names on all of their booklets. Then, they filled out a questionnaire designed to determine accuracy. The questionnaire consisted of 30 items that addressed diverse details of the wallet-snatching incident. It asked about major details, such as information about the central characters, their clothing, and their actions, and it asked about minor details, such as the surrounding environment, extraneous people, buildings, and traffic. The 30 items were declarative sentences requiring a phrase or word to be completed. To complete these sentences, a five-alternative multiple-choice test was given. For example, one question was, "The thief wore a _____. (a) heavy shirt (b) long winter coat, (c) short winter coat, (d) light jacket, (e) down vest."

The self-preoccupation scale (Sarason & Stoops, 1978) measures the degree to which an individual is preoccupied by task-irrelevant thoughts. The scale yields two scores: Scale 1 consists of the subjects' responses to items dealing specifically with fears about performance (e.g., I thought about how poorly I was doing); Scale 2 consists of the subjects' judgments concerning how much their minds wandered during the preceding task.

In addition to the measures completed during the experimental session, scores on the Life Experiences Survey (LES) (Sarason et al., in press), a measure of life stress, were also available for each subject. The LES is a 57-item self-report inventory to which subjects respond by endorsing those events they have experienced in the past year (e.g., death of a close friend, marriage, new job). Respondents rate both the desirability (positive or negative) of each event they have experienced and the magnitude of the impact (0 to 3). The inventory is scored by summing the impact ratings for those events rated as undesirable by the respondent. Previous research has suggested that undesirable life changes are consistently related to psychological problems (Sarason et al., in press; Vinokur & Seizer, 1975), not to change per se, as suggested by earlier work (cf. Holmes & Rahe, 1967).

RESULTS

The mean correct on the 30-item eyewitness accuracy test was 14.58. The mean score on the anxiety scale of the MAACL was 7.67. Subjects scored an average of 24.19 on Scale 1 of the preoccupation measure and 2.83 on the item assessing how much their minds wandered during the task (scored on a 7-point scale).

Of central interest in the present research was the relationship between eyewitness ability and the other individual measures. Pearson product-moment correlations were computed between performance on the eyewitness task and the measures of anxiety, preoccupation, and life stress. As predicted, performance on the test of eyewitness ability was negatively correlated with anxiety [r (84) = −.20, $P < .05$], with preoccupation Scale 1 [r (84) = −.24,

$P < .01$], and with preoccupation Scale 2 [$r(84) = -.26$, $P < .01$]. Although the results for life stress were suggestive, the correlation was not statistically significant [$r(84) = -.12$, $P < .13$]. Thus, the results indicate that persons who are more anxious and preoccupied tend to perform more poorly on a test of eyewitness ability.

DISCUSSION

The results of this study suggest that eyewitness ability is affected by the psychological state of the witness. Specifically, anxiety and preoccupation seem to result in less efficient performance. As suggested by both Easterbrook (1959) and Sarason (1975), the highly anxious individual may not be vigilant to important task-relevant cues, and thus may miss some of the information that is crucial for the eyewitness task.

While these findings are useful for future laboratory studies of eyewitness ability, the important question is the degree to which this information can be integrated into the courtroom setting. The data provide some tentative evidence that recent life stresses may contribute to inaccurate eyewitness testimony. Although this finding is only suggestive, it is likely that there are other variables that moderate this relationship. For example, Smith, Johnson, and Sarason (1978) have found that the accumulation of life stress exerts a detrimental impact primarily on individuals who try to minimize their level of stimulation, or low-sensation seekers (Zuckerman, Kolin, Price & Zoob, 1964). It is the task of future research to refine our knowledge concerning those individual variables that contribute to eyewitness accuracy and to provide the avenues for employing this information in the courtroom setting.

REFERENCES

Dohrenwend, B. S., & Dohrenwend, B. P. *Stressful life events.* New York: Wiley, 1974.

Easterbrook, J. A. The effect of emotion on cue utilization and the organization of behavior. *Psychology Review,* 1959, *66,* 183–201.

France, A. *Penguin Island.* New York: Dodd, Mead, 1909.

Holmes, T. H., and Rahe, R. H. The social readjustment rating scale. *Journal of Psychosomatic Research,* 1967, *11,* 213–218.

Sarason, I. G. Anxiety and self-preoccupation. In I. G. Sarason & C. D. Spielberger (Eds.), *Anxiety: Current trends in theory and research* (Vol. 2). New York: Wiley (Halsted), 1975.

Sarason, I. G., Johnson, J. H., & Siegel, J. M. Assessing the impact of life change: The development of the Life Experiences Survey. *Journal of Consulting and Clinical Psychology,* in press.

Sarason, I. G., & Stoops, R. Test anxiety and the passage of time. *Journal of Consulting and Clinical Psychology,* 1978, *46,* 102–109.

Smith, R. E., Johnson, J. H., & Sarason, I. G. Life change, the sensation seeking motive, and psychological distress. *Journal of Consulting and Clinical Psychology,* 1978, *46,* 348–349.

Vinokur, A., & Selzer, M. L. Desirable versus undesirable life events: Their relationship to stress and mental distress. *Journal of Personality and Social Psychology,* 1975, *32,* 329–337.

Zuckerman, M., Kolin, E. A., Price, L., & Zoob, I. Development of a sensation seeking scale. *Journal of Consulting Psychology,* 1964, *26,* 250–260.

Zuckerman, M., & Lubin, B. *Manual for the multiple affect adjective checklist.* San Diego, Calif: Educational and Industrial Testing Service, 1965.

CHAPTER EXERCISES

10.1. Assume you replicated the experiment reported by Siegel and Loftus using ten friends as subjects and their memory for scenes from a movie as the memory task. Make up your own data for each of these ten subjects by giving each a hypothetical anxiety score between 0 and 100 and a hypothetical memory score between 0 and 100. When you are inventing these scores, see if you can use numbers that will produce a Pearson correlation of approximately −.5. Calculate the Pearson r on your hypothetical data to see how close you came to this figure.

10.2. Can you think of any confounded third variables in the correlation design reported by Siegel and Loftus that also account for the variance in memory that they attribute to high levels of anxiety?

10.3. As indicated in Chapter 10, a second major problem with correlation designs is the directionality problem. Does this problem exist in the Siegel and Loftus experiment?

10.4. Do you see any threats to the external validity of the correlation results reported by Siegel and Loftus?

CHAPTER 11

QUASI-ANALYTIC EXPERIMENTS: MULTIVARIATE CORRELATION DESIGNS

I n my particular version of heaven, there would be a restaurant that carried charcoal-broiled swordfish on its menu—served with a mild horseradish sauce and fresh steamed broccoli. Or at least this would have been my dream dish until a few years ago, when the government announced that swordfish was contaminated with mercury. More recently, government officials changed their minds. They now claim that the mercury in swordfish is below toxic levels. Unfortunately, my appetite has failed to return, and I now imagine a celestial smoked haddock.

Swordfish is only one example of a story that is all too common these days. The news this week began with an item about a truck that had leaked polychlorinated biphenyls (PCBs) along a highway near Kenora, Ontario. A car following the truck was sprayed with PCBs, and there was concern about the health of its passengers: a man, his pregnant wife, and two young children. The week ended with a story claiming that the water supplies of three small towns in Nova Scotia had been contaminated by indiscriminate disposal of toxic waste produced by the dry-cleaning industry.

Such stories have placed a great deal of pressure on scientists in recent years. The public wants to know if these chemicals are dangerous to human health, and scientists are expected to provide quick, definitive answers. By now you probably realize that it will not be easy to meet this demand. Questions about the effects of many of these substances rule out the use of our most effective methodology, the analytic experiment. People cannot be assigned at random to treatment conditions in which some are exposed to potentially dangerous chemicals and others are not. If ethical judgments permit the exposure of laboratory animals to these substances, we are still left with doubts about the external validity of the results.

These ethical problems inevitably force us to use the various ex post facto and correlation designs that we have been discussing in the two preceding chapters, and you are now aware of the problems associated with making causal inferences from these quasi-analytic methods. The difficulties are further compounded when you consider the problem of detecting and measuring the effects of toxic substances at low levels of exposure. Low-level effects can be delayed and the symptoms can be very subtle and difficult to measure. For example, an exposure to methylmercury that has no apparent effect upon a pregnant adult female is sufficient to produce developmental retardation in the child she is carrying (Clarkson et al., 1981).

Measures of behavior often prove to be very sensitive to the low-level toxic effects of substances like lead and mercury, which are known to disrupt the functions of the nervous system. Motor tremor, reaction times, and various perceptual skills are sometimes adversely affected long before more serious medical symptoms become evident. The use of these behavioral measures to detect low-level toxicity has expanded so rapidly over the last decade that Weiss (1983) has coined the term *behavioral toxicology* to describe the various behavioral techniques that have been developed in this context.

For reasons that you will discover very shortly, research done in the area of behavioral toxicology provides a particularly good example of the more complicated multivariate correlation designs that we will consider in the present chapter. The purpose will be to introduce you to two related multivariate procedures: partial correlation and multiple correlation. Some of these multivariate procedures require rather formidable and complex methods of computation. My goal will *not* be to teach these to you. Instead, I hope to explain the reasoning behind the multivariate methods, explain why they are used, and describe how they should be interpreted when you encounter research in which they have been employed. If you require more advanced information about the computational procedures, you should consult books by Cozby (1984), Tabachnick and Fidell (1983), Cohen and Cohen (1975), and Ferguson (1971). These will help you with the mechanics of computation for the methods discussed in this chapter.

PARTIAL CORRELATION

The PCBs mentioned earlier are chemicals used in a wide variety of industrial situations. These substances are gradually accumulating in our environment as pollutants. For example, some researchers (Schwartz et al., 1983) have demonstrated that fish from Lake Michigan are a source of PCB exposure to people who consume the fish. This exposure is particularly worrisome to pregnant women, because research on laboratory animals indicates that PCBs cross the placenta and can disrupt the normal development of the fetus (Chou et al., 1979).

Suppose you wanted to determine if children born to women who consumed fish from Lake Michigan were affected by exposure to PCBs. In other words, are the typical dietary levels of these substances dangerous to the developing human fetus? Although an analytic experiment is obviously not possible, it should not be too difficult to design a correlation experiment. Interviews with a sample of pregnant women known to have eaten fish caught in Lake Michigan during their pregnancies should be sufficient to determine how much fish they have consumed. This information, in turn, would permit us to calculate an estimate of the PCB exposure suffered by the fetus in utero. Assume, for the purpose of discussion, that this PCB index ranges from a score of 0 to 100, with a score of zero indicating that no fish was consumed. Assume also that the Ballard Examination for Fetal Maturity is administered shortly after the birth of each child in this sample. The Ballard score provides an index of fetal development. A low score indicates that the normal development of the fetus has been retarded to some extent (Ballard, Novak, & Driver, 1979). Given these two measures, the question of interest is whether or not there is a correlation between the level of exposure to PCBs during pregnancy and the scores on the Ballard examination.

Although a much larger sample of subjects would be used in an actual correlation of this sort, consider the hypothetical data for ten pregnant women and their newborn infants presented in Figure 11.1. As the scatterplot of these data indicates, the infants' scores on the Ballard examination tend to decrease as the exposure of the mother to PCBs increases. If you calculate a Pearson r bivariate correlation coefficient for these ten subjects, it will confirm the story told by the scatterplot with a value of $-.75$. These results should immediately raise a mental warning flag telling you to ask a question. Are any third variables confounded in this bivariate correlation? Could some other factor confounded with PCB exposure explain the adverse effects on fetal development? If there is, any claim that PCBs retard fetal development would obviously be questionable.

One possible third variable that could play a role in this correlation is the amount of red meat consumed by the female during pregnancy. If the amount of fish consumed is an index of PCB exposure, it seems reasonable to assume that the more fish a person consumes, the less red meat (e.g., lamb, pork, beef, etc.) there is in the diet. Hence, the amount of fish consumed would be systematically confounded (negatively correlated) with the amount of red meat consumed. It is also possible that red meat consumption during pregnancy is positively correlated with infant growth and development as measured by the Ballard Examination. The hypothetical data in Figure 11.1 illustrate the confounded third variable just described. Variable X is the PCB exposure index (amount of fish consumed); variable Y is the Ballard Examination score; and variable C is an index of red meat consumption by these ten pregnant women.

We have already calculated the bivariate correlation between PCB exposure (X) and the Ballard score (Y), and we know that this correlation (r_{xy}) is $-.75$. If we now calculate the bivariate correlation between PCB exposure (X) and red meat consumption (C), we find that this correlation (r_{xc}) is $-.78$. Finally, the

Mothers	Mother's PCB index	Infant's Ballard score
A	60	35
B	100	15
C	70	10
D	90	25
E	80	5
F	30	50
G	50	30
H	20	45
I	40	20
J	10	40

Pearson $r = -.75$

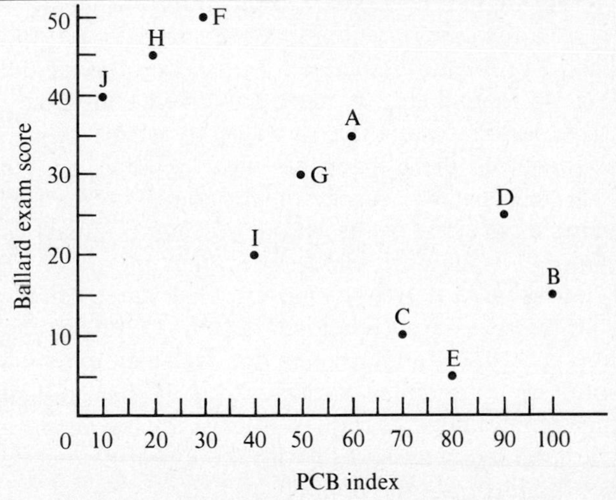

Figure 11.1 Hypothetical data describing negative correlation between amount of PCBs consumed by pregnant women and the scores of their newborn infants on the Ballard Examination for Fetal Maturity.

bivariate correlation between red meat consumption (C) and the Ballard score (Y) is calculated, and this correlation (r_{cy}) is $+.70$. The hypothetical data demonstrate, just as we suspected, that red meat consumption is a third variable confounded with PCB exposure and logically just as eligible to explain the variance in the Ballard scores as PCB exposure.

Given this ubiquitous third-variable problem with the bivariate correlation data, there are two basic improvements offered by more complex multivariate correlation methods. One improvement is called a *partial correlation* procedure, the other a *multiple correlation* procedure. We will consider the partial correlation in the context of our PCB example and return to multiple correlation later in the chapter. As you will discover, the latter procedure is just a more complex version of the former.

Stated very simply, a partial correlation procedure permits us to determine the extent to which two variables, X and Y, are correlated when we *eliminate* the contribution of a third variable, C, to the relationship. In the example we have been discussing, the partial correlation permits us to measure the correlation between PCB exposure and fetal development under conditions in which all women can be assumed to have consumed the same amount of red meat. In other words, the statistical manipulations permit us to hold constant (i.e., control) the red meat variable when measuring the correlation between PCB exposure and the Ballard scores. Although I promised not to burden you with any complex multivariate computational procedures, you should realize that the calculation of a partial correlation is a relatively simple extension of the simple bivariate computations that you learned in Chapter 10.

When students are first introduced to this interesting multivariate technique called partial correlation, they assume that they have found the solution to one of the fundamental problems associated with correlational designs, the third-variable problem. In fact, there are more advanced techniques that extend the basic logic of the partial correlation to cases in which we can systematically eliminate the influence of more than one third variable in a correlation design. Indeed, every variable that you suspect might contribute to a correlation can be examined by using extensions of the partial correlation analysis. The basic reasoning is the same, only the "arithmetic" becomes more complicated.

Does the partial correlation or its more sophisticated relatives actually solve the third-variable problem in correlational designs? Not completely. This multivariate technique is certainly an improvement over a simple bivariate correlation that ignores potential confounded variables, but it does not provide the same insurance against confounded variables offered by an analytic experiment in which subjects are randomly assigned to different treatment conditions. Our PCB example will help to illustrate the point.

Suppose you found that after you had used multivariate techniques to *eliminate* the potential contribution of every conceivable confounded variable, a significant correlation remained between PCB exposure and the Ballard scores. It would be very tempting to make a strong causal claim at that point, but you should still exercise considerable caution. No matter how many third variables you consider with these techniques, there can always be one more that is, in fact, confounded and is the important factor in the relationship. One of the appealing features of random assignment in analytic experiments (when they can be used) is that both *detected* and *undetected* potential confounded variables are controlled by random distribution to treatment conditions. Indeed, it is the *undetected* variables that worry us most in correlation designs.

A recent experiment reported by Jacobson, Fein, Jacobson, Schwartz, and

Dowler (1984) helps to underline the point made in the preceding paragraph. Appropriately enough, these investigators were concerned (among other things) with the relationship between the consumption of PCB-contaminated fish by pregnant women and the Ballard scores of their newborn infants. They discovered that increased levels of dietary PCB exposure were significantly related to lower Ballard scores and that "the lower Ballard scores were related primarily to greater neuromuscular immaturity among the exposed infants" (Jacobson et al., 1984, p. 318).

The point to appreciate in the present context is that this significant relationship between PCB exposure and Ballard scores remained after multivariate techniques were used to eliminate the contribution of some 37 different third variables confounded in the relationship. Unfortunately, Jacobson et al. do not provide a complete list of these variables. However, in spite of this impressive effort to overcome the third-variable problem with extensions of the partial correlation technique, the fact remains that they could have missed "variable 38," and it might account for the variance in Ballard scores just as effectively as PCB exposure. It would be interesting to know, in this respect, if red meat consumption was one of the 37 variables they considered.

To summarize briefly, the problem of confounded variables in correlation designs can be corrected to some extent by techniques like partial correlation and its multivariate relatives. In practice, however, the logic of these more complex correlation designs does not justify as much confidence in causal claims as does the logic of analytic experiments.

MULTIPLE CORRELATION

In the preceding example, we used a partial correlation method to eliminate the contribution that a third confounded variable was making to the correlation between PCB exposure and measures of fetal development. There is another side to this same coin which is called multiple correlation. Instead of eliminating the potential influence of a third variable, the basic purpose of the multiple correlation procedure is to determine the extent to which a *combination* of several different variables is correlated with a particular dependent variable. To help explain the basic reasoning behind the multiple correlation technique, we can use yet another example from the domain of behavioral toxicology.

A substantial amount of evidence has accumulated suggesting that alcohol consumed during pregnancy has adverse effects on fetal development (Abel, 1980). As you might have guessed, most of these data come from either correlation or ex post facto designs, and some concern has been expressed that other substances also consumed during pregnancy are probably confounded with alcohol consumption (cf. Jacobson et al., 1984). One approach to this problem, with which you are now familiar, would be to use partial correlation techniques to eliminate the potential contribution of other substances, such as nicotine and caffeine, that might be confounded with alcohol consumption and also influence fetal development. Jacobson and co-workers (1984) used essentially this approach and found that alcohol does have adverse effects on fetal development and continued to have these effects after the potentially confounded contributions of smoking and caffeine consumption were "partialled out" of the relationship.

However, we might also like to know the extent to which a combination of all three of these variables is related to fetal development. The multivariate method called multiple correlation permits us to answer this question. In the jargon of multiple correlation, the three variables alcohol, smoking, and caffeine are called *predictor* variables and the measure of fetal development is called a *criterion* variable. Although we will not consider the computational procedures, a multiple correlation analysis essentially combines the three (or more) predictor variables (alcohol, smoking, and caffeine) into one *composite* variable. It is then possible to calculate the extent to which this composite variable is related to the criterion variable, fetal development. In other words, does too much of the "good life" during pregnancy have adverse effects upon fetal development? The multiple correlation coefficient is usually designated as R to differentiate it from its bivariate relative (r), and the amount of variance accounted for by the relationship between the composite predictor variables and the criterion variable is designated as R^2.

Interpretation of the Multiple Correlation R

Why would anyone want to calculate a multiple correlation? The answer, in general, is that we often want to improve our ability to predict certain outcomes to which several variables might contribute. If you decide to pursue graduate studies in psychology, many graduate schools will require you to take two examinations called the Graduate Record Examination and the Miller Analogies Test. They assume that both these tests taken together will provide better information on which to predict your success in graduate school than either one alone. In the language of multivariate methods, the multiple correlation based on the two predictor tests will be larger (account for more variance) than either of the bivariate correlations that could be calculated. In our example concerned with fetal development, a partial correlation can tell a mother whether alcohol alone (in the absence of smoking and caffeine) is related to fetal development, but the multiple correlation will inform her of the risk produced by a combination of smoking, alcohol, and caffeine, with the importance of each predictor appropriately weighted. This latter information is obviously of considerable value to the mother and to health professionals advising her. In the real world, pregnant women who consume alcohol often smoke and drink coffee as well.

If you find yourself interested in a particular research problem in which multiple correlation methods have been used, there are several other properties of the multiple correlation you should consider. First, unlike the Pearson r, the computations that generate the multiple R can only have values ranging from 0 to +1. A perfect R of +1 would be impressive in our fetal development example, or any other example for that matter. It means that an appropriately weighted combination of the three variables (smoking, alcohol, and caffeine) can account for all the variance observed in the fetal development of the offspring produced by these mothers.

A second point, which is perhaps intuitively obvious, is that the multiple R can never have a value that is *less than* the largest bivariate correlation that exists between any of these variables. If, for example, the largest bivariate correlation happens to be between alcohol consumption and fetal development and it has a value of .7 (ignore the sign), the multiple R cannot be less than this, and it should be larger if the other variables you consider are also related to fetal development.

A third and related point of interpretation is that each variable added to your composite predictor variable has the potential to increase the size of the multiple R (and your ability to make predictions) only to the extent that the new predictor variable is *not* correlated with other predictor variables. If, for example, there is a multiple R of .5 that describes the correlation between fetal development and a composite of the two variables alcohol and smoking, the addition of a third predictor variable (i.e., caffeine) will *not* improve the R if caffeine happens to be perfectly correlated with one of the other two predictor variables (i.e., smoking). Stated very simply, the two sources of information are completely redundant. Alternatively, if the correlation of the new variable caffeine and the other two variables is low, the information provided by caffeine is not redundant and can potentially increase the size of R.

Finally, and most important with respect to the interpretation of the multiple R, you must not forget that this tactic is a quasi-analytic method. Although the multiple R is a formidable tool for the scientist, it does not completely escape the two basic criticisms that we leveled against the simple bivariate correlation discussed in Chapter 10. If, for example, you were to discover a perfect multiple R of 1 which described the relationship between the composite predictor variable of smoking, drinking, and caffeine and your measure of fetal development, this finding would be of tremendous interest to pregnant women and health professionals all over the world. However, they should also realize that some other undetected factor could still be the culprit accounting for part or all of the variance in fetal development. Such is the nature of the correlational study when it comes to making causal arguments. On the other hand, the existing evidence on this matter (while it does not approach the perfect multiple R value) should not be ignored by pregnant women or health professionals. It is obviously prudent to pay attention to any data, correlation or otherwise, suggesting that a substance might have adverse effects upon the infant's development.

Note also that the multiple R, like the bivariate r, does not always permit claims about the direction of the presumed causal relationship. In many cases it is just as reasonable to argue that the criterion variable could be causing the differences observed in the predictor variables as vice versa. In our particular example, this directional problem would not seem to arise. It is not reasonable to suggest that the criterion variable (fetal development in utero) is causing differences in the amount of alcohol, smoking, or caffeine intake exhibited by the pregnant mother.

In conclusion, I hope that you can now see that multivariate correlation designs basically extend the reasoning behind simple bivariate correlation designs in order to deal with relationships between more than two variables. In doing so, the multivariate methods provide us with more information about various relationships in nature, but they do not completely escape the basic problems encountered by correlation procedures in general. As you may recall, my goal throughout the preceding chapter was to introduce you to the reasoning behind the multivariate methods so that you could better understand claims that are based on these methods. Should you be interested in knowing more about them or want to use them yourself, you should not be discouraged by my apologetic references to the formidable computational procedures. Most advanced treatments of these methods, referenced throughout the chapter, will carry you along step by step and introduce you to various computer programs that are very easy (perhaps dangerously easy) to use.

In the meantime, I have reprinted, on the following pages, portions of an article published by Rodin and Rodin (1972). I think both you and your instructor may find this example of correlational research particularly interesting. It attempts to measure the relationship between student ratings of their instructor and the amount that students have learned in a course. These data provoked a lot of controversy after they were published (cf. Rodin, Frey, & Gessner, 1975), and they still raise some interesting questions about how one should measure good teaching. The research also illustrates how a partial correlation method can be employed in a context very different from the behavioral toxicology examples we have been considering in the present chapter. As such, it should test your ability to generalize what you have learned to a new situation.

In order to focus your attention on the logic and architecture of this multivariate correlation design, I have omitted the somewhat lengthy introduction to this research and reprinted only the directly relevant portions of the "Method," "Results," and "Conclusions." Read these portions of the study and see if you can do the Chapter Exercises that follow.

STUDENT EVALUATIONS OF TEACHERS

M. RODIN AND B. RODIN

California State University, San Diego 92115

Note to Reader

As indicated above, these authors were interested in the extent to which student ratings of their calculus instructor were related to the amount of calculus that was learned in the course. Much of the introduction is devoted to a discussion of how one might measure the amount a student learns in a course and the student's opinion of the instructor. The particular solutions to these problems that Rodin and Rodin adopted are described below in the "Method" section of their report.

METHOD

The instructors were teaching assistants in a large (293 students) undergraduate calculus course. All of the students met 3 days a week for a large lecture by the professor In charge of the course. They met with individual teaching assistants in small recitation sections on the remaining 2 days. One recitation hour was devoted to answering questions about the lectures and homework. The other was devoted exclusively to administering test problems and going over preceding ones.

The course content was defined by 40 paradigm problems. Comprehension of a paradigm problem was tested with a specific problem. If the student missed that problem, he was allowed to retake variants of it (up to 6 times) until he passed. All the students received a uniform sequence of variants constructed by the professor. The teaching assistants were not permitted to see the problems before the hour in which they were administered. The grading was done by the teaching assistants, but was completely objective. If any portion of the problem was done incorrectly, or if there was any error, no matter how trivial, the entire problem was scored as a miss. The final grade was completely determined by the number of problems passed. The number of attempts necessary to pass a problem had no effect on the grade.

The above procedure yields a fair and careful measure of what has been learned. In the first place, the test problems exhausted the content domain of the course. Most traditional examinations only sample the course content, and different samples are very likely to yield different estimates of how much was learned. Second, because of the opportunity for multiple administrations, the measure of how much was learned was highly reliable. Scores on one-shot testing procedures are subject to a great deal of variability connected with factors such as personal problems, fatigue, gloomy compared to sunny rooms and the like. The secrecy of the test problems was another important factor. If instructors have prior information about the contents of tests, they may, intentionally or unintentionally, pass it on to the students. It is always good practice to eliminate such potential bias from testing procedures. In this case, it is particularly important, since otherwise an obtained positive correlation may merely reflect the tendency of popularity-minded teaching assistants to hint at or "teach to" test items.

Criterion Measures

There were 12 sections, two of which were taught by the same instructor. Three measures were obtained for each of the sections: initial ability in calculus, amount learned by the students (objective measure of teacher effectiveness), and student evaluation of the instructor (subjective measure of teacher effectiveness). Since these data were collected in the third quarter of the course, a measure of the students' initial ability was available from their previous performance. Each section was assigned an initial ability score based on the mean grade obtained by the students in that section in the preceding quarter. (The students may or may not have had the same instructor in earlier quarters.) The amount learned in each section of the current quarter was defined by the mean grade obtained in that section. The instructor for each section received a student evaluation score based on the mean rating given him by students in that section. The student evaluations of the instructors were made and collected during the large lecture section at the end of the quarter. Anonymous ratings were requested in the interest of obtaining honest responses. A number of subquestions were asked on the rating sheet. The question used in the analysis was: "What grade would you assign to his total teaching performance?" (This is the question most similar to the one item which previous investigators found significant.) Numbers were assigned to letter grades in the usual way with A equal to 4, B to 3, and so on, and with an adjustment of .5 made for borderline ratings.

Note to Reader

Most of the preceding section basically describes the operational definitions that Rodin and Rodin adopted for the variables that are to be correlated in this study. Note that the two variables of primary interest are (1) the measure of how much is learned in the course and (2) the students' evaluation of the instructor in their section. Note also that Rodin and Rodin are concerned that the students in some sections will be better than students in other sections, and that these differences in initial ability will be a confounded third variable in their correlation. Hence, they have also measured the students' initial ability in calculus in order to monitor this variable. In the next section they describe the multivariate method they decided to use to deal with their third-variable problem.

Since students were allowed to choose recitation sections compatible with their preferences and schedules, the sections might be expected to vary in initial ability. Initial ability could affect the amount learned by the students. Therefore, in preference to a simple correlation between objective and subjective measures of teaching effectiveness, a partial correlation between the two measures was obtained. This statistic "partials out" the effect due to initial ability, or, in effect, describes the relation between amount learned from the instructor and student rating of the instructor with initial ability held constant.

RESULTS AND CONCLUSIONS

The partial correlation between the objective and subjective measures of teaching ability, with the initial ability held constant, was equal to $-.746$. The ordinary correlation between the two measures was $r = -.754$.

Figure 1 is a scatter diagram for the two measures. Such a diagram does not correct for the differences in the initial ability of the classes; nevertheless, it is useful because the ordinary and partial correlation coefficients happened to be nearly identical. The points labeled a represent the outcome for the two sections taught by the same instructor; their closeness is informal evidence for the reliability of the data.

Note to Reader

The bivariate correlation coefficient for these data was highly significant (i.e., the relationship was very unlikely to have been produced by chance alone). Hence, there appears to be a *negative* relationship between how highly a professor is evaluated and how much a student learns! Rodin and Rodin speculate about the reasons for this negative relationship in the final section of their discussion, which is reprinted below. You might have some ideas of your own on this matter.

The explanation for the negative correlation between the amount learned from an instructor and the student's evaluation of his teaching performance is not obvious. Perhaps students do not wish so much to maximize the

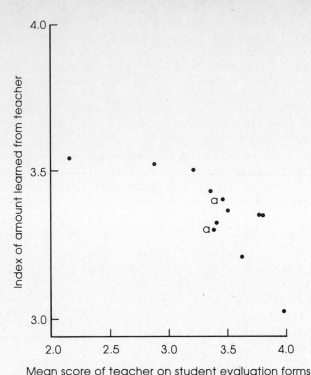

Mean score of teacher on student evaluation forms

Figure 1   Relationship between objective and subjective criteria for good teaching ($r= -.75$). The points labeled *a* are for two sections taught by the same instructor. Reprinted with permission of The American Association for the Advancement of Science and the authors from Rodin, M., and Rodin, B. 1972. Students evaluations of teachers. *Science, 177,* 1164–1166. Copyright 1972 by The American Association for the Advancement of Science.

amount learned as to reach an equitable compromise between the effort involved in learning and the perceived importance of what is being learned. Or, in short, perhaps students resent instructors who force them to work hard and who force them to learn more than they wish. It may be that as students learn more, they become better able to detect the weaknesses in their instructors. Many other hypotheses could be advanced, but it seems fruitless to speculate without further evidence. Similarly, information about the extent to which the present results may be generalized to different types of course must await further experimentation.

     A correlation in the vicinity of .7 accounts for about one half of the variance in student evaluation of their teachers. What accounts for the residual variance? There is evidence that student evaluations to a large extent tend to reflect the personal and social qualities of the instructor, "Who he is" rather than "What he does."

How should good teaching be measured? The major defense for defining good teaching in terms of good scores on the student evaluation forms is based on an analogy between the student and the consumer—the student, as primary consumer of the teaching product, is in the best position to evaluate its worth. However, the present data indicate that students are less than perfect judges of teaching effectiveness if the latter is measured by how much they have learned. If how much students learn is considered to be a major component of good teaching, it must be concluded good teaching is not validly measured by student evaluations in their current form.

CHAPTER EXERCISES

11.1. Rodin and Rodin report that the simple (ordinary) bivariate correlation between the student ratings of the instructor and the amount learned was $-.754$; the partial correlation between these two variables with initial ability held constant was $-.746$. What do these results tell you about the extent to which initial ability was a confounded third variable in this correlation design?

11.2. Can you think of any other third variables that might be confounded in the relationship between student ratings of the instructor and the amount they learn in a course?

11.3. Does the correlation reported by Rodin and Rodin make any directional claims about which factor might be causal in this relationship? If so, are these directional claims justified?

11.4. Do the results of this correlation design have external validity, in your opinion?

11.5. If you recall the example of a bivariate correlation design reported by Siegel and Loftus (1978), reprinted at the end of Chapter 10, there were three measures of the psychological state of anxiety in that experiment. The authors correlated each measure of anxiety with a measure of memory called the "eyewitness testimony task." Now that you have read Chapter 11, can you think of other, more informative ways to have discussed the data from the Siegel and Loftus experiment? What additional information might have emerged from their experiment if it had been treated as a multivariate correlation design?

CHAPTER 12

CITIZEN SCIENCE: AN EPILOGUE

Jerry White lives in New Brunswick, Canada. Thirty years ago he was part of a crew hired to spray herbicide along power lines in New Brunswick. This same herbicide was used later by the U.S. military to defoliate large areas of jungle in Vietnam. Known as Agent Orange, it contains a substance called *dioxin* that is suspected to have a wide variety of toxic effects on people exposed to it.

Jerry White is now the president of a group called SODA, short for Sprayers of Dioxin Association. He formed the group after discovering that many of the people who had worked on spray crews were having serious health problems. SODA is now planning a legal action; and as part of this process, it must deal with scientific evidence that has accumulated on the toxic effects of Agent Orange. Jerry White described his experience over the past year as follows:

> I started out with no formal education in this field and I started out with no literature on the field, and today, the literature would take up enough space to cover a room about 9 by 10. And I've talked to and met with a good many of the top scientists from all over the world in this particular field. So I naturally have at least a very good level of expertise from a layman's standpoint. (Canadian Broadcasting Corporation Transcript 41d108, 1985, p. 5)

Jerry White's decision to become familiar with the toxic effects of Agent Orange have had a large impact on his life. As he stated during his interview:

> It's totally changed my life, actually, because I had spent most of my adult life in either sales for national companies or in small businesses of my own, so I never would have classified myself as an environmentalist a year ago. I would probably

look upon the kind of person I have become as a radical. (Canadian Broad-casting System Transcript, 41d0108, 1985, p. 6)

Margherita Howe is a store owner in Southern Ontario and the head of a group called Operation Clean Niagara. In 1979 she discovered that a large chemical company was going to build a pipeline to carry toxic wastes to the Niagara River. This marked the beginning of a long and continuing fight she has waged against pollution of the Niagara water system. She described her early experiences in this role as follows:

I gradually became aware that you didn't really have to be an expert. There really are very few experts around, for one thing, and if you have 12 scientists looking at a report, you'll probably have 12 different interpretations. And depending on who the scientists or experts work for, that determines the policy. I think a scientist or an expert would admit to that. So what you'd have to use is your good common sense. (Canadian Broadcasting Corporation Transcript 41d108, 1985, p. 7)

Elizabeth May is a lawyer living in Halifax, Nova Scotia. Like Jerry White and Margherita Howe, she has also been concerned with an environmental health problem. Much of Nova Scotia is covered by virgin spruce forests owned or leased by multinational pulp and paper companies. The companies feel that there are two major threats to this natural resource. First, they compare the hardwood trees in the spruce forest to weeds in a vegetable garden because the hardwoods compete with the spruce. Second, spruce trees can be killed by an insect called the spruce budworm; in recent years the budworm has devastated large areas of spruce forest. The solutions proposed by the pulp and paper companies are (1) to spray the forests with an herbicide (Agent Orange) that will selectively kill competing hardwoods and (2) to spray a pesticide to kill the spruce budworm. Many people, particularly those living in target areas, are against such wholesale use of chemicals because of the potential health hazards. Recently, a small group of residents in a rural area of Nova Scotia went to court against one of the largest pulp and paper companies in the world in an attempt to prevent the use of these chemical substances. Elizabeth May was their lawyer. They lost. In a recent interview, Elizabeth May expressed some interesting thoughts about the case:

That was often a charge levelled against us—listen to the experts, you people aren't experts. And experts was always in quotes and capitalized, and really, when you come right down to it, there is not an expert on the spruce budworm spraying issue. There are people who know one fragment of that issue. There are entomologists who know something about budworms and how to kill them. There are toxicologists who know something about how those chemicals are going to affect a human being. There are foresters who know something about how much wood they want for the pulp and paper industry. And all of these people can pronounce themselves experts, but to put the whole picture together, citizens in the area were essentially in just as good a position as anyone with a string of

Ph.D.'s to figure out that this was not a good idea, either for the industry, for the environment, or for the people who lived in the area. (Canadian Broadcasting Corporation Transcript 41d108, 1985, p. 17)

The preceding information was taken from a series of radio programs prepared by Donna Smyth, a professor of English at Acadia University in Wolfville, Nova Scotia. Called "Finding Out: The Rise of Citizen Science," they were broadcast as part of the Canadian Broadcasting Corporation's *Ideas*.

As I listened to these radio programs, I thought about the material I had written in Chapter 1. There, if you recall, I suggested that the primary value of this book for most students would be to improve their critical skills as consumers of scientific information. If I then had any doubts about the importance of these critical skills, the words of people like Jerry White, Margherita Howe, and Elizabeth May have since eliminated them. These people have gone well beyond being passive consumers of scientific information. Donna Smyth, with a note of genuine respect in her voice, calls them "citizen-scientists." Personal circumstances and a strong sense of civic duty have placed them in an adversarial relationship with experts and authorities; one weapon they use to fight their battles is scientific evidence. Given the promises I made to you in Chapter 1, it seems appropriate to offer an epilogue that briefly considers the role of citizen scientists.

THE DILEMMA OF CITIZEN-SCIENTISTS

As I listened to the stories told by the 43 citizen-scientists that Donna Smyth introduced in this series, they all seemed to be actors in the same three-act play. The scenery and dialogue changed from performance to performance, but the story line remained the same. In the first act, they became concerned about a particular substance or procedure and the effect that it might have on people. In the second act, they consulted scientists for answers to their questions. The scientists disagreed among themselves and the available evidence was inconsistent or incomplete. In the third act, the citizens confronted authorities who questioned their credibility because they were not experts. As Marie-Syms Grehan, one of the citizen-scientists from Saskatchewan, said with reference to the decision process on one of these issues:

What it does is it ties up people in a process which is just so heavily loaded for the companies, who have the experts, who have the time, who have the money, and can really discredit anything we can say very easily by pulling out another paid chemist or another paid toxicologist to say these things are fine. I have found that it's frustrating, it burns out environmentalists who try to study and get all sorts of very good information, but which does not stand up in court. It does not stand up in hearings because you're really only an interested citizen, you are not an expert, and so you're not respected. What you say has no respect, it has no weight. (Canadian Broadcasting Corporation Transcript 41d108, 1985, p. 23)

Of course, the unfortunate problem with this three-act drama is that it ends in a dilemma. Scientists fail to provide definitive answers, and the authorities assume that the concerned citizen is unable to make credible judgments. In the end, some government authority is forced to make a decision, and the grounds on which such decisions are made can be very arbitrary. This is perhaps understandable. Politicians and government officials elected to make such decisions are often no more qualified than the citizen-scientists whose credibility they question.

RESOLVING THE DILEMMA

I think everyone would agree that we must find some effective way to resolve the dilemma of the citizen-scientist; the question is how? Should the decisions on such issues be made in a courtroom, as it was in the case of the Nova Scotia herbicide trial discussed earlier by Elizabeth May? If so, should we trust a jury of peers or place our faith in judges? Or perhaps a committee of scientists and citizens independent of the legal system could be given jurisdiction over such matters? To be perfectly candid, I can't think of any specific process for resolving the dilemma that does not have serious drawbacks. I can, however, make one point without reservation: *a minimal necessary condition for any such process to work effectively is that the participants have a basic knowledge of the strategies that scientists use to answer these contentious questions about nature.* Although this knowledge cannot guarantee that rational decisions will be made, any decisions made without such knowledge will inevitably be risky and questionable. To emphasize this point and leave you with some food for future thought, consider the following example.

Aspartame is a sugar substitute that is manufactured by the G. D. Searle Company and marketed under the trade names *Equal* and *Nutrasweet*. The product is widely used in diet soda, dairy products, cereals, and many diet foods. Recently, the Community Nutrition Institute, a consumer organization based in Washington, D.C., has expressed concern about the alleged effects of this substance on basic brain functions. Their concern was spread to a more general audience in an article published in *Vogue* magazine (Stern, 1984). It describes the results of some of the initial scientific research on aspartame. One set of experiments in particular was distressing in that aspartame was observed to produce substantial changes in brain chemistry (Wurtman, 1982). These experiments were conducted on laboratory rats using dosages of aspartame comparable to those a child might receive in several cans of diet soda consumed with a sandwich. On the other hand, Stern (1984) reports that the manufacturer has found no evidence of dangerous side effects in its own research program.

This story line should sound very familiar to you at this point. It is the first act of the ubiquitous three-act play described earlier. I suspect that the second and third acts will develop rapidly. The major players will be the G. D. Searle Company and those food manufacturers that use aspartame; various scientists whose research is concerned with the properties of aspartame; government agencies like the Food and Drug Administration that license the distribution of such substances; and, last but not least, citizen-scientists like the Community Nutrition Institute. Indeed, according to Stern's article, the Community Nutrition Institute is planning to petition the courts so as to force the Food and Drug Administration to examine the use of aspartame in carbonated beverages. It seems that the second act is about to begin.

My reason for introducing this example is not to indicate whether or not aspartame has potentially dangerous side effects. Instead, I want you to think about how the issue will be resolved. Having just read several hundred pages of material concerned with the strategies that scientists use to answer this kind of question, can you imagine anyone making reasonable judgments about the scientific evidence on this issue without understanding the difference between analytic and quasi-analytic experiments? Can you conceive of making such judgments without being aware of the basic threats to the internal and external validity of a retrospective ex post facto experiment? Can you imagine anyone discussing the results of a correlation design without being aware of the ever-present third-variable problem? A familiarity with the problems associated with the use of operational definitions, sampling procedures, and measurement bias would also seem to be of fundamental importance in considering claims made about the properties of aspartame.

I cannot imagine making these decisions without such knowledge, and I think you also now understand why this knowledge is essential if you want to be an informed consumer of scientific information or an active participant in the many issues raised by citizen-scientists these days. If consumers, citizen-scientists, politicians, and government officials can develop a basic knowledge of the strategies scientists use to answer such questions and the way in which these strategies succeed and fail, we will have taken an important step toward resolving the dilemma generated by these three-act plays affecting our lives. Although I am not so naive as to think that this knowledge alone will suffice to resolve all such problems, I believe it is one of the necessary first ingredients for any effective solution. My sincere hope is that this book has provided at least a basic introduction to it.

THE PSYCHOLOGY LITERATURE

You will recall from Chapter 2 the data reported by Hess (1975) indicating that, in human interactions, changes in pupil size serve to communicate feelings and attitudes. Hess reported that people tend to interpret relatively large pupils as positive, pleasant, and friendly, whereas small, constricted pupils are interpreted as negative, aggressive, and unpleasant. If this claim is true, it would seem that there is a very subtle and important nonverbal communication system at work when people interact. Suppose you wanted to know more about this phenomenon. How should you proceed?

The question of how to proceed is important. If you want to think critically about the scientific claims that affect your life each day, the first step is obviously going to be finding the original information on which such claims are based. Or if you want to conduct research on some phenomenon, you will have to conduct a literature search to find other relevant information. The best place to start is a good university library. In the case of scientific information, it is useful to know some of the tricks of the trade that scientists and librarians have devised over the years in order to make sense of the vast amount of data generated in any scientific field. Of course, you may already be familiar with some of these "tricks," in which case you can skip quickly over the material in the following discussion. Alternatively, if the rows of dusty books and journals in the typical science library discouraged you long ago, it is time to come back for another look. The next few pages are intended to give you a basic introduction to the problem of finding a specific type of information in the behavioral science library.

For the purpose of discussion, we shall continue to consider the problem of pupil size and nonverbal communication. Most of the material available to you on any scientific topic will fall into two categories: (1) scientific books and (2) scientific periodicals (journals). You should know that each book in any library can be accessed according to the author's name, the title of the book, or the subject matter on cards in a central file known as the *card catalogue*. If you don't know how to use this, ask the librarian to show you.

SCIENTIFIC BOOKS

When you first develop an interest in a particular topic, it is best to start with the subject catalogue to see if the library lists any books on this specific topic. Libraries use standardized subject headings in their catalogues, so it is wise to begin by finding the proper heading to use. In our example, you might wish to look at a reference book called *Library of Congress Subject Headings,* under words such as pupil, communication, nonverbal, etc. This will direct you to the proper terms for the subject catalogue. Do not be discouraged if you do not find the perfect book covering all the latest information on your specific topic. You should look through any book that might have some relevant information. If you are fortunate enough to know the name of one of the prominent researchers in the field, you can also check the author catalogue for any listings under his or her name.

If you do manage to locate a book on the topic of nonverbal communication and pupil size, you should note that scientific books generally tend to have two shortcomings as sources of information. First, the information they contain will almost certainly be somewhat out of date. The process of writing, publishing, and distributing a textbook is a lengthy one. Consequently, some of the information you find even in a recent book on pupil size and nonverbal communication may be several years old. Newer evidence can supersede or invalidate some of the "facts" described in the book. Knowledge in most sciences is developing at a tremendous rate. In short, be aware of the fact that the information you read in almost any book will be somewhat dated.

The second shortcoming of most scientific books is that they typically do not present the information in enough detail to permit a critical examination of the procedures and results. This is particularly true of textbooks in science. They tend to summarize the existing state of knowledge and do not go into any detail about the experiments on which the information is based. As this book tries to show, there are good and bad experiments; if you want to be able to differentiate between them, you must have access to the original experimental reports. Scientific books, textbooks in particular, do not typically provide adequate information for this purpose.

In spite of these two shortcomings, books covering particular areas of scientific research are very useful in providing an overview of the existing state of knowledge. They will introduce you to the literature on the topic and lead you to some of the important people and research reports. Hence you should look for such books as a *first step* in the process of developing an understanding of the literature on a topic. Once you have this overview, you can focus your efforts on developing a more detailed and critical understanding. To do so will inevitably lead you to the scientific journals, which we will consider next. Before proceeding, I might note that I went to the card catalogue in the local library with the word "pupil" as a subject term. Sure enough, in between the words "pupae" and "puppet making" I found a card titled "pupillometry," under which the following relevant book was listed:

Michael, Pierre. Pupillometry: the psychology of the pupillary response. Washington: Hemisphere Pub., 1977.

SCIENTIFIC JOURNALS

The most common sources of original scientific reports are scientific journals. These periodicals are published weekly, monthly, bimonthly, and quarterly, depending on the publication. Subscriptions are expensive, so you will find that most scientists use the journals in the university library collection and subscribe to only those few that focus on their most specialized interests.

Scientific journals are an interesting phenomenon in themselves. To the novice, they look like row after row of uninteresting, uniformly bound, dusty books. They do not exactly invite browsing! Not so for the scientist. Each is a recognizable entity. Some are known for their exceptionally high standards, some for their low standards. Some are known for their biases, others for their objectivity and fairness. Many have nicknames, and the careers of many scientists rise and fall on the judgment of the editors who manage these periodicals. The editors also acquire nicknames, which are not always repeatable!

Perhaps the first thing to note about the journals in the behavioral sciences is that they fall into clusters based upon the function and/or area of research that they serve. There are, for example, a number of different journals specializing in publishing research concerned with animal behavior; others specialize in research concerned with sensory functions. *Animal Behavior* and *Perception and Psychophysics* are examples from each of these categories. Other journals serve specialized functions in their sciences and are not particularly restricted with reference to content or subject matter. If, for example, you have developed a new psychological theory concerned with human memory, you would very likely try to publish it in the *Psychological Review*. This is one of the more influential journals in psychology and is devoted primarily to publishing new and interesting theoretical ideas. Alternatively, if you have just written a critical review of the literature concerned with pupil size and nonverbal communication, you might try to publish it in the *Psychological Bulletin*. This is another influential journal and is devoted primarily to publishing critical reviews of specific research topics in the psychology literature. As you might suspect, it is always pleasant to discover an article in *Psychological Bulletin* devoted to a topic that has recently caught your interest. This means someone has done a tremendous amount of work searching and critically reading the literature on this topic. It will give you a real headstart in approaching the literature.

These are just a few examples of the different clusters of journals. In Table A.1, at the end of this discussion, I have listed some of the journals most frequently used by my students and the Library of Congress call number of each journal so that you can find it in your library. Note that the journals are listed according to the content areas and/or functions that they are generally considered to serve. Note also that most libraries keep the most recent (current) issues of their journals in a special place for a short time after they have been received. Older issues are bound into book form and placed in the library stacks according to the call numbers listed in Table A.1. Finally, for a complete listing of all scientific journals, ask your librarian for the index of periodicals for your particular library.

PSYCHOLOGICAL ABSTRACTS

If you have glanced at Table A.1, you will see that it lists a substantial number of journals, and this is only a small sample. If you want to find information on a specific topic, how do you wade into this sea of information and find exactly those reports that are relevant to your topic? It is not always easy, but perhaps the most effective approach for the beginner (at least until you know your way around the scientific literature better) is to use one of the indexing or abstracting journals that are essentially summaries of the information contained in a large number of different journals. *Psychological Abstracts* is one title that falls into this category. It is essentially a "superjournal" that publishes brief summaries (abstracts) of articles appearing in a wide variety of other psychology journals. *Psycho-*

logical Abstracts is perhaps the best way to get into the published literature on a specific topic in the behavioral sciences. We shall consider it in some detail to show how one uses this type of publication.

Once you have located *Psychological Abstracts* in your library, you will note that six monthly issues of the journal comprise one volume and that each such volume contains thousands of abstracts of journal articles. These abstracts are organized into sixteen different categories based upon the general content of the articles, and these categories are very broad. For example, there is a category called "Physiological Psychology," a category called "Experimental Social Psychology," and a category called "Communication Systems." It is quite a job to scan each of these general categories, so you will probably want to look for a much more specific, narrow heading.

In order to find abstracts of articles dealing with more specific topics in *Psychological Abstracts,* you can use the index published for each volume. This index has both a subject index and an author index to all of the abstracts published during the six months covered by that volume. You can consult the subject index and the author index with subject terms and proper names to find articles on particular topics or by particular authors, respectively. If this is confusing you, stop reading now and go to the library. Locate *Psychological Abstracts;* then continue reading.

On the chance that all this sounds very foreign to you and at the risk of being pedantic, I think it is perhaps worthwhile to turn now to a specific example and describe exactly how you might approach *Psychological Abstracts* to find information on a specific topic. We will continue with our example of pupil size and nonverbal communication and assume that you have walked into your library and found *Psychological Abstracts.*

1. Once the volumes are located, you will want to start by selecting some of the recent volumes and work your way back in time.
2. Assume you decide to start looking in the year 1978. First, look for the *index volume* for that year. There will be two of them, one for the first six months of the year and one for the last six months. If you pick up Vol. 60, you will find that it covers the last six months of 1978.
3. If you open the volume, you will see that it is divided into two major sections: one an author index, the other a subject index. Since we do not have any author names at our disposal at this point, we shall skip through the author index.
4. As you enter the subject index, assume that you decide to use the key word "pupil" for your first search. If you leaf through the alphabetized subject index, you will find the headings, *pupil (eye)* and *pupil dilation.* Under these terms, you find a total of 12 different abstracts listed; if you read through each of them, one of the listings will sound as if it might be directly relevant to your interests. It reads as follows:

> pupil dilation and constriction, attitudes about alcoholic beverages, female college students, 11110

5. You now go to the shelves and find Vol. 60 of *Psychological Abstracts* for 1978, which contains abstract 11110, and you will find on page 1188 of that volume the following abstract:

> 11110 Beall, Sue. (Texas A.&M.U.) Pupillary response as a measure of attitudes about alcoholic beverages. *Perceptual and Motor Skills,* 1977 (Dec.), Vol. 45(3), 751–756.
>
> Pupillary and verbal responses of 39 female college students were not significantly associated, although mean pupillary responses while viewing slides of a seascape, an automobile accident, and a control slide were significantly different. There was a positive relation between a stated dislike

of the accident scene and pupillary constriction. Pupillary responses and Bell Alcohol Scale scores correlated −0.42.

6. Congratulations! You have managed to find one reference relevant to the topic in which you were interested. It appeared in the journal *Perceptual and Motor Skills* in 1977 and was abstracted in Vol. 60 of *Psychological Abstracts* for 1978.

This is at least a start, and it should give you some idea of how your entry into the journal literature can be made using *Psychological Abstracts*. Once you have gone into the stack to dig out the particular journal article you have discovered, you will find that this article refers to others in the same area, and so the search goes.

This little excursion into the *Psychological Abstracts* is only the beginning of a trip that can be very extensive depending upon the topic under attack. Additional volumes of *Psychological Abstracts* must be consulted; other subject terms must be explored; authors' names, as they are discovered, must be checked through the author index; and so on. I should also note, contrary to the preceding example, your search would usually start with the most recent abstracts and work backward in time. This way you find the most up-to-date information first.

INDEX MEDICUS

Psychological Abstracts, as indicated earlier, tend to focus on journals of interest to psychologists and behavioral scientists in general. *Index Medicus* performs a similar function for over 2000 different biomedical journals. As the name implies, one should check *Index Medicus* when the topic of interest is medical or health-related. You may recall our friend from Chapter 1 who was concerned about the addictive properties of the drug Valium—also the student being treated for a phobia. If you are searching for references relevant to either of these topics, you would certainly want to include *Index Medicus* as a possible source of information.

I shall not go through the procedure for using *Index Medicus* in any detail. It is relatively simple to use, and once you have mastered the *Psychological Abstracts*, the others tend to be much easier to learn. Any librarian can give you all the guidance you will need in a few minutes. You should note, perhaps, that *Index Medicus* does not provide abstracts of the articles it lists. Instead, it gives you the title, author, and journal. Hence, you will have to estimate from a particular title how relevant a particular journal article might be. As you will discover when you search out a journal article with a very relevant title, titles can sometimes be misleading.

SCIENCE CITATION INDEX AND SOCIAL SCIENCES CITATION INDEX

As the names suggest, these two general sources, like *Index Medicus,* list titles of articles published in either the natural and physical sciences (biology, chemistry, physics, etc.) or the social sciences (sociology, economics, psychology, etc.). These sources are actually composed of three different indexes. If you want to find articles listed under a specific topic (e.g., addiction) you consult the *Subject Index.* If you want to find articles written by a specific scientist, you consult the *Source Index* for the time periods in which you are interested. Finally, there is the *Citation Index,* which is interesting and unique among source materials. The *Citation Index* will provide you with a list of all the journal articles that make reference to any journal article in which you might be interested. If, for example, you discover an interesting article on changes in pupil size published by Hess in 1975, you can consult the *Citation Index* for a list of all the articles that referred to Hess's article subsequent to its publication.

As you can imagine, the *Citation Index* is a popular device among scientists. If a scientist named Jones published a paper in 1979, Jones can monitor the *Citation Index* for any papers that appear subsequently and make reference to the Jones paper. Obviously, papers that refer to Jones are directly relevant to Jones. I suspect that the *Citation Index* also serves as a "vanity meter." Scientists like to think that their research is important, and some judge its importance in terms of the frequency with which their published papers are cited by *other* important papers. Important papers are cited very frequently, whereas unimportant papers might not receive any citation! Although there are dangers in using the *Citation Index* as a measure of the scientific importance of a particular journal article, it is fair to say that such judgments are often made.

Once again, if you can find your way through a source like *Psychological Abstracts,* five minutes with the librarian will make you familiar with *Science Citation Index* and *Social Sciences Citation Index.*

Finally, other source volumes that would be of more specialized interest to individuals doing behavioral research in certain specific fields include the *Cumulative Index of Hospital Literature, International Nursing Index, Abstracts of Studies in Public Health, Education and Information Research Center, Rehabilitation Literature,* and *Abstracts of Health Care Management Guides.*

The library is really a very efficient institution for those who know its secrets!

JOURNAL LISTS AND CALL NUMBERS

The following is a guide to frequently used publications in the psychology literature and their Library of Congress call numbers.

General Information Sources

These publications are essentially used as guides to the journal literature. Most contain subject and author indexes that permit you to track down journal articles published on specific topics and/or by specific authors.

BF 1 P9	Psychological Abstracts
Z 7401 S365	Science Citation Index
AS 30 M62	Dissertation Abstracts
QP 351 C6	Behavioral Biology Abstracts
AI 3 R281	Social Sciences Citation Index
QL 750 B4	Animal Behaviour Abstracts

General Science Journals and Reviews

These publications are not restricted to particular content or topics; in some cases, they function primarily to publish critical reviews of the literature on various topics.

T 1 S41	Scientific American
Q 1 N282	Nature
BF 30 A61	Annual Review of Psychology

BF 1 A51	American Psychologist
BF 1 C2	Canadian Journal of Behavioural Science
BF 1 C212	Canadian Psychological Review
BF 1 J83	Journal of Experimental Psychology: General
BF 1 P96	Psychological Bulletin
BF 1 P97	Psychological Review
Q 1 S41	Science

Applied Psychology

These publications are devoted primarily to topics concerned with the application of psychological principles to a wide variety of problems. They range from journals concerned with the effectiveness of particular therapeutic procedures to those concerned with the development of efficient mass-production procedures in modern factories.

B 637 B4 P66	Progress in Behavior Modification
RC 475 P97	Psychotherapy
BF 636 A1 07	Organizational Behavior and Human Performance
BF 309 C65	Cognitive Therapy and Research
BF 637 C6 C64	The Counseling Psychologist
RC 467 C87	Current Topics in Clinical and Community Psychology
BF 1 C5	The Clinical Psychologist
HM 251 J52	Journal of Applied Social Psychology
BF 1 J7	Journal of Applied Psychology
BF 199 J6	Journal of Applied Behavior Analysis
RC 321 J86	Journal of Clinical Psychology
RC 467 J65	Journal of Community Psychology
BF 1 J8	Journal of Consulting and Clinical Psychology
BF 637 C8 J86	Journal of Counseling Psychology
RC 489 B4 A78	Advances in Behavior Research and Therapy
HM 251 A5	American Journal of Community Psychology
RC 489 B4 B435	Behavior Therapy
QP 351 B56	Biofeedback and Self-Regulation

Developmental Psychology

These publications are concerned primarily with changes that take place as an organism develops. Much of the research falls into the categories of neonatal development, child development, and the psychology of the aged.

HQ 768.8 R4	Review of Child Development Research
BF 721 J862	Journal of Experimental Child Psychology
BF 1 D4	Developmental Psychology
QP 86 E9	Experimental Aging Research
QP 1 H84	Human Development
BF 723 I6 U5	Infant Behavior and Development
BF 1103 S67	Monographs of the Society for Research in Child Development

Physiological Basis of Behavior

A broad range of physiological factors have been studied with reference to their effects upon behavior. Much of this research is devoted to neurological and neurophysiological factors. These publications are concerned with this general area of research.

QP 1 A5	American Journal of Physiology
QP 356 P73	Progress in Neurobiology
QP 351 P75	Progress in Psychobiology and Physiological Psychology
QP 356.4 P8	Psychoneural Endocrinology
QP 351 J59	Journal of Neurobiology
QP 351 J6	Journal of Neurophysiology
RC 321 N45	Neuroscience and Behavioral Physiology
QP 351 N44	Neurosciences Research Symposium Summaries
QP 351 P5	Physiological Psychology
QP 1 P57	Physiology and Behavior
QP 1 E96	Experimental Brain Research
RC 321 E94	Experimental Neurology
QP 187 A1 H63	Hormones and Aggression
QP 356 H6	Hormones and Behavior
BF 1 J75	Journal of Comparative and Physiological Psychology
QP 351 P79	Psychophysiology

Biological Basis of Behavior

These journals are primarily concerned with animal behavior, evolution, genetics, and other biological factors that are assumed to be of fundamental importance in the study of behavior.

QL 750 A59	Animal Behaviour
QL 785 W6	Journal of Biological Psychology
BF 671 B41	Behaviour
QH 431 A1 B44	Behavior Genetics
QP 351 C6	Behavioral and Neural Biology
QK 351 K92	Biological Cybernetics
QP 351 B5	Biological Psychology

Tests and Measurement

These publications are devoted primarily to studies of various psychological tests and the procedures used to develop tests to measure psychological characteristics such as intelligence, personality traits, and other psychological processes. Also included are journals concerned with statistical procedures and mathematical models in psychology.

BF 1 P985	Psychometrika
BF 1 J862	Journal of Mathematical Psychology
BF 431 A1 J8	Journal of Personality Assessment
BF 1 M96	Multivariate Behavioral Research
BF 1 E24	Educational and Psychological Measurement
BF 1 B862	British Journal of Mathematical and Statistical Psychology

Psychological Processes

Experimental psychologists are interested in understanding the basic processes that underlie behavior. Therefore the areas of research in experimental psychology can be divided into categories based on the particular process of interest. Some psychologists are interested, for example, in sensory processes; others in memory. Some use animal subjects to study these processes; others use humans. The subheadings listed below are intended to organize the periodicals concerned with specific processes into some of the most prominent categories.

Sensory and Perceptual Processes

QP 431 S452	Sensory Processes
QP 474 V83	Vision Research
BF 1 J835	Journal of Experimental Psychology: Human Perception and Performance
BF 311 P4	Perception
BF A4 P42	Perception and Psychophysics

Learning and Memory Processes

BF 1 J832	Journal of Experimental Psychology: Anim. Beh. Pro.
BF 1 J834	Journal of Experimental Psychology: Hum. Learn. Mem.
LB 1051 J86	Journal of Verbal Learning and Verbal Behavior
QL 785 A5	Animal Learning and Behavior

Cognitive Processes

BF 1 M4	Memory and Cognition
RC 321 N49	Neuropsychologia
BF 311 C545	Cognition
BF 1 C55	Cognition Psychology
BF 309 C63	Cognition Science

Personality, Social, and Abnormal Processes

BF 698 P964	Progress and Experimental Personality Research
HM 1 S54	Social Behavior and Personality
BF 728 J65	Journal of Cross-Cultural Psychology
HM 251 J863	Journal of Experimental Social Psychology
BF 1 J863	Journal of Personality
HM 251 J86	Journal of Personality and Social Psychology
BF 1 J87	Journal of Research in Personality
BF 173 A2 J86	Journal of Abnormal Psychology

Motivational Processes

LB 1051 P79	Psychology of Learning and Motivation
QP 351 J86	Journal of the Experimental Analysis of Behavior
BF 199 L4	Learning and Motivation
BF 683 M6	Motivation and Emotion

ETHICAL PROBLEMS IN EXPERIMENTATION

Most of the psychological research you will read has two protagonists, the experimenter and the subject, and behavioral scientists face the perpetual problem of finding subjects who are willing to participate in their research. Since most of the research is conducted in a university setting, it is understandable that students are the most frequently used subjects. Therefore you should not be at all surprised if someday you receive a phone call from a psychologist asking you to participate in a research project. I can remember the first such call I received, and my reaction is still very vivid in my mind. It made me nervous. I was not sure what to expect, and the idea that some psychologist wanted to use me as a "guinea pig" did not appeal to me at all. Now that I am at the other end of the phone, I think that I have a little better perspective on the matter. I realize now that a participant in psychological research generally has nothing to fear. Many concerned people have spent considerable time and effort struggling with questions about ethical principles in this context. The net result is that a contemporary behavioral scientist is required to keep the subject's best interest in mind at all times. When problematic procedures are used, they are usually subjected to considerable scrutiny before they can be adopted. All research protocols are monitored very carefully by most universities, and failure to adhere to existing ethical guidelines can have severe consequences for the scientist.

Ethical questions, however, do not always have precise, clear-cut answers. Like most rules, those ethical rules that govern psychological research are subject to different interpretation in different contexts. At one extreme, people would argue that much of the research being conducted in psychological laboratories should be banned. They claim that it invades privacy, creates unwarranted emotional stress, and is potentially damaging to the well-being of the participants. At the other extreme, it has been argued that there is no need for special ethical rules to govern psychological research. It is assumed by some that the existing "laws of the land" are adequate protection for any citizen, and that any procedure within the limits of these laws is permissible. Somewhere between these two extremes is a rational position recognizing that much of value is to be gained from behavioral research and that all interests must be protected in the process of reaping these benefits. The purpose of the following discussion is to make you aware of these ethical problems and enable you to find your own position somewhere between the two extremes. There will never be precise answers to the ethical questions that arise in the context of psychological research; there can only be rational, informed individuals who make decisions about ethical matters according to their best judgment.

ETHICAL APPETIZERS

Perhaps the best way to start thinking about the ethical questions that can arise in psychological research is to consider a few examples illustrating the range and variety of possible ethical problems. Although these examples are hypothetical, it is not too difficult to find actual research projects that are variations on each of the themes.

As an approach to these examples, assume that your phone rings and, after appropriate introductions and so on, a psychologist asks you to volunteer to be a subject in a research project. What experiences might await you?

Example 1: The Memory Experiment

You agree to participate and you arrive at a specified place and time. A research assistant greets you and seats you in front of a video display terminal designed to present lists of words, one at a time, at a fixed rate of presentation. You are told that the experiment is concerned with human memory and that you are part of a group to whom the words are presented at a very fast rate. The scientist hopes to determine whether or not the rate of presentation during the learning procedure will affect subsequent memory performance. You proceed to learn the list and are subsequently given a memory test. After the tasks are completed, the research assistant thanks you for your participation and you leave, somewhat bored but content to have contributed to the research program.

Example 2: Deception and Stress

The research assistant tells you that the experiment is concerned with your attitudes toward various social organizations on the university campus. You agree to participate and, once again, you arrive at the laboratory at a specified time and are greeted by a research assistant. You are then seated at a table and the research assistant asks you to complete a questionnaire. She also explains that some physiological measurements are required and these will be taken after the questionnaire is completed. She also notes that the physiological measurements can be painful, but she is sure you will be able to tolerate the discomfort. On the other side of the room, you notice some rather ominous pieces of electrical equipment that are connected to a rather frightening metal helmet, obviously intended to fit the human head. The assistant informs you that you have 15 minutes to complete the questionnaire and then leaves. Fifteen minutes later, she returns and informs you that there is a problem with the equipment and the physiological measures will not be possible. Instead, she asks you to complete another questionnaire, after which you will be excused from the experiment. Once the second questionnaire has been completed, the assistant returns and informs you that the true purpose of the experiment was to determine the effects of stress and anxiety on the attitudes measured by the questionnaires. You would not, under any condition, have been exposed to painful procedures. The experimenter thanks you and, if you have no other questions, bids you goodbye. You go home, feeling perhaps a little disgruntled over the deception but relieved that you did not have to wear that metal helmet!

Example 3: Coercion and Stress

Again you agree to participate, this time with some enthusiasm, because the psychologist tells you that she needs you to serve as an assistant in a project concerned with how well students learn under stress. When you arrive at the laboratory, a distinguished gentleman in a white laboratory coat greets you and thanks you for donating your time. He explains that he wants you to play the role of "teacher" in this experimental procedure. As such, you will be seated at a control panel and will administer an electric shock each time a subject, seated in an adjacent room, gives an incorrect answer during a learning session. You are seated at the panel and the experiment begins. The research assistant notes that several intensities of shock can be administered to the subject. They extend from mild discomfort into the dangerous range. The researcher will tell you which intensities to administer on any particular trial. As the experiment progresses, the subject makes errors and you administer shocks. The experimenter tells you to increase the intensity every so often and, eventually, to administer the dangerous levels, in spite of the fact that you can hear the subject in the adjacent room screaming in pain. Finally, the experiment is terminated and the researcher explains that the procedure had nothing to do with learning under stress and that you had not been shocking the person in the adjacent room. Instead, the experiment was actually studying the extent to which a person would be obedient under the influence of authority and social pressure. The degree to which you were willing to inflict painful shocks is assumed to be a measure of this tendency. Once again, after the research assistant has answered any additional questions, you leave the laboratory. What are your feelings on this occasion?

Given these three examples, stop for a moment and ask yourself a seemingly simple question? Is there anything unethical about any of these procedures as I have described them?

I have reprinted below ten basic ethical principles listed in the American Psychological Association's publication *Ethical Principles in the Conduct of Research with Human Participants*. Read these, think about the three examples just discussed, and we shall then discuss some of the problems that will arise in your mind.

THE ETHICAL PRINCIPLES*

The decision to undertake research should rest upon a considered judgment by the individual psychologist about how best to contribute to psychological science and to human welfare. The responsible psychologist weighs alternative directions in which personal energies and resources might be invested. Having made the decision to conduct research, psychologists must carry out their investigations with respect for the people who participate and with concern for their dignity and welfare. The Principles that follow make explicit the investigator's ethical responsibilities toward participants over the course of research, from the initial decision to pursue a study to the steps necessary to protect the confidentiality of research data. These principles should be interpreted in terms of the context provided in the complete document offered as a supplement to these principles.

1. In planning a study the investigator has the personal responsibility to make a careful evaluation of its ethical acceptability, taking into account these principles for research with human beings. To the extent that this appraisal, weighing scientific and humane values, suggests a deviation from any principle the investigator incurs an increasingly serious obligation to seek ethical advice and to observe more stringent safeguards to protect the rights of the human research participant.
2. Responsibility for the establishment and maintenance of acceptable ethical practice in research always remains with the individual investigator. The investigator is also responsible for the ethical treatment of research participants by collaborators, assistants, students, and employees, all of whom, however, incur parallel obligations.
3. Ethical practice requires the investigator to inform the participant of all features of the research that reasonably might be expected to influence willingness to participate and to explain all other aspects of the research about which the participant inquires. Failure to make full disclosure gives added emphasis to the investigator's responsibility to protect the welfare and dignity of the research participant.
4. Openness and honesty are essential characteristics of the relationship between investigator and research participant. When the methodological requirements of a study necessitate concealment or deception, the investigator is required to ensure the participant's understanding of the reasons for this action and to restore the quality of the relationship with the investigator.
5. Ethical research practice requires the investigator to respect the individual's freedom to decline to participate in research or to discontinue participation at any time. The obligation to protect this freedom requires special vigilance when the investigator is in a position of power over the participant. The decision to limit this freedom increases the investigator's responsibility to protect the participant's dignity and welfare.
6. Ethically acceptable research begins with the establishment of a clear and fair agreement between the investigator and the research participant that clarifies the responsibilities of each. The investigator has the obligation to honor all promises and commitments included in that agreement.
7. The ethical investigator protects participants from physical and mental discomfort, harm, and danger. If the risk of such consequences exists, the investigator is required to inform the participant of that fact, secure consent before proceeding, and take all possible measures to minimize distress. A research procedure may not be used if it is likely to cause serious and lasting harm to participants.
8. After the data are collected, ethical practice requires the investigator to provide the participant with a full clarification of the nature of the study and to remove any misconceptions that may have arisen. Where scientific or humane values justify delaying or withholding information, the investigator acquires a special responsibility to assure that there are no damaging consequences for the participant.
9. Where research procedures may result in undesirable consequences for the participant, the investigator has the responsibility to detect and remove or correct these consequences, including, where relevant, long-term after effects.
10. Information obtained about the research participants during the course of

an investigation is confidential. When the possibility exists that others may obtain access to such information, ethical research practice requires that this possibility, together with the plans for protecting confidentiality, be explained to the participants as a part of the procedure for obtaining informed consent.

A human research program would be judged ethical to the extent that the experimenter could adhere to the principles stated above. It will, however, be of some value to reconsider the three hypothetical experiments proposed earlier in this discussion.

Consider, first, example 1, the memory experiment. I think that we can dispense with this example without too much controversy. Literally hundreds of similar experiments are conducted in psychology laboratories on a daily basis. In these experiments, the subjects are informed of the purpose of the experiment, the procedure is explained, and the subjects consent to participate. No problems with deception or distress are evident. For the most part, no contentious ethical questions arise.

Examples 2 and 3 are another matter. A number of ethical questions arise in these two examples and in many similar procedures. They are as follows: (1) in both examples, the subject has been deceived by the experimenter about the real purpose of the experiment; (2) in both cases, the subject can be exposed to considerable distress or anxiety while participating in the experiment, and these feelings may persist once the experiment has been completed; and (3) there is considerable explicit and implicit coercion to continue in the experiment—hence the subject does not feel free to terminate participation at any time during the experiment.

I suspect that a substantial percentage of the population would object to these aspects of the experimental procedures described in examples 2 and 3. Given complete knowledge of the procedure and a completely free choice, many potential subjects would not agree to participate. Are these procedures unethical, in your opinion?

According to the code of ethics described earlier, each of these examples would be considered, at best, undesirable, and an experimenter would be encouraged not to conduct an experiment employing these tactics. If, however, we judge these procedures questionable on ethical grounds, a good many psychologists will find themselves in a difficult dilemma. Consider, first, the question of deliberately deceiving and misleading a subject. Paragraph 4 of the code of ethics frowns on this practice. The fact is, however, that a considerable amount of psychological research would be rendered meaningless if the subject were informed of the "true" purpose of the experiment. Indeed, in certain types of research, it is absolutely necessary that subjects not know that they are being observed. When subjects know that they are being observed, or when they are informed of the purpose of a particular experiment, they will very often fail to act "normal" during the procedure. The two most common problems that emerge are those of "subject compliance" and the "screw-you effect." Both are well known to social psychologists. In the former case, the subject will go to any length to please the experimenter. Subjects have been known to perform the most trivial, boring tasks for hours on end, just because that is what they thought the experimenter wanted them to do. There is also a certain percentage of subjects who will do exactly the opposite. If they suspect that the experimenter wants them to work fast, they will proceed as slowly as possible. The label mentioned earlier seems to fit these subjects very well. If you do not give the subjects explicit instructions, you not only violate the code of ethics to some extent but also invite guessing on the part of the subjects, and this can lead to the most bizarre behavior. I once arranged an experiment in which subjects were required to come to a "game room" for one hour each day. They were permitted to spend their time playing with one of four items in the room: a pool table, a pinball machine, a dart board, and a video game. After a couple of weeks, we removed one item from the room; we were interested in how this would affect the time spent on the remaining activities. We explained the purpose of the experiment to each subject, invited questions, and reassured them of the simple purpose of the procedure. At the end of the experiment, we questioned them about their choices and their thoughts during the experiment. It turned out that a substantial number of these subjects simply did not believe our instructions. For example, one girl spent all her time during the experiment playing pool. Afterward, I asked her why she did not try some of the other activities. She looked at me as if I were crazy and said that she knew better than to mess with anything electrical in a psychology experiment! One fellow spent all his time playing pinball. His explanation was simple. He knew we were studying frustration and he was out to prove that there was no way in which we ever could frustrate him. When we assured him that he had misstated our motives, he gave us a knowing grin, winked, and departed!

As you can see from this anecdote, dealing with human subjects can be a difficult task under the best of conditions. It should therefore be easy to understand why certain types of research require that the experimenter make use of deception as part of the procedure. In order to avoid the contaminating effects of "subject compliance" and "screw-you effects," the experimenter attempts to mislead the subject so that the true purpose of the experiment can be accomplished. As noted earlier, this leaves the experimenter with the ethical dilemma of either using deception or risking contaminated results. I think you can understand the dilemma. But how do you resolve it?

Take next the problem of exposing a subject to the type of fear, stress, and anxiety that would very likely be produced in example 2 and to some extent in example 3. As you might expect, procedures such as these are also questionable under the code of ethics (cf. paragraph 9), which forbids procedures that inflict mental or physical duress on a subject. If the procedure used in example 2 proved effective, most subjects would experience considerable anxiety at the prospect of the "unspecified painful physiological measurements" promised by the experimenter. They had not been informed of this aspect of the procedure prior to volunteering to participate.

There is considerable interest in studying the effects of stress and anxiety on behavior. We know that these basic motivational states are very important determinants of behavior in a wide variety of situations. However, for the psychologist interested in studying the properties of these motivational states, the code of ethics once again poses a dilemma. How can one study the properties of fear, stress, and anxiety if it is considered unethical to expose subjects to these conditions?

Finally, you should note that all three of the examples have elements of coercion that are implicit or explicit in the procedures employed with the subjects. In each case, the subject is under some pressure to participate in the experiment and to continue to participate once the experiment is under way. A strict interpretation of the code of ethics (see in particular paragraph 5) suggests that the experimenter give the subject every opportunity to decline to participate or to leave the experiment at any time. To the extent that the subject is not given this opportunity and that subtle pressures are exerted, the procedure can be considered coercive and unethical.

Obviously, the coercive role of the experimenter is most evident in example 3 where the subject is directly instructed to inflict pain on another person. Such experiments (see Milgram, 1963) demonstrate that subjects are very vulnerable to this type of coercion and very hesitant to ignore demands made by authority figures. Generally speaking, there is no justification for the use of such coercive procedures in an experiment unless its purpose is to study the properties of coercion per se. In any other situation, you should strictly comply with the rules of paragraph 5 of the code of ethics. Once again, however, these rules do pose a dilemma for the psychologist who wishes to study the properties of coercion and social influence.

COMMON SENSE, CONCERN, AND DEBRIEFING

It should be clear from the preceding examples that there will be cases in which it is not possible to adhere to the strictest interpretation of a code of ethics. As stated at the outset, there are no precise, simple answers to ethical questions—only common sense and interpretation by knowledgeable people. There will be experiments in which deception is required, a certain amount of anxiety and distress are induced, or a certain amount of coercion is used. If you find yourself confronted with the dilemmas posed in the preceding discussion (as either a subject or an experimenter), perhaps you should consider the following points in coming to a conclusion:

1. Is the purpose or goal of this research sufficiently important to justify the degree to which it deviates from the principles outlined in the code of ethics?
2. Has the experimenter considered every possible alternative to the use of the questionable procedures in the experiment?
3. Has the experimenter sought independent, "outside" opinions from informed people about the ethical problems under consideration?
4. Has the experimenter been very thorough in debriefing the subjects to correct any misconceptions and alleviate any anxiety or distress provoked by the experimental procedures? (See particularly paragraphs 3 and 9 of the code of ethics.)

I would also suggest, for the interested reader, a more systematic and thorough discussion of these problems by Carlsmith, Ellsworth, and Aronson (1976).

ANIMAL SUBJECTS IN PSYCHOLOGICAL RESEARCH

Most people are aware of the fact that many behavioral scientists study the behavior of nonhuman animals in their research. Two reasons are most often given for doing such research. The first is generally referred to as the "comparative assumption." Comparative psychologists, for example, believe that a complete understanding of human behavior can be obtained only if the human animal is studied in the context of the evolutionary pressures assumed to mold the characteristics of all species. This means that it is important to understand the human in relation to other animals, in terms of both the similarities and the differences. To illustrate the perspective taken by the comparative psychologist, consider a psychologist who spends a lifetime studying the honeybee—in particular the intricate chemical communication system that seems to control the behavior of every bee in the hive. What does this psychologist hope to gain by devoting so much time and energy to this task? There are perhaps three answers to this question, and the answers are to some extent generalizable to any comparative psychological research. First, it is assumed that it is important to understand the honeybee as a part of nature sui generis. Obviously, these insects are of considerable ecological importance, and their survival in nature may depend on our knowledge of their behavior and biology. So the psychologist studies honeybees to understand honeybees. Second, the comparative psychologist assumes that any information about the delicate mechanisms of chemoreception discovered in the honeybee may give us direct insights into the chemosensory functioning of other organisms, including the human senses of taste and smell. Third, as the label implies, the comparative psychologist is constantly looking for similarities and differences in the mechanisms that control the behavior of various species. For example, the discovery of chemical odors controlling the social behavior of the honeybee gives rise to questions about the role of chemical odors in other species. To what extent do you think that "odor" signals play a role in your interactions with another person?

The second reason most often given for using animals in behavioral research is both more pragmatic and more controversial. There are certain experimental procedures, particularly those concerned with the physiological bases of behavior, in which it is impossible to use human subjects. If, for example, you want to determine whether a particular area of the brain is involved in the control of sexual behavior, two of the most effective ways of approaching the question are to lesion that area or to stimulate the tissue directly. Clearly it would not be ethical to expose humans to the dangers of these experimental manipulations and few people would knowingly volunteer for such research, no matter what the long-term benefits for humanity. This raises a very difficult and fundamental question for every individual and for society in general. Can we justify using such procedures with animals?

There are two extreme points of view on this question which are relatively easy to define. At one extreme are certain antivivisectionists who say that we have absolutely no right to inflict any distress or discomfort on any living organism for any purpose. The very thought of using animals for research is repugnant to them. Obviously, this decision is a moral-ethical one, and people have the right to argue for it to the degree that they are willing to regulate their own behavior according to such principles.

At the other extreme are those who take the view that absolutely no constraints should be placed on scientific research with animals. Again, the decision is a moral-ethical matter, and one must respect an individual's right to argue from this position.

Between these two extreme positions, there is a less well-defined point of view that accepts the need for constraints on the use of animals for research yet also recognizes that there are tremendous benefits to be gained by both humans and other animals through such research.

The difficulty of taking a position between these two extremes was vividly illustrated to me recently when a local news and public affairs program carried an item concerned with the use of cats and dogs in medical research. These animals, strays and wild dogs, were being purchased from the local pound by the university for use in various medical research projects. Having been captured on the streets and taken in, they were maintained at the shelter for five days. If they were not claimed within that time, the animals were either destroyed or sold to the university. In a city the size of Montreal, close to 100,000 such animals are destroyed every year, and the number is increasing.

The news item implied that animals sent to the university for research undergo all sorts of torture and agony at the hands of medical researchers. The report was sensationalized by interspersing unpleasant pictures, as of monkeys suffering from leprosy, throughout. A concerned and sincere local citizen came on the program to ask that this practice of supplying animals to the university be stopped.

On the other hand, medical researchers who saw this program were irate. They consider their research to be of fundamental importance and stated that it would be disrupted if they could not obtain animals. They also objected strenuously to being portrayed as "evil" scientists torturing helpless animals. For the most part, they are physicians trained to heal and relieve pain, not to inflict it. Hence their dismay over the program was also understandable.

Who was correct on this issue, the concerned citizen or the medical researchers? Should the animals be supplied for research purposes or not? The answers to such questions do not come easy, but it helps me to deal with the issue if I think about it in the following way. There are really two parties trapped in the middle—between the medical researcher and the antivivisectionist. One party is the dog, cat, monkey, or rat that is subjected to the actual experimental procedures. Such procedures obviously vary in the amount of distress and discomfort an animal might experience, just as your treatment at the hands of a physician will vary in the amount of distress and discomfort you experience.

The other party trapped between scientist and antivivisectionist is the child with terminal bone cancer, the young man with multiple sclerosis, or the housewife who discovers she has leukemia. It is a fact, for example, that medical science does not at present know enough about pain management to guarantee that the dying child will not suffer terribly.

Perhaps, in the best of all possible worlds, the dog and the young child with bone cancer could sit down together and negotiate the matter. How much distress, discomfort, and danger would the dog decide to endure? How much would the young child ask of the dog? Unfortunately, we do not live in the best of all possible worlds in this respect, or in many others. The dog cannot communicate its feelings, and many would argue that the young child does not have an adequate grasp of the concepts and principles involved. Someone must, therefore, negotiate these ethical questions, and it is obvious that it will not be easy. The medical researcher cannot always guarantee results—only probabilities. A human cannot really presume to judge the distress or discomfort of another human or another animal. Who would you place in the position of making this decision: scientist or antivivisectionist?

Despite these problems, everyone would probably agree on at least one ethical principle in this situation—specifically, that pain and suffering should be eliminated from the world of humans and other animals whenever and wherever possible. At the risk of sounding like an insensitive economist, perhaps I could start from this principle and suggest that we make such decisions according to a cost-payoff principle that gives us the greatest gains for the least cost. To the degree that any experimental procedure is costly in terms of distress and discomfort, that procedure should also maximize our chances of minimizing pain, suffering, and disease over the long term. This strikes me as our only realistic choice in dealing with ethical questions concerning animal experimentation. It also strikes me as the only possible workable position between the two extremes discussed earlier. It takes into account the concerns of both the antivivisectionist and the scientist—and, more importantly, it takes into account the problems of the two parties caught in the middle of the argument.

As you read through this textbook, you will encounter some examples of research using animals as subjects. Some of the procedures will involve painful stimulation, others will not. In all cases, these are examples that can be found in the scientific literature; as such, they have been approved as ethical. I would invite you to think about these examples as you read them. Ask yourself the ethical questions discussed in the preceding paragraphs and come to your own conclusions.

Some Ethical Rules for Animal Research

Of the various attempts to specify a set of rules to guide animal experimentation, those proposed in 1978 by the Canadian Council on Animal Care come as close as any (in my opinion) to recognizing the complexity of the problem and the cost-payoff principle discussed in the preceding section. These rules are reprinted below. You should read through them, think about the various issues involved, and try to come to a rational decision about these matters. Perhaps you will adopt one of the two extreme positions with which we started the discussion, or perhaps you will develop your own position. Someday you may find yourself in the position of acting on this decision—as a scientist, as an antivivisectionist, or quite simply as a concerned citizen.

ETHICS OF ANIMAL EXPERIMENTATION*

These principles are presented to provide guidance and assistance to all those utilizing vertebrates in the conduct of research, teaching or testing.

In the establishment of ethical principles concerning animal experimentation, an effort has been made to incorporate the majority of the suggestions made by members of the Canadian Council on Animal Care, the Canadian Federation of Humane Societies, and other individuals concerned with the humane treatment of animals.

The polarized views of those at the extreme ends of the spectrum on the question of animal usage have, of necessity, been precluded, i.e., those wishing to conduct experiments with little or no constraints regarding infliction of pain [and] those opposed, on humanitarian principles, to any suffering whatsoever.

Those using conscious animals should apply to their studies such tenets as Russell and Burch's "3R" principle of reduction, replacement and refinement,[1] Dr. Carol Newton's "3S" principle of good science, good sense and good sensibility,[2] and Dr. H. C. Rowsell's "3R" tenet: the right animal for the right reasons.[3]

1. In studies involving animals there must be reasonable expectation that such studies will contribute significantly to knowledge which may eventually lead to the improvement of the health and welfare of either man or animals.
2. Investigators have a moral obligation to abide by the humanitarian dictate that experimental animals are not to be subjected to unnecessary pain or distress.
3. If pain or distress are necessary concomitants of the experimental study, then these should be minimized both in intensity and duration.
4. An animal that is observed to be in a state of severe pain which cannot be alleviated should be immediately destroyed, using a humane, acceptable method for euthanasia which must include, as an initial action, rapid production of unconsciousness.
5. Studies such as toxicological and biological testing, cancer research and infectious disease investigation may require continuation until the death of the animal. This requirement, in the face of distinct and irreversible signs that toxicity, infectious processes, or tumour growth have been reached and are causing severe pain and distress, would clearly violate the principles outlined above. In such cases, alternative end points should be sought which would not only satisfy the objectives of the study but also give human consideration to the animal.
6. In test procedures the investigator should be especially cautious with tests which may cause pain and distress. Acceptance should not be based on cheapness and ease of application.
7. Experiments involving the withholding of food and water should be short-term and have no detrimental effect on the health of the animal.
8. Prolonged physical restraint procedures which result in distress or ill effects should only be used after alternative procedures have been considered and found inadequate.

[1]Russell, W. M. S., and Burch, R. L. 1959. The Principles of Humane Experimental Technique. Charles C Thomas. Springfield, Ill.
[2]Proceedings of the symposium on The Future of Animals, Cells, Models and Systems in Research, Development, Education and Testing, NAS-ILAR, Washington, D.C. 1975.
[3]Proceedings of the 1978 Convention of the Canadian Association for Laboratory Animal Science (to be published).
*Reprinted by permission of the Canadian Council on Animal Care.

9. The use of painful experiments solely for the instruction of students or for the demonstration of established scientific knowledge in, e.g., exhibits, conferences or seminars cannot be justified.

10. It is accepted that where the animal is anesthetized and insensitive to pain during an entire experimental study and euthanized before regaining consciousness, there is no conflict of opinion concerning the acceptability of experimental procedures as long as the studies abide by the principles enunciated in this document. This applies also to the conduct of an experiment which involves no pain or distress to the animal.

However, in the use of conscious animals an informed assessment of the degree of pain and its duration is required, in order to relate these to acceptable, or unacceptable, limits. Investigators must be especially prudent in their use of the following procedures:

   a. experiments involving withholding pre- or post-operative pain-relieving medication;
   b. paralyzing and immobilizing experiments where there is no reduction in the sensation of pain;
   c. electric shock as negative reinforcement;
   d. extreme environmental conditions such as low or high temperatures, high humidity, modified atmospheres, etc.

It must be understood that the degree of pain involved should never exceed that determined by the humanitarian importance of the problem to be solved by the experimental study. The following procedures must be restricted and used only when, on the basis of expert opinion, it is anticipated that their utilization will undoubtedly contribute knowledge or benefit to man or animals;

   i. prey killing and fighting experiments;
   ii. experimental burn studies and fracture studies. These studies require anesthesia during procedures, followed by analgesia.

11. Certain experimental procedures are known to inflict excessive pain and are thus unacceptable. These include:

   a. utilization of muscle relaxants or paralytics (curare and curare-like) alone, without anesthetics, during surgical procedures;
   b. traumatizing procedures involving crushing, striking or beating on unanesthetized animals or on animals allowed to recover from the anesthesia.

The above principles should be applied in conjunction with the guiding principles for the Care and Use of Experimental Animals as prepared and distributed by the Canadian Council on Animal Care.

The Canadian Council on Animal Care's Special Committee on Ethics of Animal Experimentation:

Dr. Florent Deopocas (Chairman),
National Research Council
(Division of Biological Sciences)

Dr. Angela Hefferman,
Canadian Federation of Humane Societies

Dr. Larry Belbeck,
Canadian Heart Foundation
(McMaster University)

Dr. H. C. Rowsell (ex-officio),
Canadian Council on Animal Care,
(University of Ottawa)

WRITING A RESEARCH REPORT

When a research project has produced results of interest to the scientific community, a scientist must prepare the information for publication and it must be written up in a specific style. Although different journals have different formats, those that publish behavioral research follow the rules recommended by the American Psychological Association (APA). This format is described in the *Publications Manual of the American Psychological Association* (1983), which can be purchased directly from the APA offices, 1200 Seventeenth Street, Washington D.C. 22201, or can be found at most university libraries.

If you are required to write research reports in your methodology course, you will probably be asked to prepare them in the APA style. The purpose of this section is to help you with this task. In the following pages, I will summarize the most important information from the APA publications manual, and reprint a student's research report that has been prepared according to the APA rules. If you require more detailed information, you should consult the APA's publications manual directly and/or examine a journal that follows these rules. If you intend to actually submit your manuscript for publication, it is worthwhile to write the journal's editor and request a copy of its instructions to authors. Editors are happy to provide this information free of charge, since it saves them a great deal of time in processing manuscripts later on.

SCIENTIFIC WRITING STYLE

Scientific writing has a particular style best described as *succinct*. Journal editors are constantly trying to save space and publication costs, so your manuscript should say everything required in the fewest words possible. I believe that the best way to learn this unique writing style is by *imitation*. Find relevant published journal articles and study the writing style. When you are preparing your own research reports, you should have a copy of a journal article beside you. As you begin special sections of your own report (e.g., the introduction, the apparatus description, etc.), consult the published article and try to imitate the style.

Even if you follow the preceding advice, experience tells me that your first efforts will be less than acceptable. Do not be discouraged. It seems that scientific writing does not come easily to most people. People who can write beautiful prose and poetry often fail miserably at their first attempt to produce a scientific manuscript, and people who have published dozens of journal articles often struggle through several drafts of each new manuscript before submitting it to a journal editor.

THE APA FORMAT

A manuscript suitable for submission to an APA journal is divided into seven major sections in the order listed below:

Title, author(s), and affiliation
Abstract
Introduction
Method
Results
Discussion
References

Consider now the material that should be included in each of these seven sections.

Title, Author(s), and Affiliation

On the first page of your report, you should center the title of the manuscript and place your name and affiliation directly below it. A title that refers to the independent and dependent variables in your research is not very poetic, but it is usually succinct and very informative. The student research report reprinted later in this discussion is titled "The Effect of Caffeine on Recall and Recognition Memory at Various Delays." This is a good title. It is immediately obvious that the writer manipulated caffeine as an independent variable and measured its effect on recall and recognition memory after several different retention intervals. The title is both *succinct* and *informative*. Below the title she has listed her name as author and her affiliation.

Abstract

The second page of the research report is the abstract. An abstract is usually not permitted to exceed 150 words and should provide the reader with a short summary of the entire article. If potential readers are attracted to the title of an article, they will immediately consult the abstract to determine whether or not their interest is justified. In other words, the abstract should help them to decide whether or not this article is relevant to their interests and worth reading. In writing an abstract, the general rule is to state the basic question being addressed by the research, describe the most important results relevant to that question, and finally describe the most important implication of these results. The abstract that is reprinted later in the discussion follows the first two parts of this formula but omits the final part. The author described her basic question and her most important results, but she failed to summarize the most important implication of these results.

Introduction

Your introduction should provide the reader with a brief overview of the background information that is most relevant to your research. The loaded words in the preceding sentence are "background information that is most relevant." It is often difficult to decide what should be included and excluded. Two tactics can be used to help make this decision. First, there are usually a few published articles directly relevant to your own research. You will have no doubts about including these articles as background information in your introduction. I would also suggest that you look at the introductions to these directly relevant articles and determine what they have included as background information. These published examples should provide you with guidelines for selecting the material that should be included in your own introduction.

A second rule of thumb in organizing your introduction is to proceed from general to more specific information. The student report reprinted on the following pages does this very well. When you read it, you will find that the author starts with a general description of caffeine and its properties. She then proceeds to focus on more specific information about the effects of caffeine on memory in laboratory animals and humans. Finally, she concludes by stating the specific purpose of her own experiment in the context of the literature that she has reviewed.

Although the student has organized her introduction well, there are some problems with it that should be mentioned. After reading the background information on caffeine and discovering that caffeine research on humans has produced inconsistent results, the reader is ready to hear two things: (1) the specific purpose of this research project and (2) how this purpose relates to the research described earlier in the introduction. The student did tell us the purpose of her research, but she did not tell us how this purpose relates to the information she presented earlier. Will, for example, the results of her experiment help us to understand the inconsistent results obtained in previous research? If so, how will it increase our understanding? The introduction would be improved by a more definite statement of the way in which this project will advance our understanding. The student could have informed us that existing research on the effects of caffeine had not differentiated between two different types of memory, recognition and recall, and that the purpose of her project was to extend the existing research in this direction. An even more impressive conclusion to her introduction might also have told us why she suspected that caffeine would have differential effects on recognition and recall memory.

Method

There are typically three subsections in the method section of a report: subjects, apparatus, and procedure. The same rule of thumb holds in all three subsections. You should present the information in enough detail to permit someone else to replicate your research.

With reference to your subjects, the people used in the research should be described in terms of their sex, age, and other relevant demographic characteristics (e.g., that they are college students). You should also include the source of the subjects and the way in which they were assigned to different treatment conditions in your experiment. Any special ethical procedures are also described in this section of the report. If you are using laboratory animals, you should describe the genus, species, strain, and supplier of these animals. The animals' maintenance conditions in the laboratory are also discussed at this point.

In the apparatus subsection, you should describe all the specialized equipment and materials used in the experiment in enough detail to permit duplication by other scientists. For standard, commercial equipment, it is often sufficient to provide the brand name, supplier, and model number. For specialized custom equipment, it may be necessary to provide drawings and measurements (metric).

In the procedure subsection, it is helpful to describe the experimental design and the independent and dependent variables as they have been operationally defined for your experiment. This is followed by a description of each step of the procedure to which your subjects were exposed. One useful tactic is to summarize the elements of the procedure that were common to all the treatment groups in your experiment and follow this with a description of the procedures that were unique to each of the different treatment conditions.

One way in which you can appreciate the importance of presenting detailed information in the method section is to read that section of the student's report reprinted on the following pages. Assume you want to replicate her research project. If all of the information you would require is reported, she has done a good job. If important information is missing, she has done a poor job. Indeed, you might find it useful to read her method section and note any missing information before I tell you what I thought was missing. Between us, we should be able to identify most of the important omissions.

In my opinion, some important information was left out of the student's method section. First, the instructions to the subjects were not clear to me. Did the subjects know the treatment condition to which they would be exposed? Did they know that some subjects received a drug and some did not? Did they know what the drug was? In order to replicate her experiment, we would have to obtain this information. Perhaps the best way to answer all these questions would be to include a verbatim copy of the instructions that were given to the subjects.

The student also failed to provide a detailed description of the apparatus used to present the random consonants. Was a slide projector used? Were the consonants presented on a video display terminal by a computer? How large were they? What color were they? And so on.

Finally, the student failed to describe the testing procedure in sufficient detail. Were the subjects put through the procedure individually, or were the treatments administered in a group situation? If it was a group treatment procedure, how many and which subjects were included in each group?

It has been my experience that people are often surprised to discover that they have forgotten to include very important, basic information in the method section of their reports. In fact, I think this ubiquitous problem is easy to understand. By the time students have planned, executed, and analyzed a research project, it seems so familiar to them that they assume too much knowledge on the part of the reader. The writer's very intimate knowledge of the procedure prevents him or her from noticing major omissions in the written description. One helpful trick is to ask someone not familiar with your procedure to read it. Such a person will occasionally spot the most glaring omissions.

Results

This section of the report presents the results you obtain from your experiment and the outcome of any inferential statistics you have applied to these results. Once again, a good rule of thumb is to progress from the general to the specific. The reader will want to know the answer to the most important question first. For example, did the drug have an effect? If so, what was the nature of this effect? Once the primary results of the research have been described, you can discuss additional, more specific observations that you want to include. Note also that you should not *interpret* your results at length in this section of the paper. Simply present the data, then describe and summarize them briefly. Interpretation and discussion are reserved for a later section of the report.

Graphs and tables are very useful devices for summarizing and presenting data in the results section of the report. You should study the ways in which these devices are used in published articles. A mistake students commonly make is to present a graph that describes the data and assume that they do not need to refer to this graph in their written text. This is incorrect. In addition to presenting the graph (or table), you should include a summary statement describing it (e.g., "The data presented in Figure 1 illustrate the effects of different drug dosages on memory. As the graph indicates, memory was disrupted only at the largest dosage . . ." etc.) Once again, imitation is your best strategy. Look at published articles and see how various authors make use of graphs and tables.

If you pause now and examine the results section reprinted on the following pages, it would appear that the student has done a reasonable job of describing her data succinctly, using both the written text and several graphs. I had only one criticism of the organization in this section of the report. The question of primary interest (as indicated in the introduction to the report) was whether or not caffeine has an effect on memory. Therefore, I think she should have begun her results section by addressing this question first. Did the caffeine have any effect on memory? Once this variable has been described, it makes sense to discuss the effects of the less important variables (recall vs. recognition and delay times). The primary results of interest should always be given top billing, whether they support your hypothesis or not!

Discussion

The first sentence in the discussion should briefly describe the most important result you obtained. Did this result support your hypothesis or not? You can then proceed to interpret these results for the reader. You should explain why the results are important and what they have added to our understanding of the phenomenon under consideration. A properly organized interpretation of your results will usually refer directly back to the purpose of the experiment and to the published research that was reviewed in the introduction. Did you accomplish this purpose? If so, what does this add to the research that has already been published on this topic? The discussion section also provides an opportunity to describe any misgivings you have about your data. For example, were there any mistakes in your experiment that should be corrected in subsequent research? Finally, it is useful to suggest any additional research that might be done in the future. I think the most impressive parts of the student's discussion are those in which she describes problems and mistakes that were made in her procedure. It is not a cardinal sin to make mistakes in your research. It is, however, important to recognize those mistakes. This student is a very good critic.

In my opinion, the discussion would have been improved by giving top billing (i.e., first sentence) to the effect of caffeine. The drug, not the other variables, was the center of attention in the research. A second problem with the discussion is that the student fails to relate these results to some of the published research described in the introduction. There are many studies on caffeine; some have observed interesting effects and others have not. Does her research provide us with any new insights into the existing inconsistencies? Her comments comparing introverted and extroverted subjects were a good start in this direction.

References

The *APA Publication Manual* has a specific format that must be followed in listing the references cited in your research report. Again, imitation is your most efficient and convenient strategy—assuming that the person you imitate knows the rules! With one exception, the references at the end of the student report are done in proper format. If you need more information than they provide, consult the *APA Publication Manual* directly.

STUDENT REPORT

The report on the following pages has been reprinted in the same format that it was submitted. You can see the remarks that the instructor has made where the student made mistakes. These remarks, along with the criticisms that were presented in the preceding discussion, should indicate how the report might have been improved. As it stands, this report received an "A," and it should provide you with a standard against which to judge your own efforts.

The Effect of Caffeine on Recall

and Recognition Memory at Various Delays

Andrea Fanjoy

Psychology Department

Dalhousie University

Abstract

This study was designed to determine the effect of caffeine
on memory. Three groups of subjects (10 subjects/group) were
given either 150 mg of caffeine, a placebo, or nothing and were
subsequently asked to perform paired-associate recall and
recognition memory tasks. Accuracy in both tests was measured for
each of the groups at each of three delays, 0 s, 6 s, or 12 s,
interposed between the presentation of the paired-associates and
the test. There was no significant difference in performance
among the three groups. Subjects performed significantly better
on the recognition tests than on the recall test and this
accuracy significantly declined as delays increased.

Caffeine is classified as a central nervous system stimulant
that has been found to affect not only our physiological systems
but also memory and performance. Among its physiological effects,
respiratory rate, blood pressure, anxiety, and restlessness have
been found to increase due to caffeine. In large doses, periods
of depression, tremors, flushing, and even death can occur after
caffeine intake. It also affects the cardiovascular system but
often there is compensatory vagal activity that plays a role in
determining whether it has a stimulating or inhibiting effect on   OMIT
the system (Sawyer, D.A., Julia, H.L., Turin, A.C., 1982).   ◯ — INITIAL

The underlying mechanism of how caffeine affects memory is
not yet completely understood. Switzer (1935a in Weiss & Laties,

1962) studied the effects of caffeine on "inhibition of delay" in rats. After receiving 300 mg of caffeine, rats were trained to associate a light (CS) that was presented for 21 s, and a shock (US) that was presented at the 16th s of the CS. Galvanic skin response served as the measure of conditioning. He found that the administration of caffeine resulted in shorter response latencies and a greater amplitude of response. These results may be due to the physiological arousal that caffeine is known to cause. They may also indicate, however, that caffeine promoted a stronger association of the CS–US pair so that the CS was a better indicator of the US.

Switzer (1935b in Weiss & Laties, 1962) performed another experiment to determine the effects of caffeine on extinction. Rats were trained to associate a light (CS) and then a shock (US) that was administered 0.8 s after the CS presentation and lasted for 1.05 s. Then, they were given 300 mg caffeine and the extinction sessions began. These consisted of a number of unreinforced CS's followed by 1 or 2 CS–US pairs. The amplitude of the responding during extinction was greater upon the administration of caffeine. This may suggest that the acquired association was so strong that it would have required a longer extinction period to break the association.

Studies on the effects of caffeine on operant conditioning yield results similar to those of the classical conditioning experiments of Switzer. Webb and Levine (1978) trained mice on a differential reinforcement of low rates schedule. With this

schedule, a response was reinforced only if 18 s had elapsed
since the subject's last response. They found an increase in
interresponse times (IRT) at doses between 12 and 24 mg/Kg and a
decrease at higher doses. Caffeine also increased response bursts
(IRT <3 per session). No overt behavior effects such as   *MEANING IS NOT CLEAR TO READER*
hyperactivity or atoxia were observed.

Castellano (1976) studied the effects of caffeine on
discrimination learning, long-term memory consolidation, and
learned behavior in mice. The experiment was carried out in a
Y-water-maze in which mice either had to swim towards a light or
a dark end. The corresponding end to which they were being
trained was raised to water level so that the mice could escape
the water. It was found that caffeine, when administered to naive
mice, improved acquisition of the discrimination task. Also,
posttrial administration of caffeine showed a facilitatory effect   *SPELLING?*
on the consolidation processes into long-term storage.

These studies on rodents may suggest that caffeine improves
both learning and retention in memory. This improvement may be a
result of the biochemical effects of caffeine in the brain
(Flexner & Flexner, 1974). Some of these actions include an
increase in cyclic adenosine-3'-5' monophosphate which may affect
synaptic transmissions. It also increases the rate of synthesis
of norepinephrine from tyrosine in the brain, which has been
found to influence memory. Finally, it causes a release of Ca
from intracellular pools which alters the physical properties of
membranes and thus influences synapses.

Due to the proposed physiological basis of the effect of caffeine on memory, one might predict that caffeine would have the same effect in humans as in rodents. However, the results of most studies with humans are inconsistent. Thus, there are many theories that explain both the positive and negative effects of caffeine on human performance.

Caffeine appears to increase both arousal and anxiety. It has been proposed that these factors decrease performance on memory tests. Arousal may decrease efficiency by narrowing the subject's attention (Easterbrook, 1959; Wally & Weiden, 1973 in Eysenck & Folkhard, 1980). Anxiety may decrease performance by causing concern or worry to problems outside of the test and thus [*CONFUSING?*] decrease the subject's concentration (Morris, Brown, & Halbert, 1977; Sarason, 1975 in Eysenck & Folkhard, 1980).

A recent study has found results that are congruent with this hypothesis that caffeine impairs performance (Erikson, G., Hager, L.B., Houseworth, C., Dungan, J., Petros, T., Beckwith, B.E., [*OMIT INITIALS*] 1985). College students were administered either 0 mg/Kg, 2 mg/Kg, or 4 mg/Kg of caffeine and then memorized a series of word lists. These word lists were presented at either a slow (one word every three seconds) or a fast rate (one word a second). Caffeine was found to inhibit females' recall during the slow rate but not the fast rate. These results suggest that arousal may reduce the efficiency with which females rehearse information in working memory.

On the other hand, Ritchie (1975 in Sawyer, D.A. et al., [*OMIT INITIALS*]

1982) suggested that caffeine improves performance by producing a
"clearer and more rapid flow of thought," "a greater capability
of sustained intellectual effort," "a more perfect association of
ideas," and a "keener appreciation of sensory stimuli." This
theory was based on a study of typists who worked faster and made
fewer mistakes upon the administration of caffeine.

Many other studies have found the effect of caffeine to be
highly dependent on dosage and personality. The arousal theory of
introversion/extroversion (Eysenck, 1967 in Revelle, Humphreys,
Simon & Gilliland, 1980) states that a specific level of arousal
must be achieved for optimum performance. According to this
theory, two different types of personalities, introverts and
extroverts, have a different baseline of arousal, such that the
former are more aroused than the latter. The addition of
caffeine, which increases arousal, will affect the performance
only in accordance with the subject's base level. If one is an
introvert, either no caffeine or only moderate amounts are needed
to increase the arousal to its optimal performance level. Large
doses of caffeine would decrease performance because the subject
would have exceeded the desired level. If one is an extrovert,
large amounts of caffeine are needed to increase the arousal to
the desired level.

If there is a physiological basis for the effect of caffeine
on human memory, one would not think that personality factors
interact. The purpose of this study was to examine whether

moderate caffeine doses increase or decrease performance on a memory task involving recall and recognition tasks. The delay between presentation of the task and the test was manipulated to see whether accuracy would be affected by delay.

Method

Subjects

Thirty undergraduate students (15 males and 15 females) volunteered to be subjects in this experiment. Twenty-seven of these were introductory psychology students and received a bonus point for their psychology course. They were between 18 and 25 years old and were arbitrarily assigned before arrival to one of the three groups: the control group, the placebo group, or the caffeine group. Each group had 5 males and 5 females. All were asked not to ingest any caffeine 5 hrs prior to the experiment. None of the subjects had prior experience with this memory test.

Apparatus

Those subjects who were not in the control group were given either a lukewarm drink consisting of 1/8 tsp each of sugar and salt in 150 ml water (placebo group) or 150 mg of caffeine in 150 ml of water (caffeine group). All subjects were then asked to fill out a questionnaire. This included questions of age, sex, weight, previous experience in memory tests, and caffeine and smoking history. They were also asked about their regular caffeine consumption per day, whether or not they were taking any medication, and whether or not they had eaten a big meal just prior to the experiment. This is because tolerance, certain

drugs, and the amount of glucose in the system may influence the

effect of caffeine (Gibbons, R.J. et al., 1976). The memory test   OMIT INITIALS

was presented to each subject on a monitor in a dark room. This

was to minimize any external distractions. The letters in the

memory test were 5 mm tall and 3 mm wide.

Procedure

The subjects were given an outline of the experiment and then

the placebo and caffeine groups were asked to ingest their

corresponding beverage. Then all subjects were given instructions

to the memory task followed by six practice trials. The responses

for the practice were not recorded.

Twenty minutes after ingesting the beverage for the caffeine

and placebo groups, and immediately after for the control group,

subjects were shown the memory task. Four pairs of random

consonants were shown, one pair at a time, for 2 s each. Between

each pair there was a 1 s delay. After the fourth pair had been

shown, there was either no delay or a 6 s or 12 s delay, during

which the subject read a random-number table from the screen.

Then, a test of either one or two consonants was presented. If

one consonant was presented the subject was required to give its

paired associate (recall test). If two consonants were presented,

the subject had to respond "yes" or "no" regarding whether or not

that pair was in the previous four pairs (recognition test). The

subjects had 5 s to give their response followed by a 5 s

interval before the next trial. The entire memory test consisted of 60 trials.

Results

The number of correct responses in the memory task were analyzed using a two-way analysis of variance (ANOVA). An ANOVA on the accuracy for recall and recognition tests over the 3 delays showed a significant interaction among the variables, $F(2,54) = 8.03$, $p < .01$. Analyses on the recall and recognition tests across the 3 groups and on the 3 delays across the 3 groups showed no significant interaction across any of the variables.

Figure 1 shows the average correct responses for the recall and recognition tests at each of the delays. The overall mean for the recall test was 4.94/10 whereas the overall mean for the recognition test was 8.31/10. This difference was significant, $F(1,54) = 90.036$, $p < .01$.

In both recall and recognition tests, the greatest accuracy was with no delay where the mean correct responses was 7.88/10. The mean correct responses for the 12 s delay was 6.25/10 and the mean correct responses for the 6 s delay was 5.75/10. This was a significant difference, with $F(2,54) = 24.95$, $p < .01$. The Tukeys honestly significant difference test showed that there was no difference in mean correct responses between the 6 s and 12 s delays. These two delays, however, showed a significant decrease in accuracy from the 0 s delay ($p < .01$).

Among the drug groups the mean correct responses were 6.47/10

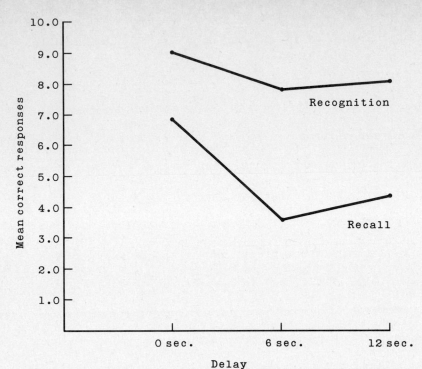

Figure 1 The mean correct responses of all subjects on
the recall and recognition tests at each of the three
delays. Reprinted with permission of author of student
paper submitted, Psychology 2500, Dalhousie University,
by Andrea Fanjoy, 1985.

for the control group, 6.03/10 for the placebo group, and 7.10/10

for the caffeine group (see Figures 2 and 3). The difference

among these groups was insignificant.   NOT STATISTICALLY
                                                      SIGNIFICANT

Discussion

The significant difference among the recall and the

recognition tests is consistent with findings from other similar

studies (Eysenck in Puff (ed.), 1982). Recognition is much easier

for the subjects and hence, has a greater degree of accuracy than

the recall tests. This difference occurred regardless of caffeine

and regardless of the delay before test presentation.

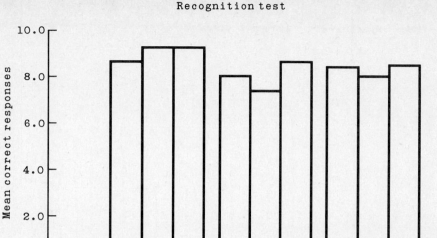

Figure 2 The mean correct responses of the control (c), placebo
(p), and caffeine (d) groups at each of the three delays for
the recognition test. Reprinted with permission of author
of student paper submitted, Psychology 2500, Dalhousie University, by Andrea Fanjoy, 1985.

The significant difference among the delays is also
consistent with previous studies (Bower, 1977). The greatest
accuracy was achieved with no delay before test presentation.
This decline in performance over delayed test presentation
occurred regardless of the caffeine and the type of test.

This experiment showed no significant effect of moderate
doses of caffeine on memory performance. The caffeine group did,
however, perform slightly better than the control and the placebo
groups. It is possible that a larger sample would have yielded a
significant difference.

Also, the subjects in the caffeine group consumed an average

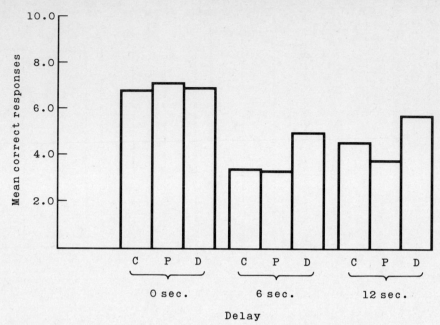

Figure 3   The mean correct responses of the control (c), placebo
(p), and caffeine (d) groups at each of the three delays for
the recall test. Reprinted with permission of author of student
paper submitted, Psychology 2500, Dalhousie University, by
Andrea Fanjoy, 1985.

of 136 mg of caffeine per day. Some habituation to this moderate

amount may have occurred. In that case, a higher dosage of

caffeine would have been necessary to increase the subjects'

performance enough to make it significant.

Another possible reason for the insignificance among the drug

groups would be because the amount of caffeine within each group

wasn't controlled. Even though all subjects were asked not to

ingest any caffeine 5 hrs prior to the experiment, 2 subjects in

the control group ingested 30 and 40 mg of caffeine, 2 subjects

in the placebo group ingested 30 and 50 mg of caffeine, and 3 subjects in the caffeine group ingested 50, 60, and 170 mg of caffeine.

Also, previous studies have indicated that dosage does not have a linear relationship with memory performance. Therefore, it should have been carefully controlled. The caffeine should have been administered according to the body weight of each subject so that they would all be under an equal influence of the drug. The natural variance in people's weights could have caused a wide range of actual caffeine influence, even though all members of the caffeine group received the same amount of caffeine.

Finally, this memory test was designed to determine the effects of caffeine on short-term memory. It was assumed that the subjects would not use imagery in trying to remember the pairs if they weren't told to use it. However, all the subjects eventually used imagery whenever possible. The point of the test when they started to use it varied. The fact that imagery was used makes the experiment no longer a study of short-term memory but of a mixture of that and long-term memory (Gleitman, 1981). Future studies should either use a test in which imagery could not possibly be used or inform all subjects about imagery prior to the test.

It is also possible, however, that caffeine does not have a significant effect on performance, over and above the interacting personality factors. These factors weren't measured in this experiment. It as assumed that the arbitrary assignment of subjects to groups would create an average representation of the population in each group. It is possible that the normal variation among the subjects' personalities produced a range of significant effects, some increasing and some decreasing performance, that averaged out to no significant effect.

These differential effects would support the arousal theory of introversion and extroversion (Eysenck, 1967 in Revelle, Humphreys, Simon, & Gilliland, 1980). If the administration of caffeine causes a performance decrement, then one could conclude that the subjects were initially overaroused and exceeded the specified level. Alternatively, if the administration of caffeine caused an improvement in performance, the subjects must have been initially underaroused. If this theory is accurate, my results would suggest that the subjects of this experiment were underaroused. Hence, those who received 150 mg of caffeine became slightly more aroused and thus were closer to the specified level for optimal performance. However, the personalities of the subjects weren't measured so the results cannot lend support to this theory.

References

Bower, G. (1977). Human memory: structures and processes. New
    York, NY: Academic Press, Inc.

Castellano, C. (1976). Effects of caffeine on discrimination
    learning, consolidation, and learned behavior in mice.
    Psychopharmacology, 48, 255–260.

Erikson, G., Hager, L.B., Houseworth, C., Dungan, J., Petros, T.,
    Beckwith, B. (1985). The effects of caffeine on memory for
    word lists. Physiology & Behavior (in press), July.

IMPROPER REFERENCE FORMAT

Eysenck, M.W., & Folkhard, S. (1980). Personality, time of day,
    and caffeine: some theoretical and conceptual problems in
    Revelle et al. . Journal of Experimental Psychology, 109, 32–
    41.

Flexner, J.B., & Flexner, L.B. (1975). Puromycin's suppression of
    memory in mice as affected by caffeine. Pharmacology,
    Biochemistry & Behavior, 3, 13–17.

Gibbons, R.J., Israel, Y., Kalant, H., Popham, R.E., Schmidt, W.,
    Smart, R.G. (1976). Research advances in alcohol and drug
    problems. New York, NY: John Wiley & Sons, Inc.

Gleitman, H. (1981). Psychology. New York, NY: W.W. Norton & Co.

Revelle, W., Humphreys, M.S., Simon, L., & Gilliland, K. (1980).
    The interactive effect of personality, time of day, and
    caffeine: a test of the arousal model. Journal of
    Experimental Psychology, 109, 1–31.

Revelle, W., Humphreys, M.S., Simon, L., & Gilliland, K. (1980).
    Individual differences in diurnal rhythms and multiple
    activation states: a reply to M.W. Eysenck and S. Folkhard.
    Journal of Experimental Psychology, 109, 42–48.

Sawyer, D.A., Julia, H.L., Turin, A.C. (1982). Caffeine and human
    behavior: arousal, anxiety, and performance effects. Journal
    of Behavioral Medicine, 5, 415–439.

Webb, D., & Levine, T. (1978). Effects of caffeine on DRL
    performance in the mouse. Pharmacology, Biochemistry &
    Behavior, 9, 7–10.

Weiss, B., & Laties, V.G. (1962). Enhancement of human
    performance by caffeine and the amphetamines. Pharmacological
    Review, 14, 1–36.

INFERENTIAL STATISTICS

I assume that you have recently read Chapter 5 and have a basic understanding of the information it presents. The purpose of Appendix D is to elaborate upon the concept of inferential statistics that was briefly introduced near the end of Chapter 5. To begin the discussion, I will briefly review the reasons that we use inferential statistics and then proceed to give you two examples that will illustrate their use. This material will not turn you into a fully trained statistician, but it should help you understand some of the basics. If you find yourself in a situation that requires a more thorough introduction to inferential statistics, I would suggest that McCall (1980) provides an excellent introduction.

"CHANCE" VS. "TRUTH"

The question that dominated our discussion throughout Chapter 5 was whether or not a severe emotional shock would disrupt memory. Our hypothesis was that such a shock would, in fact, disrupt memory, and we designed a simple analytic experiment to test this hypothesis. Assume, for a moment, that you conducted this simple analytic experiment and compared the memories of two different groups of subjects. One group was exposed to an emotional shock; the other was not. There were ten subjects in each of the two groups. Assume also that you obtained the data presented in Table D.1. (The reader with a good memory will recognize this as Table 5.2 from Chapter 5!)

If you assume that a high score indicates a good memory, the data in Table D.1 would seem to support our hypothesis. The average memory performance following emotional shock was 4.1 items recalled, whereas the average memory performance in subjects *not* exposed to emotional shock was 5.2 items recalled.

As a scientist you have two choices at this point. You can accept this difference

Table D.1 HYPOTHETICAL RESULTS OF AN
EXPERIMENT DESIGNED TO MEASURE
THE EFFECTS OF EMOTIONAL SHOCK
UPON MEMORY

Emotional shock condition		No emotional shock condition	
S-1	2	S-1	7
S-2	3	S-2	6
S-3	1	S-3	8
S-4	1	S-4	7
S-5	4	S-5	3
S-6	9	S-6	2
S-7	7	S-7	1
S-8	8	S-8	4
S-9	1	S-9	9
S-10	5	S-10	5
Σ	41	Σ	52
$\overline{X}$	4.1	$\overline{X}$	5.2

between the two treatment conditions as a "true" difference caused by the emotional shock treatment. If you make this choice, we say that you have *accepted the experimental hypothesis*. Alternatively, you can assume that the difference was *not* produced by the emotional shock and instead occurred by chance. If you make this choice, we say that you have *accepted the null hypothesis* (i.e., that there is no difference between the treatment conditions). Now, look again at the data in Table D.1 and think about it for a moment. Should you accept the experimental hypothesis, or should you accept the null hypothesis? Which does your intuition tell you to choose?

As indicated in Chapter 5, in the context of an analytic experiment, the purpose of *inferential statistics* is to help you decide whether or not a difference between two treatment conditions occurred by "chance" or is a "true" difference. There are a large number of different inferential statistical procedures that you can use to help you decide between the experimental hypothesis and the null hypothesis. They have many esoteric names like *t-test, F-test, chi square, sign test,* and my all time favorite, the *Bonferroni test!* One reason that there are so many different inferential statistics from which to choose is that each statistic is intended for use under certain specific conditions. It goes beyond the scope of the present discussion to describe all the factors you must consider when you try to determine if a particular statistic is appropriate for a particular set of data; however, the two examples that will be used in the subsequent discussion will clarify at least one aspect of this problem for you.

With reference to the data in Table D.1, one of several inferential statistics that we can use to decide between the experimental hypothesis and the null hypothesis is called the Mann-Whitney *U* test. This particular statistical test is a good one for the novice to learn because it is relatively easy to see the basic reasoning upon which the calculations are based. As we go through the example, you will find it useful to keep the basic purpose of the analysis in mind. Specifically, we are trying to calculate the likelihood that the difference we see in Table D.1 has occurred by chance alone. If there is a very small likelihood that our difference occurred by chance alone, we will feel more comfortable about accepting our experimental hypothesis.

THE MANN-WHITNEY U TEST

Applied to the data in Table D.1, the Mann-Whitney U test is embarrassingly easy to use. The first step requires you to rank-order from highest to lowest all 20 memory scores from both treatment conditions. Note that there are a lot of tied ranks in these data, and that in case of ties you must assign the average rank to the tied values. Also note that you should *circle* each score in the rank-ordered list that comes from the emotional shock condition. This rank-ordered list of scores is presented for your convenience in Table D.2. You can ignore the column of numbers labeled "frequency" for the time being.

Before we proceed to the next step, you should pause for a moment and consider this rank-ordered list of scores in Table D.2. You will notice in particular that the *circled* scores are mixed throughout the ranks, and that there are many tied ranks. Recall that

Table D.2   A RANK-ORDERED LIST OF THE 20
MEMORY SCORES TAKEN FROM
TABLE D.1

Rank	Memory score[a]	Frequency
1.5	9	0
1.5	⑨	
3.5	8	1
3.5	⑧	
6	⑦	
6	7	2
6	7	2
8	6	3
9.5	5	3
9.5	⑤	
11.5	④	
11.5	4	4
13.5	③	
13.5	3	5
15.5	2	6
	②	
15.5	①	
18.5	①	
18.5	①	
18.5	1	7
18.5		

$$U = 33$$

[a]The scores that are *circled* are subjects who were exposed to the emotional shock condition.

our hypothesis predicts that the memory scores will be lower in the emotional shock condition. Hence, if our hypothesis is correct, we would expect to see most of the *circled* scores near the bottom of this list. It would appear from the data in Table D.2 that our hypothesis is not going to fare very well!

The next step in the Mann-Whitney *U* test consists of counting the number of *circled* scores that are *ranked higher* than each *uncircled* score in the rank-ordered list. If you examine the rank-ordered list in Table D.2, the first uncircled score you encounter is a 9. There is no *circled* score ranked higher than this 9, so we give it a frequency score of 0 in the column labeled *frequency* in Table D.2. The next *uncircled* memory score on the list is an 8. If we count the number of circled scores ranked higher than 8, we see a circled 9. Hence, we give the uncircled 8 a frequency of 1. The next uncircled score is a 7. If you count the number of circled scores ranked higher than this uncircled 7, you find two of them (a circled 8 and a circled 9). Hence, you assign the uncircled 7 a frequency count of 2. This rather tedious process continues down the rank-ordered list until you have assigned a frequency score to each of the ten uncircled scores.

Next, you add up the frequency column in order to obtain a value called the Mann-Whitney *U*. In our particular example, *U* equals 33. Before we proceed to consider the *U* value, I want you to pause for a moment and think about the process you have just completed. You will recall our hypothesis predicted that subjects exposed to the emotional shock (the circled scores) would perform less well (be ranked lower in this list). If our predictions were perfect, what should the rank-ordered list in Table D.2 look like? I think you can see that all of the circled scores would be ranked in the last ten positions of the rank-ordered list. If the *circled* scores occupied the last ten positions in the rank-ordered list, what would happen to the *U* value? Again, I think you can see that the value of *U* would be 0. Alternatively, the more frequently you find circled scores mixed throughout the list, the higher the value of *U* will be. It also follows that the more the circled scores are mixed throughout the list, the less confidence we will have in our experimental hypothesis.

The moral of the story at this point is quite simple. The *U* value is a number that tells us the degree to which scores from one treatment condition in our experiment are mixed together with scores from the other treatment condition. If they are thoroughly mixed together, the *U* value will be large and we will have little reason to be confident that the different treatments had an effect in our experiment. If the scores are not thoroughly mixed and most of the scores in one treatment condition fall at the predicted end of the list, the *U* value will be small and we can be more confident that our treatment had the predicted effect.

The final step in the Mann-Whitney *U* test is perhaps the easiest to do but the most difficult to understand. As you look at the data in Table D.2, you realize that there is a slight tendency for more of the circled scores to occur in the bottom half of the rank-ordered list; but, for the most part, the circled scores can be found throughout the list. We are now faced with a final decision. We must decide at what point the scores are sufficiently separated into the bottom half of the list to allow the conclusion that the emotional shock made memory worse. Stated another way, we must decide how low this *U* value must be before we feel confident about accepting our experimental hypothesis (i.e., that emotional shock disrupts memory).

In practice it is easy to make this decision. At the back of almost any basic statistics book you will find a table much like Table D.3. This table will tell you how low the *U* value must be in order for you to feel confident that your experimental hypothesis can be accepted. However, before I show you how to use Table D.3, it is important that you understand a little bit about the basic reasoning behind the numbers you find in statistical

Table D.3   TABLE OF CRITICAL VALUES OF U IN THE MANN-WHITNEY TEST

Critical values of U for a one-tailed test at $\alpha = .05$ or for a two-tailed test at $\alpha = .10$

x_2 \ x_1	9	10	11	12	13	14	15	16	17	18	19	20
1												
2											0	0
3	1	1	1	2	2	2	3	3	3	4	4	4
4	3	4	5	5	6	7	7	8	9	9	10	11
5	6	7	8	9	10	11	12	14	15	16	17	18
6	9	11	12	13	15	16	18	19	20	22	23	25
7	12	14	16	17	19	21	23	25	26	28	30	32
8	15	17	19	21	24	26	28	30	33	35	37	39
9	18	20	23	26	28	31	33	36	39	41	44	47
10	21	24	27	30	33	36	39	42	45	48	51	54
11	24	27	31	34	37	41	44	48	51	55	58	62
12	27	31	34	38	42	46	50	54	57	61	65	69
13	30	34	38	42	47	51	55	60	64	68	72	77
14	33	37	42	47	51	56	61	65	70	75	80	84
15	36	41	46	51	56	61	66	71	77	82	87	92
16	39	44	50	55	61	66	72	77	83	88	94	100
17	42	48	54	60	65	71	77	83	89	95	101	107
18	45	51	57	64	70	77	83	89	96	102	109	115
19	48	55	61	68	75	82	88	95	102	109	116	123
20	51	58	65	72	80	87	94	101	109	116	123	130
	54	62	69	77	84	92	100	107	115	123	130	138

Source: Adapted and abridged from Tables 1, 3, 5 and 7 of Auble, D. 1953. Extended tables for the Mann-Whitney statistic. *Bulletin of the Institute of Educational Research at Indiana University,* 1, No. 2, with the kind permission of the author and the publisher. Reprinted with permission of McGraw-Hill Book Company, from *Nonparametric Statistics* by S. Siegel. Copyright 1956.

tables like this. We will therefore take a somewhat lengthy digression to discuss this matter before returning to the decision on the data in Table D.2.

As a scientist, you must look at the memory scores in Table D.2 and find some basis for deciding whether or not to accept your experimental hypothesis. This hypothesis predicts that the circled scores should occur at the bottom of the rank-ordered list. Although the scores tend to cluster at the bottom of the list, you will always be haunted by the possibility that this arrangement of scores might simply be the product of chance. One way of dealing with this dilemma would be to calculate the exact probability that this arrangement of scores would occur by chance alone. If we knew, for example, that this probability was .5, we would be hesitant to suggest that the emotional shock had any effect. Alternatively, if the probability that this arrangement would occur by chance alone was .05, we might be willing to accept the hypothesis that emotional shock disrupts memory. There would only be five times in every hundred that we would be wrong in the latter case, whereas we could be wrong as frequently as fifty times in every hundred in the former case.

It so happens that it is possible to calculate the exact probability that any particular arrangement of these 20 scores will occur by chance alone. Hence, we do have some basis for knowing how confident we should feel about claiming that our experimental hypothesis is correct. Furthermore, such calculations tell us that the *less mixed together* our scores from the two treatment conditions are, the lower the probability that these particular results have occurred by chance. Stated another way, the lower the *U* score for a particular set of data, the less likely the particular rank ordering has occurred by chance alone. Table D.4 has been designed to illustrate this point for you in more detail.

In Table D.4 there are three different hypothetical memory experiments of the type we have been discussing. Each experiment has a total of 10 subjects, with 5 exposed to each treatment condition. If you look first at Experiment 1, you will note that all subjects in the emotional shock condition have a lower memory score than any subject not exposed to emotional shock. These data represent an extremely impressive level of support for our experimental hypothesis. Immediately below these data from Experiment 1, I have

Table D.4 THREE HYPOTHETICAL MEMORY EXPERIMENTS THAT COMPARE EMOTIONAL SHOCK TREATMENT TO NO EMOTIONAL SHOCK TREATMENT.[a]

Experiment 1		Experiment 2		Experiment 3	
Emotional shock	No emotional shock	Emotional shock	No emotional shock	Emotional shock	No emotional shock
S-1 3	S-1 9	S-1 3	S-1 9	S-1 3	S-1 4
S-2 4	S-2 6	S-2 4	S-2 6	S-2 9	S-2 6
S-3 2	S-3 5	S-3 5	S-3 2	S-3 5	S-3 7
S-4 1	S-4 7	S-4 1	S-4 7	S-4 1	S-4 2
S-5 1	S-5 8	S-5 1	S-5 8	S-5 1	S-5 8
$\Sigma = 10$	$\Sigma = 35$	$\Sigma = 14$	$\Sigma = 32$	$\Sigma = 19$	$\Sigma = 27$
$\overline{X} = 2$	$\overline{X} = 7$	$\overline{X} = 2.8$	$\overline{X} = 6.4$	$\overline{X} = 3.8$	$\overline{X} = 5.4$

Rank	Memory score	Frequency	Rank	Memory score	Frequency	Rank	Memory score	Frequency
1	9	0	1	9	0	1	9	
2	8	0	2	8	0	2	8	1
3	7	0	3	7	0	3	7	1
4	6	0	4	6	0	4	6	1
5	5	0	5	5	0	5	5	
6	4		6	4		6	4	3
7	3		7	3		7	3	
8	2		8	2		8	2	3
9.5	1		9.5	1	3	9	1	
9.5	1		9.5	1		10	1	
		U = 0			*U* = 3			*U* = 8
	p<.004			*p*<.028			*p*<.274	

[a] In each case, we predict that memory will be worse after emotional shock. Each experiment has 10 subjects, with 5 assigned to each treatment condition. *U* values are calculated for each experiment from the rank-ordered lists of memory scores. See text for explanation and interpretation.

rank-ordered the subjects and calculated a U value using the procedures described earlier. As you can see, all of the circled scores (emotional shock subjects) occur at the lower end of the rank-ordered list. The U value for this arrangement of scores is obviously 0.

What is the likelihood of obtaining this particular arrangement of scores by chance alone? You can probably see that it would be unlikely. To illustrate this point, suppose I gave you a deck of 10 cards (instead of 10 subjects in a memory experiment). Of these cards, 5 are white and 5 are black. Now I ask you to shuffle the cards thoroughly and deal them to me one at a time off the top of the deck. If the deck is well shuffled, chance alone should determine how the cards are arranged. I suspect you would be very surprised if all the white cards came off the deck first and were followed by all the black cards. If you have any experience with cards at all, you will realize that there is some probability that the cards will fall this way, but it is very small to say the least.

I think you can see the analogy between the deck of 10 cards and the 10 subjects in Experiment 1 of Table D.4. There is a small chance of obtaining the arrangement of scores with a U value of 0 by chance alone, but it is very small indeed. If you actually calculate it, you would expect to obtain the U value of 0 for this set of scores by chance along only four times in a thousand. At this point, the scientist would look at the results of Experiment 1 and decide to reject the *null hypothesis* and accept the *experimental hypothesis*, even though this particular result might be one of the four times in every thousand that chance was operating. In fact, most scientists are willing to operate at a *.05 level of confidence*, which is to say that they are willing to accept an experimental hypothesis even if it might have been chance operating five times in every hundred.

If you look next at Experiment 2 in Table D.4, you can see that the results are not quite so clear-cut. The rank-ordering of these scores reveals some degree of mixing instead of the perfect separation seen in Experiment 1. The slightly larger U value of *3* reflects this greater degree of mixing. Once again, however, it is possible to calculate the exact probability of obtaining a U value of 3 *or less* from this set of data. If you recall the analogy with the black and white cards, it should not surprise you to find that there is a higher probability of obtaining this kind of arrangement. The probability of a U value of 3 or less is .028, very low, but higher than in Experiment 1.

Finally, you can complete the story by looking at Experiment 3 in Table D.4. The extent to which the scores are mixed throughout the distribution is greatest in this particular experiment and the U value is 8. The probability of observing a U value of 8 *or less* is .274. As you know, a probability of .274 exceeds the arbitrary lower level of .05, which most scientists demand before they will reject the null hypothesis and accept their experimental hypothesis. Hence, there is too much "mixing" of the treatment conditions in Experiment 3 to accept the hypothesis that emotional shock disrupts memory.

The essential point of this rather lengthy digression was to illustrate that it is possible to calculate the probability that any particular arrangement of scores in a rank-ordered list has occurred by chance. Hence, it is possible to calculate the probability that any particular U value (or less) has occurred by chance. The nice thing about most inferential statistics textbooks is that they do all these calculations for you (they use computers rather than decks of black and white cards!). Table D.3 represents such an effort. It requires you to determine the size of each group in your experiment (n_1 and n_2). In the case of our original experiment in Table D.1, $n_1 = 10$; and, $n_2 = 10$. Given this information, you enter the table with these two values and find that a U of 27 or less is required for you to reject your null hypothesis with at least a .05 level of confidence. According to the data in Tabel D.2, the U value is 33, hence, we were above the required value and must accept the *null hypothesis* that there is no "true difference" between the two treatment conditions. This should not come as a surprise to you. You knew from very early in our discussion that there was a lot of mixing of the scores from the two treatment conditions.

Before we consider the next example, I should note that there are a number of features of the Mann-Whitney U test that were not considered in the present discussion. There is, for example, a computational procedure for larger numbers of subjects that is easier to use than the rather tedious frequency counting that we have employed. For a more complete discussion of the Mann-Whitney U test and its characteristics, I would suggest you begin with Siegel's (1956, pp. 116–127) treatment of this statistical procedure.

THE SIGN TEST

Suppose, for a moment, that we decide to make a basic change in the design of the simple analytic memory experiment that we have been discussing. Instead of using two independent groups of subjects in our two different treatment conditions, suppose that we randomly selected just five subjects from the population and exposed these five subjects to *both* treatment conditions. You will recall that we called this a *within-subjects* bivalent experiment in Chapter 5. In this experiment, each subject will be exposed to the *emotional shock condition* and the *no emotional shock condition* and memory will be measured twice, once after each treatment.

Assume that we conduct this bivalent within-subjects experiment and obtain the memory scores presented in Table D.5. When you look at the average memory score in each condition, it suggests once again that our experimental hypothesis can be accepted; the average memory score is lower following emotional shock. Indeed, if you look at each individual subject in Table D.5, you see that four of the subjects forgot more after emotional shock than they did in the absence of emotional shock. Only subject 3 did better after emotional shock.

Now ask yourself how confident you feel about rejecting the null hypothesis and accepting our experimental hypothesis. Four of the five subjects showed inferior memory after emotional shock. This seems impressive, but it could have occurred simply by chance. If, for example, we had flipped a coin to decide which memory score would be lower for each subject, it is possible that the coin would land *heads-up* on four of the five

Table D.5   HYPOTHETICAL RESULTS OF A WITHIN-SUBJECTS BIVALENT MEMORY
EXPERIMENT WITH FOUR SUBJECTS
(Maximum memory score for any subject is 10.)

Subject	No emotional shock	Emotional shock	Sign
1	6	4	+
2	4	3	+
3	3	5	−
4	5	3	+
5	7	2	+
	Σ 25 $\overline{X}$ 5	Σ 17 $\overline{X}$ 3.4	

$$P < .188$$

flips and produce the same results we see in Table D.5—only subject 3 came up a *tail*. Indeed, if we flipped a coin for each subject, it is possible that we could get five heads in a row, in which case we would give all subjects a lower score in the emotional shock condition.

This example illustrates the same basic problem we encountered when we were discussing the Mann-Whitney U test. Any difference you see between these two treatment conditions could be the product of chance and have nothing to do with the way you treated the subjects. This possibility bothers scientists; they need some way to determine how likely it is that these results are due to chance and not to the variables that they have manipulated. Once again, this is one basic purpose of inferential statistics.

One appropriate inferential statistic to use with the data in Table D.5 is called the *sign test*. Like the Mann-Whitney U test, the sign test is nice because it is relatively easy to see the reasoning behind the calculations.

When applied to the data in Table D.5, the sign test proceeds as follows: First, for each pair of memory scores in which the emotional shock treatment score was lower, you should assign that pair a *plus sign*. These plus cases are consistent with the direction of your experimental hypothesis. Next, for each pair of scores in which the memory score was higher, you should assign the pair a *minus sign*. Finally, any cases in which the two scores are tied are dropped from the analysis when using the sign test.

These first steps are surprisingly simple. Again, however, we should digress briefly to consider what would happen if you had assigned your plus and minus signs by flipping a coin instead of using the subjects' memory scores. If, for a head, you assigned a plus sign, and for a tail, you assigned a minus sign, it should be obvious to you that your results can only be due to chance, assuming a fair coin. You also probably have enough experience flipping coins to know that it would be reasonably rare to get five heads in five flips of a coin. In fact, the probability of obtaining a head on any one flip is ½, and you can calculate the probability of getting five heads in five successive flips as $\frac{1}{2} \times \frac{1}{2} \times \frac{1}{2} \times \frac{1}{2} \times \frac{1}{2} = (\frac{1}{2})^5 = .0311$.

The sign test works on similar reasoning. In the actual scores seen in Table D.5, we found that four of the five subjects were given a plus sign. It is possible that these results are the product of a process like "coin flipping" chance and not our experimental treatments. In fact, it is possible once again, as it was with the Mann-Whitney U test, to calculate the probability that you would obtain *four plus signs or more* by chance alone. Indeed, Table D.6 contains this information already calculated for an N as large as 25. To use this table, N is the number of signed pairs. If a pair has no sign (tied scores), N is reduced appropriately. The numbers along the top of the table designated as X are equal to the number of the fewer signs.

With reference to the data in Table D.5, $N = 5$ and $X = 1$. Hence, the probability of obtaining four *or more* plus signs by chance in this data is .188. This exceeds the arbitrary .05 *level of confidence* that scientists require in order to reject the *null hypothesis*. Hence, based upon these data we would accept the null hypothesis and reject our notion that emotional shock disrupts memory.

Now that I have described the sign test and the basic reasoning behind this inferential statistic, you should find it easy to apply to data in which there are fewer than 25 pairs in your data table. Unfortunately, it is not uncommon to encounter experiments for which the sign test is an appropriate statistic and there are more than 25 pairs of data. I shall, therefore, briefly describe the procedure for using the sign test with such a large number of subjects. This procedure, which is often called the *large N sign test*, is based on a mathematical relationship statisticians call *a normal approximation of the binomial distribution*. If you are interested in knowing more about this and how it plays a role in the

Table D.6 TABLE OF PROBABILITIES ASSOCIATED WITH VALUES AS SMALL AS OBSERVED VALUES OF X IN THE BINOMIAL TEST

Given in the body of this table are one-tailed probabilities and H_0 for the binomial test when $P = Q = \frac{1}{2}$. To save space, decimal points are omitted in the p's.

N \ z	0	1	2	3	4	5	6	7	8	9	10	11	12	13	14	15
5	031	188	500	812	969	†										
6	016	109	344	656	891	984	†									
7	008	062	277	500	733	938	992	†								
8	004	035	145	363	637	855	965	996	†							
9	002	020	090	254	500	746	910	980	998	†						
10	001	011	055	172	377	623	828	945	989	999	†					
11		006	033	113	274	500	726	887	967	994	†	†				
12		003	019	073	194	387	613	806	927	981	997	†	†			
13		002	011	046	133	291	500	709	867	954	989	998	†	†		
14		001	006	029	090	212	395	605	788	910	971	994	999	†	†	
15			004	018	059	151	304	500	696	849	941	982	996	†	†	†
16			002	011	038	105	227	402	598	773	895	962	989	988	†	†
17			001	006	025	072	166	315	500	685	834	928	975	994	999	†
18			001	004	015	048	119	240	407	593	760	881	952	985	996	999
19				002	010	032	084	180	324	500	676	820	916	968	990	998
20				001	006	021	058	132	252	412	588	748	868	942	979	994
21				001	004	013	039	095	192	332	500	668	808	905	961	987
22					002	008	026	067	143	262	416	584	738	857	933	974
23					001	005	017	047	105	202	339	500	661	798	895	953
24					001	003	011	032	076	154	271	419	581	729	846	924
25						002	007	022	054	115	212	345	500	655	788	885

† 1.0 or approximately 1.0.

Source: From *Statistical Inferences* by Helen M. Walker and Joseph Lev, copyright © 1953 by Holt, Rinehart and Winston, Inc., reprinted by permission of Holt, Rinehart and Winston; as adapted by S. Siegel in *Non-Parametric Statistics* (New York: McGraw-Hill, 1956), p. 250, reprinted by permission of McGraw-Hill.

Large N sign test, you can consult Siegel (1956, pp. 36–42; 68–75). If not, you can simply apply the method in much the same manner that you would follow a recipe in a cookbook. You should, however, realize that the same fundamental reasoning that is behind the small N sign test is also at work in this more elaborate version.

The rationale for the large N sign test goes as follows:

1. Arrange all of your data in a table much like Table D.5 so that pairs of memory scores for each subject can be easily compared.
2. Count the numbers of pairs in your data table which have either a plus sign (consistent with hypotheses) or a minus sign (inconsistent with hypotheses). Remember that N equals the number of *signed* pairs and ties are dropped from the analysis.
3. At this point you can check your data table. If the number of signed pairs is 25 or fewer, you can use the small N method described earlier and consult Table D.6. Note that in Table D.6, N stands for the number of signed pairs and X stands for the number of "fewer" signs.
4. If your N is greater than 25, you must use equation D.1 to calculate a value of Z.

$$Z = \frac{(X \pm .5) - \frac{1}{2} N}{\frac{1}{2} \sqrt{N}} \qquad (D.1)$$

In equation D.1, X is the number of plus signs (i.e., the number of pairs in which the direction of the difference is consistent with your hypothesis) and N is the total number of signed pairs. Given these two values, you must next decide whether or not to add or subtract the constant .5 from the value of X in the equation. The rule for making this decision is as follows. Assume you have 100 signed pairs in your data table. If only chance factors are operating in your experiment, you would expect about half of the pairs (50) to produce a plus sign and about half (50) to produce a minus sign. Hence, the expected value of X, given that your independent variable had absolutely no effect, would be 50. If the actual value of X is higher than this expected value, you subtract .5 from X in equation D.1. If the actual value of X is lower than the expected value, you add .5 to X in equation D.1. To illustrate the rule, suppose you have 100 signed pairs in your data table and 60 of these pairs have a plus sign. Since the actual value of X (60) is greater than the expected value of X, you should subtract .5 from the actual value of X in equation D.1.

5. Finally, given the values of X and N, you can substitute in equation D.1 and calculate a value for Z. Once Z is calculated, you can enter Table D.7, which is very easy to use. Assume for a moment that we completed the procedure on some actual data from a within-subjects memory experiment and obtained a Z value of 2.46. If you find the value in Table D.7 associated with a Z of 2.46, you will discover that the odds of obtaining a Z value this large are at least .0069 (approximately seven times in a thousand). As such we would reject our null hypothesis with considerable confidence and assume that the difference in memory scores supported our experimental hypothesis.

CHOOSING THE APPROPRIATE STATISTIC

One last point needs to be made now that we have considered both of the examples in this brief discussion of inferential statistics. Students often look at the data in Table D.1 (a between-subjects memory experiment) and in Table D.5 (a within-subjects memory experiment) and ask a simple question: "Why can't I use a Mann-Whitney U test on the data in both these experiments?"

As I mentioned early in the discussion, a statistic that is appropriate for use with the data from one experiment may not be appropriate for data obtained in a different experiment. There are a wide variety of factors to consider in choosing any inferential statistic, and it goes well beyond the scope of the present discussion to describe all of them. However, the two examples that we considered in the preceding discussion do manage to illustrate at least one such factor, which we will consider briefly as a way of making the more general point.

There is a simple reason why the Mann-Whitney U test cannot be used with the data in Table D.5. In any within-subjects experimental design, the measures taken on each subject are clearly *related*. In the case of our memory experiment, I take two measures of your memory during the experiment and I have every reason to believe that these two measures cannot be considered independent of each other. This is a reasonable assumption when you realize they are made on the *same* individual. Alternatively, if you are a subject in a between-subjects experiment, I obtain only one measure of your memory and this measure is then compared to a totally unrelated or *independent* measure taken

Table D.7 TABLE OF PROBABILITIES ASSOCIATED WITH VALUES AS EXTREME AS OBSERVED VALUES OF *Z* IN THE NORMAL DISTRIBUTION

The body of the table gives one-tailed probabilities under H_0 of z. The left-hand marginal column gives various values of z to one decimal place. The top row gives various values to the second decimal place. Thus, for example, the one-tailed p of $z \geq .11$ or $z \leq - .11$ is $p = .4562$.

z	.00	.01	.02	.03	.04	.05	.06	.07	.08	.09
.0	.5000	.4960	.4920	.4880	.4840	.4801	.4761	.4721	.4681	.4641
.1	.4602	.4562	.4522	.4483	.4443	.4404	.4364	.4325	.4286	.4247
.2	.4207	.4168	.4129	.4090	.4052	.4013	.3974	.3936	.3897	.3859
.3	.3821	.3782	.3745	.3707	.3669	.3632	.3594	.3557	.3520	.3483
.4	.3446	.3409	.3372	.3336	.3300	.3264	.3228	.3192	.3156	.3121
.5	.3085	.3050	.3015	.2981	.2946	.2912	.2877	.2843	.2810	.2776
.6	.2743	.2709	.2676	.2643	.2611	.2578	.2546	.2514	.2483	.2451
.7	.2420	.2389	.2358	.2327	.2296	.2266	.2236	.2206	.2177	.2148
.8	.2119	.2090	.2061	.2033	.2005	.1977	.1949	.1922	.1804	.1867
.9	.1841	.1814	.1788	.1762	.1736	.1711	.1685	.1660	.1635	.1611
1.0	.1587	.1562	.1539	.1515	.1492	.1469	.1446	.1423	.1401	.1379
1.1	.1357	.1335	.1314	.1292	.1271	.1251	.1230	.1210	.1190	.1170
1.2	.1151	.1131	.1112	.1093	.1075	.1056	.1038	.1020	.1003	.0985
1.3	.0968	.0951	.0934	.0918	.0901	.0885	.0869	.0853	.0838	.0823
1.4	.0808	.0793	.0778	.0764	.0749	.0735	.0721	.0708	.0694	.0681
1.5	.0668	.0655	.0643	.0630	.0618	.0606	.0594	.0582	.0571	.0559
1.6	.0548	.0537	.0526	.0516	.0505	.0495	.0485	.0475	.0465	.0455
1.7	.0446	.0436	.0427	.0418	.0409	.0401	.0392	.0384	.0375	.0367
1.8	.0359	.0351	.0344	.0336	.0329	.0322	.0314	.0307	.0301	.0294
1.9	.0287	.0281	.0274	.0268	.0262	0256	.0250	.0244	.0239	.0233
2.0	.0228	.0222	.0217	.0212	.0207	.0202	.0197	.0192	.0188	.0183
2.1	.0179	.0174	.0170	.0166	.0162	.0158	.0154	.0150	.0146	.0143
2.2	.0139	.0136	.0132	.0129	.0125	.0122	.0119	.0116	.0113	.0110
2.3	.0107	.0104	.0102	.0099	.0096	.0094	.0091	.0089	.0087	.0084
2.4	.0082	.0080	.0078	.0075	.0073	.0071	.0069	.0068	.0066	.0064
2.5	.0062	.0060	.0059	.0057	.0055	.0054	.0052	.0051	.0049	.0048
2.6	.0047	.0045	.0044	.0043	.0041	.0040	.0039	.0038	.0037	.0036
2.7	.0035	.0034	.0033	.0032	.0031	.0030	.0029	.0028	.0027	.0026
2.8	.0026	.0025	.0024	.0023	.0023	.0022	.0021	.0021	.0020	.0019
2.9	.0019	.0018	.0018	.0017	.0016	.0016	.0015	.0015	.0014	.0014
3.0	.0013	.0013	.0013	.0012	.0012	.0011	.0011	.0011	.0010	.0010
3.1	.0010	.0009	.0009	.0009	.0008	.0008	.0008	.0008	.0007	.0007
3.2	.0007									
3.3	.0005									
3.4	.0003									
3.5	.00023									
3.6	.00016									
3.7	.00011									
3.8	.00007									
3.9	.00005									
4.0	.00003									

Source: From *Statistical Inferences* by Helen M. Walker and Joseph Lev, copyright © 1953 by Holt, Rinehart and Winston, Inc., reprinted by permission of Holt, Rinehart and Winston; as adapted by S. Siegel in *Non-Parametric Statistics* (New York: McGraw-Hill, 1956), p. 247, reprinted by permission of McGraw-Hill.

from some other individual in the other treatment condition. Hence, these two measures of memory that we plan to compare are unrelated or *independent*.

The sign test is appropriately used when the measures that are going to be compared are *related*. When the probability of the various outcomes is calculated using the sign test, the degree to which they are related is taken into consideration. The Mann-Whitney *U* test is appropriately used only when the measures that are going to be compared are *independent* or *unrelated*. Hence, in deciding which of these two statistics you should use with any particular set of data, you must consider whether the measures to be compared are related (i.e., come from the same individual) or independent (i.e., come from different individuals).

In conclusion, let me suggest that you consult a good introductory statistics book for a discussion of other statistical procedures, the factors to consider when choosing an appropriate procedure, and how to do the calculations. I hope you will discover that the basic concepts introduced in the preceding discussion will help you to understand the reasons for using many of the inferential statistics you will encounter.

ANSWERS TO SELECTED CHAPTER EXERCISES

Chapter 2

2.1 Consider two examples from the list of suggested concepts: aggression and dreaming. There are many different operational definitions of aggression in the psychological literature. For example, in comparative studies of animal behavior, definitions usually isolate some particular stereotyped pattern of behavior exhibited toward another organism. When a crab raises its claws and spreads them apart in response to the presence of another crab, this particular stereotyped response is called *meral spread*, and it is often used as an operational definition of aggression in crabs and other crustacean species. The frequency and/or duration of these stereotyped activities provides a reliable and publicly repeatable method of measuring aggressive interactions in these species, and most ethologists would view the definition as having construct validity.

Describing aggressive behavior in humans is a more contentious matter. Our aggressive behavior manifests itself in a variety of ways, and not all versions of aggressive behavior are readily subsumed by a single operational definition. For example, at first thought, few would dispute the suggestion that aggression can be defined as any interaction between two humans in which one inflicts physical pain on the other. The definition is reliable and publicly repeatable. Note, however, that its construct validity is likely to be questioned. There are cases in which pain is inflicted for the welfare of the recipient (a tetanus inoculation) and instances of aggressive behavior in which no pain is inflicted (i.e., mental duress). It should therefore come as no surprise to find that there are many different operational definitions of aggression in the psychological literature dealing with human behavior. While many of them meet the reliability requirement discussed in Chapter 2, you will find that most of them suffer somewhat in terms of construct validity.

Alternatively, there seem to be relatively few operational definitions of dreaming in the psychological literature, and most of these seem to have acceptable levels of construct validity among psychologists. The most widely used operational definition is people's verbal reports upon awakening. If they say they have been dreaming, you accept this as evidence that dreaming has occurred.

The second definition, which is often used in conjunction with the above, is more difficult to implement. Basically, it involves monitoring, *simultaneously*, both the electrical activity of the brain (with an electroencephalogram) and the muscles that control eye movements during sleep. It is generally accepted that when a person's eyes are moving rapidly (with lids closed!) and the electroencephalogram is dominated by low-voltage, high-frequency brain waves, that person is dreaming. (These measurements correlate highly with verbal reports to that effect.) The rapid eye movements and low-voltage, high-frequency brain wave state is typically called REM (rapid eye movement) sleep. Unlike the definition of aggression or that of pornography discussed in Chapter 2, REM sleep is a widely accepted operational definition of dreaming, with a considerable amount of construct validity.

2.3   The hospital employees described by Rosenhan offer classic examples of the distortion rule. Their observations of the patients are obviously distorted by what they expect of a person who is a patient in a mental hospital. Normal behavior is perceived as abnormal (with reference to the pseudopatients), and abnormal behavior is sometimes diagnosed as normal (when employees are told that some patients might be pseudopatients). Like the planet Uranus, insanity would appear to be in the eye of the beholder.

With reference to the second question, a number of different measures were used to define the concept of depersonalization operationally. In one case, physical segregation from the patients was used as an operational definition. Specifically, the amount of time that the nurses spent outside the "staff cage," interacting with patients, and the frequency with which they left the "staff cage" were publicly repeatable, reliable definitions of the degree to which the staff were assumed to play a role in the depersonalization of the patients. Rosenhan makes a strong plea for the construct validity of this "staff cage" measure. Does he convince you? A second set of measurements used to define the process of depersonalization was directed specifically at the social responsiveness of the hospital staff. Measures of eye contact, time spent talking to a patient, gaze aversion, and other social responses listed in Table 1 all constitute reliable, repeatable operational definitions of depersonalizing behavior exhibited by the hospital employees. Once again, Rosenhan argues that these measures have construct validity in that they are an index of the degree to which hospital patients are treated as individuals and not depersonalized by the hospital staff.

Alternatively, many of the anecdotal stories that are reported by the pseudopatients are simply personal descriptions of the staff-patient interactions, and they do not provide highly reliable measurements of the depersonalization concept. Interpretation of these events is very subjective; in many cases it would be difficult to repeat the measurements and be confident that the same events were being observed.

Chapter 3

3.1 1. Ratio scale. 2. Psychologists usually treat these measures as if they were an interval scale, but strictly speaking they are more accurately viewed as an ordinal scale. 3. Ordinal scale. 4. Nominal scale. 5. Nominal scale . . . .

3.2 The statement "My wife was beautiful in childbirth" is clearly a positive statement. A man saying this would be making a definitive positive statement about his experiences in this context. Note also that this statement would not seem to be too strong (criterion 1); it states an opinion, not a fact (criterion 2); the statement does not use universal words like *always* and *never* (criterion 4); it focuses directly on the topic of childbirth (criterion 6), and so on. On the whole, this statement seems to meet the criteria outlined in Table 3.1 rather well.

Chapter 4

4.1 There are no right or wrong answers to this exercise. You should view it as a test of your creative powers. If Chapter 4 teaches you anything, it shows you that it is not easy to come up with questions that are worthwhile. I have often thought that it would be interesting to examine the questions that are asked about the depression experienced by rape victims. Specifically, if one compared the questions (i.e., hypotheses) proposed by males to those proposed by females, it might reveal some interesting differences in attitudes about rape in the different sexes.

4.2 If you manage to outline a theory, one way to determine how well you have done the job is to make a list of operationally valid, testable hypotheses that can be deduced from the theory. If you cannot deduce any, chances are that your theory is not going to enjoy much success on the "open market."

Chapter 5

5.1 Experiment 1 in this series is a bivalent, between-subjects design. The subjects were assigned to one of two different treatment groups and each group saw a different version of the film: one with a violent ending, one without a violent ending. Experiments 2 and 3 were multivalent, between-subjects designs. If you had trouble determining the architecture of these designs, try to construct a schematic diagram like those presented in Figures 5.2, 5.3, and 5.4 of this chapter. Insert the independent, dependent, and controlled variables into the diagram.

5.2 In each experiment, the independent variable is the type of film shown to the subjects in each group. Two different films are used in Experiment 1 and three different films in Experiments 2 and 3.

5.3 The dependent variable of primary interest in all the experiments was whether or not the subjects could remember the number 17 on the boy's jersey. Subjects were also asked to provide a confidence rating from 1 to 5 on their answer. In addition, Loftus and Burns measured the subjects' memories for several other pieces of information on the film. Each different memory task would be listed as a different dependent variable.

5.4 One variable that Loftus and Burns held constant across the different treatment conditions was the time interval between viewing the film and answering questions about it. This is called the "retention interval" in a memory experiment, and it should be identical in each of the different treatment groups. Otherwise, one group might enjoy an advantage (e.g., a shorter retention interval) over the other. You should be able to list several other variables that were held constant across the different treatment conditions in each experiment.

5.5 Recall that Loftus and Burns were comparing memory for an event preceding a violent scene in the film or preceding a nonviolent scene. They intepret the deficit in memory observed following exposure to the violent scene as an example of retrograde amnesia produced by exposure to emotional shock. It also seems reasonable to suggest that a second variable was covarying with the independent variable (i.e., confounded with the independent variable). Specifically, not only was the ending of one film violent compared to the other film, it was *unexpected* compared to the ending of the other film. Hence, it is possible that the unexpectedness of the ending, not the emotional shock, made it difficult to remember the details near the end of the film. Therefore, the element of unexpectedness is confounded with emotional shock. How did the investigators determine if the confounded variable of unexpectedness was the cause of the memory deficit?

Chapter 6

6.1 There are two independent variables in the experiment of Tomlinson et al. One variable has two levels, the other has three. The first variable is the sex of the model in the photograph; the second is the size of the model's pupils. The three pupil sizes are designated as small (6 percent), medium (29 percent), and large (46 percent). When the two levels of sex and three levels of pupil size are combined, they will generate six different treatment combinations in the experiment. In practice, this means that each subject will see six different photographs and be asked to rate each. One photograph will be a female with small pupils, one will be a male with large pupils, and so on. Note that each subject is exposed to each of the six photographs (i.e., six different treatment conditions); hence the experimental design is a *within-subjects* design. If a different group of subjects had viewed each of the six photographs (six groups each viewing one photo), the design would have been a *between-subjects* design.

6.2 The dependent variable in this experiment was the subject's rating of each photograph.

6.4 Two independent variables with one at two levels and the other at three levels make this a 2 × 3 factorial design. As noted earlier, all subjects were exposed to all six of the treatment conditions, so it would be called a within-subjects 2 × 3 factorial design.

6.5 One main effect is the sex of the model. If you compare the ratings of male and female models presented in Table 1 of the article (ignoring pupil size), it is obvious that the students rated the female model as more attractive. If you have trouble extracting the other main effect in the experiment, you should plot the data on a graph similar to those illustrating main effects and combined effects in this chapter (see Figures 6.7 and 6.8). With the data in the form of these graphs, they may be easier for you to interpret. With reference to the combined effects, Tomlinson and co-workers state in the results section of their article that the "sex of model by pupil size interaction" was significant. Try to describe the interaction in your own words. Again, it may be useful for you to plot their data from Table 1 as a factorial graph.

Chapter 7

7.1 The experiment reported by Zimbardo and Andersen is best described as a between-subjects multivalent design. There were three different treatment levels: deafness with awareness of source; deafness without awareness of source; and the control condition, which did not involve deafness.

7.2 There were many different dependent variables in the Zimbardo and Andersen experiment, most of which were attempts to measure feelings of paranoia. These measures are listed in Table 1 of the article, and they include personality tests (MMPI and TAT) as well as self-ratings on their feelings by the subjects and ratings of the subjects' behavior by the judges.

7.3 One example of a controlled variable was the hypnotizability of the subjects. Zimbardo and Andersen went to considerable trouble to make sure that all subjects in the experiment were highly hypnotizable.

7.6 One of the threats to the external validity of the Zimbardo and Andersen experiment involves their subject selection procedure. As indicated above, they went to considerable trouble to make sure that each subject in their experiment was very easy to hypnotize. One might ask whether the results they obtained can be generalized beyond this very special population of subjects. For example, it is possible that paranoia is more readily observed in highly hypnotizable subjects than it is in the general population.

7.7 If the subjects in the two control conditions (deafness with awareness group and itchy ear group) also showed increased symptoms of paranoia, there would be reason to suspect that the subjects had guessed the purpose of the experiment and were behaving in a manner that complied with the experimenters' wishes. Since these groups did not show increased symptoms of paranoia, Zimbardo and Andersen argue that the results in the experimental group could not be explained by demand characteristics.

Chapter 8

8.1 The design used by Maurer and Young is best described as a within-subjects multivalent quasi-analytic experiment. Each infant is exposed to four different stimulus conditions.

8.2 The four different stimulus conditions (face stimuli) represented four levels of this independent variable.

8.4 Maurer and Young suggested that Goren and co-workers had a confounded variable in their earlier research on this same problem. Specifically, it was suggested that the experimenter could directly influence the degree to which the infant followed the stimulus in the experiment by Goren et al. Hence, one could not determine whether the experimenters' influence or the differences in stimulation were causing the differences in the infants' responsiveness in this experiment.

8.5 As a way of controlling for order effects in their experiment, Maurer and Young randomized the order in which each infant was exposed to the different stimuli. They could have used a counterbalancing procedure and treated the experiment as a mixed within- and between-subject factorial design. Can you figure out how they might have arranged the factorial design?

8.6 Tomlinson et al. controlled for treatment-order effects by randomizing the order in which each subject saw the six different stimulus cards.

Chapter 9

9.1 The Jacobs and Charles experiment is best described as a retrospective ex post facto quasi-analytic experiment. These scientists started with the "effect" (i.e., cancer) and searched backward in time for the causal factor (i.e., life stress). The subjects were selected on the basis of their condition, not randomly assigned to different treatment conditions.

9.2 The logic of the design demands that a population of children with cancer and children without cancer do not differ in any respect other than the life-stress measure. Obviously, it is difficult to make this claim. These two populations of people might also differ in terms of the extent to which they are exposed to a variety of cancer-causing agents. For example, parents of these children may also have a lot of stress in their lives and consequently may smoke more than the comparison-group parents. Thus the children in the cancer group would not only have had more stress in their lives, but would also have been exposed to more smoke in their environments. Can you think of other ways in which these two populations might differ—other than the differences in stress on which Jacobs and Charles have focused?

9.3 A sampling bias toward selecting more high-stress children in the cancer group could have occurred. Jacobs and Charles noted that there was more cancer in the families of the children diagnosed with cancer. Cancer in the immediate family or in close relatives would probably create more stress in the lives of these same children. Consequently, the chances of selecting a high-stress child in the cancer group would be higher than the chances of selecting a high-stress child in the noncancer comparison group.

9.5 Detection bias is perhaps the biggest single threat to the internal validity of this experiment reported by Jacobs and Charles. As noted in Chapter 9, the people in the cancer group were probably more highly motivated to think about and remember stressful events in their life histories than the people in the control group. A person diagnosed with cancer would certainly think very hard about possible causes and propose *more* possible causes than someone without the motivation supplied by the disease. This biases the results in favor of discovering more life stress in the cancer group and offers a classic example of the detection bias that can contaminate retrospective ex post facto research designs.

9.6 Jacobs and Charles attempt to avoid the danger of confounded variables in their design with two tactics. First they selected control subjects that were *matched* to the cancer group in terms of age, sex, and socioeconomic status. Second, they attempted to *measure* a number of variables that they thought might be confounded with the differences in life stress. Some of these measurements are presented in Table 2 of the article. They include such confounded differences as the number of unplanned pregnancies in each group, the frequency with which various other diseases were reported in each group, and the frequency of cancer in the family histories of each group. Each of these was confounded with the difference in life stress and prevent one from making any strong causal claims based on the stress factor alone. Matching and measuring potential confounded variables is useful, but it does not, as you can see, completely solve the problem of confounded variables in ex post facto designs.

Chapter 10

10.2 The data reported by Siegel and Loftus suggest a negative relationship between measures of anxiety and memory performance. The higher the score on various measures of anxiety, the lower the memory score on their memory task. In looking for possible third variables that are confounded in this correlation design, you should try to think of some variables that might covary positively with anxiety. One possibility is that people who score high on anxiety measures are more likely to be taking various forms of medication to control anxiety, and this medication may impair memory. Hence, a third variable in the bivariate correlation might be dosage of medication to control anxiety. Can you think of others?

10.3 The directionality problem involves the direction of the causal claim made from a correlation design. Siegel and Loftus would like to claim that the anxiety is causing the memory deficit on their memory task. You can also examine the possibility of a relationship between these two variables in the opposite direction. Suppose, for example, that the first thing the subjects did when they arrived for the experiment was to view the material and take the memory test. After they had completed the memory task, they proceeded to complete the different questionnaires Siegel and Loftus used to measure anxiety level. It seems possible that poor performance on the memory task (experienced first) could also be producing high scores on some of the subsequent tests for anxiety. A subject that did well on the memory task would feel good and score low on the anxiety measures; a subject that did poorly on the memory task might feel anxious about it and score high on the anxiety measures. Under these conditions, one could just as easily claim that poor performance on the memory test caused the high anxiety. Siegel and Loftus are claiming the opposite.

Of course the above arguments against the directional claims made by Siegel and Loftus would not hold up if they measured the subject's anxiety levels before administering the memory task. It is difficult to know from their description of the experiment which procedure was followed.

10.4 Two threats to the external validity of this experiment might be suggested. Siegel and Loftus would like to argue that these results can be generalized to the courtroom situation in which eyewitness reports are made. One threat to this generalization is that the students used in the experiments were all college students. Their memory processes may be somewhat different than those found in the general population. The second threat concerns the memory test. A sequence of slides was used to tell the story that was to be recalled by the subjects. This is an unusual way to present the material. Most eyewitness accounts would not be based on a series of snapshots of the events.

Chapter 11

11.1 The data suggest that the correlation between teacher ratings and amount learned was virtually identical whether the confounded variable of *initial ability* was partialled out of the relationship or not. This would indicate that initial ability was not an important third variable in the correlation design. If initial ability had been an important third variable, the partial correlation of teacher ratings with amount learned would be reduced when initial ability was partialled out of the relationships.

11.3 This correlation design is interesting in that the authors do seem to argue one directional claim over the other. They do not argue that popular teachers cause the student to learn less, or that learning less causes more popular teachers. In fact, they seem to offer explanations for their data in both directions.

11.4 Rodin and Rodin are cautious in their claims about the external validity of these correlational results. Specifically they state, ". . . information about the extent to which the present results may be generalized to different types of course must await further experimentation." Their caution is prudent. These results are perplexing to say the least, and it may be that they will hold true only under very specific conditions (e.g., the same calculus course taught in multiple sections).

GLOSSARY

absolute threshold   The minimum amount of physical energy that an organism can reliably detect. For example, a loudness threshold is the minimum sound intensity that an organism can hear.

additivity   In a factorial experiment, when the effects of one independent variable are equivalent across the different levels of the other independent variable, we call these results *additive*.

associative learning paradigms   Any procedure for measuring learning that requires the subject to form an association between two items usually designated as the stimulus item and the response item. Paired-associate verbal learning procedures are one example.

bivalent analytic experiment   An analytic experiment that compares two different values of the independent variable.

classical conditioning   Any procedure in which a motivationally neutral stimulus (e.g., a tone) is paired with a motivationally significant stimulus that reliably elicits a response (e.g., food elicits salivation). If repeated pairings are associated by the organism, the neutral stimulus will eventually elicit the response (e.g., tone elicits salivation). The tone is called a conditional stimulus; the food, an unconditional stimulus; the salivation, an unconditioned response.

concept learning paradigms   Any procedure for measuring learning that requires the subject to learn some concept or rule which will solve a problem. Anagram tasks are an example.

confounded variable   In a simple analytic experiment, any factor that covaries with the independent variable is a confounded variable. The logic of the experiment demands that confounded variables be controlled.

controlled variable   In a simple analytic experiment, any factor that is held constant across different treatment conditions is called a controlled variable. Various methods can be used to make certain that a variable is controlled and does not covary with the independent variable in an experiment.

convenience event sampling   The process of selecting a smaller sample of individuals from a larger population in order to estimate the frequency of some event (e.g., bruxism)

331

in that population. This particular type of sampling is defined by the use of any convenient procedure for selecting subjects.

convenience time sampling   A time-sampling procedure in which the observer attemtps to observe the occurrence of a behavior during "convenient" observation periods.

demand characteristics   Any aspect of an experiment that inadvertently causes a subject to behave in a particular manner expected by the experimenter. This is a form of unwanted experimenter influence on subjects that can threaten both the internal and external validity of an experiment.

dependent variable   The factor in an analytic experiment that is predicted to change in the presence and absence of the independent variable. In a simple analytic experiment, several dependent variables can be measured simultaneously.

descriptive statistics   Various calculations that serve to describe the properties of a particular set of measurements. The mean and the standard deviation are examples that describe the central tendency and the variability of a group of measurements respectively.

detection bias   The assumption made in both prospective and retrospective ex post facto designs is that it is equally easy to detect the presence of the presumed causal factor in the different groups of the experiment. When, for any reason, it is easier to detect this factor in one of the groups, this bias is called detection bias.

distortion rule   The rule of observation in science stating that procedures used to make our observations should not introduce distortions and artifacts.

dummy coding   Assignment of an arbitrary number to a dichotomous (nominal scale) variable for the purpose of certain statistical treatments (e.g., male = 1, female = 0), like a point-biserial correlation coefficient.

ecological validity   The extent to which rules obtained with a particular experimental laboratory procedure can be generalized to "real life" or naturalistic situations.

event-sampling procedures   Any procedure that selects a smaller group of individuals from a larger population in order to estimate the characteristics of the larger population.

ex post facto designs   A type of quasi-analytic experiment in which subjects are assigned to different groups on the basis of some characteristic they already exhibit. (e.g., males vs. females; schizophrenics vs. normals). The independent variable in these designs is defined "after the fact."

external validity   The extent to which an experimental observation will be valid for subjects and conditions other than (external to) those used in the experiment per se.

fixed-time sampling   A time-sampling procedure in which the observer attempts to observe the occurrence of a behavior during intervals prearranged at fixed points in time throughout an observation period.

formal hypothesis   A tentative specification of the condition or set of conditions suspected to be necessary and/or sufficient for the occurrence of a particular phenomenon.

formal quantitative hypothesis   A formal hypothesis that specifies the functional relationship between a causal variable and its effect in quantitative terms.

hypothesis   A proposed tentative explanation for a phenomenon.

hypothesis myopia   The notion that previously held ideas or beliefs prevent the scientist from seeing important events or asking important questions that go beyond existing assumptions.

independent variable   The factor in an analytic experiment that is identified as a causal agent. It is contrasted across different treatment conditions in the experimental design.

instrumental conditioning   Any procedure that requires an organism to perform a specified sequence of responses in order to obtain a reward (or avoid a negative event). For example, running through a maze to obtain food or pressing a lever to avoid electric shocks.

interaction   When examining the results obtained with a factorial design, if the effects of one independent variable are different at different levels of the other independent variable, the results are described as an interaction.

internal validity   When all of the logical conditions of an experimental design have been arranged to identify a causal factor and there are no confounded variables, an experiment has internal validity.

interval level of measurement   A level of measurement that permits one to rank-order events along some dimension and specify the distance between events in terms of equal units. This scale does not have an absolute zero point, although it can be assigned an arbitrary zero. Temperature on the Fahrenheit scale is an example.

Likert scale   An attitude-measuring device on which respondents indicate the extent of their agreement or disagreement with statements that express positive or negative attitudes toward some topic. Also called a summative scale because the final score is based on the sum of responses to a list of items or statements.

linear regression analysis   Statistical procedure for defining a straight line that minimizes the deviations of the data points around that line.

main effects   In a factorial experiment, the net performance associated with each independent variable, ignoring or summing across all levels of the other independent variables, is called a main effect in the experiment.

mean   A measure of central tendency calculated by dividing the sum of a set of measurements by the total number of measurements.

median   A measure of central tendency calculated by determining the middle value in a list of measurements ordered from lowest to highest.

method of limits   A method for measuring sensory thresholds by presenting the organism with a sequence of increasing and decreasing physical values and measuring the values that are reliably detected.

Milner's syndrome   The inability to transfer information in immediate memory into long-term memory. This memory deficit is often associated with damage to the temporal lobes and hippocampal regions of the brain.

mixed within- and between-subjects design   A factorial experiment in which some treatments are administered to all subjects (within-subjects) and other treatments are administered to separate groups of subjects (between-subjects).

mode   A measure of central tendency that is simply the most frequently occurring value in a set of measurements.

multimodal frequency distribution   A distribution in which there is more than one "peak" frequency, indicating that there is more than one most common or "typical" value in the distribution.

multivalent analytic experiment   An analytic experiment that compares more than two levels of a single independent variable in the same experiment.

negatively skewed frequency distribution   A distribution in which there are relatively more values at the low end of the abscissa, causing the curve to slope in the direction of the lower values.

nominal scale of measurement   A level of measurement in which events are simply assigned to different categories. Redheads vs. blonds or males vs. females would represent nominal measurements of hair color and sex respectively.

null hypothesis   The assumption that no "true" difference exists between measures taken under different treatment conditions.

one-zero sampling   A time sampling procedure in which some interval of time (e.g., ten seconds) is designated during which an observer looks for the occurrence of a behavioral event (e.g., smoking). If the event occurs, a "1" is recorded for that interval; if the event does not occur, a "0" is recorded. Repeated observations are used to estimate the frequency of the behavior in actual continuous time observations.

operational definition A description of a phenomenon stated in terms of operations that are publicly repeatable and necessary to measure the phenomenon (e.g., "red"—a wavelength of light that will pass through a designated 600 nanometer filter).

operational definition rule In observing and describing events, this rule states that the events we observe must be defined in terms of the operations used to measure them (e.g., "hot" must be defined in terms of degrees on a thermometer system used to measure it).

ordinal scale of measurement A level of measurement in which events can be rank-ordered along some dimension without providing information on the distance between successive events. Asking a judge to rank-order four bottles of wine in terms of sweetness would produce an ordinal scale of sweetness.

organismic variables Measurable characteristics of organisms that are often used as independent variables in ex post facto designs. Examples include sex, race, age, intelligence, and various personality characteristics.

paradigm measurements Special measurement procedures developed by behavioral scientists to measure specific types of behavioral or psychological processes. For example, psychophysical paradigms are specifically concerned with measuring sensory and perceptual functions.

parameter values The value that each variable in an experiment is given is called a parameter value (e.g., temperature, time of day, amount of food, size of room, sex of subjects, etc.).

partial correlation A statistical procedure that permits one to determine the amount of variance shared by two variables when the contribution of a third variable is eliminated.

Pearson *r* A statistical computation used to quantify the linear relationship that exists between two variables in a correlational design.

personality inventory A method for measuring personality characteristics in which the individual is required to circle or check statements on a list that correctly describes the individual (e.g., Beck Depression Inventory or Minnesota Multiphasic Personality Inventory).

personality trait A tendency to react in a defined way to a definite set of stimuli (e.g., an introvert tends to avoid social situations).

Peterson STM paradigm A procedure for measuring short-term memory in which a single verbal item is presented to the subject and the subject then counts backward during a very short retention interval (e.g., 18 seconds), after which he or she is required to recall the item.

point-biserial correlation analysis A procedure for calculating the correlation between two variables, one of which is measured on a nominal scale and the other on at least an interval scale.

population Any group of people or events that can be clearly delineated from other groups and listed as a group (e.g., North Americans).

positively skewed frequency distribution A distribution in which there are relatively more values at the high end of the abscissa, causing the curve to slope in the direction of the higher values.

principle of converging evidence   To the extent that available evidence, taken together, suggests that the conditions of an experiment and the subjects used are not unique, this principle suggests that the experiment has external validity.

projective personality test   A method for measuring personality characteristics in which the individual is required to make responses to unstructured stimuli such as pictures (TAT) or abstract stimuli (Rorschach ink blots).

prospective ex post facto designs   An ex post facto experiment in which one looks *forward in time* to determine if membership in a particular ex post facto group "causes" a particular effect (e.g., whether smokers are more likely to develop cancer than nonsmokers).

psychophysical methods   A group of standardized procedures for measuring sensory capabilities. They include the method of limits, method of constant stimuli, method of average error, signal detection methods, and magnitude estimation methods.

r^2 The Pearson r correlation coefficient squared. It is used to estimate the amount of shared variance between two variables.

random event sampling   The process of selecting a smaller sample of individuals from a larger population in order to estimate the frequency of some event (e.g., baldness) in that population. The random procedure requires that every individual in the population have an *equal* chance of being selected.

range   A descriptive statistic obtained by subtracting the smallest value in a distribution from the largest value.

ratio level of measurement   A level of measurement in which one rank-orders events along some dimension with equal units between event and an absolute zero that equals the absence of the dimension. Distance measurements are on a ratio scale.

recall paradigm   Any procedure for measuring memory that requires the subject to recall or generate previously learned material without prompting or assistance.

recognition paradigm   Any procedure for measuring memory that requires the subject to select or recognize previously learned material embedded in a list of choices.

relative risk ratio   In prospective ex post facto experiments, the ratio of subjects that show a particular effect in one treatment group is divided by the ratio of subjects that show the same effect in another (control) group.

retention interval   The time interval between original learning and a subsequent memory test.

retrograde amnesia   An inability to remember information and events that immediately precede the onset of a convulsive seizure episode.

retrospective ex post facto designs   An ex post facto experiment in which one searches *backward in time* from a particular effect (e.g., lung cancer) to determine if it was preceded by a particular cause (e.g., smoking).

sample   Any group of people who have been selected according to some defined rules from a population of people. The typical purpose of the exercise is to obtain a sample that is a smaller *representative* of the population.

shared variance   The variability in one variable (x) that can account for the variability observed in a second variable (y).

symmetrical frequency distribution   A distribution in which the values are more or less equally distributed above and below some central or average value.

systematic event sampling   The process of selecting a smaller sample of individuals from a larger population in order to estimate the frequency of some event in that population. This particular procedure systematically takes one in every so many individuals from a list of the entire population.

test reliability   The ability of the testing instrument to produce consistent measurements.

test validity   The ability of the test to measure what it claims to measure.

theory   A collection of hypotheses about some phenomenon that is organized into a logically consistent conceptual framework.

time-sampling procedures   Any procedure in which segments of a continuous time observation period are selected as sample observation periods in an attempt to estimate the characteristics of the continuous time record.

two-by-two factorial design   An analytic experiment that examines the effects of two independent variables each at two different levels. Variations follow the same labeling convention. For example a 2×3 factorial has two independent variables, one at two levels and one at three levels; a $2 \times 2 \times 2$ has three independent variables, all at two levels.

variance   A descriptive statistic used to estimate the dispersion of a set of scores around the mean of those scores. It consists essentially of the sum of squared deviations around the mean divided by the numbers of values in the distribution minus one.

volunteer event sampling   The process of selecting a smaller sample of individuals from a larger population in order to estimate the frequency of some event (e.g., red hair) in that population. Any such procedure that permits individuals to *volunteer* rather than be selected is called *volunteer* sampling.

REFERENCES

Abel, E. L. 1980. Fetal alcohol syndrome: Behavioral teratology. *Psychological Bulletin, 87*, 29–50.

Altmann, J. 1974. Observational study of behavior: Sampling methods. *Behaviour, 9*, 227–267.

Anastasi, A. 1976. *Psychological testing* (4th ed.). New York: Macmillan.

Atkinson, J. W. 1957. Motivational determinants of risk-taking behavior. *Psychological Review, 64*, 359–372.

Atkinson, J. W. 1964. *An introduction to motivation*. Princeton N.J.: Van Nostrand.

Bachrach, A. J. 1981. *Psychological research: An introduction* (4th ed.). New York: Random House.

Ballard, J. L., Novak, K. K., & Driver, M. 1979. A simplified score for assessment of fetal maturation of newly born infants. *Journal of Pediatrics, 95*, 769–774.

Barbero, G., & McKay, N. 1969. Failure to thrive. In W. E. Nelson (Ed.), *Textbook of pediatrics*. Philadelphia: Saunders.

Beck, A. T. 1970. *Depression: Causes and treatment*. Philadelphia: University of Pennsylvania Press.

Beck, A. T., Ward, C. H., Mendelson, M., Mock, J., & Erbaugh, J. 1961. An inventory for measuring depression. *Archives of General Psychiatry, 4*, 561–571.

Berkowitz, L. I. 1971. The "weapons effect," demand characteristics and the myth of the compliant subject. *Journal of Personality and Social Psychology, 20*, 332–338.

Berkowitz, L., & Donnerstein, E. 1982. External validity is more than skin deep. Some answers to criticisms of laboratory experiments. *American Psychologist, 37*, 245–257.

Berkowitz, L., & LePage, A. 1967. Weapons as aggression eliciting stimuli. *Journal of Personality and Social Psychology, 7*, 202–207.

Boulanger, G., Kadushin, C., & Martin, J. 1981. *Legacies of Vietnam. Vol 4: Long term stress reactions*. Washington, DC: U.S. Government Printing Office.

Bower, T. 1982. Development in infancy (2nd ed.). San Francisco: Freeman.

Bridgeman, P. W. 1927. *The logic of modern physics*. New York: Macmillan.

Buros, O. K. 1974. *Tests in print two*. Highland Park, NJ: Gryphon Press.

Buros, O. K. (Ed.). 1978. *The eighth mental measurements yearbook*. Highland Park, NJ: Gryphon Press.

Campbell, D. T., & Stanley, J. C. 1963. *Experimental and quasi-experimental designs for research*. Chicago: Rand McNally.

Carlsmith, J. M., Ellsworth, P. C., & Aronson, E. 1976. *Methods of research in social psychology*. Reading, Mass.: Addison-Wesley.

Castelli, W. P. 1979. How many drinks a day. *Journal of the American Medical Association, 242,* 2000.

Chou, S. M., Miike, T., Payne, W. M., & Davis, G. J. 1979. Neuropathy of "spinning syndrome" induced by prenatal intoxication with a PCB in mice. *Annals of the New York Academy of Sciences, 320,* 373–381.

Clarkson, T. W., Cox, C., Marsh, D. O., Myers, G. J., Al-Tikriti, S. K., Amin-Zaki, L., & Dabbagh, A. R. 1981. Dose response relationships for adult and prenatal exposure to methylmercury. In G. G. Berg & H. D. Maille (Eds.), *Measurement of risks*. New York: Plenum Press.

Cohen, J., & Cohen, P. 1975. *Applied multiple regression/correlation analysis for the behavioral sciences*. New York: Erlbaum.

Cook, T. D., & Campbell, D. T. 1979. *Quasi-experimentation: Design and analysis issues for field settings*. Boston: Houghton Mifflin.

Cooper, L. A. 1975. Mental rotation of random 2 dimensional shapes. *Cognitive Psychology, 7,* 20–43.

Cozby, P. C. 1984. *Using computers in the behavioral sciences*. Palo Alto, Calif.: Mayfield Publishing.

Cronbach, L. J. 1970. *Essentials of psychological testing* (3rd ed.). New York: Harper & Row.

Cronenwett, L. R., & Newmark, L. L. 1974. Fathers' responses to childbirth. *Nursing Research, 23,* 210–216.

Cunningham, A. J. 1985. The influence of mind on cancer. *Canadian Psychology, 26,* 13–29.

D'Amato, M. R. 1970. *Experimental psychology: Methodology, psychophysics, and learning*. New York: McGraw-Hill.

Davidson, M. B. 1981. *Diabetus mellitus: Diagnosis and treatment*. New York: Wiley.

Dean, R. S., & Rothlisberg, B. A. 1983. Lateral preference patterns and cross-modal sensory integration. *Journal of Pediatric Psychology, 8,* 285–292.

Donahoe, J. W., & Wessels, M. G. 1980. *Learning, language, and memory*. New York: Harper & Row.

Downs, F. J. 1982. Editorial. *Nursing Research*.

Dunham, P. J. 1977. *Experimental psychology: Theory and practice*. New York: Harper & Row.

Dunham, P. J. 1978. Sex pheromones in crustacea. *Biological Reviews, 53,* 555–583.

Edwards, A. L. 1957. *Techniques of attitude scale construction*. New York: Appleton Century Crofts.

Edwards, A. L. 1985. Experimental design in psychological research. New York: Harper & Row.

Ellsworth, P. C. 1977. From abstract ideas to concrete instances: Some guidelines for choosing natural research settings. *American Psychologist, 32,* 604–615.

Fantino, E., & Logan, C. A. 1979. *The experimental analysis of behavior: A biological perspective*. San Francisco: Freeman.

Feingold, B. F. 1975. *Why is your child hyperactive?* New York: Random House.

Feinstein, A. R. 1971a. Clinical biostatistics X: Sources of "transition bias" in cohort statistics. *Clinical Pharmacology and Therapeutics, 12,* 704–721.

Feinstein, A. R. 1971b. Clinical biostatistics XI: Sources of "chronology bias" in cohort statistics. *Clinical Pharmacology and Therapeutics, 12,* 864–879.

Feinstein, A. R. 1977. *Clinical biostatistics.* St. Louis: Mosby.

Feinstein, A. R., & Horowltz, R. I. 1982. Double standards, scientific methods, and epidemiologic research. *New England Journal of Medicine, 307,* 1611–1617.

Fenz, W., & Epstein, S. 1967. Gradients of physiological arousal of experienced and novice parachutists as a function of an approaching jump. *Psychosomatic Medicine, 29,* 33–51.

Ferguson, G. A. 1971. *Statistical analysis in psychology and education.* New York: McGraw-Hill.

Freeman, D. 1983. *Margaret Mead and Samoa: The making and unmaking of an anthropological myth.* Cambridge, Mass.: Harvard University Press.

Gatchel, R. J. 1977. Therapeutic effectiveness of voluntary heart rate control in reducing anxiety. *Journal of Consulting and Clinical Psychology, 45,* 689–691.

Gatchel, R. J., & Proctor, J. D. 1976. Effectiveness of voluntary heart rate control in reducing speech anxiety. *Journal of Consulting and Clinical Psychology, 44,* 381–389.

Gholson, B., & Parker, P. 1985. Kuhn, Lakatos, & Laudan: Applications in the history of physics and psychology. *American Psychologist, 40,* 755–769.

Glaros, A. G., & Rao, S. M. 1977. Bruxism: A critical review. *Psychological Bulletin, 84,* 767–781.

Harvey, M., Horwitz, R., & Feinstein, A. R. 1982. Toxic shock and tampons. *Journal of the American Medical Association, 248,* 840–846.

Hayes, R. L., Bennet, G. J., Newlon, P. G., & Mayer, D. J. 1978. Behavioral and physiological studies of non-narcotic analgesia in the rat elicited by certain environmental stimuli. *Brain Research, 155,* 69–90.

Hennekens, C. H., Willet, W., Rosner, B., Cole, D. S., & Mayrent, S. L. 1979. Effects of beer, wine, and liquor in coronary deaths. *Journal of the American Medical Association, 242,* 1973–1974.

Henshel, R. L. 1980. The purposes of laboratory experimentation and the virtues of deliberate artificiality. *Journal of Experimental Social Psychology, 16,* 466–478.

Hess, E. H. 1975. The role of pupil size in communication. *Scientific American, 233,* 110–119.

Hier, D. B., & Crowley, W. F. 1982. Spatial ability in androgen-deficient men. *New England Journal of Medicine, 306,* 1202–1205.

Huff, D. 1973. How to lie with statistics. Middlesex, England: Pelican books.

Hulka, B. S. 1982. Tampons and toxic shock syndrome. *Journal of the American Medical Association, 248,* 872–874.

Hyman, H. H. 1954. *Interviewing in social research.* Chicago: University of Chicago Press.

Jacobs, T. J., & Charles, E. 1980. Life events and the occurrence of cancer in children. *Psychosomatic Medicine, 42,* 11–24.

Jacobson, S. W., Fein, G. G., Jacobson, J., Schwartz, P. M., & Dowler, J. K. 1984. Neonatal correlates of prenatal exposure of smoking, caffeine, and alcohol. *Infant Behavior and Development, 7,* 253–265.

Jick, H., Walker, A., Rothman, K., Hunter, J., Holmes, L. Watkins, R., D'Ewart, D., Danford, A., & Madsen, S. 1981. Vaginal spermicides and cogenital disorders. *Journal of the American Medical Association, 245,* 1329–1332.

Justice, A., 1985. Review of the effects of stress on cancer in laboratory animals: Importance of time of stress application and type of tumor. *Psychological Bulletin, 98,* 108–138.

Kagan, J. 1982. The idea of spatial ability. *New England Journal of Medicine, 306,* 1225–1226.

Kajosaari, M., & Saarinen, V. M. 1983. Prophylaxis of atopic disease by six months total food elimination: Evaluation of 135 exclusively breast fed infants of atopic families. *Acta Pediatrica Scandinavica, 72,* 411–414.

Kling, J. W., & Riggs, L. (Eds.). 1971. *Woodworth and Schlosberg's experimental psychology.* (3rd ed.). New York: Holt, Rinehart, and Winston.

Kuffler, S. W., & Nicholls, J. G. 1976. *From neuron to brain.* Sunderland, Mass.: Sinauer.

Kuhn, T. S. 1962. *The structure of scientific revolutions.* Chicago: University of Chicago Press.

Laufer, R. S., Gallops, M. S., & Frey-Wouters, E. 1984. War stress and trauma: The Vietnam veteran experience. *Journal of Health and Social Behavior, 25,* 65–85.

Law, C. E. 1980. Yes Virginia, drinking is good for your health. *MacLeans Magazine,* Feb. 11.

Leavitt, R. R., Sykes, B., & Weatherford, E. 1975. Aboriginal women: Male and female anthropological perspectives. In R. R. Reiter (Ed.), *Toward an anthropology of women.* New York: Monthly Review Press.

Lehner, P. N. 1979. *Handbook of ethological methods.* New York: Garland Press.

Loftus, E. F., & Burns, T. E. 1982. Mental shock can produce retrograde amnesia. *Memory and Cognition, 10,* 318–323.

Luria, A. R. 1969. *The mind of a mnemonist.* L. Solotaroff (trans.). New York: Avon Books. (Original work published 1965).

Mandler, J. M., & Johnson, N. S. 1979. Remembrance of things passed: Story structure and recall. *Cognitive Psychology, 9,* 111–151.

Manicas, P. T., & Secord, P. F. 1983. Implications for psychology of the new philosophy of science. *American Psychologist, 38,* 399–413.

Marek, G. R. 1975. *Toscanini.* London: Vision Press.

Marx, M. H. 1963. *Psychological theory: Contemporary readings.* New York: Macmillian.

Maurer, D., & Young, R. 1983. Newborn's following of natural and distorted arrangements of facial natures. *Infant Behavior and Development, 6,* 127–131.

McCall, R. B. 1980. *Fundamental statistics for psychology* (2nd ed.). New York: Harcourt, Brace, Jovanovich.

Milgram, S. 1963. Behavioral study of obedience. *Journal of Abnormal and Social Psychology, 67,* 371–378.

Milner, B. 1968. Amnesia following operation on the temporal lobes. In O. I. Zangwill & C. W. M. Whitty (Eds.), *Amnesia.* London: Butterworths.

Milner, B. 1974. Hemispheric specialization: Scope and limits. In F. O. Schmitt & F. G. Worden (Eds.), *The neurosciences.* Cambridge, Mass.: M.I.T. Press.

Mook, D. G. 1983. In defense of external invalidity. *American Psychologist, 38,* 379–387.

Mook, D. G. 1983. *Psychological research: Strategy and tactics.* New York: Harper & Row.

Nathan, P. E. 1983. Failures in prevention: Why we can't prevent the devastating effect of alcoholism and drug abuse. *American Psychologist, 38,* 459–467.

Neisser, V. 1982. *Memory observed: Remembering events in natural contexts.* San Francisco: Freeman.

Nunnally, J. C. 1970. *Introduction to psychological measurement.* New York: McGraw-Hill.

Orne, M. T., & Evans, F. J. 1965. Social control in the psychological experiment: Antisocial behaviour and hypnosis. *Journal of Personality and Social Psychology, 1,* 189–200.

Ostrom, T. M. 1984. The role of external invalidity in editorial decisions. *American Psychologist, 39,* 324.

Page, M. M., & Scheidt, R. J. 1971. The elusive weapons effect: Demand awareness, evaluation apprehension, and slightly sophisticated subjects. *Journal of Personality and Social Psychology, 20,* 304–318.

Plutchik, R. 1983. *Foundations of experimental research* (3rd ed.). New York: Harper & Row.

Puff, C. R. (Ed.). 1982. *Handbook of research methods in human memory and cognition.* New York: Academic Press.

Robinson, J. P. & Shaver, P. R. 1973. *Measures of social psychological attitudes.* Ann Arbor, Mich.: University of Michigan Press.

Rodin, M., Frey, P. W., & Gessner, P. K. 1975. Student evaluation. *Science, 187,* 555–559.

Rodin, M., & Rodin, B. 1972. Student evaluations of teachers. *Science, 177,* 1164–1166.

Rosenthal, R. 1967. Covert communication in the psychology experiment. *Psychological Bulletin, 67,* 356–367.

Rosenthal, R., & Rosnow, R. 1969. Artifact in behavioral research. New York: Academic Press.

Rosenthal, R., & Rosnow, R. 1984. *Essentials of behavioral research: Methods and data analysis.* New York: McGraw-Hill.

Schwartz, P. M., Jacobson, S. W., Fein, G. G., Jacobson, J. L., & Price, H. A. 1983. Lake Michigan fish consumption as a source of polychlorinated biphenyls in human cord serum, maternal serum, and milk. *American Journal of Public Health, 73,* 293–319.

Shaw, M. E., & Wright, J. M. 1967. *Scales for the measurement of attitudes.* New York: McGraw-Hill.

Sidman, M. 1960. *Tactics of scientific research.* New York: Basic Books.

Sidowski, J. B. 1966. *Experimental methods and instrumentation in psychology.* New York: McGraw-Hill.

Siegel, S. 1956. *Non-parametric statistics for the behavioral sciences.* New York: McGraw-Hill.

Singer, L. T., & Fagan, J. F. 1984. Cognitive development in the failure to thrive infant: A three year longitudinal study. *Journal of Pediatric Psychology, 9,* 363–382.

Smyth, D. 1985. Finding out: The rise of citizen Science. *Canadian Broadcasting Corporation,* Transcript 4-1D-108.

Sperry, R. W. 1964. The great cerebral commissure. *Scientific American,* 42–52.

Spevak, R. A., & Suboski, M. D. 1969. The retrograde effect of electroconvulsive shock on learned responses. *Psychological Bulletin, 72,* 66–75.

Springer, S. P., & Deutsch, G. 1981. *Left brain, right brain.* San Francisco: Freeman.

Stern, J. S. 1984. Sweet dilemma: An expert examines current concerns about the newest sugar substitute. *Vogue,* Dec., p. 214.

Surwit, R. S., Feinglos, M. N., & Scovern, A. W. 1983. Diabetes and behavior: A paradigm for health psychology. *American Psychologist, 38,* 255–262.

Tabachnick, B., & Fidell, L. S. 1983. *Using multivariate statistics.* New York: Harper & Row.

Todd, J., Fishaut, M., Kapral, F., et al. 1978. Toxic shock syndrome associated with phase-group-1 staphylococci. *Lancet, 2,* 1116–1122.

Visintainer, M. A., Volpicelli, J. R., & Seligman, M. E. P. 1982. Tumor rejection in rats after inescapable or escapable shock. *Science, 216,* 437–438.

Wagenaar, A. C. 1982. Raised legal drinking age and automobile crashes: A review of the literature. *Abstracts and Reviews in Alcohol and Driving, 3,* 3–8.

Wagenaar, A. C. 1982. Aggregate beer and wine consumption: Effects of changes in the minimum legal drinking age and a mandatory beverage container deposit law in Michigan. *Journal of Studies on Alcohol, 43,* 469–487.

Warner, W. W. 1976. *Beautiful swimmers: Watermen, crabs, and the Chesapeake Bay.* New York: Penguin Books.

Weiss, B. 1982. Food additives and environmental chemicals as sources of childhood behavior disorders. *Journal of the American Academy of Child Psychiatry, 21,* 144–152.

Weiss, B. 1983. Behavioural toxicology and environmental health science. *American Psychologist, 38,* 1174–1187.

Willer, J. C., Dehen, H., & Cambier, J. 1981. Stress-induced analgesia in humans: Endogenous opiods and naloxone-reversible depression of pain reflexes. *Science, 212,* 689–691.

Wurtman, R. J. 1982. Biochemical changes following high-dose aspartame with dietary carbohydrates. *New England Journal of Medicine, 309,* 429–430.

AUTHOR INDEX

SUBJECT INDEX